The All-Conquering Lamb

A Comprehensive and Devotional

Exposition of the Book of Revelation

Brian A. Russell

EP BOOKS (Evangelical Press)
Registered Office: 140 Coniscliffe Road, Darlington, Co Durham, UK DL3 7RT

www.epbooks.org
admin@epbooks.org

EP Books are distributed in the USA by:
JPL Books, 3883 Linden Ave. S.E.,
Wyoming, MI 49548

www.jplbooks.com
orders@jplbooks.com

First published 2019

British Library Cataloguing in Publication Data available

ISBN 978-1-78397-268-5

Printed and bound in Great Britian by Bell & Bain Ltd.

To
Pastors and Bible College students in the Third World
who do not have the means to purchase Christian
books which 'contend earnestly for the faith
which was once for all delivered to the saints'

(Jude 6)

Contents

❦ Introduction

The number of commentaries on the book of Revelation are legion, but many fall into the category of being unduly technical or unhelpfully brief. This commentary will seek to have a more popular approach by giving comprehensive exposition to both the exegetical and devotional content of this portion of Scripture which we generally find difficult to understand and leave largely unread.

Individually, we know it is a divinely-inspired book in the sacred library of Holy Scripture and therefore we give it due recognition. But we remain uneasy and hesitant to step into its strange, unfamiliar world of angels and demons, of lambs and dragons, and two malicious monsters, one emerging out of the sea with seven heads and ten horns, and the other coming from the earth with a lamb's horns and a dragon's voice. There are also extraordinary events, like the turning of one-third of the sea into blood, which are impossible to visualize. So we turn our backs on its grotesque images and spend our time instead on the stories of Jesus in the Gospels and the teaching of His apostles in their letters.

But we cannot leave the matter there, and pay less attention to the study of the book of Revelation than we would to any other book of

Scripture. This book has much to teach Christians of every generation. Indeed, it promises at its beginning a special blessing to the person who reads, hears and keeps the words of this prophecy (1:3). Moreover, the promise is repeated at the end of the book (22:7). We would therefore be foolish to neglect it. So let us not be intimidated by its mysteries, but rather turn to its pages with this prayer:

> Break Thou the bread of life,
>   Dear Lord, to me,
> As Thou didst break the loaves
>   Beside the sea:
> Beyond the sacred page
>   I seek Thee, Lord;
> My spirit pants for Thee,
>   O living Word!
>
> O send Thy Spirit, Lord,
>   Now unto me,
> That He may touch my eyes,
>   And make me see:
> Show me the truth concealed
>   Within Thy word,
> That in Thy book revealed
>   I see Thee, Lord.
>
> (*v. 1 Mary Lathbury, 1841–1913; v. 2 Alex. Groves, 1843–1909*)

The place of Revelation in the Bible

It is not by chance that Revelation is the last book of the Bible to be written and the book with which the Bible ends. No other book among the sixty-six that make up the canon of Scripture could more fittingly bring the Bible to its proper conclusion. Thus the Bible opens with the statement that 'In the beginning God created the heavens and the earth', and it ends with John seeing 'a new heaven and a new earth' (Genesis 1:1; Revelation 21:1). The river watering the Garden of Eden reappears in the New Jerusalem as the 'river of the water of life, clear as crystal, proceeding from the throne of God and of the Lamb' (Genesis 2:10; Revelation 22:2). 'The tree of life' from which man was barred because of his disobedience is again accessible for the blessing of all the redeemed in the new city of God (Genesis 2:9; 3:22–24; Revelation 22:2). The 'curse' of sin pronounced upon the entire creation in Genesis 3:17–19 is forever removed from the new heaven and the new earth (Revelation 22:3). The image of God marred in man by the Fall is perfectly restored when at the throne of God and the Lamb His glorified saints see His face and His name is on their foreheads (Genesis 1:27; Revelation 22:4). There is no devil in the first two chapters or in the last two chapters of God's word.

All in all, the book of Revelation brings the story of *Paradise Lost* to a perfect conclusion with *Paradise Regained* forever to an infinitely greater degree.

The author of Revelation

The writer identifies himself simply as 'John'. He does not give us any other clue to his identity such as 'John the apostle' or 'John, the brother of James'. In chapter 1:1 we are told that Jesus sent an angel to pass on the revelation of Himself 'to His servant John'. In verse 4 he says, 'John, to the seven churches which are in Asia.' In verse 9 he describes himself as, 'I John, both your brother and companion in tribulation, and in the kingdom and patience of Jesus Christ.' And then in chapter 22:8 he says, 'Now I, John, saw and heard these things.' That is all we learn about the author from the book itself.

Who then is this John? Is he the apostle John who wrote the fourth gospel and the three epistles? Tradition has always claimed he is, and the fact that the author of Revelation simply calls himself 'John' confirms that he was a very well-known person. No additional designation was necessary, because only one John was famous enough among the early Christians to require any further qualification. Among

the early Christian writers to ascribe the authorship of the book of
Revelation to the apostle John are Justin Martyr (c. 100–165) and
Irenaeus (c. 130-c. 202), a disciple of Polycarp (c. 70–155/160) who
knew the apostle.[1]

True, it must be admitted that there is a striking difference in the
style of writing between the Revelation, and the gospel and the epistles
which John wrote. But this can be accounted for by the fact that
Revelation is a *prophecy* conveyed through symbols and images like
Daniel, and not a *history* like the gospel or a *correspondence* like the
epistles. What is significant to most students of Revelation is that the
writer of the fourth gospel and the writer of Revelation are the only
ones in the New Testament who speak of Jesus as 'the Lamb of God'
and the 'Logos' or 'Word'. The 'Lamb of God' is referred to twice in the
gospel (John 1:29,36) and twenty-seven times in the Revelation simply
as the 'Lamb' with a capital 'L' (5:6,8,12,13; see your concordance). The
title 'the Logos' is found in John 1:1; 1 John 1:1 and Revelation 19:13.
These similarities also support the tradition that the John who wrote
the Revelation is the apostle John.

The recipients of Revelation

For whom was it intended? Like the apostolic letters of the New
Testament, the book of Revelation is laid out in the traditional form
of a letter. After the opening words of introduction in verses 1–3, the
author identifies himself as John in verse 4 and then follows with a
word of greeting: 'John, to the seven churches which are in Asia: Grace
to you and peace from Him who is and who was and who is to come,
and from the seven Spirits who are before His throne, and from Jesus
Christ, the faithful witness, the firstborn from the dead, and the ruler
over the kings of the earth.' In addition, the book ends like the other
New Testament letters with a *benediction*: 'The grace of our Lord Jesus
Christ be with you all. Amen.' (22:21). To whom then did John send
this letter? Verse 4 says, 'To the seven churches which are in Asia';

namely, to Ephesus, to Smyrna, to Pergamum, to Thyatira, to Sardis, to Philadelphia, and to Laodicea (v. 11).

Now the 'Asia' mentioned here is not the Asia of today consisting of the continent of Russia, China and India, but the Roman province of Asia that was located on the western seaboard of what we now know as Turkey. And the seven cities to which the letter was addressed were situated in the central western part of Turkey. They all lay on what the British archaeologist Sir William Ramsay called 'the great circular road that bound together the most populous, wealthy and influential part of the Province.'[2] They are listed in the order in which the messenger carrying the book would have visited the cities in which these churches were located.

He would have sailed north from the island of Patmos where John had been exiled, and disembarked at the port of Ephesus which was the capital city of the province of Asia. He would then travel further north in a clockwise direction to Smyrna and Pergamum, and then bending round to the east and down to the south again, he would come to Thyatira, Sardis, Philadelphia and finish his journey at Laodicea. Although addressed to these seven churches living in a particular geographical area at a particular point in time with particular circumstances, the book of Revelation cannot be limited to those who first read it. Verse 1 says that God gave it 'to show His servants things which must shortly take place', and God's servants are to be found in every place and in every age. Besides, just as Paul's letters were to be passed on to other churches (Colossians 4:16), so John's letter to the *Asians* is as much God's word to us as to any of them. God's holy, inspired, revealed word is universal and timeless (Psalm 119:89).

The time and circumstances of Revelation

On its own evidence Revelation was written during one of two periods of great persecution experienced by the early church in the first century. There are those who think it was written in the days of the

Emperor Nero who ruled the Roman Empire from AD 54 to 68. It was during his reign that Christians were first persecuted, not because they would not worship Nero, but because he had to find scapegoats for the great fire that destroyed half of Rome, for which it is almost certain that he himself was responsible. But Nero's persecutions were sporadic and confined to Rome, whereas 25 years later a second phase of official persecution was initiated by the Emperor Domitian who reigned from AD 81 to 96.

As his reign progressed, Domitian became more and more hungry for divine honours and the persecution spread as far as Asia. Christians were commanded to worship before the Emperor's shrine in their town once a year. But no true Christian could call Caesar Lord when the only Lord he owned was Christ. There are many indications in the book of Revelation that persecution had already broken out, for John has been exiled to the rocky island of Patmos, a penal colony about ten miles long and five miles wide. In addition, 'Antipas' is singled out from those who have been martyred (2:13); some of the Christians at Smyrna are about to be thrown into prison (2:10), and those in Philadelphia are warned of 'the hour of trial which will come upon the whole world' (3:10). The whole book is full of warnings of increasing persecution, and so most conservative scholars agree with Bishop Irenaeus who wrote that Revelation was written towards the end of Domitian's reign in c. AD 96.[3] The words of Irenaeus are later quoted by Eusebius (c. 265–c. 339), the father of church history, who also affirms John's return from the Isle of Patmos and dates it immediately following the death of Domitian, which occurred in AD 96.[4]

The literary style of Revelation

The book of Revelation belongs to a particular class or *genre* of literature that is known as *apocalyptic*. We may not fully appreciate it, but it is very important in properly interpreting any Scripture to take note of the type of literature it is. There is, for example, a difference in *prose* and *poetry*, and the difference does not merely lie in the fact that the one rhymes and the other does not. Essentially the difference lies in the way the ideas or truths are expressed. Prose would describe a beautiful girl like this: 'Your eyes are blue, your hair is blond and long; your teeth are straight and white, your lips are red; your neck is ivory and slim.' That is a very prosaic description of a beautiful girl. But here is a poetic description in the Bible of the same beautiful girl. 'Behold, you are fair, my love! … You have dove's eyes behind your veil. Your hair is like a flock of goats, going down from Mount Gilead. Your teeth are like a flock of shorn sheep which have come up from the washing … Your lips are like a strand of scarlet … Your neck is like the tower of David' (Song 4:1–4).

Literary style is important. The same things are being described, but they are expressed differently. Pictures are drawn in poetry in a way that prose does not. So we must not interpret the pictures drawn for us in poetry literally, but instead seek to lay hold of the ideas that the pictures are trying to convey. That has to be borne in mind whenever we look at a passage of Scripture: is it prose or poetry? But when we come to books like Daniel, Ezekiel, Zechariah and Revelation, there is a third class of literature we need to deal with which is called *apocalyptic* literature. The name comes from the title of John's book: 'The Revelation [Greek is *apokalupsis*] of Jesus Christ' (1:1). The Greek word means 'an unveiling' or 'a disclosure'. This is a form of Jewish religious literature that appeared in the dark period of history when Israel was oppressed first by the Babylonians and then by the Persians, the Greeks and the Romans. Apocalyptic literature is highly symbolic and full of all kinds of bizarre imagery involving weird beasts and mysterious numbers. To be precise, it is *code writing*, which can only be understood by those for whom it is written.[5] In times when God's people were under attack, it was important that they should be comforted by a word from God that assured them that they would prevail over their enemies. But the writer had to make sure that God's message was not intelligible to the enemy, otherwise they would be charged with sedition.

So Daniel and Ezekiel and John the seer all wrote in symbols that would be understood by those who needed the message, but too obscure to be used against them by the enemy. Now the key to the symbolic code is in the rest of Scripture, and that is why the Jews who first read it were able to interpret the symbols with the help of the Old Testament. H.B. Swete cites Westcott and Hort to the effect 'that of the 404 verses of the Apocalypse [or Revelation], there are 278 which contain references to the Jewish Scriptures ... with Daniel having the greatest number of references.'[6] We today are not so fortunate because we are not steeped in the Old Testament as they were, and some of us have never studied Daniel and Ezekiel and Zechariah. What will be of help, however, is to keep in mind that John does not intend us to take the symbols literally. The symbols are used to convey realities far greater than words can describe. To understand the meaning of the symbol, it must be deciphered by using the plain teaching elsewhere in Scripture to make clear what is obscure.

Moreover, John is seeking to communicate to us not just the *meaning* but also the *feeling* of what he saw as he saw it. Revelation, therefore, is a divinely revealed word of a different sort: an acted word, a word dramatized, a word you can see and feel. We are to experience the emotional impact of the truth being symbolized as well as its meaning, whether it is 'a Lamb as though it had been slain', or 'a great, fiery red dragon.' The reality of revealed scenes like these is transcendental in character, and cannot be fully described in human language which is bound by time. But human language is our only means for conveying these revelations of the transcendental realm, and so the prophet or seer must use symbols which point beyond themselves to communicate what he has seen.

The purpose of Revelation

There are many people in evangelical churches today who read the book of Revelation as if it were a biblical almanac. They want to identify the signs of Christ's return, the arrival of Antichrist, the outcome of the Arab-Israeli conflict, and so on. Of course, it is true that the book of Revelation does warn us of events that will take place at the end of the world. I do not think it is possible to understand it in any other way. But the attempt to link John's symbols with political entities in the twenty-first century and make detailed forecasts of those events is fraught with uncertainty and subjectivity. It has led groups like Jehovah's Witnesses and Seventh-Day Adventists to make confident predictions of the time of Jesus Christ's second coming which have only proven false.

Rather, the main purpose of Revelation is to give hope and spiritual strength to Christ's church in every land and in every age in its struggle with the forces of evil who seek to destroy it by means of persecution, error and sin. And it does so by variously portraying the Son of God as the Lamb of God who by the offering of Himself as an atonement for sin has overcome Satan's power over the world. Moreover, because of His victory at the cross of Calvary, it is not incongruous for the 'Lamb' to also be called 'the Lion of the tribe of Judah', for God raised Him from the grave and exalted Him to His right hand where all authority has been given to Him in heaven and on earth (5:1–12; 12:1–11; 19:11–21).

Throughout the visions of this precious book the Lamb is gloriously portrayed as the Victor (1:18; 2:8; 5:9–12; 6:2; 7:9–10; 11:15; 12:10; 14:14–16; 15:2; 17:14; 19:11–21; 22:3). William Hendriksen spells it out most appealingly:

> He is victorious; hence, so are we! Even when we seem to be hopelessly defeated. Do you see that band of believers? Are their garments splashed and filthy? They wash their robes, and make them white in the blood of the Lamb (7:14; 22:14). Are they 'in great tribulation'? They come out

of it (7:14). Are they killed? They stand upon their feet (11:11). Are they persecuted by the dragon, the beast, and the false prophet? In the end you see them standing victoriously on Mount Zion. Rather you see the Lamb, and with Him a hundred and forty-four thousand, having His name, and the name of His Father, written on their foreheads (14:1). They triumph over the beast (15:2).

Does it *seem* as if their prayers are not heard (6:10)? The judgments sent upon the earth are God's answer to their prayers (8:3–5). ... Do they *seem* defeated? In *reality* they *reign!* Yes, they reign upon the earth (5:10); in *heaven with Christ a thousand years* (20:4); *in the new heaven and earth for ever and ever* (22:5).

And what happens to those who *seem* to be conquerors? I see them arise out of the abyss, the sea, the earth. Yes, I see them: the dragon (12:3); the beast (13:1); the false prophet (13:11); and Babylon (14:8), in that order! And then? I see them go down in defeat: Babylon (18:2); the beast and the false prophet (19:20); and the dragon (20:10), in that—exactly reversed—order![7]

No wonder John clearly states twice: 'Here is a call for the endurance and faith of the saints' (13:10; 14:12, ESV).

The interpretation of Revelation

In Revelation 1:1, John says, 'The revelation of Jesus Christ which God gave Him to show His servants—things which must shortly take place.' The claim is repeated in chapter 22:6. So by its own testimony Revelation is about historical events. How then does this sequence of visions which John describes correlate to real history? How are we to interpret its contents? There are four main schools of thought.

The first view is called the *preterist* view, because it comes from the Latin word for that which has gone by. These scholars believe that most of the prophecies of this book were fulfilled in the events leading up to the destruction of Jerusalem and the temple in AD 70. The great merit of this approach is that it interprets the plight of the first-century church in terms of the crisis of emperor worship and persecution which it was experiencing at that particular time. And its significance for us lies largely in the fact that we can look back at what God had to say to the church at that time and see what lessons we can draw from it. Its major weakness, however, is that the decisive victory of Christ over all evil portrayed in the visions was never achieved, not even nineteen centuries later.

The second view, the *historicist* view, holds that John's visions show the struggles of the church in a sequence of events that stretch successively from Christ's first coming to His second. So we can see the fulfilment of some events in the past history of the church, and others as coming to pass in our day, and still others as occurring in the future.

The third view is the *futurist* view, and as the name indicates, it holds that everything from chapter 4 to the end of the book is describing events that will only come to fulfilment at the end of the world. This is the view of popular prophetic writers like Hal Lindsey who wrote *There's a New World Coming*, and Tim LaHaye, co-author of the famous *Left Behind* series. The weakness of this view is that it robs the book of all significance for the Christians in John's day and for all subsequent generations since then right up to the last.

The fourth view is termed the *idealist* view. It holds that the events described are not to be thought of as successive historical occurrences. Rather, they are to be seen as pictures of spiritual principles upon which God acts throughout human history, and so it is relevant to Christians of every age.

The structure of Revelation

My own position is basically that of the historicist view. But with Reformed scholars like B.B. Warfield and William Hendriksen, I also believe that the history of the church from Christ's first coming to His second is *progressively revealed* in seven main parallel visions. So the events are not recorded in strict, successive chronological order, but repeated again and again. For example:

Vision One (1:9–3:22) contains the seven letters from Christ the exalted Judge to the *seven churches* in Asia. These seven churches existed in John's day and they needed to receive these words of praise and rebuke from Christ, the head of the church. But seven is the symbol of completeness, and the fact that only seven churches out of at least ten in Asia were selected, makes them representative of the whole church's struggle spanning the entire dispensation.

Vision Two (4:1–8:1) also covers the entire age of the church in which Christ, as the Lord of human destiny, opens the *seven seals* that end with the final judgment (6:12–17) and all the redeemed in heaven (7:9–17).

Vision Three (chapters 8–11) consists of the *seven trumpets* of warning ending again with a clear reference to the final judgment (11:15–18).

Vision Four (chapters 12–14) is made up of seven signs of cosmic conflict showing how the church is persecuted by the dragon for the entire dispensation which ends with Christ coming with His sickle to judge the world (14:14–16).

Vision Five (chapters 15–16) describes *seven bowls* of wrath poured out on the world during the church age, and ends predictably with a reference to the final judgment when every island flees away (16:20; see also 6:14; 20:11).

Vision Six (chapters 17–19) depicts the fall of the great harlot called Babylon (the seductive power of materialism), as well as the punishment of the Beast (the Antichrist) and the False Prophet, culminating yet again in Christ's coming to judge the world (19:11–21).

Vision Seven brings us to the last three chapters (20–22). The subject here is the destiny of Satan. He will be bound during the church age so that the world can be evangelized (20:1–6). At the end of the church age the devil is loosed for a short season, and immediately makes war on the church to destroy it (20:7–10). Christ, however, returns to cast him into hell and judge the world (20:11–15). He then creates a new heaven and a new earth for believers of all ages to enjoy forever and ever (21:1–22:21).

All seven divisions of the book deal with the same period of time between Christ's first and second comings. Each division looks at it from a different aspect, but every one ends with the overthrow of evil at the last judgment when Jesus returns to the earth. So in the final analysis, although the book has seven major divisions, it is a complete unity emphasizing the absolute triumph of the crucified, risen and reigning Lord Jesus Christ over all His enemies. That is the message that has brought and still does bring great comfort to every generation of Christians who *read* and *hear* the words of this prophecy, and *keep* those things that are written in it.

It is a pattern of writing that is distinctively Eastern. Westerners prefer to start at the beginning of an epoch and continue without interruption to the end. We, however, must check this straight-line presentation of history if we are to feel the full weight of the message of Revelation (and also, of course, the prophecy of Daniel and the Olivet Discourse of our Lord in Matthew 24 and Mark 13). It is a pattern of writing called 'progressive parallelism': the repetition of a sequence of events in different ways. 'One might liken the structure', says Sinclair Ferguson, 'to a spiral staircase, turning around the same central point on more than one occasion, yet rising higher and higher at the same time.'[8]

It is the ardent prayer of the author that by the gracious working of God through the Holy Spirit every reader will not only have their head filled with divine truth, but their heart consequently fired with wonder, love and praise to our Lord Jesus Christ, the all-conquering Lamb of God.

Brian A. Russell, Glen Allen, VA, U.S.A.

1 The opening curtain rises

^{1:1}The Revelation of Jesus Christ, which God gave Him to show His servants—things which must shortly take place. And He sent and signified it by His angel to His servant John, ²who bore witness to the word of God, and to the testimony of Jesus Christ, to all things that he saw. ³Blessed is he who reads and those who hear the words of this prophecy, and keep those things which are written in it; for the time is near.

⁴John, to the seven churches which are in Asia:

Grace to you and peace from Him who is and who was and who is to come, and from the seven Spirits who are before His throne, ⁵and from Jesus Christ, the faithful witness, the firstborn from the dead, and the ruler over the kings of the earth. To Him who loved us and washed us from our sins in His own blood, ⁶and has made us kings and priests to His God and Father, to Him be glory and dominion forever and ever. Amen.

⁷Behold, He is coming with clouds, and every eye will see Him, even they who pierced Him. And all the tribes of the earth will mourn because of Him. Even so, Amen.

⁸'I am the Alpha and the Omega, the Beginning and the End,' says the Lord, 'who is and who was and who is to come, the Almighty.'

(Revelation 1:1–8)

The book of Revelation is also known as *The Apocalypse*, a name taken from the Greek word *apokalupsis* which is translated in the very first verse as 'revelation' (literally, unveiling). For the Apocalypse is an unveiling by God of the central players in the history of the world, particularly the history that spans the entire period from the first to the second coming of the Lord Jesus Christ, the Lamb of God who is the Chief Player. It is like a highly dramatised play in which, to quote the famous lines of the bard, Shakespeare:

All the world's a stage,
And all the men and women merely players.
They have their exits and their entrances.[1]

In Revelation 1:1–8 the curtain rises for the opening scene of Act One (or, if you like, Vision One), which serves as a backdrop for all the scenes and visions to come. All will be filled with images and symbols and words which disclose God's absolute control of history: past, present and future. History is His-story. What happens in the world is not by chance, but by divine decree. What God has willed in His infinite goodness and inscrutable wisdom will be done, not somehow, but triumphantly. The theme of the drama of Revelation is: The Lamb wins!

The invincibility of God and of the Lamb who shares His throne will be the focus of our attention as we take up the difficult but rewarding task of studying the book of Revelation. It is the last book in the canon of the Bible and the last book of Scripture to be written. It is not, however, a mere appendix to the collection of books which make up God's word. It is in fact as relevant to the modern world as any of the other books in the Bible. Indeed, the book ends with this warning from Jesus Christ, its divine author, 'For I testify to everyone who hears the words of the prophecy of this book: If anyone adds to these things, God will add to him the plagues that are written in this book; and if anyone takes away from the words of the book of this prophecy, God shall take away his part from the Book of Life, from the holy city, and from the things which are written in this book. He who testifies to these things says, "Surely I am coming quickly." Amen. Even so, come, Lord Jesus!' (22:18–20).

This is a warning to everyone that the book of Revelation is not to be tampered with. *Nothing is to be added,* because there is nothing missing that God meant should be there; and *nothing is to be taken away,* because there is nothing there that God did not put there or that is no longer true. When taken in conjunction with chapter 1:1, no book in the Scriptures opens and closes with such an uncompromising statement of its own direct inspiration.

The superscription to the letter

Verses 1–3 form the opening statement that gives us the *title, origin* and *purpose* of this last book of the New Testament canon. The book begins in verse 1 with its *title,* 'The Revelation of Jesus Christ.' The word *revelation* comes from the Latin word *revelatio,* the title given to the book in the *Vulgate,* the Latin version of the Bible. The word in the original Greek text is *apokalupsis* and both the Latin word and the Greek word simply mean 'the unveiling.' Thus the book is known either as the Revelation or the Apocalypse. The Greek word, *apokalupsis* is used in Scripture of the unveiling by God of hidden or partially hidden truths which would otherwise remain unknown to man (Romans 16:25; Galatians 1:12; Ephesians 1:17; 3:3).

However, the title makes it clear that the book is not just an unveiling of things in general, but 'the Revelation of Jesus Christ.' The phrase 'of Jesus Christ' could mean *from* Jesus Christ, but that cannot be its primary sense, for the verse goes on to say 'which God gave Him.' It is from God the Father that this revelation ultimately comes. He is its source and originator. So it is best to take the preposition *of* as an objective genitive meaning 'about Jesus Christ.' For Jesus Christ is the central figure of this book and the clue to its true meaning. The unveiling of Jesus Christ implies the veiling He underwent in His incarnation, when the full glory of His divine majesty was veiled in His humanity, suffering and penal substitutionary death for sinners.

But since His resurrection and ascension, the glorious unveiling of the Son of God and the Son of Man has begun. He is the One 'who loves us and has freed us from our sins by His blood' (1:5, ESV). He is the eternal God, 'the Alpha and the Omega, the First and the Last' (1:11). He is the Conqueror of Death who 'was dead', but can say: 'behold, I am alive for evermore. Amen. And I have the keys of Hades and death' (1:18). He is the supreme Head of the church 'who walks in the midst of the seven golden lampstands' (1:20). He is worshipped in heaven by saints and angels who cry out, 'Worthy is the Lamb who was slain to receive power and riches and wisdom and strength and honour and glory and blessing' (5:12). He is the One who overcomes all His enemies, for 'He is Lord of lords and King of kings' (17:14). He is our returning Judge who says, 'Behold, I am coming quickly, and My reward is with Me, to give to every one according to His work' (22:12). How that should whet our spiritual appetites! Nobody can read the Apocalypse without gaining a clearer view of Jesus Christ and His ultimate triumph over evil.

So God the Father is the *origin* of this revelation, and He gave it to Jesus Christ, His incarnate Son, because, being one with God and one with us, He is the only Mediator between God and man (1 Timothy 2:5–6). Not only that, because He is at the Father's right hand, He is now able to lift the curtain (or veil) of time and reveal the glory which His redeemed people are destined to share. So verse 1 says that the purpose for which John is given the revelation, is 'to show His servants.' Although the revelation was sent in particular to the seven churches in the Roman province of Asia (v. 4), here in verse 1 it is addressed to all who love and serve Christ without distinction.

This is true of all the books of the New Testament. Luke, for example, compiled his gospel and the book of Acts for a single individual named Theophilus, yet what he wrote was copied by the church for readers in every age. There are, however, two other links in the chain of communication, if we can skip the next phrase for a moment. 'And He (that is, Jesus) sent and signified it by His angel to His servant John.' There is no further identification of the angel. Whoever he was, he was simply doing what he was created to do. He was a *messenger* (which is the meaning of the term 'angel') and he was sent by Jesus 'to minister for those who will inherit salvation' (Revelation 22:16; Hebrews 1:14). This is the only book in the Bible that was entirely communicated by an angel.

Moreover, the *method* of communication was by means of signs or symbols conveyed through a series of visions. That is the meaning of the phrase, 'and signified it by His angel', for to signify means to communicate a message by means of signs or to explain the meaning of the signs, either by the context or by the addition of some words of explanation. For example, 'the seven candlesticks' are defined as 'seven churches' (1:20). To understand the message of Revelation, then, we must grasp the significance of these signs or symbols, not only by considering the clues that are given, but also by seeking light from the context of Scripture as a whole. This was the way the angel communicated Christ's message to John who in turn recorded it in writing for the seven churches of Asia and for all the servants of God in every generation.

We must now go back to the clause we temporarily skipped: 'to show … things which must shortly take place' (v. 1). The *revelation* about Jesus Christ is also a *prophecy* about 'things which must shortly (i.e. soon, ESV) take place' concerning Christ and the consummation of His kingdom. This note of urgency is reinforced by the further warning that 'the time is near' (v. 3). The fact that these two warnings are addressed to people in John's day, should discourage *futurist* views of events in the book that place them all in the last generation of world history before Christ returns. These warnings were meant to be relevant for the churches in John's day (c. AD 95). It is true that the word 'shortly' could also be translated 'suddenly'. But to give it that meaning would rob the book of its relevance to the people in John's day. Besides, to translate the word 'shortly' or 'soon' agrees better with the pronouncement that 'the time is near.'

The fearful judgments that are going to be so graphically depicted in John's prophecy are real and impending. Our Lord Himself also spoke repeatedly of the *imminence* of His return, for He will come unexpectedly. No one can read all the signs of His second coming with pinpoint accuracy. So His warning to the church in the first generation is just as relevant to the church in every generation: 'Watch therefore, for you do not know what hour your Lord is coming ... therefore you also be ready, for the Son of Man is coming at an hour you do not expect' (Matthew 24:42,44). Now if the objection is raised that the prophecies of the book of Revelation have not taken place 'soon', for nearly two thousand years have passed and still Christ has not returned, we need to remember two important facts: first, history is advancing in accordance with God's timetable, not man's, and 'that with the Lord one day is as a thousand years, and a thousand years as one day' (2 Peter 3:8). There has been, and there will be no failure in the fulfilment of the promise of Christ's return. Revelation is about 'things which *must* come to pass.' There can be no escaping them.

The second important thing to remember is that the word 'shortly' and the phrase 'the time is near' are also saying what the rest of the New Testament says; namely, that we are living in 'the last days' (Acts 2:17; 1 Corinthians 10:11; 2 Timothy 3:1; Hebrews 1:2). The first coming of Christ was the inauguration of God's kingdom on earth (Mark 1:14–15). Already, everything is moving by divine appointment towards its consummation. And so as soon as John's letter reaches its destination in the churches of Asia, his readers will be able to say, 'The time is indeed near. These things are happening now. They are in the process of being fulfilled, the length of which is in God's hands.' Every Christian in every generation who reads the book of Revelation should have this sense of immediacy. We are not waiting for the process of consummation to start. It has already begun and its climax will come unexpectedly and suddenly.

Verse 2 tells us that John not only received this revelation from and about Jesus Christ, but also faithfully reported it for all God's servants. Through the five stages of its transmission from God the Father to God the Son to the angel to John to those he wrote to, he 'bore witness to the word of God, and to the testimony [lit., witness] of Jesus Christ, to all things that he saw.' John was already suffering in exile on the island of Patmos 'for the word of God and for the witness of Jesus Christ' (v. 9), for this witness is borne by life and conduct, no less than by preaching or writing. But here John says that the word of God and the witness of Jesus Christ which he saw and heard was duly recorded in writing (v. 3) and sent to the churches of Asia to be read aloud in church meetings like the other inspired, apostolic Scriptures (Colossians 4:16; 2 Peter 3:15–16). This, however, was to be the last time that God would directly, visually and verbally communicate His truth to a man, and He was to do so with even greater power and splendour than He had done with Moses on Mount Sinai.

That brings us to verse 3, 'Blessed is he who reads and those who hear the words of this prophecy, and keep those things which are written in it; for the time is near.' John is inspired by the Holy Spirit to send forth his prophecy with a *beatitude* promising blessing on the reader and the hearers of the words of this prophecy. The reader is *singular* while the hearers are *plural*, because John intends that the book will be read aloud by one of the elders to the congregation of each church when it arrives. Obviously, several copies had to be made so that each church to which the messenger was sent, could have their own copy of the prophecy. The beatitude, moreover, is pronounced not merely on those who read and hear the prophecy, but in particular on those who 'keep those things which are written in it.' The reading and hearing, of course, is a preliminary necessity. But to heed its warnings and obey its commands is the main response required, apart from which all reading and hearing is futile. Revelation contains moral instruction and not just prophetic predictions.

The apostolic greeting

Verse 4, 'John, to the seven churches which are in Asia.' We have already dealt in our introduction to the book with the questions of *who* this John is, and *where* these churches were situated. It is the same John who was one of the apostles of Jesus and the writer of the fourth Gospel and the three letters that bear his name. The prophecy of Revelation was written in the form of a letter addressed to seven specific churches in the Roman province of Asia (the western, central portion of modern Turkey). Although in chapters 2 and 3 seven letters are addressed to seven particular churches in different towns, there were other churches, including Troas (Acts 20:5ff), Colossae (Colossians 1:2) and Hierapolis (Colossians 4:13) which were of equal importance in Asia when John wrote Revelation. The reason for limiting the number to seven is symbolic. In Scripture the number seven signifies divine activity and appointment. Thus we have the seven days of creation, the seven Spirits of God, the seven bowls of wrath and so on These seven churches then stand for all Christ's churches in every place and in every century. Indeed, that is why each letter ends with the declaration: 'He who has an ear, let him hear what the Spirit says to the churches' (i.e. to all churches, not just these particular ones).

To come back to the form of the letter, verses 4–8 contain the usual *salutation* and the last verse in Revelation contains the usual *benediction* found in most of the New Testament letters. The rest of the book, however, is utterly unlike any other letter in the New Testament, and can hardly be classified as such, yet it is. The greeting continues with the words, 'Grace to you and peace.' Grace is God's love showing mercy and favour to sinners who not only do not deserve such kindness, but instead deserve His wrath and condemnation.

The words are addressed to Christians because our need of God's grace does not stop after we have been converted. We need grace every day for cleansing from current sin and power to walk with God (1 John 1:5–10). 'Peace' is the fruit of God's grace that calms our fears and anxieties with the assurance that we are right with God and He has given us more than enough resources to see us safely to glory (Philippians 4:6–7).

John now goes on to more fully describe the source from which all grace and peace flows. They come from the Triune God: 'Grace to you and peace from Him who is and who was and who is to come.' This paraphrase of the divine name ('I AM', Exodus 3:14–15), calls attention to the eternal self-existence of God the Father, but it is equally true of God the Son and God the Holy Spirit. Secondly, grace and peace come 'from the seven Spirits who are before His throne.' Again, the number seven is symbolic. It refers to the completeness of the Holy Spirit's ministry to every church in every place and in every age. His sevenfold fullness (Isaiah 11:2) are equally present in the universal body of Christ's church. Michael Wilcock suggests that 'the unusual order of the Trinity here (Father, Spirit, Son) corresponds to the plan of the earthly sanctuary, where the ark in the Holy of Holies represents the throne of God, the seven-branched lampstand in the Holy Place before it represents the Spirit, and in the courtyard before that stands the altar, with its priest and its sacrifice both representing the redeeming work of Christ.'[2]

In verse 5 the second member of the Trinity is now given the fullest description: 'Grace and peace … from Jesus Christ, the faithful witness', because He is the living Word of God and the embodiment of truth (John 14:6). He is, furthermore, 'the firstborn from the dead.' Others have been resuscitated, only to do their dying all over again at a later time. Jesus Christ, however, was the first to be raised with a glorified, immortal body. Furthermore, the firstborn implies later-born children; namely, Christians whom He will raise from the dead

when He returns (John 6:44; 1 Corinthians 15:20–26). Thirdly, as
the firstborn and heir (Romans 8:17; Galatians 4:7), the Son is also
described as 'the ruler over the kings of the earth' (Psalm 89:27). For
the rulers of the world will try their hardest to destroy His church, but
they will never succeed (Matthew 16:18). He rules supreme, and on the
last day He will destroy all His enemies (17:14; 19:16).

A most fitting doxology

Such a wonderful Saviour deserves the praise of His people. So John
bursts spontaneously into this doxology: 'To Him who loved us and
washed us from our sins in His own blood, and has made us kings [lit.
a kingdom] and priests to His God and Father, to Him be glory and
dominion forever and ever. Amen' (vv. 5b–6). Some manuscripts have
'to Him who loves us' (present tense), for although He has washed or
'freed us' (ESV) once for all from our sins by His blood shed on the
cross as an atonement (Matthew 26:28; 1 John 1:7), Christ's love for
us is eternal. It preceded the cross and it continues after the cross as
He allows us to reign with Him in His kingdom and serve as priests
offering spiritual sacrifices acceptable to God through Him (1 Peter
2:5). This concept of God's people constituting a kingdom of priests is
found in Exodus 19:6 where God says to the Jews, 'You shall be to Me
a kingdom of priests and a holy nation.' It is also mentioned in 1 Peter
2:9, 'But you are a chosen generation, a *royal priesthood*, a holy nation,
His own special people, that you may proclaim the praises of Him who
called you out of darkness into His marvellous light' (italics added).

Our royal and priestly activity is something we already enjoy on
earth. Indeed as Philip Edgcumbe Hughes correctly points out:
'The ascription proper that now follows, "to Him be the glory and
the dominion for ever and ever. Amen", is itself an outpouring of
priestly praise, for, since we owe everything to God, the blessing
of our creation, the grace of our redemption, and His providential
care of our every need, all the praise and glory is due to Him and

none at all to ourselves. Our glorying is always and only in the Lord
(1 Corinthians 1:30).'[3]

The grand theme of Revelation

The grand theme of the Apocalypse is the absolute triumph of the
Lord Jesus Christ over evil and His judgment of it. This long-awaited
climax of history will only take place at the promised return (John
14:1–3; Acts 1:10–11) of God our Saviour which John now affirms.
Verse 7, 'Behold, He is coming with clouds [Daniel 7:13; Matthew
24:30], and every eye will see Him, even they who pierced Him' (v.
7). This is a very important verse. It tells us that the second coming
of Christ is not going to be secret, witnessed only by the Christians
who on that day will be caught up alive to heaven. John says, 'every
eye will see Him' including the wicked who are living at the time. This
is supported by the words that follow, 'and all the tribes of the earth
will mourn because of Him.' Those who all their lives looked upon
Jesus with contempt and repudiation, will now look upon Him with
terror and sorrow; not the godly sorrow that leads to repentance, but
with the self-pity and mourning of those who have been found out,
yet remain impenitent. The weeping and wailing will be *universal* for
'all the tribes of the earth will mourn because of Him.' At His coming
every impenitent member of the human race will see their culpability
in the rejection and execution of Jesus Christ. Moreover, there will be
no hiding from the resplendent glory of His sudden appearance, and
no escaping the fierce anger of His divine judgment on all who have
persisted in unbelief and impenitence. It will be the ultimate fulfilment
of the prophecy in Zechariah 12:10 (see John 19:37).

But while the wicked who pierced Him will bewail the misery
of their lot, Christ's own penitent people whose sins also nailed
Him to the cross will joyfully welcome Him. That is the force of
John's exclamation, 'Even so, Amen.' It is just two words, *nai* and
amen, the Greek and Hebrews words for expressing affirmation and

approval: 'Yes, indeed! So let it be!' Now it will not be vindictive for Christians to welcome the Judge of all the earth. We do not rejoice in the judgment of the wicked, but we do wholeheartedly approve the vindication of Christ in the overthrow of all His enemies at His return.

The divine authentication of Christ's triumph

Only here and in chapter 21:5 does God, the Father, Himself speak to make us absolutely confident about this vindication of Christ. He declares that He is 'the Alpha and the Omega, the Beginning and the End' (v. 8). *Alpha* is the first letter, and *Omega* the last letter of the Greek alphabet. The title tells us that God is 'the First, the Beginning' in the sense that He brought the whole created order into existence; and He is 'the Last, the End' in the sense that after He has destroyed His enemies, He will bring heaven and earth to the glorious end or purpose for which it was originally created. For He alone is 'the Almighty'. That is brought out in the relative clause that follows: 'says the Lord, who is and who was and who is to come, the Almighty.' In other words, although He has a past (the God who was) and a future (the God who is to come), He is first and foremost *eternal* (the God who is). He is the God who is eternally present; no one has preceded Him and no one will survive Him. Therefore none can resist His power and none can thwart His purposes. He alone can designate Himself 'the Almighty'. The contemplation of such a glorious God should evoke unshakable faith in the triumph of His Son, and unending worship to the praise of His glory.

> Praise to the Lord, the Almighty, the King of creation;
> Oh my soul, praise Him, for He is thy health and salvation:
> All ye who hear,
> Brothers and sisters, draw near,
> Praise Him in glad adoration.
>
> Praise to the Lord, who o'er all things so wondrously reigneth,
> Shelters thee under His wings, yea, so gently sustaineth:

Hast thou not seen?
All that is needful hath been
Granted in what He ordaineth.

Praise to the Lord, who doth prosper thy work, and defend thee!
Surely His goodness and mercy here daily attend thee:
Ponder anew
What the Almighty can do,
Who with His love doth befriend thee.

Praise to the Lord! O let all that is in me adore Him!
All that hath life and breath come now with praises before Him!
Let the amen
Sound from His people again;
Gladly for aye we adore Him.   (*Joachim Neander, 1650–80*)

2 The all-majestic Judge overseeing His church

1:9I, John, both your brother and companion in the tribulation and kingdom and patience of Jesus Christ, was on the island that is called Patmos for the word of God and for the testimony of Jesus Christ. 10I was in the Spirit on the Lord's Day, and I heard behind me a loud voice, as of a trumpet, 11saying, 'I am the Alpha and the Omega, the First and the Last,' and, 'What you see, write in a book and send it to the seven churches which are in Asia: to Ephesus, to Smyrna, to Pergamos, to Thyatira, to Sardis, to Philadelphia, and to Laodicea.'

12Then I turned to see the voice that spoke with me. And having turned, I saw seven golden lampstands, 13and in the midst of the seven lampstands One like the Son of Man, clothed with a garment down to the feet and girded about the chest with a golden band. 14His head and hair were white like wool, as white as snow, and His eyes like a flame of fire; 15His feet were like fine brass, as if refined in a furnace, and His voice as the sound of many waters; 16He had in His right hand seven stars, out of His mouth went a sharp two-edged sword, and His countenance was like the sun shining in its strength. 17And when I saw Him, I fell at His feet as dead. But He laid His right hand on me, saying to me, 'Do not be afraid: I am the First and the Last. 18I am He who lives, and was dead, and behold, I am alive forevermore. Amen. And I have the keys of Hades and of Death. [19]Write the things which you have seen, and the things which are, and the things which will take place after this. [20]The mystery of the seven stars which you saw in My right hand, and the seven golden lampstands: The seven stars are the angels of the seven churches, and the seven lampstands which you saw are the seven churches.

(Revelation 1:9–20)

The Apocalypse is made up of seven glorious and awesome visions that reveal the triumph of Jesus Christ over evil. The first is a vision of our all-majestic Judge in the midst of His church dictating seven letters, requiring seven essential marks which He wants to see in all His followers on earth (1:9–3:22). These letters underline the seriousness of the commitment that God demands from His people in His covenant of redemption (Deuteronomy 11:26–28; 30:18–20). To those who overcome Jesus promises blessings (2:7,11,17,26–27; 3:5,12,20–21). To those who fail to repent He threatens judgment (2:5,16,22–23; 3:3,16,19). It is a sobering prospect, but judgment must begin at the house of God (1 Peter 4:17).

It is the grandest and most detailed depiction of the divine-human Saviour of the world to be found in Scripture. Moreover, from the time of the Fall, the world has been and still is a hostile place for God's followers to live in, and so what Christians of every generation need more than anything else, is a faith-sustaining view of the glory, majesty and power of their risen, exalted and ever-present Lord who is both Saviour and Judge (Matthew 13:36–43; 24:45–51; John 5:21–30). Leon Morris comments, 'In doing this John persistently makes use of words and concepts associated in the Old Testament with God. He does not hesitate to employ divine attributes to describe the glorious Christ. And he does not do this and then forget it. The titles used of Christ in this vision are taken up and used elsewhere, notably in the addresses to the churches in chapters 2 and 3 (only that to the church of Laodicea is not drawn from this chapter).'[1]

Your brother and companion in tribulation

The apostle John did not write the book of Revelation of his own accord because he was the last remaining apostle and thought it was important to do so. Rather he wrote it because the Head of the church commissioned him to do so: 'What you see, write in a book [lit. a scroll] and send it to the seven churches which are in Asia' (v. 11). So he humbly identifies himself with the Asian Christians as 'your brother': not their brother in the flesh, but their brother in the spirit through their common union by faith with Jesus Christ, their elder brother (Hebrews 2:11–14). Our Lord, 'the only Son from the Father', came to earth to give His life a ransom for many, and 'to all who did receive Him, who believed in His name, He gave the right to become children of God, who were born, not of blood, nor of the will of the flesh, nor of the will of man, but of God' (John 1:14,12–13, ESV).

This identification with his Christian readers, present and future, is heightened by John calling himself, 'your ... companion [or fellow-partaker, NASB] in the tribulation and kingdom and patience [or perseverance, NASB] of Jesus Christ' (v. 9). Tribulation (lit. sore-pressure) is part of the cost of belonging to Jesus Christ and being a member of His kingdom. Thus our Lord said, 'A servant is not greater than his master. If they persecuted Me, they will also persecute you' (John 15:20). And Paul, who suffered much for Christ's sake, gave similar warnings to his Christian converts, saying, 'We must through many tribulations enter the kingdom of God'; 'For to you it has been granted on behalf of Christ, not only to believe in Him, but also to suffer for His sake'; 'that you may be counted worthy of the kingdom of God, for which you also suffer' (Acts 14:22; Philippians 1:29; 2 Thessalonians 1:5).

John then informs his readers that he 'was on the island that is called Patmos for the word of God and for the testimony of Jesus Christ' (v. 9). That is to say, he had been banished by the Roman Emperor to this penal colony on a little barren, rocky island some 60 miles south-west of Ephesus. The Roman authorities in Asia apparently regarded the apostle's preaching as seditious and banished him from the mainland in an attempt to stifle the growth of the churches in the Province. The hard labour in the quarries and the deprivation of his exile justified his claim to be a fellow-partaker in the tribulation common to all Christians. Their common lot is described as the 'tribulation and kingdom and patience of Jesus Christ.' And as Robert H. Mounce explains, 'The order of the three is instructive. Since the present is a time of tribulation and the kingdom a period of future blessedness, believers must during the interim period exercise that kind of patient endurance which was exemplified by Jesus.'[2]

Verse 10, 'I was in the Spirit' means 'I came to be in the Spirit.' It is a phrase which means more than being 'filled' with the Spirit. It was a special endowment of the Holy Spirit that was necessary for all the faculties of the seer to be enabled to see and hear and remember things that would otherwise be impossible to experience. The expression is unique to Revelation and occurs again in chapters 4:2; 17:3 and 21:10. In each case Spirit should be spelt with a capital 'S' rather than a small 's' as in the Authorized Version. Peter and Paul had similar visions (Acts 10:10; 11:5; Acts 22:17; 2 Corinthians 12:1–4). John also tells us that this experience involving all the visions of Revelation, not just some, took place 'on the Lord's Day', an expression not found anywhere else in the New Testament.

Elsewhere it is simply said that it was 'on the first day of the week when the disciples came together to break bread' and hear the word of God (Acts 20:7; see also John 20:19; 1 Corinthians 16:2). The Lord's Day here is therefore a reference to the first day of the week commemorating our Lord's resurrection from the dead and the outpouring of the Holy Spirit upon the church at Pentecost. For this reason, it would seem, it became the weekly Christian Sabbath in place of the Jewish Sabbath. And just as 'the breaking of bread' was later rightly called 'the Lord's Supper' (Acts 2:42; 1 Corinthians 11:20), so 'the first day of the week' was later rightly called 'the Lord's Day' (1 Corinthians 16:2).

Did it really matter to John on which day the Spirit came upon him in this extraordinary way? Could not any day of the week have been just as good? The answer from verse 10 is that it did matter. Even though he was unable to enjoy the privilege of worshipping with other believers, John remembers that it happened on the Lord's Day. This aged servant of God obviously treasured this special day of the week, and in spite of his isolation made the most of the time available to him to draw near to God. And as he turned his heart and thoughts away from the quarry and upwards to heaven, God spoke to him in this series of visions. These words are surely written for our instruction. The same God who met with John on that Lord's Day is the God who continues to meet with all His people every Lord's Day.

Our Lord's words to John

Uniquely possessed by the Holy Spirit, John says, 'And I heard behind me a loud voice, as of a trumpet' (v. 10). Trumpets are mentioned more often in Revelation than in the rest of the New Testament put together, and they were blown to call attention to an important announcement. The loud voice is the voice of Christ (vv. 17ff). And as Thomas F. Torrance quaintly puts it, 'the voice spoke like a trumpet with no uncertain sound, and with one blast the whole earthly panorama was transformed. The apostle's eyes became young with eternity, and he saw as he never saw before … the heavens above unfolded like a scroll before his eyes.'[3]

Our Lord then introduces Himself by saying, 'I am the Alpha and the Omega, the First and the Last' (v. 11). These words are omitted by the other modern versions using earlier Greek manuscripts. But there is no need to omit them, because whether these words used of God in verse 8 are appropriated here by Christ or not, they are used by Him in verse 17 and again in chapter 22:13. Moreover, it is important that both at the beginning of Revelation and at the end Christ is seen as equal with God the Father. For the Christians to whom this book was first publicly read, needed to hear that claim by Jesus right upfront in order to draw the full comfort of the visions that follow. They needed to know that He is the Alpha and the Omega: the One who is before all and after all; who finishes what He begins; who had the first word and will also have the last word; whose purposes can never fail.

Next, the voice of Christ says, 'And what you see write in a book [lit. on a scroll] and send it to the seven churches which are in Asia' (v. 11b). Everything written is to be contained in one scroll. The seven letters are not to be seen as seven separate letters, each one to be read only by the particular church to which it was addressed. The entire scroll was to be read at each church for the spiritual enlightenment and benefit of all 'the churches' (2:7,11,17,29; 3:6,13,22). The seven are then named by the cities in which they were located: 'to Ephesus, to Smyrna, to Pergamos, to Thyatira, to Sardis, to Philadelphia, and to Laodicea.' The order in which the churches are addressed is strictly geographical. They do not portray the spiritual condition of the universal church in seven successive periods of church history, as dispensational premillennialists maintain. To quote Hal Lindsey: 'Here in seven typical churches we see the predominant characteristics of seven successive eras of Church history. The prophetic aspects were never understood clearly until much of the church history had unfolded, but now as we look back we can see striking similarities between the characteristics of each church in Revelation and the various periods of church history up to our present day.'[4]

As stated above (see v. 4), the number 'seven' is a symbol of divinity. The significance of seven was established by God right from the beginning of time. God could have completed His plan of creation in one day or in one second, but He did not. We are not told why He did so, but simply that it is so. By divine appointment seven days complete a man's working week, and seventy years his allotted span of life. So these seven churches stand for Christ's church throughout its history in every land and in every generation. As noted above, there were more than seven churches in the province of Asia by the time this book was written. Why were the churches at Troas, Colossae and Hierapolis not addressed by letter? Did they have no sins to be condemned and no virtues to be commended? No! The seven were chosen because their strengths and weaknesses are characteristic of individual churches throughout this church age.

The awesome appearance of our Saviour and Judge

Verse 12, 'Then I turned to see the voice that spoke with me.' The loud voice, as of a trumpet, had come from behind John, so he turned to see who it was that was speaking to him. But the first thing he sees is not the speaker but 'seven golden lampstands.' That is to say, seven separate stands on which lamps might be stood or hung, and not one stand with seven branches like the menorah in the temple. This is probably because the separate lampstands, which verse 20 says stand for 'the seven churches', depict the church as the world sees it, scattered and vulnerable. But the church as God sees it is united and indestructible, for she is also 'the seven stars' in Christ's right hand that cannot be plucked from His almighty grasp (vv. 16,20; John 10:27–30).

Verse 13, 'And in the midst of the seven lampstands One like the Son of Man.' That is to say, whose form was that of a human being, but who is more than a man. For the Person, as verse 18 shows, is none other than the risen Christ, the incarnate Son of God now resplendent in the glory which He had with the Father 'before the world was' (John 17:5). He is also the same 'Son of Man' in Daniel 7 whom the prophet saw 'coming with the clouds of heaven ... [to whom] was given dominion and glory and a kingdom ... which shall not be destroyed' (vv. 13–14). It is the same picture of Christ who after receiving the kingdom from 'the Ancient of Days' is seen 'coming with clouds' in Revelation 1:7 and again in chapter 14:14 where John says, 'Then I looked, and ... on the cloud sat One like the Son of Man, having on His head a golden crown.' Notice, too, that the glorified Christ is seen 'in the midst of the seven lampstands', for He is the Head of the church who watches over it and superintends all its activities.

As John continues His description of Christ, he says that He was 'clothed with a garment down to the feet and girded about the chest with a golden band.' Some say this is the garment of a priest, but in ancient times a long robe with a golden girdle about the breast could also be the garment of a very high dignitary, like a king or judge, or even both: a king who also acts as judge.[5] So 'His head and hair were white like wool, as white as snow' (v. 14). Whiteness in Revelation nearly always stands for absolute *purity* and *integrity* (3:4; 6:11; 7:9; 15:6; 19:8,14; see also Isaiah 1:18). So the whiteness of Christ's head and hair denote the absolute purity and integrity of His character and judgments. And here again, something that is attributed only to God the Father in Daniel 7:9 is attributed also to Jesus Christ His Son. For in Daniel's vision it is said of 'the Ancient of Days ... His garment was white as snow and the hair of His head was like pure wool', for they share the same divine essence.

To complete the picture of the absolute purity and integrity of the character and judgments of the reigning Christ, we are told that He has 'eyes like a flame of fire.' No one can conceal their sins from the burning, penetrating gaze of His fiery eyes: 'There is no creature hidden from His sight, but all things are naked and open to the eyes of Him to whom we must give account' (Hebrews 4:13). Not only does He see all men, but He also sees through all men. Verse 15, 'His feet were like fine brass, as if refined in a furnace.' Feet of gleaming brass or bronze is a symbol of the *splendour* and *strength* of Christ as the returning Judge. He is pictured as relentless and irresistible. When He tramples His enemies under His feet, none will escape. They will be thoroughly crushed (6:12–17; 19:11–16; 20:11–15). Moreover, John says, 'His voice was like the sound of many waters' (v. 15), like the thunder of the mighty waves beating the rocky coast of Patmos. It is also a description applied by Ezekiel to the voice of God (43:2), and it symbolizes the fact that Christ's judgments will go unchallenged. Any protest against the sentence He passes will be drowned out by His loud, unequivocal voice. The church, however, has nothing to fear. The salvation of His people is secure, for Christ has 'in His right hand seven stars' (i.e. the church, vv. 16,20) where no harm can befall them.

Verse 16 carries on the attributes of the Judge of all the earth by saying: 'out of His mouth went a sharp two-edged sword.' In the Bible the sword in the mouth of God's servants or Son is always the word of God. In Isaiah 49:2 the Servant of the Lord (who is Christ) says, 'The Lord has made My mouth like a sharp sword.' In Ephesians 6:17 Paul writes of 'the sword of the Spirit which is the word of God'; and in Hebrews 4:12 we read that 'the word of the Lord is living and active and sharper than any two-edged sword, piercing even to the division of soul and spirit, and of joints and marrow, and is a discerner of the thoughts and intents of the heart.' Philip Edgcumbe Hughes brings out the meaning of this analogy best: 'Such sharpness far surpasses the sharpness of any man-made sword. That the sword which is the Lord's word has two edges means that it never fails to cut. If it does not cut with the edge of salvation it cuts with the edge of condemnation; for the word of redemption to all who believe is at the same time the word of destruction to those who refuse to believe, as in 2:16 and 19:15 (see in particular John 12:47f).'[6]

Verse 16 ends, 'and His countenance [face, ESV] was like the sun shining in its strength.' After all, in Malachi 4:2 Christ is called 'the Sun of Righteousness.' The sun in our planetary system is only a huge ball of fiery lava, and therefore cannot match the absolutely brilliant transcendental splendour of the innate glory of the divine Christ, which instantly blinded Saul of Tarsus on the road to Damascus to persecute the church (Acts 26:13ff). It is the same glory that suffused His face and clothes on the Mount of Transfiguration and will burst forth upon the world when He returns on the Day of Judgment (Matthew 17:2; Revelation 6:16). On that day all Christians, both the living and the dead, will rise up to meet Him in the air. We will not be terrified to look at Him for we will be sinless. 'We shall be like Him, for we shall see Him as He is' (1 John 3:2). Or as our Lord promised, 'The righteous shall shine forth as the sun in the kingdom of their Father' (Matthew 13:43). Those, however, who remain in their sins will say 'to the mountains and rocks, "Fall on us and hide us from the face of Him who sits on the throne and from the wrath of the Lamb. For the great day of His wrath has come, and who is able to stand?"' (6:16–17).

John's response to the glorified Christ

Verse 17, 'And when I saw Him, I fell at His feet as dead.' This was not John prostrating himself before Christ in worship. This was the physical effect upon John of the awesome appearance of His exalted Lord and the awareness of his own utter unworthiness and sinfulness. We see this same effect throughout the Bible. When God revealed His glory to Moses on Mount Sinai, we read: 'So terrifying was the sight that Moses said, "I am exceedingly afraid and trembling"' (Hebrews 12:21). So it was with Isaiah and Ezekiel and Saul of Tarsus when they saw the glory of Christ (Isaiah 6:1–6; John 12:41; Ezekiel 3:23; Acts 9:3–4). The lesson we learn from all this is that the higher the view we have of Christ, the lower the view we have of ourselves. There is something wrong in the church when we can be superficial and self-centred in our worship services, both in our songs and in our sermons. More and more we need to be in the Spirit on the Lord's Day, so that we might see more of the glory of the exalted Christ.

Mercifully, the exalted Christ 'laid His right hand' on John, saying, 'Do not be afraid.' Derek Thomas aptly comments, 'One of the things that the book of Revelation teaches us is that there are many appropriate ways of responding to Christ, but if the fear of God is not one of them, we have never fully responded to Him. It was not inappropriate for John to fall before Jesus as though he were dead, yet Jesus says to John, "Fear not" (1:17). These two things go together. We fall down before His exalted majesty, and we feel the reassurance of His hand upon our shoulder encouraging us not to be afraid. There is no other Jesus and there can be no other adequate response. We are awed by His majesty and drawn by His grace.'[7]

Our Lord then identifies Himself. We have assumed all along it was Christ, but here He makes it clear. He says, 'I am the First and the Last', affirming His eternal being and power as God. But then Jesus adds, 'I am He who lives, and was dead, and behold I am alive for evermore. Amen' (v. 18). This can only refer to our Saviour who claimed to be 'the Life', because He is the Creator of all life (John 14:6; 1:1–3; 10:10; Colossians 1:16). More importantly, the Son of Man came to earth to die and 'give His life a ransom for many'; for the penalty of sin demanded by God's law is eternal death, the death of the body and the soul in hell. Jesus suffered this God-forsaken death on the cross for all who will believe in Him as their Saviour (Mark 10:45; Romans 6:23; 1 Peter 1:18–19; 3:18). Moreover, as the Lord of life, He suffered this death victoriously: 'I lay down My life that I may take it again. No one takes it from Me, but I lay it down of Myself. I have power to lay it down, and I have power to take it again' (John 10:14–18). The power of a divinely sufficient atonement which fully and eternally paid the penalty for all the sins of all His people. Death could have no more hold on Him (Acts 2:24).

That is why Christ goes on to say, 'And behold, I am alive forevermore. Amen. And I have the keys of Hades and of Death.' Hades is the realm of departed or disembodied spirits to which death reduces us all. It is not just the grave where the body decays. When Christians die their spirits go to heaven (2 Corinthians 5:6–8; Philippians 1:21–23; Hebrews 12:22–24), while the spirits of unbelievers go to hell (Luke 16:22–26). Christ alone has the keys to unlock the gates of Hades and reunite the spirits of the righteous and the wicked with their resurrected bodies; the righteous with bodies of *glory* and the wicked with bodies of *ignominy*. The 'keys' are symbols of His authority and power to do so as the Saviour of the world whose atonement on the cross has delivered believers from the curse of sin and the bondage of death (Galatians 3:13; Romans 8:18–23; Hebrews 2:14–15). This truth is repeated in Revelation 20 when at the final judgment we are told that 'Death and Hades [personified in the total number of the damned] were cast into the lake of fire. This is the second death' (i.e. the everlasting destruction of body and soul in hell).

In verse 19 John is instructed to 'write the things that you have seen [namely, the vision of the exalted Christ as the Judge of all the earth], and the things which are [the present state of the church which Christ will disclose in chapters 2 and 3], and the things which will take place after this' (i.e. His victory over the devil, and the creation of a new heaven and a new earth). John presumably wrote all these visions he saw and the words he heard when the 'Revelation of Jesus Christ' was completed. Let me stress, however, that because the unveiling of these things is in symbols our understanding of them is *partial* and not *precise*. Only at Christ's return will everything become fully clear to those who are alive at that time.

Verse 20, 'The mystery of the seven stars which you saw in My right hand, and the seven golden lampstands: The seven stars are the angels of the seven churches, and the seven lampstands which you saw are the seven churches.' Here the two symbols of the lampstands and the stars are interpreted for us. Taking the lampstands first, the symbol is saying that the prime function of the church on earth is to be a bearer of Christ's light. Christ Himself is 'the light of the world', (John 8:12), and we are to bear that light by showing Him to the world through the Christlike life we live and the words of Christ we speak. Thus the apostle Paul urges the Christians at Philippi to 'become blameless and harmless, children of God without fault in the midst of a crooked and perverse generation, among whom you shine as lights in the world, holding fast the word of life' (2:15–16). 'It is not the church's business', says Richard Brooks, 'to make truth, alter truth or improve truth, but to receive it, stand firm upon it, contend earnestly for it, preach it, adorn it with holy living, and—if necessary—die for it.'[8] The lampstands are 'golden' because gold is a symbol of their preciousness in Christ's sight.

Next, our glorified Lord says, 'The seven stars are the angels of the seven churches.' But what does He mean by the term 'angels'? Three main interpretations have been given. Some think that what is meant is angelic beings. After all, they say, if individuals and nations have guardian angels (Matthew 18:10; Acts 12:15; Psalm 91:11; Daniel 10:13; 12:1), why should not every church have one? Moreover, even if we exclude chapters 1–3, the seventy remaining references to angels in Revelation all refer to spirit beings. The difficulty with this view, however, is what would be the point of addressing a letter to an angel who stands in the presence of Christ in heaven, and calling him to repent of his sins?

The second view is that they are the seven *pastors* overseeing the churches, for the word 'angel' literally means a 'messenger.' But every New Testament church had several pastors or elders (Philippians 1:1)—why address the letter to only one? And again, why should the pastor of each church be the only one to enjoy the blessing of being held safe and secure in the hand of Christ? The third view makes the most sense. If we interpret Scripture by Scripture, we read in John 10:27–30 that all Christ's sheep are held in His hand and not just their under-shepherds. So the third view is to regard the angels as a symbol of the whole church rather than one person. For as the angels are the messengers of God, so the churches are messengers of Christ to the world. In other words, each church is a bearer of light, whether you liken it to a star or a lampstand. The lampstands are isolated, but the stars are held together safely in Christ's right hand. The lampstands are symbols of the *individual responsibility and accountability* of the churches to bear Christ's light to the world. The stars are symbols of the *unity and the safety* that the churches enjoy because they are in the right hand of Christ from which they can never be plucked.

The placing of this vision of the exalted Christ as the Judge of the living and the dead right at the beginning of the book is very significant. The church is Christ's 'little flock' (Luke 12:32), outnumbered by formidable foes in the form of the world and the devil. To all outward appearance our situation most of the time seems hopeless. It is only as our Lord Jesus is seen for what He really is as the Victor of sin and death, and the Judge of Satan and the world, that everything else can be seen in its true perspective. Moreover, to accentuate the matter, the divine attributes of the Judge who is returning to earth to right all wrongs are not just described here and forgotten, but repeated in chapters 2 and 3. With Jesus as the captain of our salvation and the commander of the Lord's army, we have nothing to fear. Victory is certain. It is around the corner. Until then, our God and Saviour, the 'Sun of Righteousness', will enable us to endure patiently all tribulation, hold fast to the truth, resist the devil and obey the commandments of God. How dark and dreadful is the future for those who continue to resist the Holy Spirit's work of unveiling the glory of Christ's person and the triumph of His work of redemption; who see Him only as the Jesus of history, the carpenter of Nazareth, and have never fallen down before Him as their merciful Saviour and returning King!

3 Christ's letters to Ephesus and Smyrna

As we turn our attention to the letters Christ wrote to the seven churches in the province of Asia (chapters 2 and 3), it is important to note that they have a basic structure:

First, they all begin with the same *greeting*: 'To the angel of the church in Ephesus', and so on.

Second, Christ identifies Himself appropriately to each church through one of the *attributes* unveiled in the vision of Himself given to John (1:12–20).

Third, Christ then *commends* the church concerned (except in the case of Laodicea).

Fourth, we have a *complaint* about some of the churches (Smyrna and Philadelphia being the exceptions).

Fifth, comes a solemn *warning* to the impenitent.

Sixth, our Lord then issues an *exhortation* which is identical in each case: 'He who has an ear, let him hear what the Spirit says to the churches.'

Seventh, each letter concludes with a *promise* to those who overcome.

Something else of note is that although these letters are addressed to seven particular churches in John's time, they convey a message to every church for all time. So the letter to *Ephesus* tells us that Christ wants His church to *love* Him above and beyond everything and everyone else. The letter to *Smyrna* tells us that Christ wants His church to be *faithful* to Him even to the point of being prepared to die for him. The letter to *Pergamum* tells us that Christ wants His church to stand up for the *truth* He has given it through His apostles and their writings. The letter to *Thyatira* tells us that Christ wants His church to be *holy* and take every precaution not to compromise with the evil that surrounds it in the world.

The letter to *Sardis* tells us that Christ wants His church to be *sincere* and not pretend to be something outwardly that it is not inwardly. The letter to *Philadelphia* tells us that Christ wants His church to be *evangelistic* and take advantage of every door of opportunity He opens for it. And the letter to *Laodicea* tells us that Christ wants His church to be wholehearted about the things of God and not cold or even lukewarm. These are seven marks of every true church, and they impress upon us from the outset the timelessness of the book of Revelation. It is for every church and every Christian in every generation.

The church in Ephesus

2:1To the angel of the church of Ephesus write, 'These things says He who holds the seven stars in His right hand, who walks in the midst of the seven golden lampstands: 2"I know your works, your labour, your patience, and that you cannot bear those who are evil. And you have tested those who say they are apostles and are not, and have found them liars; ³and you have persevered and have patience, and have laboured for My name's sake and have not become weary. ⁴Nevertheless I have this against you, that you have left your first love. ⁵Remember therefore from where you have fallen; repent and do the first works, or else I will come to you quickly and remove your lampstand from its place—unless you repent. ⁶But this you have, that you hate the deeds of the Nicolaitans, which I also hate.

⁷He who has an ear, let him hear what the Spirit says to the churches. To him who overcomes I will give to eat from the tree of life, which is in the midst of the Paradise of God."' (Revelation 2:1–7)

Ephesus was some 60 miles north by sea from the island of Patmos, and the first city the bearer of the letter would come to. It was the largest and most important city of the Roman province of Asia. Because much of the trade from the East to Rome came through the port of Ephesus, it was also a very prosperous centre of business. Its magnificent temple in honour of the goddess Diana was one of the seven wonders of the ancient world. The Christian church there was founded by the apostle Paul with the help of Aquila and Priscilla 'about AD 52 when Paul left them there en route from Corinth to Antioch'[1] on the return leg of his second missionary journey (Acts 18:18–21). The apostle rejoined the couple when he made Ephesus the first stop on his third journey. He spent altogether three years (Acts 20:31) in the city preaching to Jews and Gentiles, and in the end a riot broke out because of a drop in the sale of silver models of the temple of Diana (Acts 19:1–20:1). But when Paul had to leave Ephesus, he left Timothy behind to supervise the growing work (1 Timothy 1:3). According to an early tradition, John replaced Timothy around AD 66 and eventually died there, after being released from Patmos when Domitian was assassinated around AD 96.

The church at Ephesus was therefore about 40 years old by this time and another generation had arisen that did not share the ardent devotion for Jesus that the first generation of converts had. The risen

Lord, however, is in a position to accurately evaluate the condition of each church, for He says: 'These things says He who holds the seven stars in His right hand, who walks in the midst of the seven golden lampstands' (v. 1). This claim is even stronger than the one Jesus makes in chapter 1:13 and 16. He not only 'has' the stars; He 'holds' them. He not only 'stands in the midst' of the lampstands; He 'walks in the midst' of them. He is the divine overseer of the churches who dwells with His people; who walks among them; who inspects them, and therefore knows their good as well as their bad works, their favourable and their unfavourable circumstances.

So He begins with a word of *commendation*. The church at Ephesus exhibited three virtues that Jesus could praise. 'I know your works', He says, and then adds by way of explanation, 'your labour' (or toil, ESV). The Greek word means strenuous and exhausting activity serving their Lord and each other. Not only that, Jesus says: 'I know your patience.' That is to say, their 'perseverance' (mg.) in the face of fierce local opposition. For although Paul had left Ephesus and died some 30 years before this, the hostility of Jews and Gentile idol-worshippers in Ephesus towards Christians still lingered (Acts 19:8–9, 23–41). John Stott comments, 'They knew what it was to be hated, to be snubbed in public and maligned in private. Some found business hard, since they were losing customers. Others found shopping a problem, as a number of tradesmen would not sell to them.'[2]

The third thing that Jesus commends is their orthodoxy. The church at Ephesus had been visited by some men who falsely claimed to be apostles: 'I know ... that you cannot bear those who are evil. And you have tested those who say they are apostles and are not, and have found them liars' (v. 2). In verse 6 they are also called Nicolaitans: 'But this you have, that you hate the deeds of the Nicolaitans, which I also hate', and in verse 14 they are identified as those who promoted sexual immorality. In his farewell to the elders of the church at Ephesus, Paul had warned them that fierce wolves would come in among them, not sparing the flock (Acts 20:29). As predicted, the wolves had come, but the Ephesians to their credit had 'tested' their teaching by comparing it with that of Christ and His apostles, and found the Nicolaitans to be 'liars.' Although they did not hate the Nicolaitans themselves, they hated their works and totally repudiated them.

Verse 3 resumes and increases the commendation in verse 2, 'And you have persevered and have patience, and have laboured for My name's sake and have not become weary.' They had not abandoned the cause of Christ under the stress of persecution and false teaching. The secret of their steadfastness was that their loyalty and suffering had been for the sake of Christ's name. They had not done it for their own sake, to be well thought of by the other churches. If they had, they would soon have abandoned the struggle. Nor had they done it because they imagined that their sufferings would put God in their debt. Rather they worked hard and endured affliction patiently because they wanted to bring honour and not disgrace to His matchless name. They felt privileged to be 'counted worthy to suffer shame for His name' (Acts 5:41).

In all these respects, Ephesus was an admirable church, but in the sight of Christ who walks in the midst of His churches something crucial was missing, and so praise had to be followed by *reproof:* 'Nevertheless I have this against you, that you have left your first love' (v. 4). Loyalty to Jesus Christ and His truth must never come at the cost of love for the Saviour Himself. Hard-working and long-suffering Christians can become joyless and introverted, if they are not constantly motivated by responsive grateful love for His incomparable dying love for us (Romans 12:1; 1 Jn. 4:19). Now some define 'first love' as honeymoon love, or our love for Christ at conversion. But though such love can be passionate, it is often not enduring when it becomes engrossed with other secondary and yet good things. Honeymoon love can soon cool after the first flush of ecstasy has died down and one party takes the other for granted. Israel is an Old Testament example:

'Thus says the LORD, "I remember the devotion of your youth, your love as a bride, how you followed Me in the wilderness, in a land not sown. Israel was holy to the LORD … What wrong did your fathers find in Me that they went far from Me?"' (Jeremiah 2:2–5, ESV).

That is not the kind of love Jesus is talking about here. It is a growing love that is not primarily first in *time*, but first in *place*. He clearly taught this in Matthew 22:37–38, 'You shall love the Lord your God with all your heart, with all your soul, and with all your mind. This is the first and great commandment.' Toil without ardent love for Christ will soon degenerate into drudgery. 'Jacob served seven years for Rachel', the Scripture says, 'and they seemed only a few days to him because of the love he had for her' (Genesis 29:20). Toil must be motivated by love. Endurance of persecution can become grievous and bitter if it is not softened and sweetened by 'love undying' for Him who suffered nothing less than damnation for us. They endured with stoicism, but without love. And orthodoxy can be harsh and unappealing if we do not speak 'the truth in love' (Ephesians 4:15); a love that hates the deeds of sinners like the Nicolaitans, while at the same time seeking their good through bringing them to repentance.

Love is the pre-eminent virtue in our relationship with Christ and men. It is the chief 'fruit of the Spirit' at work in us (Galatians 5:22), the one quality without which all others have no value. Thus Paul can say in 1 Corinthians 13:1–2, 'If I speak in the tongues of men and of angels, but have not love, I am a noisy gong or a clanging cymbal. And if I have prophetic powers, and understand all mysteries and all knowledge, and if I have all faith so as to remove mountains, but have not love, I am nothing.' The only virtues that abide are 'faith, hope and love, these three; but the greatest of these is love' (v. 13). The failure to love the Triune God first and foremost will always impoverish our relationship with Him.

That is the *counsel* our Lord gives the Ephesians in verse 5,

'Remember therefore from where you have fallen; repent and do the first works.' Philip Edgcumbe Hughes is very helpful here:

> Departure from first love is a falling; it is symptomatic of a decline in practice as well as in devotion, for first love and *first works* belong together; the latter spring naturally from the former. Consequently, the disappearance of the first love entails the disappearance also of the first works, which are works distinguished by selfless zeal and joyful dedication. To recapture the first love is to return to the first works, and this is what the church in Ephesus needs to do if it is to recover its well-being before God. Although still toiling and enduring in the Lord's cause, the Ephesian church is in a state of decline, and culpably so. Hence the admonition to *remember* the original intensity of zeal and devotion from which it has *fallen* and to *repent* of its declension and return to that first intensity.[3]

Our Lord then adds a warning to further motivate them: 'or else I will come to you quickly and remove your lampstand from its place—unless you repent' (v. 5). We must be careful to understand the threat that the Son of God is making here. It is not a threat against individual true believers. The Good Shepherd's sheep are eternally secure (John 10:27–30). None will ever be lost (John 6:37; 17:12). When they sin they will repent. So they are described as belonging to God's invisible church, for only 'the Lord knows those who are His' (2 Timothy 2:19). This invisible church which is made up of true believers must therefore be distinguished from the *visible churches* that claim to be a part of it. No local church can assume permanency. Every professing church in every place is continuously on trial and by its impenitence may lapse into the darkness of extinction. Ephesus today is a sad example. There is nothing there except a small railway station, a hotel and a few houses. Their lampstand was 'removed from its place.' For though the locality where God's light once burned brightly may be left in darkness, His light does not cease to burn. It is 'removed' and placed elsewhere. This is a serious complaint and threat. It is significant that only in the

first and last of the seven letters is a church threatened with actual
extinction, and in each case the reason is that it lacks fervent devotion.

To encourage the church in Ephesus to heed His warning, Christ
now adds a *promise* to those members who do repent: 'He who has
an ear, let him hear what the Spirit says to the churches. To him
who overcomes I will give to eat from the tree of life, which is in
the midst of the Paradise of God.' To hear and obey responsively
is imperative because it is God who is speaking, and what the Holy
Spirit says to the church at Ephesus He says to all 'the churches'; not
just to the churches in the Roman province of Asia, but to all the
churches throughout the world till the end of time. The pronouns are
all singular, because each church is made up of individual members
whose responsibility it is to obey the Spirit's summons individually.
Accordingly, the promise to 'overcome' their neglect of loving
Christ supremely is also addressed to each individual member of
His churches.

Moreover, the promise is particularly apt. Instead of forfeiting the
presence and blessing of God in Paradise or heaven, every overcomer
will inherit them. Heaven is the abode of love, for heaven is where
God is, and God is love. This is a fitting reward for those who want to
love God more, for heaven is the only place where we will ever be able
to love God perfectly without any rivals. No hint, however, is given in
this letter as to how first love may be rekindled, but John does give us a
clue in his First Epistle where he says, 'We love Him because He first
loved us.' The only way to really rekindle 'first love' for Christ, is to go
back to the cross where in utter self-giving love He bore the guilt and
punishment of our sin to put us in the right with God. He gave His all
for us when we were at our worst. No one has or ever could show us
greater love than that (Romans 5:6–8).

The church in Smyrna

2:8 And to the angel of the church in Smyrna write, 'These things says the

First and the Last, who was dead, and came to life: ⁹"I know your works, tribulation, and poverty (but you are rich); and I know the blasphemy of those who say they are Jews and are not, but are a synagogue of Satan. ¹⁰Do not fear any of those things which you are about to suffer. Indeed, the devil is about to throw some of you into prison, that you may be tested, and you will have tribulation ten days. Be faithful unto death, and I will give you the crown of life. ¹¹He who has an ear, let him hear what the Spirit says to the churches. He who overcomes shall not be hurt by the second death."' (Revelation 2:8–11)

If the first mark of a true church is *first love*, the second is *faithfulness* until death (v. 10c). The town of Smyrna was situated some 35 miles north of Ephesus along the coast, and it is the only one of the seven cities that still exists. Its modern name is Izmir, and it is the third largest city in Turkey today. To this church our Lord offers no word of rebuke, not because it is perfect, but because it is faithful. So although it receives the shortest letter (only four verses), it gets the warmest praise. Appropriately, Christ begins by choosing a title from the vision of Himself in chapter 1 that is perfectly suited to the situation of persecution that is about to overtake them: 'These things says the First and the Last, who was dead, and came to life' (v. 8). In other words, take heart, your Head 'became obedient to the point of death' (Philippians 2:8). I allowed them to put Me to death so that I could pay the penalty of your sin and deliver you from the curse of death. But then, 'I came to life.' I rose from the dead, for nothing can destroy Me or those I love. 'I am the First and the Last.' Nothing precedes Me and nothing can succeed Me.

What a wonderful way to start a letter to a church, some of whose members are going to be martyred! No matter what our enemies threaten to do to us, Christ always has the last word. Verse 9, 'I know your works, your tribulation and your poverty (but you are rich).' The word 'tribulation' literally means 'sore pressures.' Leon Morris paraphrases it as 'the burden that crushes.'[4] There were those in the city who were doing their utmost to squeeze the life out of their Christian neighbours. So Jesus says, 'I know your poverty.' They were probably quite poor to begin with. By God's design the Gospel attracts in the main the nobodies of society, not the wealthy. But now things were worsening as Christians were terminated from their jobs and refused service when they went to buy food from Jewish shopkeepers. If they went to Gentile shopkeepers they were probably forced to pay more for food, so it became increasingly difficult to provide for their families.

'I know your poverty (but you are rich).' They were not materially rich, but spiritually rich. They were 'rich towards God' (Luke 12:21). They had 'treasure in heaven': namely, the forgiveness of their sins, peace with God, eternal life, a Saviour-High Priest praying for them at God's right hand, and the Holy Spirit dwelling in them as their heavenly Helper. Let men despise our material poverty! It matters not if Christ can add His reassuring parenthesis 'but you are rich.' Only He knows what true, lasting riches are. Sadly, notice who it was that was stirring up all this opposition: 'I know the blasphemy [slander, ESV] of those who say they are Jews and are not, but are a synagogue of Satan' (v. 9; cf. Romans 2:25–29). It came from unconverted Jews who hated Christ and branded all Jews who followed Him as traitors to their religion, their culture and their nation. Though they boasted of having Abraham as their father, by their evil deeds they showed themselves to be the children of 'Satan' (the term is Hebrew and means 'adversary', but its Greek equivalent ('devil' v. 10) means 'slanderer' or 'false accuser', see John 8:33–44). They were indeed a synagogue carrying out the activities of God's supreme adversary, Satan.

As their fellow-Jews did to Paul, so these Jews sought to get the Christians into trouble with the Roman authorities. Smyrna was renowned for its loyalty to Rome, 'and in 195 BC it became the first city in the ancient world to build a temple in honour of *Dea Roma* [Rome personified as a goddess]. Later, in 23 BC, Smyrna won permission (over ten other Asian cities) to build a temple to the emperor Tiberius (Tacitus, *Ann.* iv.55–56). This strong allegiance to Rome, plus a large Jewish population which was actively hostile to the Christians made it exceptionally difficult to live as a Christian in Smyrna. The most famous martyrdom of the early church fathers was that of the elderly Polycarp, the "twelfth martyr in Smyrna", who, upon his refusal to acknowledge Caesar as Lord, was placed upon a pyre to be burned' [c. AD 156].[5] So when the Smyrnean Christians refused to sprinkle incense on the fire that burned before the emperor's bust and say, 'Caesar is Lord', the local Jews reported them to the authorities. The Jews were only too happy to do this, because they were exempt from this religious obligation on the grounds that they were too fanatical about their religion to conform and prone to rioting. In reality, therefore, these Jews who rejected Christ and persecuted His followers in Smyrna were God's adversaries. Their house of worship was nothing less than 'a synagogue of Satan.' Those are strong words, but they are true even to this day of every house of worship that rejects Christ and does not worship Him exclusively as God and Saviour.

Verse 10, 'Do not fear any of those things which you are about to suffer. Indeed, the devil is about to throw some of you into prison … Be faithful until death.' Here is an appeal to be loyal to Christ whatever the cost in suffering. *Fear* is the opposite of *faith*. They cannot co-exist. Faith banishes fear and faith produces faithfulness. When our faith is fully in Christ, we shall be faithful even to the point of death. How then can our faith in Christ grow so strong that it will not deny Him in order to spare us suffering? By remembering His promises and trusting Him to keep them without fail (Romans 10:17). Our Lord has already given them some reasons why their faith should be strong. He is 'the First and the Last.' He is from everlasting to everlasting. We change as we grow old and become frail, but His power to keep His people is 'the same yesterday and today and forever' (Hebrews 13:8). When fear grips our hearts, and our reputation and possessions and life are threatened, nothing can keep us steadfast and true like faith in Christ who is before all things and continues after all things.

Again, He told them that He is victor over death which is the penalty of sin. He died not for His own sins but for the sins of His people, 'and He came to life.' He rose from the grave. So even if they have to be faithful until death, they can trust Him. He will raise them up again on the last day just as He raised Himself from the dead on the third day. Four times in John 6 Jesus told His disciples that He would raise them up 'at the last day' (vv. 39,40,44,54). 'The keys of Death and Hades' are in His hand (1:18). They must 'not fear those who kill the body, but cannot kill the soul' (Matthew 10:28).

But now Jesus gives them three more good reasons why they are to trust Him and be faithful. The first is that He has a *purpose* for allowing them to be persecuted in this way. He says, it is in order that 'you may be tested' (v. 10b). Satan's design was to *destroy* their faith. Christ's design is to *strengthen* their faith. This is true of every Christian going through trial. And so our duty is to look beyond the trial to its purpose; beyond the pain to its profit. The next additional reason is that Christ is in *control*. He is sovereign. The tribulation that they are about to pass through will be limited in *scope* as well as *duration*. Not all of them will be thrown into prison, only 'some'. Moreover, the tribulation will not go on forever, but only for 'ten days'. This is a symbolical, not a literal period of time. Ten or multiples of ten signify magnitude determined by God (ten toes or ten fingers). Here it symbolises a period of time under God's control that will fulfil His perfect purpose for that period. That is a great comfort to all God's saints. Our faith can remain strong as long as God is in full control of the scope and the duration of our trial. God will allow the devil to go so far, but no further; for so long, but no longer (Job 2:4–6).

And then the third added reason for being faithful in times of tribulation is that if we remain faithful until we die, Christ has a wonderful gift in store for us: 'Be faithful until death, and I will give you the crown of life ... He who overcomes shall not be hurt by the second death' (vv. 10–11). 'I will give you' is what Jesus says. Heaven is not a merit award, it is a *gift*. Our Lord is gracious and generous in His gifts to His people. If by our faithfulness through all our trials we prove the genuineness of our faith in Christ, our body and our soul shall escape hell which is 'the second death' and we shall enter heaven which is 'the crown of life.' The first death is the death of the body and it only lasts until the resurrection. The second death is the death of the body and soul in hell which will last forever. The second death cannot hurt the Christian. That is Christ's promise, but it will hurt every unbeliever. Revelation 21:8 says, 'But the cowardly, unbelieving, abominable, murderers, sexually immoral, sorcerers, idolaters, and all liars shall have their part in the lake which burns with fire and brimstone, which is the second death.'

This is the message of the letter Christ sent to the church in Smyrna. It is as searching for us now as it was for them then. If we are going to be faithful and true to Christ, we shall suffer. But we are not to fear, however severe the test our sovereign Saviour permits us to pass through. For He is still the First and the Last, who died and lived again, who controls all that befalls us, and will give us the crown of everlasting life if we are faithful until death. When the venerable old pastor, Polycarp, was arrested by the Roman authorities in Smyrna for refusing to offer incense to Caesar and own him as Lord, the officer in charge urged him to recant. 'What harm can it do', he asked, 'to sacrifice to the emperor?' Polycarp refused. He was then brought before the proconsul in the amphitheatre, who also pleaded with God's servant: 'Respect your years! ... Swear by the genius of Caesar ... Swear, and I will release you; revile Christ!' To which Polycarp replied: 'For eighty-six years I have served Him, and He has done me no wrong; how then can I blaspheme my King who saved me?' The proconsul persisted: 'Swear by the genius of Caesar ... I have wild beasts; if you will not change your mind, I will throw you to them ...' 'Call them', Polycarp replied. 'Since you make light of the beasts, I will have you destroyed by fire, unless you change your attitude.' Polycarp was brought to the pyre and the fire was lit, but as the wind drove the flames away from him and prolonged his suffering, a soldier put an end to his misery with a sword.

4 Christ's letters to Pergamum and Thyatira

The church in Pergamum (Pergamos, KJV)

2:12 And to the angel of the church in Pergamos write, 'These things says He who has the sharp two-edged sword: 13"I know your works, and where you dwell, where Satan's throne is. And you hold fast to My name, and did not deny My faith even in the days in which Antipas was My faithful martyr, who was killed among you, where Satan dwells.

14"But I have a few things against you, because you have there those who hold the doctrine of Balaam, who taught Balak to put a stumbling block before the children of Israel, to eat things sacrificed to idols, and to commit sexual immorality.

15"Thus you also have those who hold the doctrine of the Nicolaitans, which thing I hate.

16"Repent, or else I will come to you quickly and will fight against them with the sword of My mouth.

17"He who has an ear, let him hear what the Spirit says to the churches. To him who overcomes I will give some of the hidden manna to eat. And

I will give him a white stone, and on the stone a new name written which no one knows except him who receives it.'" 　　(Revelation 2:12–17)

Each letter our Lord addresses to the seven churches in the Roman province of Asia highlights an important spiritual characteristic that He, as the Head, wants to see in His church universal. So the letter to the church in Ephesus requires Christ's people to give Him their *first love*; to give Him first place in their affections and love Him with all their heart. The second letter to Smyrna requires all Christians to be *faithful* to Jesus and His cause, even to the point of death. Now in His letter to Pergamum Jesus requires concern for the preservation and spreading of His *truth*.

The Head of the church is all-knowing

The city of Pergamum was about 55 miles north and inland of Smyrna, and it was a citadel of paganism. Its name in Greek (Pergamon) means 'citadel', for it was built on a cone-shaped hill that rose one thousand feet above the plain.[1] No traveller could visit the city and not be impressed by the multitude of its temples. Moreover, because it was the seat of Roman imperial power in the province of Asia, the cult of emperor worship was also well established in the city. The church there was truly besieged on all sides by false doctrines, and the exalted Christ who walks in the midst of the seven golden lampstands that are the seven churches, is very well acquainted with their situation. He says, 'I know your works [all the good deeds you do as well as the bad], and where you dwell [the difficult spiritual conditions you have to live in], where Satan's throne is ... where Satan dwells' (v. 13). Satan, their adversary, not only inhabited the place where they lived, but ruled it. People today may dismiss the devil as a mythical figure with horns and hooves and a tail, but God's word presents him as the chief evil spirit in the universe who is highly intelligent, immensely powerful and utterly unscrupulous. Our Lord calls him 'the ruler of this world', for he has a throne and a kingdom consisting of 'principalities', 'powers' and 'spiritual hosts of wickedness in the heavenly places' (John 16:11; Ephesians 6:12).

It is true that Satan and his minions were critically defeated by Christ at the cross of Calvary where, figuratively speaking, Satan's head was crushed at the cost of Christ's heel being bruised (Genesis 3:15). In anticipation of that victory, our Lord told the seventy disciples when they returned from a preaching and healing mission in which they had cast out demons in His name, 'I saw Satan fall like lightning from heaven' (Luke 10:18). That fall was a curtailing of his power, for through the atoning death of Jesus on the cross and His sending of the Holy Spirit to open blind eyes and soften hard hearts, Satan would be bound and prevented from deceiving the nations until the end of the age (Revelation 20:1–3). In Matthew 12:29 Jesus makes the same point when He says that He is the One who has bound 'the strong man' so that He might 'plunder his goods', and release those he holds captive. But although Satan has been defeated, he and his fellow-demons continue to defend every inch of their territory in the world. The kingdom of Satan retreats only as the kingdom of God advances.

The truth concerning salvation

Pergamum was obviously a city where Satan continued to exercise much influence. Indeed, it was probably through a refusal to burn incense on the fire before a bust of the Roman emperor and say 'Caesar is Lord', that 'Antipas' was martyred (v. 13c). That was the penalty Rome imposed upon those who refused to worship the emperor. Antipas was given grace to hold fast the truth and not deny his faith in Christ. He would render to Caesar the things that were Caesar's, but not the title of 'Lord' that belonged to Christ. As a result, his courage cost him his life, and Jesus honours Antipas with His own title, 'faithful martyr' (lit. witness; cf. 3:14).

That was the diabolical environment in Pergamum where these Christians lived, and Jesus commends them with the words, 'You

hold fast to My name, and did not deny My faith even in the days
in which Antipas ... was killed among you' (v. 13b). What does He
mean by 'My name'? As elsewhere in Scripture, Christ's name stands
for Himself. The angel said to Joseph, 'You shall call His name Jesus,
for He will save His people from their sins' (Matthew 1:21). The name
Jesus means 'Jehovah our Saviour.' It proclaims His divine person and
His saving work. So to 'hold fast My name' means to hold firmly the
truth that Jesus is God come in human flesh to be the Saviour of the
world, and never let it go. Intellectual assent to the truth, however, is
not enough. We must act upon the truth if we truly believe it. Thus the
phrase, 'and did not deny My faith' refers to 'your faith in me' (NIV).
For if our *intellectual conviction* about Jesus Christ is genuine, it will
lead to *personal commitment* to Him. If Jesus is Jehovah (or Lord), I
must submit to Him as my Lord. If He is the only Saviour of sinners,
I must trust Him as my Saviour who alone can forgive my sins and
change my life.

These fundamental truths cannot be compromised no matter
what the cost of standing up for them is, and Jesus commends these
Christians for standing firm in the place where Satan lives and rules.
It may be that Antipas was a notable leader in the church, and his
martyrdom was intended to intimidate the Christians in Pergamum
into giving up their faith and denying Christ. But their spirit had
remained undaunted. 'I know where you dwell, where Satan's throne
is. And you hold fast to My name, and did not deny My faith.' There
is a vital lesson for us to learn here. To quote John Stott, 'We cannot
regard as Christians any who deny either the divine-human person of
Jesus or His unique saving work. There is no room for negotiation or
appeasement here. To deny that Jesus is "the Christ come in the flesh"
is antichrist, wrote John, while to preach any gospel other than the
gospel of Christ's saving grace is to deserve Paul's anathema (1 John
2:22; 4:2; 2 John 7–11; Galatians 1:6–9).'[2]

The truth concerning holiness

The all-knowing Head of the universal church saw not only something to *commend*, but also something to *condemn*: 'But I have a few things against you, because you have there those who hold the doctrine of Balaam, who taught Balak to put a stumbling block before the children of Israel, to eat things sacrificed to idols and to commit sexual immorality. Thus you also have those who hold the doctrine of the Nicolaitans, which thing I hate' (vv. 14–15). The church at Pergamum stood firm on the doctrine of salvation, but compromised on the doctrine of sanctification or holiness. Creed and conduct, however, cannot be divorced. The apostles are as scathing in their denunciation of immoral professors of Christianity as they are in their repudiation of those who deny the divine person and saving work of Christ. According to John, a Christian is someone who both 'walks in the truth' and 'walks in the light' (1 John 1:7; 2 John 4; 3 John 3,4). To deny Christ is to be a liar, and to disobey His commandments is to be a liar also (1 John 2:22; 1 John 4:20–21). Similarly, Paul chides the Corinthian Christians, saying, 'Do you not know that the unrighteous will not inherit the kingdom of God? Do not be deceived. Neither fornicators, nor idolaters, nor adulterers, nor homosexuals, nor sodomites, nor thieves, nor covetous, nor drunkards, nor revilers, nor extortioners will inherit the kingdom of God' (1 Corinthians 6:9–10).

But this strong rejection of sin and this passionate love of righteousness was being compromised in the church in Pergamum, for they tolerated among their number some who held the teaching of Balaam. Balaam was the false prophet who, greedy for the reward offered by Balak, king of Moab, to bring God's wrath upon the Israelites, advised the king to use the women of Moab to seduce the men of Israel by inviting them to take part in their idolatrous and immoral festivities. Sadly, Balaam's evil scheme worked and 24,000 Israelites 'died in the plague' (Numbers 25:1–9; 2 Peter 2:15; Jude 11). The Balaamites and the Nicolaitans were teaching the same thing:

namely, it is alright to go to a family party or social celebration in a pagan temple. You cannot be unsociable to your family and friends, just because they are unbelievers. Besides, you get the best meat and wine there. There are also ladies who are happy to entertain you. Where's the harm in it? Everyone else in the city does it; why shouldn't you? Are we not faced with a similar situation today when invited to attend a same-sex marriage ceremony? Is it rude to decline or right?

Christ's hatred of any tolerance of immorality is unequivocal: 'the doctrine of the Nicolaitans, which thing I hate' (v. 15). The church in Ephesus, you remember, was commended for its holy hatred of 'the deeds of the Nicolaitans' (1:6), but what was *hated* in Ephesus was *tolerated* in Pergamum. So Jesus calls the church (v. 16) to 'repent' of this error, for He deeply disapproves of a church that accommodates those who have a lax view of sexual immorality. Evil must not be countenanced by Christians. This was made clear to all Gentile Christians coming out of paganism. Among the admonitions given to Gentile Christians at the first church council in Jerusalem was the exhortation 'to abstain from things polluted by idols' (i.e. food sacrificed to pagan gods), and from 'sexual immorality' (Acts 15:20,29). Our Lord is therefore concerned that the church in Pergamum recognises the seriousness of compromising with false doctrine, and warns them that if they do not discipline the heretics, He will: 'Repent, or else I will come to you quickly and fight against them with the sword of My mouth' (v. 16). Our Lord is not totally dependent on human instrumentality. He Himself can and does discipline error in His church.

The only warfare Christians are engaged in is a spiritual warfare; and the only weapon that can overcome error is the sword of Christ's word. Thus He began this letter by designating Himself as 'He who has the sharp two-edged sword', for those who pervert Christ's word will be smitten by that same word. It is a two-edged sword because with one side it saves those who repent, and with the other edge it cuts off from the body of believers those who remain impenitent. False doctrine can never be suppressed by torture or by restrictive government legislation, or even by war. Force of arms cannot conquer ideas. Only truth can defeat error. So Christ's church must be marked by its faithfulness to His truth, and by its commitment to using sound doctrine to uproot heresy in its midst and expose evil in the world for what it is.

Having issued this warning, our Lord goes on to *promise* a blessing for those who remain true to His word: 'He who has an ear, let him hear what the Spirit says to the churches' (v. 17a). Christ reminds us again that His word to the church in Pergamum is a word to all churches in every country and in every century. He wants all His churches to live by the truth of His word and advance by it. Those who do, will receive a wonderful gift: 'To him who overcomes I will give some of the hidden manna to eat' (v. 17b). Every Jew would know that this is a reference to the manna hidden in the golden urn and stored permanently in the Ark of the Covenant. It was a symbol of God's promise that the Messiah He is going to send will be 'the true bread from heaven … which … gives life to the world' (John 6:33). Like all the other gifts promised at the end of each letter, Christ's gift of eternal life will only be fully inherited in heaven. Heaven for the Christian who overcomes will be 'the marriage supper of the Lamb' which will last forever (Revelation 19:9).

But that is not all that is promised: 'And I will give him a white stone, and on the stone a new name written which no one knows except him who receives it' (v. 17c). Among the many suggestions as to the meaning of the 'white stone', the most plausible, I believe, is the practice in the ancient world of giving a white stone to someone who was approved for membership of some trade guild or social club. Here, of course, it stands for membership of the 'church of the firstborn who are registered in heaven' (Hebrews 12:23). Moreover, the 'new name' written on the white stone is a name 'which no one knows except him who receives it', for as Philip Edgcumbe Hughes explains:

God does not view the multitude of the redeemed as an undifferentiated mass. The name known only to the recipient indicates the uniqueness of each individual before God and the distinctness of the interpersonal relationship of each with Him. There will be no confusion of names in the mind of God. As the name is given by the Lord, it also, of course, signifies that the recipient of the white stone is precious to Him and His possession. What is revealed to St. John here is really the fulfilment of the age-old promise: 'You shall be called by a new name which the mouth of the Lord will give' (Isaiah 62:2) ... In the new creation every name will be a new name which because of its uniqueness establishes a sacred bond between the Lord God and its recipient; no two names will be the same.[3]

The truth, as it 'is in Jesus' (Ephesians 4:21), is an essential characteristic of Christ's church. Any professing church without it forfeits the right to be called Christ's church. Our Lord Himself said, 'If you abide in My word you are My disciples indeed. And you shall know the truth, and the truth shall set you free' (from all evil, John 8:31–32). The gospel of Christ 'is the power of God to salvation to everyone who believes' (Romans 1:16). When the gospel of Christ is watered down or tampered with, people cannot be saved and the church cannot grow. When the truth of holiness is not the means of disciplining evil in the church, evil will flourish in the congregation and the community, and the church's light will be diminished. 'God is light and in Him is no darkness at all. If we say we have fellowship with Him, and walk in darkness, we lie and do not practise the truth' (1 John 1:5–6).

Our duty as regards to the truth, then, is twofold. First, negatively, we are commanded to 'Guard what was committed to your trust, avoiding the profane and vain babblings and contradictions of what is falsely called knowledge—by professing it, some have strayed concerning the truth' (1 Timothy 6:20–21). Second, positively, we are 'to contend earnestly for the faith which was once for all delivered to the saints' (Jude 3).

The church in Thyatira

2:18*And to the angel of the church in Thyatira write, 'These things says the Son of God, who has eyes like a flame of fire, and His feet like fine brass:* 19*I know your works, love, service, faith, and your patience; and as for your works, the last are more than the first.* 20*Nevertheless I have a few things against you, because you allow that woman Jezebel, who calls herself a prophetess, to teach and seduce My servants to commit sexual immorality and eat things sacrificed to idols.* 21*And I gave her time to repent of her sexual immorality, and she did not repent.* 22*Indeed I will cast her into a sickbed, and those who commit adultery with her into great tribulation, unless they repent of their deeds.* 23*I will kill her children with death, and all the churches shall know that I am He who searches the minds and hearts. And I will give to each one of you according to your works.* 24*Now to you I say, and to the rest in Thyatira, as many as do not have this doctrine, who have not known the depths of Satan, as they say, I will put on you no other burden.* 25*But hold fast what you have till I come.* 26*And he who overcomes, and keeps My works until the end, to him I will give power over the nations—*

27*"He shall rule them with a rod of iron;*
They shall be dashed to pieces like the potter's vessels"—

as I also have received from My Father; 28*and I will give him the morning star.* 29*He who has an ear, let him hear what the Spirit says to the churches.'* (Revelation 2:18–29)

The longest letter is addressed to the church in the smallest of the seven cities. Thyatira was some 40 miles to the south-east of Pergamum. It was, however, a busy trading centre, long famous for its purple dye. Paul's first convert in Europe was Lydia, 'a seller of purple from the city of Thyatira' (Acts 16:14). Our Lord begins His letter by saying, 'I know your works, and your love, service, faith and patience' (v. 19a). These are words of warmest approval. Thyatira was actually serving Christ like Ephesus, but it also had the first love that Ephesus lacked. 'I know your love', He says with approval. It also preserved

the 'faith' (or truth) that was in peril at Pergamum, and shared with
Smyrna the virtue of 'patience' during 'tribulation'. This is a glowing
report that doesn't end there, for Jesus adds: 'and as for your works,
the last are more than the first' (v. 19b). Thyatira was a church that was
growing spiritually: 'and that you are now doing more than you did at
first' (NIV). The Christian life is not one in which the last state is not
as good as the first, but one in which we are constantly increasing in
love, knowledge, faith and holiness. Is our Christian life growing like
the believers at Thyatira, or are we standing still like the Pergameans,
or are we falling back like the Ephesians?

The church's toleration of evil

With such splendid progress, it is sad to go on and read of this
church's failure to discipline impurity in their midst: 'Nevertheless I
have a few things against you, because you allow [tolerate, ESV] that
woman Jezebel, who calls herself a prophetess, to teach and seduce My
servants to commit sexual immorality and eat things sacrificed to idols'
(v. 20). The one blemish in the life of the church in Thyatira was that
it allowed one of the women in its fellowship to teach and encourage
moral laxity; not from the pulpit, for that was clearly forbidden, but in
the privacy of some of the church's homes. Jezebel, king Ahab's pagan
wife, was responsible for the official introduction of Baal worship
(religious prostitution) to the northern kingdom of Israel (1 Kings
16:30–32; 21:25; 2 Kings 9:22) which eventually led to its destruction
150 years later. 'Jezebel', therefore, seems to be another term or label
for the cult of the Nicolaitans that troubled the Ephesians and the cult
of Balaam that troubled Pergamum. They all sanctioned attendance
at pagan temple feasts where Christians could be seduced by the
idolatry and immorality that went on there. In this regard the church
at Thyatira should have emulated the church at Ephesus who hated the
deeds of this false cult and refused to befriend them because they were
'liars' who had not been sent by God. Thyatira mistakenly believed
that it was an act of love not to question the claims of Jezebel to be

a prophetess sent by God. The church believed in peace at all costs and in not creating a scene. Here was a failure to discipline both false teaching and impurity.

This, then, is the message of Christ's letter to the church in Thyatira. Holiness of life is another indispensible mark for every true church that bears His name. *Conduct* is as important as *creed*. It is not Christian to turn a blind eye to abortion, or divorce, or sex outside of marriage, or homosexuality, or drunkenness, or dishonesty, and so on. For holiness is the purpose of the *Father's election*: 'He [the Father] chose us in Him [Christ] before the foundation of the world, that we should be holy and without blame before Him in love' (Ephesians 1:4). Holiness is also the purpose of the *Son's redemption*: 'Jesus Christ gave Himself for us that He might redeem us from every lawless deed and purify for Himself His own special people, zealous for good works' (Tit. 2:14). And holiness is the purpose for the *Holy Spirit's indwelling* of the Christian: 'God did not call us to uncleanness but in holiness. Therefore … God has also given us His Holy Spirit' (1 Thessalonians 4:7–8). Again and again it has been shown in history that if Satan cannot destroy the church's witness by persecution from without, he will resort to the more subtle assault of pollution from within.

Christ's call for repentance

'Jezebel' was a real woman who posed as a prophetess from God and claimed a knowledge of 'deep things' (v. 24) that sanctioned promiscuity under the guise of religion. But if the elders in the church allowed these sins to go unchecked, Christ would not. He is 'the Son of God who has eyes like a flame of fire, and His feet like fine brass' (v. 18). His burning eyes exposed the fact that the deep things Jezebel taught were not 'the deep things of God' (1 Corinthians 2:10, NIV), but 'the deep things of Satan' (v. 24, ESV). His feet of fine brass will justly crush the evildoers to death (v. 23). So He says, 'I gave her time to repent of her sexual immorality, and she did not repent (lit. 'she does not wish to repent', v. 21). She was resolute in her will to carry on seducing others and being seduced. Christ therefore has no other option but to 'cast her into a sickbed' (v. 22). Her punishment will fit her crime. Her bed of sin will become a bed of sickness.

There is still hope for Jezebel's followers

'I will cast ... those who commit adultery with her into great tribulation, unless they repent of their deeds' (v. 22). If this final warning is not heeded, judgment will follow them too: 'And I will kill her children with death, and all the churches shall know that I am He who searches the minds and hearts. And I will give to each one of you according to your works' (v. 23). To 'kill with death' is an Old Testament expression that means to kill 'with pestilence' (NASB). That such a literal punishment overtook Jezebel and her followers is most likely. This was the age when Ananias and Sapphira were struck dead for lying, and some Corinthians died because they defiled the Lord's Supper by their greed and drunkenness (Acts 5:1–11; 1 Corinthians 11:17–32).

This is a warning all churches need to heed today. Though we may not suffer immediate physical judgment, ultimately the New Testament says that 'the unrighteous will not inherit the kingdom of God' (1 Corinthians 6:9). We may persuade ourselves that our impurity is well hidden and will never come to light, but He 'who has eyes like a flame of fire' sees everything we do. And 'He who searches the minds and hearts' of all His creatures knows our thoughts from afar. There can be no escaping the crushing judgment from His feet that are 'like fine brass'. To know that the Son of God is coming at any moment 'to give to each one according to your works', is the strongest incentive to holy living (Matthew 16:27; Romans 2:6; 2 Corinthians 5:10).

A message for the true believers

Christ now turns His attention to the rest of the congregation in Thyatira: 'But I say to you, the rest who are in Thyatira, who do not hold this teaching, who have not known the deep things of Satan, as they call them—I place no other burden on you. Nevertheless, what you have, hold fast until I come' (v. 24–25, NASB). Our Lord is referring here to the decree of the council of Jerusalem in Acts 15:28 which said, 'It seemed good to the Holy Spirit and to us, to lay upon you no greater burden than these necessary things: that you abstain from things offered to idols … and from sexual immorality.'

This was not as easy as it sounds. Thyatira was a city of trade guilds for dyers, weavers, potters and so on. And each trade guild had its own guardian deity. If you wanted a job, you had to belong to a trade guild, which entailed going as a group to a temple to offer sacrifices to the god of that guild, and consorting with the temple prostitutes.[4] The deep things Jezebel taught encouraged Christians to go along with this for the sake of their own livelihood and to have some influence upon their fellow workers. Jesus, however, insists that Acts 15:28 be obeyed: 'I will put on you no other burden.' The way to holiness is not to keep adding more and more man-made rules to the list of taboos. The Holy Scriptures are themselves an adequate guide and a sufficient rule of faith and conduct. Until Christ comes, our duty is to hold fast to them and place no other burden on ourselves or others.

A gracious promise to the overcomer

To those who heed Christ's warning and overcome evil, two promises are given. First, 'He who overcomes, and keeps My works until the end, to him I will give power over the nations—"He shall rule them with a rod of iron; they shall be dashed to pieces like the potter's vessels"—as I also have received from My Father' (vv. 26–27). The Father gave this promise of universal authority to His incarnate Son in Psalm 2:8–9, and now here in verses 26–27 Christ promises to share that universal authority with us. Exactly how we will share in Christ's reign is not explained. What is made clear is that heaven will not only be a place of endless delights, but of awesome authority and responsibility. To the good servant in the parable of the talents who was 'faithful over a few things', Jesus says, 'I will make you ruler over many things' (Matthew 25:23). And to the good servant in the parable of the pounds, Jesus says: 'Because you were faithful in a very little, have authority over ten cities' (Luke 19:17).

The second promise of Christ to the overcomer is found in verse 28, 'And I will give him the morning star.' In Revelation 22:16 Jesus calls Himself 'the bright and morning star.' He is the star, the light of whose glory at His return will dispel the long night of sin and bring in the dawn of an endless day without the help of the sun. For in the new heaven and the new earth, 'They need no light of the sun, for the Lord God gives them light' (Revelation 22:5). So this promise is His assurance that we will share not only in His authority, but also in His divine glory. We will not only rule the nations, but possess the Lord of the nations as our Bridegroom. That is a precious blessing far, far greater than anything we may have had to renounce on earth in our pursuit of holiness. 'He who has an ear, let him hear what the Spirit says to the churches' (v. 29), even to us and the church we belong to.

5 Christ's letters to Sardis and Philadelphia

The church in Sardis

3:1And to the angel of the church in Sardis write, 'These things says He who has the seven Spirits of God and the seven stars: "I know your works, that you have a name that you are alive, but you are dead. 2Be watchful, and strengthen the things which remain, that are ready to die, for I have not found your works perfect before God. 3Remember therefore how you have received and heard; hold fast and repent. Therefore if you will not watch, I will come upon you as a thief, and you will not know what hour I will come upon you. 4You have a few names even in Sardis who have not defiled their garments; and they shall walk with Me in white, for they are worthy. 5He who overcomes shall be clothed in white garments, and I will not blot out his name from the Book of Life; but I will confess his name before My Father and before His angels. 6He who has an ear, let him hear what the Spirit says to the churches."'

(Revelation 3:1–6)

The city of Sardis was situated some thirty miles south-east of Thyatira on the great circular road that connected these seven most populated and wealthy cities in the Roman province of Asia. We do not know when or how the church was started, but it is the recipient of a severe letter which contains almost unmitigated criticism. 'I know your works', says the Head of all the churches, 'that you have a name that you are alive, but you are dead' (v. 1c). What an indictment for a church which faced so little outward opposition. There is no mention of the persecution that the Christians at Smyrna and Pergamum were enduring; no mention of having to overcome the error and evil that Pergamum and Thyatira had to face. Yet in those churches our Lord found fault only with a minority of their members. At Sardis, however, a majority of the members are at fault. Only 'a few names' have 'not defiled their garments' (v. 4).

What Christ saw that others did not

Amazingly the church in Sardis had acquired a reputation among the other churches in the province for being alive. Visitors to the church may have found a large congregation attending services marked by eloquent preaching, loud amens, good singing and plenty of weeknight activities. There was no shortage of money or manpower. But outward appearances can be deceptive, and this was certainly the case in Sardis. It seemed to be spiritually alive, but in fact it was virtually dead. The eyes of Christ saw beneath the impressive facade that covered its moribund spiritual condition underneath. Nor should we be at all surprised, 'for the Lord does not see as man sees; for man looks at the outward appearance, but the Lord looks at the heart' (1 Samuel 16:7).

Thus at the end of verse 2 Christ goes on to say, 'for I have not found your works perfect before God.' The Greek word literally means 'fulfilled'. In other words, their activities, though outwardly impressive to human eyes, did not come up to God's standard. They did not 'fulfil' God's purpose. How badly we need this message today! Many contemporary churches seem to be fixated on numbers and desperately want to be admired by their peers. They want to be known as the church on the move. But as true Christians our chief responsibility is to God. It is for Him that we live, before Him that we stand, and to Him that one day we must give an account. He can survey our motives and desires. He can see if there is any reality behind our appearances.

The root of nominal or cultural Christianity

What reduced Sardis to being a Christian church in name only? Our Lord puts it down to spiritual drowsiness. That is the implication behind the command, 'Be watchful' (v. 2) which is repeated again in verse 3. Our adversary, the devil, is very crafty or wily. If he cannot lure us into sinning overtly through 'the lust of the flesh, the lust of the eyes', then he will tempt us through the more subtle means of 'the pride of life', all of which are 'not of the Father but ... of the world' (1 John 2:16). And no sin, according to the New Testament, is more deceptive than religious pride and self-righteousness. That, I believe, was the downfall of the church in Sardis. They were proud of their reputation of being an alive church and concentrated on promoting that reputation.

The sin of religious pride is surely what Jesus is alluding to in the words, 'for I have not found your works perfect before God' (v. 2). While all the other churches praised them for being a model church, excelling in attendance, worship, preaching, praying, conduct and giving, Christ saw that these works were not perfect in God's sight. If we know our New Testament, we know that we can sin even in our observance of the Lord's Supper, and in our praying and preaching and giving (1 Corinthians 11:17–22, 27–34; James 4:1–3; 1 Corinthians 2:1–5; Acts 5:1–11). That is what the Bible teaches. As our Lord Himself said, 'When you have done all those things which you are commanded, say, "We are unprofitable servants. We have done what was our duty to do"' (Luke 17:10). The word 'perfect' means that the works of Sardis did not meet with God's approval. They were aimed at pleasing and glorifying self instead of God (John 8:29; 1 Corinthians 10:31; 2 Corinthians 5:9; Colossians 1:10; 1 Thessalonians 2:4; 4:1).

There can be no spiritual life when members are happy to simply play church. This was the great sin of the people of God in Isaiah's day, and our Lord quotes Isaiah as proof that it was also the great sin in the nation in His day: 'You hypocrites! Well did Isaiah prophesy of you when he said: "This people honours Me with their lips, but their heart is far from Me; in vain do they worship Me"' (Matthew 15:7–8, ESV). Their leaders were even worse! They disfigured their faces to show others that they were fasting and 'prayed in the streets that they may have glory from men' (Matthew 6:1–2, 16–18). So Jesus said to them, 'Woe to you, scribes and Pharisees, hypocrites! For you are like whitewashed tombs, which outwardly appear beautiful, but within are full of dead people's bones and all uncleanness. So you also outwardly appear righteous to others, but within you are full of hypocrisy and lawlessness' (Matthew 23:27–28, ESV). Paul warned Timothy to watch out for the same danger, saying, 'But know this, that in the last days perilous times will come: for men will be lovers of themselves, lovers of money, boasters, proud, blasphemers, disobedient to parents, unthankful, unholy … lovers of pleasure rather than lovers of God, having a form of godliness but denying its power' (2 Timothy 3:1–5).

The remedy for nominal Christianity

All these Scriptures tell us that form without power, reputation without reality, outward appearance without inward integrity, profession without possession of spiritual life, are a denial of true Christianity. So Christ says, 'Wake up, and strengthen what remains and is about to die' (v. 2, ESV). There is still hope if the majority of the church in Sardis would only wake up and see how Satan has duped them into a kind of self-righteous slumber. The call to 'wake-up' is repeated in verse 3. If the situation were beyond repair, there would be no point in addressing the church in Sardis in this way. So what is the church to do? They are to 'Remember, then, what you received and heard. Keep it and repent' (v. 3, ESV). Our Lord is appealing, not to the majority who were dead, but to the minority who had spiritual life: 'You have a few names even in Sardis who have not defiled their garments' (v. 4).

Within that dying congregation a godly remnant was left. It has always been so. When the spiritual life of God's people gets low, He always has a remnant to work with and bring vitality to those who profess to be His, but whose religion is an empty charade. Thus Isaiah says, 'Unless the Lord of hosts had left to us a very small remnant, we would have become like Sodom, we would have been made like Gomorrah' (1:9). It is to these few alive Christians that Jesus makes His appeal in verse 2, 'Be watchful and strengthen the things which remain, that are ready to die.' Do something before the whole church becomes nominal and spiritually dead. This is the continuing duty of every remnant within a nominal church. When we sense our church is dead, our first duty is not to leave it and go elsewhere, but to work for reformation and revitalization. God has often worked through godly minorities. By God's grace an alive and awake minority can preserve a dying church from utter extinction. Verse 3, 'Remember therefore how you have received and heard; hold fast and repent.' In other words, remember how you received the Holy Spirit when you first heard the gospel. Do not give up. Repent of your lack of faith. This is the same teaching of the apostle Paul in Galatians 3: 'Did you receive the Spirit by the works of the law, or by the hearing of faith? ... He who supplies the Spirit to you, does He do it by the works of the law or by the hearing of faith? ... Christ redeemed us from the curse of the law ... that we might receive the promise of the Spirit through faith' (vv. 2,5,13–14).

So what are these few believers to repent of? They are to repent of being taken in by all the activities in their church and the fine words of praise they hear from visitors. A spirit of complacency easily accompanies a reputation. They are to repent of forgetting the power of the gospel to bring people out of spiritual death and into life. They are to repent of not using the gospel to revive their church's prayer life,

worship, holiness and outreach to the far ends of the earth. They are
to repent of not seeking a fresh visitation of the Holy Spirit from God.
That is why Jesus describes Himself in verse 1 as 'He who has the seven
Spirits of God and the seven stars.'

In every one of these seven letters our Lord introduces Himself by
means of a title that is perfectly suited to meet the spiritual condition
of the church He is addressing. What the church in Sardis needs to
remember is that Christ, the exalted Head of the universal church, is
the One who directs the seven Spirits and the seven stars. The 'seven
Spirits' is a reference to the completeness of Christ's gift of the Holy
Spirit to His church in every land and every age, and the 'seven stars'
represent the churches who are His messengers to the world. Christ
is the giver of the Holy Spirit to the believing members of each church
who by that gift shine as stars, radiating His heavenly light to the
world. Both are in Christ's right hand, for Christ directs the Holy
Spirit to those churches that hear His word with faith and obey His
Spirit (Acts 5:32). So it is only by receiving the Holy Spirit through
the hearing of faith and by praying and preaching and worshipping
and walking and living in the Spirit that any church of Christ's can be a
living church (Jude 20; 1 Thessalonians 1:5; John 4:24; Philippians 3:3;
Galatians 5:16,25).

A solemn warning for the impenitent

Verse 3b, 'If you will not wake up, I will come like a thief, and you will
not know at what hour I will come against you.' There is no difficulty
in understanding what our Lord is saying here, because it is something
He has repeatedly warned of in the Gospels (Matthew 24:42–44;
Mark 13:33–37; Luke 12:39–40). It is a simile which the apostles also
use (1 Thessalonians 5:2,4; 2 Peter 3:10; Revelation 16:15). A thief
comes unannounced while people are sleeping. The point is that time is
not on the side of those who are being warned to repent and put their

lives and the church's life in order. If the church does not wake up to its perilous condition, Christ will unexpectedly visit them in judgment.

One way our Lord could come unexpectedly is at death. Our lives are entirely in His hands. At any moment we can be summoned into His presence, and when that moment comes there will be no opportunity to do the things we have left undone. Another coming of Christ, just as unexpected, will be His return as the Judge of all the earth. Christians cannot afford to be spiritually asleep (Romans 13:11; Ephesians 5:14). Either way, Christ's warning that if the church at Sardis does not wake up, He will come upon them as a thief, was a most fitting one. The city was built on a hill so steep that its defences seemed impregnable. Yet, because of a lack of vigilance, the city had fallen twice to its enemies; to Cyrus the Persian in 549 BC and to Antiochus the Great (III) in 218 BC. 'On both occasions enemy troops scaled the precipice by night and found that the over-confident Sardians had set no guard.'[1]

A gracious promise to the overcomer

In verses 4–6 Christ ends his letter to Sardis with a promise to the overcomers of a twofold reward in heaven that is appropriate to their situation. First, 'You have a few names even in Sardis who have not defiled their garments; and they shall walk with Me in white, for they are worthy.' The phrase 'walk with Me' signifies the restoration of the perfect fellowship man had with God before the Fall. It is another picture of paradise regained. Moreover, they will walk with God in 'white', for white is the symbol of the spotless purity of those 'who have washed their robes and made them white in the blood of the Lamb' (7:14). And that is precisely why they are seen as 'worthy'. Their worthiness is not one of their own achieving, but one received from Christ. The only way to be made worthy of heaven is to be cleansed by Christ's blood (Matthew 26:28; 1 John 1:7).

Secondly, Christ makes a further promise to the overcomer, saying, 'And I will not blot out his name from the Book of Life' (v. 5). The

Bible tells us that God keeps a register in heaven in which the names
of all His people are enrolled (Psalm 69:28; Daniel 12:1; Philippians
4:3; Revelation 13:8; 17:8; 20:15; 21:27). Of course, it's not a literal
book, for they are registered in God's mind. The book is just a symbol.
Moreover, our Lord is not suggesting that God's bookkeeping in
heaven is subject to continual change with the removal of names
previously entered, and the restoration of names previously removed.
To quote Philip Edgcumbe Hughes, 'Such a conception could only
be conducive to insecurity on the part of God's people (whose names
might be in His book today and out tomorrow) and to uncertainty
even in the mind of God Himself regarding the ultimate outcome of
His redemptive action, which is unthinkable.'[2]

So to remove all doubt the Greek sentence has a double negative
that conveys the sense: 'I will never by any means blot out his name.'
Indeed, far from removing the overcomer's name, Jesus promises to
confess it 'before My Father and before His angels.' We do not have to
worry about any mistake being made in the record-keeping of heaven.
Christ who knows all His sheep by name (John 10:3), will personally
own us as His sheep on the Day of Judgment. 'He who has an ear,
let him hear what the Spirit says to the churches.' What is He saying
to us today? Is our name written down in the Book of Life? It may
be written on our church's membership roll, and yet be missing from
God's Book of Life. Time is too short for us to settle for just having the
name of being a Christian. We need to be Christian in reality as well.
We need to be regenerated and kept spiritually alive by the presence
and power of the Holy Spirit.

The Church in Philadelphia

3:7 And to the angel of the church in Philadelphia write: 'These things
says He who is holy, He who is true, *"He who has the key of David, He
who opens and no one shuts, and shuts and no one opens"*: 8I know your
works. See, I have set before you an open door, and no one can shut it;

for you have a little strength, have kept My word, and have not denied My name. [9]Indeed, I will make those of the synagogue of Satan, who say they are Jews and are not, but lie—indeed I will make them come and worship before your feet, and to know that I have loved you. [10]Because you have kept My command to persevere, I also will keep you from the hour of trial which shall come upon the whole world, to test those who dwell on the earth. [11]Behold, I am coming quickly! Hold fast what you have, that no one may take your crown. [12]He who overcomes, I will make him a pillar in the temple of My God, and he shall go out no more. I will write on Him the name of My God and the name of the city of My God, the New Jerusalem, which comes down out of heaven from My God. And I will write on him My new name. [13]He who has an ear, let him hear what the Spirit says to the churches.'   (Revelation 3:7–13)

The city of Philadelphia was situated about 28 miles south-east of Sardis, and it derived its name from Attalus II, its founder, whose loyalty to his brother Eumenes II won him the epithet Philadelphus, 'lover of his brother'. Rome tried to encourage Attalus to overthrow his brother and become king of Pergamum, but he resolutely declined. Also of significance is the fact that the city of brotherly love was originally founded for the purpose of being a centre for spreading the language and culture of the empire of Greece eastwards in Asia Minor. William Ramsay indicates the success achieved by Philadelphia by noting that before AD 19 the Lydian language had been replaced by Greek as the only language of the country.[3] But the message of Christ to the church in Philadelphia is that He wants it to be a 'missionary city' for spreading the gospel to Mysia, Lydia and Phrygia. Robert H. Mounce says, 'The imperial post route from Rome via Troas passed through Philadelphia and continued eastward to the high central plateau [and] helped it earn the title "gateway to the East."'[4]

Unlike the previous letter to Sardis which was one of almost unmitigated censure, the letter to Philadelphia, like the letter to Smyrna, is one of almost unqualified commendation. Our Lord says,

'I know your works ... [you] have kept My word, and have not denied
My name ... You have kept My command to persevere' (vv. 8b,10a).
But notice what else He says, 'I know your works. See, I have set
before you an open door, and no one can shut it' (v. 8). An open
door in the Bible is a door of opportunity for missionary activity
(1 Corinthians 16:9; 2 Corinthians 2:12; Colossians 4:3). When the
door is closed, the opportunity has passed. That is very important.
Every true church must reach out to others with the gospel as God
opens the door. Evangelism or missionary endeavour, then, is the
sixth mark to characterize what Christ wants His church to be. And
to quote John Calvin, 'The gospel does not fall from the clouds like
rain, by accident, but is brought by the hands of men to where God has
sent it.'[5]

Philadelphia and God's open door

When Paul and Barnabas returned to Antioch after their first
missionary journey, Luke says, 'They reported all that God had
done with them, and that He had opened the door of faith to the
Gentiles' (Acts 14:27). A few years later, on Paul's third missionary
journey, he had a wonderful opportunity to spend three years in
Ephesus preaching the gospel night and day. And as he writes to the
Corinthians about this experience, he says, 'I will tarry in Ephesus
until Pentecost. For a great and effective door has opened to me,
and there are many adversaries (1 Corinthians 16:8–9). Similarly, in
Philadelphia, where there was also much opposition, Jesus Christ has
opened a door for the gospel which no hostile power can shut. That
was very encouraging, given the fact that Jesus says the church has
'little strength', probably because its members were few in number and
composed largely from the lower classes of society. They lacked the
resources that the world would regard as essential for captivating men's
hearts and minds.

This, however, was not to deter them from evangelising their town and further afield. Human weakness is no hindrance to the power of God to save souls. When Paul despaired of his human weakness, God reassured him, saying, 'My grace is sufficient for you, for My strength is made perfect in weakness' (2 Corinthians 12:9f). The church in Philadelphia was also proving this, for though they had 'little strength', Christ says, 'You have kept My word, and have not denied My name' (v. 8b). God always chooses 'what is weak in the world to shame the strong' (1 Corinthians 1:27, ESV). So our Lord says that it is not the weak Christians in Philadelphia who will be overcome, but the opponents of the gospel: 'Indeed, I will make those of the synagogue of Satan, who say they are Jews and are not, but lie—indeed, I will make them come and worship before your feet, and to know that I have loved you' (v. 9). As in Smyrna, the opposition in Philadelphia was being stirred up by Jews who no longer had any right to that name, for they were not the children of God, but the children of Satan. Their claim to be the true people of God was really a 'lie'. Paul clearly taught that 'he is not a Jew who is one outwardly ... but he is a Jew who is one inwardly, and circumcision is that of the heart, in the Spirit, and not in the letter; whose praise is not from men but from God' (Romans 2:28–29). Furthermore, by their slander and persecution of the Christians in Philadelphia, the Jews in that city had shown themselves to be 'the synagogue of Satan' (see also John 8:44; Galatians 6:16).

Now in times of persecution, Christians are often tempted to lie low and hold their peace. Discretion is the better part of valour, we say, so why stir up trouble? But our Lord encourages the church with the words, 'I have set before you an open door, and no one can shut it' (v. 8). If His followers will march believingly through that door, He says, 'I will make them [the Jews] come and worship before your feet, and to know that I have loved you' (v. 9b). Obviously not all the Jews in Philadelphia will be converted and worship Jesus with the Christians, but a significant number will. Those Jews who are not brought to salvation will at the end of the world be brought to judgment. They will not be able to avoid this. For then, whether

willingly or unwillingly, 'at the name of Jesus every knee [shall] bow …
and every tongue [shall] confess that Jesus Christ is Lord to the glory
of God the Father' (Philippians 2:10–11).

Their obedience will be tested by trial

Verse 10, 'Because you have kept My command to persevere, I also
will keep you from the hour of trial which shall come upon the
whole world, to test those who dwell on the earth.' The hour of trial
predicted here has both an immediate and an ultimate fulfilment like
that referred to in Matthew 24:21–22. Its immediate context has to
do with a period of persecution which the churches throughout the
Roman empire will shortly experience. But it also includes all Christian
persecution throughout the age, culminating in the final tribulation
to come under the Antichrist who hates Christian evangelism and
missions.

The thrust of the verse, however, is upon what is about to happen
rather than on the end of the age. And because the Philadelphian
Christians had kept Christ's command to patiently endure their
persecution as He had His, He would also keep them from falling
when their hour of trial comes. The promise is consistent with what
our Lord prayed for His church in John 17:15, 'I do not pray that You
should take them out of the world, but that You should keep them
from the evil one.' It is their preservation *in* trial that is taught, not
their rescue *out of* trial as John Walvoord asserts. Referring to verses 10
and 11, he writes, 'Many have observed also that the preposition "from"
(Gk., *ek*) is best understood as "out of" rather than simply "from"
… This implies the rapture of the church before the time of trouble
referred to as the great tribulation. Such a promise of deliverance
to them would seemingly have been impossible if the rapture of the
church were delayed until the end of the tribulation prior to the second
coming of Christ and the establishment of the kingdom. This passage
therefore provides some support for the hope that Christ will come for

His church before the time of trial and trouble described in Revelation 6 to 19.'[6] The context of the verse is against this interpretation. Jesus is promising deliverance *in* or *through*, rather than *from* trial.

The church in Philadelphia must not doubt the outcome of the struggle with the forces of Satan: 'Behold, I am coming quickly! Hold fast what you have, that no one may take your crown' (v. 11). The final judgment at the great white throne will be ushered in by Christ's return to earth, and His return will be sudden and quick, and therefore it is imminent (Revelation 20:11–15). It will come unexpectedly like a thief in the night (Matthew 24:36–44; 25:13). We must be ready for it. We do not want to forfeit the crown of life promised to those who endure to the end, because we grow faint and give up. No dismay could be greater than to see the crown we thought would be presented to us being presented to others, and to hear the Lord say to us: 'I never knew you!' (Matthew 7:21–23). Verse 11 is a necessary warning. No one can steal our crown, but that does not mean that we can be careless. The Christian life requires constant vigilance and perseverance in the midst of our trials and afflictions through the enabling of the Holy Spirit.

The promise of absolute security

Verse 12a, 'He who overcomes, I will make him a pillar in the temple of My God, and he shall go out no more.' The pillars of a magnificent building are a fitting symbol of strength and permanence. This is a promise that if we serve Christ with whatever little strength we have, it will not be on a lost cause. It will not come to nothing like those who build only for this life. Every servant of God will become a pillar in the spiritual temple God is building, and a pillar by its very nature and function is not removable. It is a permanent part of the structure: 'and he shall go out no more.'

This promise of security is backed up by a further promise that says the same thing: 'I will write on him the name of My God and the name of the city of My God, the New Jerusalem, which comes down out of heaven from My God. And I will write on him My new name' (v. 12bc). The threefold naming of those who overcome signifies divine ownership and eternal security under God's care. God jealously guards what belongs to Him. The overcomer who goes through open doors to serve Christ whatever the cost will become the Father's cherished possession (Numbers 6:22–27; Revelation 14:1; 22:4); a citizen of His eternal city (Galatians 4:26; Philippians 3:20); and a trophy of Christ's saving grace, who has redeemed him at the infinite cost of His own precious blood (1 Peter 1:18–19; 1 Corinthians 6:19–20; Revelation 7:14). In short, those who risk their lives for Christ and the gospel in this world, will belong forever to God, to Christ and to His people.

Christ has the key to open all doors

How do we find an open door to Christian service? Do we prise it open? Do we engineer an opening into a conversation where Christ is not welcome? Do we bring political or economical pressure to bear upon uncooperative governments to open their doors to the gospel? Some would say 'Yes' to all three questions. Christ's letter to the church in Philadelphia says otherwise. Only Christ can open doors of service that will glorify Him and advance His kingdom.

So Christ at the beginning of the letter claims in verse 7 to be divine: 'These things says He who is holy, He who is true.' Only God is absolutely holy and true (Isaiah 40:25; Revelation 6:10). We can believe Him. He does not lie (Numbers 23:19). Moreover, He claims to be 'He who has the key of David, He who opens and no one shuts, and shuts and no one opens.' The key of David is an expression taken out of the Old Testament where God appointed Eliakim to be the chief steward over the household of Hezekiah and says, 'The key of the house of David I will lay on his shoulder; so he shall open, and no one shall shut; and he shall shut, and no one shall open' (Isaiah 22:22). Eliakim therefore prefigured Christ who as the eternal heir to David's throne now has the authority to open or shut the door for people to enter God's everlasting kingdom (Luke 1:32f). No man can enter until Christ opens the door, and no man can enter after He has closed it (Luke 13:24–28; John 10:7–11). He wields even the keys of death (the power to separate body and soul) and of Hades (the power to keep body and soul separate) for He is Redeemer and Judge (Revelation 1:18; 20:13–14).

To conclude this exposition of our Lord's letter to the church in Philadelphia, here are some wise words of personal, practical application from John Stott:

> Christ has the keys. He opens the doors. There is no sense in trying to barge our way unceremoniously through doors which are still closed. We have to wait for Him to make openings for us. Damage is continually being done to the cause of Christ by brash or tactless testimony. It is of course right to seek to win for Christ our friends, relatives, neighbours and colleagues. But we are sometimes in a greater hurry than God. Instead, we need to be patient, pray hard and love much, and to wait expectantly for the God-given opportunity to witness.
>
> The same principle applies to any uncertainty we may have about God's will for our future. Probably more mistakes are made by speed than by sloth, by impatience than by delay. God's purposes often ripen slowly. If the door is shut, it is foolish to put our shoulder to it. We must wait till Christ takes out the key and opens it.[7]

6 Christ's letter to Laodicea

3:14 And to the angel of the church of the Laodiceans write,

'These things says the Amen, the Faithful and True Witness, the Beginning of the creation of God: ¹⁵I know your works, that you are neither cold nor hot. I could wish you were cold or hot. ¹⁶So then, because you are lukewarm, and neither cold nor hot, I will spew you out of my mouth. ¹⁷Because you say, "I am rich, have become wealthy, and have need of nothing"—and do not know that you are wretched, miserable, poor, blind, and naked—¹⁸I counsel you to buy from Me gold refined in the fire, that you may be rich; and white garments, that you may be clothed, that the shame of your nakedness may not be revealed; and anoint your eyes with eye salve, that you may see. ¹⁹As many as I love, I rebuke and chasten. Therefore be zealous and repent. ²⁰Behold, I stand at the door and knock. If anyone hears My voice and opens the door, I will come in to him and dine with him, and he with Me. ²¹To him who overcomes I will grant to sit with Me on My throne, as I also overcame and sat down with My Father on His throne. ²²He who has an ear, let him hear what the Spirit says to the churches.'

(Revelation 3:14–22)

Laodicea was the last of the seven most populous and influential cities connected by the great circular road that ran through the Roman province of Asia. It was situated some forty miles south-east of Philadelphia, being almost due east of Ephesus. Its sister cities were Hierapolis, six miles to the north across the Lycus river, and Colosse, ten miles east of Laodicea, both cities on the south bank of the river. All three cities are mentioned in the apostle Paul's letter to the Colossians (2:1; 4:13,15,16). Paul, at the same time, also wrote a letter to the Laodicean church which some think has been lost and others believe is his letter to the Ephesians (Colossians 4:16), since three of the earliest manuscripts of Ephesians omit the words, 'To the saints who are in Ephesus' in verse 1 of that letter.

The background to the church

These three churches had not been planted by the apostle Paul, for he writes of them as those who 'have not seen my face in the flesh' (Colossians 2:1). Indeed, it is most probable that Epaphras was the one who founded the Laodicean church (Colossians 1:7; 4:12–16). But now, one generation later, the church at Laodicea existed in name only. The Christianity of its members was nominal, not real or actual. They had no relationship with Christ whatever. It was just a religious club or society which did not have even 'a few names' like Sardis (3:4) whom our Lord could own. There was nothing! Jesus was simply Someone outside their lives to patronise. So the Son of God has to send it the severest of the seven letters, one which has much to criticize and nothing to commend. What had happened? It is clear from the letter that the Laodiceans had not been troubled by any gross sin or error. There is no mention of heresy or immorality. Rather, it seems that materialism had infested the church.

The city of Laodicea was very wealthy, one of the richest commercial centres in the world at that time. It was renowned, however, not only for its financial institutions, but for its manufacture of clothing and carpets from the fine sheep raised in the fertile valley, and for its medical school and their famous eye salve that reputedly cured ophthalmia. Consequently, its citizens were very satisfied with their lot, and this spirit of pride and complacency had unfortunately spilled over into the church and made its members smug and self-contented. Indeed, they were so content with their material wellbeing that they gave no thought to their spiritual wellbeing. It is a situation which we in the West today can readily identify with. None of the seven letters is more appropriate to the respectable, half-hearted Christianity that is so prevalent in the affluent and materialistic societies of the 21st century.

The verdict of the divine Judge

Christ, the Head of the church, refuses to let them be self-satisfied, and demands that these professors of Christianity heed His assessment out of respect for Him. Verse 14, 'These things says the Amen, the Faithful and True Witness, the Beginning of the creation of God.' The Hebrew root of the term 'Amen' denotes what is firm and reliable. Thus our Lord used it in the Gospels to introduce important statements: 'Amen. Amen; I say to you' ('Truly, truly, I say to you', John 1:51, NASB). A designation of God as 'Amen' is also found in Isaiah 65:16. What the title means is further explained in the additional self-declaration that Jesus is 'the Faithful and True Witness.' It implies the deity of Christ who claimed to be 'the Truth' (John 14:6), for 'God is not a man, that He should lie' (Numbers 23:19).

The final designation, 'the Beginning of the creation of God', cannot mean that God began creation by creating the Son (as Mormons and Jehovah's Witnesses maintain), for Scripture cannot contradict Scripture. Scripture clearly asserts, 'All things were made through Him [the Word], and without Him nothing was made that was made … And the Word became flesh and dwelt among us' (John 1:3,14; see also Colossians 1:13–18). Philip Edgcumbe Hughes explains the ambiguity as follows, 'The term "beginning" in this expression must not, then, be treated as a passive noun, meaning the first being created by God, but as an active noun, meaning the dynamic agent of God's creation, the One through whom the created order was brought into existence ... The fact that the Son is the beginning of all created things is the guarantee and assurance of the indefectibility of God's purposes in creation.'[1] And if He cannot have any defects or flaws in His creation, Jesus, as God manifested in the flesh, can have no defects or flaws in His church (1 Timothy 3:16).

This is the Head and Judge of the church at Laodicea who can say with absolute authority and accuracy: 'I know your works, that you are neither cold nor hot. I would that you were cold or hot.' The Greek words are striking. The word 'cold' means icy cold and the word 'hot' means boiling hot. Christ would prefer us to be either very cold or very hot in our attitude to Him. Of course, His chief preference is that we continue at spiritual boiling point. That is the thrust of Paul's command in Romans 12:11 where he exhorts us to 'be fervent in spirit, serving the Lord.' A Christian who is not zealous in loving and serving Christ is a contradiction in terms. In the light of His total self-giving for us on the cross, there can be no other appropriate response. It is upon the mercies of God shown to sinners in Christ that Paul bases his appeal to all Christians to 'present your bodies a living sacrifice, holy, acceptable to God, which is your reasonable service' (Romans 12:1). Christ's total self-giving for our salvation should unfailingly inspire our total self-giving in His service. Zeal is an essential part of Christianity. He who for our sake left all and endured all, including the God-forsakenness of the cross, has every right to lay down that 'he who does not take his cross and follow after Me is not worthy of Me' (Matthew 10:38). God our Saviour has more patience with those who treat Him with icy indifference than He has with those who insult Him with an insipid lukewarmness that nauseates Him. He can get through to the *hostile* easier than He can to the *complacent*.

'So then', says Jesus, 'because you are lukewarm, and neither cold nor hot, I will spew [spit, ESV] you out of My mouth' (v. 16). It is, of course, metaphorical language, but that does not empty these words of their meaning. Lukewarm liquids are not only *tasteless*, but positively *distasteful*. Christ's forceful expression is one of disgust. He will utterly repudiate those professing Christians whose attachment to Him is half-hearted and complacent. This was not an empty threat! How long it took to take effect we do not know. The city that was so prosperous is now a tragic waste, and this once promising church is no more. He who removed the lampstand from Ephesus, spat Laodicea out of His mouth. Their comfortable lifestyle made it difficult to take Christ seriously.

As church history has proved over and over again, *adversity* is easier to cope with than *prosperity*. You are complacent, says Jesus: 'Because you say, "I am rich, have become wealthy, and have need of nothing"' (v. 17a). Self-satisfaction had been allowed to take the place of self-renunciation. Cross-bearing had been driven out by self-gratification. The Laodiceans had been materially blessed by God, but their self-preoccupation which was a symptom of ingratitude, showed that they had yet to learn that pride is a debilitating disease of the soul (1 Corinthians 4:7f).

The true condition of the members of the church in Laodicea was quite the opposite of what they believed it to be, and our Lord's letter must have come as a rude awakening informing them of their real spiritual condition. Far from being 'rich' and 'wealthy' and 'in need of nothing', their spiritual state is one of the gravest danger: 'and do not know that you are wretched, miserable [pitiable, ESV], poor, blind, and naked' (v. 17b). They are 'wretched, pitiable, poor' sinners dying without hope, for in themselves they have no grounds on which to ask God to forgive their sins. They are morally 'naked', because they have no righteousness of their own to make them fit to live in the presence of God in heaven. And they are spiritually 'blind', because they cannot see either the poverty of their soul or the danger of eternal damnation that awaits them.

The advice Jesus offers them

Jesus is warning all churchgoers who are spiritually lukewarm and half-hearted in their commitment to Him that their profession of Christianity is spurious. It is a situation that cannot go on. Either we take action to rectify it, or He will take action to spit the tepid churchgoer out of His mouth. What advice, then, does the Son of God give to rectify this? He says, 'I counsel you to buy from Me gold refined in the fire, that you may be rich; and white garments, that you may be clothed, that the shame of your nakedness may not be revealed; and anoint your eyes with eye salve, that you may see' (v. 18). The Laodiceans were putting their trust in the riches of this world that can never pass the test of divine judgment. Money may buy us out of trouble in this life, but not in the next. The only ultimate and enduring wealth is to be 'rich toward God'; to have 'the unsearchable riches' of God's grace in Christ who is the sum of all heaven's wealth (Luke 12:21; Matthew 6:19–21; 13:45–46). To know Him as our Saviour and Lord is to have everything that counts, and lack nothing that really matters.

Moreover, this bounty of eternal salvation in Christ is offered free of charge, simply because the infinite cost of procuring it has been fully met by Christ's death for our sins on the cross (1 Peter 1:18–19). Salvation is all of grace. It is a free gift (Ephesians 2:8–9; Romans 6:23). So Christ's counsel to 'Buy from Me gold refined in the fire' must not be pressed literally. It is simply Christ's poetic way of saying: 'I advise you to give up trading with your earthly suppliers, and come and do business with Me, bankrupt as you are.' It is precisely the same invitation that God issues in Isaiah 55:1 to those who have no money. 'Come, buy and eat,' He says, 'Yes, come, buy wine and milk without money and without price.' The Laodiceans also need the 'white garment' of Christ's sinless life on earth to be imputed to them as a covering to hide the shame of the spiritual nakedness which their self-righteousness has reduced them to, as well as the heavenly 'eye salve' with which to anoint 'the eyes of their understanding' (Ephesians 1:18;

4:18). Turned in upon themselves, they had become blind to the things of God, and urgently needed the healing salve of the Holy Spirit's regenerating power to 'see the kingdom of God' (John 3:3).

The call to repent

But how can they 'buy' these things without money? They can only do so as God gives them the spiritual capital with which to secure His blessing of salvation: namely, His free gifts of repentance (Acts 5:31; 11:18) and faith (Acts 16:14; Philippians 1:29; Ephesians 2:8–9). Verse 19, 'As many as I love, I rebuke and chasten. Therefore be zealous and repent.' Christ's stern warning that He will spit them out of His mouth is not incompatible with His love for them. Indeed it is because He longs to save them from final judgment that He now reproves and chastens them. They must respond to His chastisement and cry out to Him for grace to repent and be zealous. There can still be a bright future for the church in Laodicea. The tenses of the verbs change significantly. 'Repent' is in the past tense, and the verb 'be zealous' is a present active imperative.

So Jesus is calling on them to repent at once, irrevocably, in order to be continually fired with godly zeal. The adjective 'hot' in verse 15 and the verb 'be zealous' in verse 19 have a common root meaning, 'to boil'. To be zealous, then, is to be at spiritual boiling point. Repentance, however, must come first, for to repent is to turn with firm resolution from everything we know to be contrary to God's will, and we can only do that with God's help. Smug self-satisfaction does not become one who professes to be a Christian. Jesus demands and deserves an enthusiasm that is boiling over. *He* must be our supreme treasure and joy, not the riches of this world. We must spit *them* out of our mouths, before He spits *us* out of His.

The call to believe

The second step to recovery is God's free gift of *faith*. If repentance is to renounce living for self, faith is to commit our lives to loving and serving Christ supremely. So the Saviour says, 'Behold, I stand at the door and knock. If anyone hears My voice and opens the door, I will come in to him, and dine with him, and he with Me' (v. 20). As our Creator, Jesus Christ is the owner of the house of our life. He is the architect who designed it and the builder who made it. We are only tenants in the house. It would be perfectly within His rights to force His way in. Instead, He knocks gently and speaks lovingly to us. He wants to come into our innermost being, not as some temporary guest, but as a welcome resident to enjoy our company and devotion forever. Thus Paul, as a believer, can say: 'Christ lives in me' (Galatians 2:20). He can assure the Colossians that the mystery of the gospel is 'Christ in you, the hope of glory' (1:27). And his prayer for the Ephesians is that 'Christ may dwell in your hearts by faith' (3:17). Personal spiritual communion with Jesus Christ indwelling us is the essence of real Christianity.

'Behold, I stand at the door', says Jesus. The preposition 'at' means 'up to'. He comes right up to the threshold of the door of our heart. His offer of salvation is not made from a distance. It is close and personal. The verb 'to stand' is in the perfect tense and indicates that He came and stood at the door and is still standing there. The next verb 'to knock' is in the present tense, for Jesus not only came some time ago and continues to stand at the door of our heart, but is continually knocking. Let us not keep such a loving and patient Saviour waiting any longer, but open the door of our heart in faith at once.

Dining and overcoming with Christ

When we by the gracious and effectual calling of Jesus Christ open the door of our heart to Him, life will not be easy. To become the friend of Jesus is to become the enemy of the 'world' (James 4:4). To deny the lusts of the 'flesh' is to stir up the opposition of the flesh (Romans 7:21–25). To be freed from captivity to the 'devil' does not mean that he will not try to recapture us (Luke 22:31–32). But however formidable the opposition, with Christ in our hearts 'we are more than conquerors' (Romans 8:37). That is what verses 20 and 21 are saying. Our Lord speaks of dining and overcoming. The Guest we invite in becomes the true Host and supplies us with 'living bread' and 'living water' (John 6:51; 7:37–38; Revelation 22:17). The dining strengthens us and leads to overcoming the enemies of our soul.

Moreover, to those who overcome is given a promise that exceeds all the promises of an afterlife made in the other letters. Verse 21, 'To him who overcomes I will grant to sit with Me on My throne, as I also overcame and sat down with My Father on His throne.' Exactly what that authority will entail is not disclosed, but in some way Christ's enthronement as the God-Man will be shared by His people who are one with Him. What an incredible offer to 'wretched, pitiable, poor, blind, and naked' sinners (v. 17, ESV)! If we open the door for Jesus Christ to sit with us at our table, He will let us sit with Him on His throne.

The letter ends with the same postscript attached to the other letters: 'He who has an ear, let him hear what the Spirit says to the churches' (v. 22). The message varies according to the problem in each church, but the purpose of the Divine Writer never varies. The personal requirement of each church is a general requirement of all. Every congregation of every age and every place must be characterized by these spiritual qualities: they must love Christ supremely; be faithful to Him even to the point of death; contend earnestly for the truth; seek after holiness, without which no one will see the Lord (Hebrews 12:14); shun hypocrisy; witness wherever God provides the opportunity to do so; and serve Him wholeheartedly. 'He who has an ear, let him hear what the Spirit says to the churches', and therefore to us individually in our day and in our church.

7 Is the church raptured before chapter 4?

The term 'rapture' does not occur in our English translations of the Bible. It is a term which comes from the Latin Vulgate translation's use of *rapiemur* to render the verb 'caught up' in 1 Thessalonians 4:17, and is generally used by dispensational premillennialists to designate the first stage of their doctrine of a two-stage return of Christ.[1] The first stage is called the secret rapture, and the second stage His coming in power and glory. Because the book of Revelation does not speak of a secret rapture of the church, dispensational premilliennialists have to posit the theory that *after* chapter 3 and *before* chapter 4 the church is removed from the earth.

Hal Lindsey, the author of the best-selling book, *The Late Great Planet Earth*, makes the case this way:

> It is important to note that the church has been the main theme of Revelation until chapter 4. Starting with this chapter, the church is not seen on earth again until chapter 19, where we suddenly find it returning to earth with Christ as He comes to reign as King of kings and Lord of lords … Part of the confusion on this issue rises from a failure to

distinguish *two stages* in Jesus' second coming. One passage of Scripture speaks of Christ's coming *in the air* and in *secret*, like a thief coming in the night. Another part of the Scripture describes Christ's coming in power and majesty *to the earth*, with *every eye* seeing Him ... Although Revelation 4:1 does not specifically refer to Christ's reappearance at the Rapture, I believe that the apostle John's departure for heaven ['Come up here', 4:1] *after* the church era closes in chapter 3 and before the Tribulation chronicle begins in chapter 6 strongly suggests a similar catching away for the church.[2]

John Walvoord, former president of Dallas Theological Seminary, basically echoes the same thinking:

> From a practical standpoint, however, the rapture may be viewed as having already occurred in the scheme of God before the events of chapter 4 and the following chapters of Revelation unfold. The word *church*, so prominent in chapters 2 and 3, does not occur again until 22:16, though the church is undoubtedly in view as the wife of the Lamb in Revelation 19:7. She is not a participant in the scenes of the tribulation which form the major content of the book of Revelation ... At the beginning of chapter 4, then, the church may be considered as in heaven and not related to events which will take place on the earth in preparation for Christ's return in power and glory.[3]

Now the chief problem with premillennial dispensationalism is that it runs counter to the biblical view of a single return of Jesus Christ which ushers in a general resurrection and judgment of the righteous and the wicked on the last day of history. The church in its early creeds held this view (see *The Apostles' Creed*, c. AD 215–225; *The Nicene Creed*, c. AD 325; and *The Athanasian Creed*, c. AD 381–428).

One return, one resurrection, one judgment

Here are some important biblical references upon which the traditional view of the church is based. In Daniel 12 the prophet predicts a general resurrection of humankind, some to everlasting life and some to everlasting contempt:

> And there shall be a time of trouble, such as never was since there was a nation even to that time. And at that time your people shall be delivered, everyone who is found written in the book. And many of those who sleep in the dust of the earth shall awake, some to everlasting life, some to shame and everlasting contempt. Those who are wise shall shine like the brightness of the firmament, and those who turn many to righteousness like the stars forever and ever' (vv. 1–3).

Our Lord also spoke of one return, one resurrection, and one judgment in several passages as follows, beginning with the parable of the wheat and the tares:

> He who sows the good seed is the Son of Man. The field is the world, the good seeds are the sons of the kingdom, but the tares are the sons of the wicked one. The enemy who sowed them is the devil, the harvest is the end of the age, and the reapers are the angels. Therefore as the tares are gathered and burned in the fire, so it will be at the end of this age. The Son of Man will send out His angels, and they will gather out of His kingdom all things that offend, and those who practise lawlessness, and will cast them into the furnace of fire. There will be wailing and gnashing of teeth. Then the righteous will shine forth as the sun in the kingdom of their Father'   (Matthew 13:37–43).

It is the same order. At the end of this age Christ comes with His angels to reap the harvest of the final judgment. The wicked are not left behind, but taken out of the world first and cast into hell. Simultaneously, the righteous will inherit the everlasting kingdom of God and shine like the sun with the glory of Christ.

> Again, the kingdom of heaven is like a dragnet that was cast into the sea and gathered some of every kind, which, when it was full, they drew to shore; and they sat down and gathered the good into vessels, but threw the bad away. So it will be at the end of the age. The angels will come

forth, separate the wicked from among the just, and cast them into the furnace of fire. There will be wailing and gnashing of teeth

(Matthew 13:47–50).

Here too, in the parable of the dragnet, one general judgment is being taught that takes place at the end of this age when Christ and His angels return. Simultaneously the wicked are cast into hell, while the righteous are preserved for God's enjoyment.

Then Jesus said to His disciples, 'If anyone desires to come after Me, let him deny himself, and take up his cross, and follow Me. For whoever desires to save his life will lose it, and whoever loses his life for My sake will find it. For what is a man profited if he gains the whole world and loses his own soul? Or what will a man give in exchange for his soul? For the Son of Man will come in the glory of His Father with His angels, and then He will reward each [that is, each and every person] according to his works' (Matthew 16:24–27).

The context is that of a general judgment at Christ's return with His holy angels. Those who have traded their souls for worldly gain and those who have denied themselves to follow Christ will be separated and receive their due reward.

'For as the lightning comes from the east and flashes to the west, so also will the coming of the Son of Man be ... Then the sign of the Son of Man will appear in heaven, and then all the tribes of the earth will mourn, and they will see the Son of Man coming on the clouds of heaven with power and great glory. And He will send His angels with a great sound of a trumpet, and they will gather together His elect from the four winds, from one end of heaven to the other ... But of that day and hour no one knows, not even the angels of heaven, but My Father only. But as the days of Noah were, so also will the coming of the Son of Man be. For as in the days before the flood, they were eating and drinking, marrying and giving in marriage, until the day that Noah entered the ark, and did not know until the flood came and took them all away, so also will the coming of the Son of Man be. Then two men will be in the field: one will be taken and the other left. Two women will be grinding at the mill; one will be taken and the other left. Watch therefore, for you do not know what hour your Lord is coming' (Matthew 24:27–31,36–42).

Who were taken away by the judgment of the flood? The wicked were. Who survived that universal judgment? Righteous Noah and his family. When our Lord Jesus Christ returns there will be a general judgment of the wicked and the righteous.

> Behold, He is coming with clouds, and every eye will see Him, even they who pierced Him. And all the tribes of the earth will mourn because of Him. Even so, Amen (Revelation 1:7).

The return of Christ will be public, not secret. Every eye will see Him. And He will judge the righteous and the wicked together. The wicked will 'mourn', the righteous will say 'Amen' (let it be so).

> 'When the Son of Man comes in His glory, and all the holy angels with Him, then He will sit on the throne of His glory. All nations will be gathered before Him, and He will separate them one from another, as a shepherd divides his sheep from the goats. And He will set the sheep on His right hand, but the goats on the left. Then the King will say to those on His right hand, "Come, you blessed of My Father, inherit the kingdom prepared for you from the foundation of the world" … Then He will also say to those on the left hand, "Depart from Me, you cursed, into the everlasting fire prepared for the devil and his angels"' (Matthew 25:31–41).

Once more, there is only one return of Christ to judge the righteous and the wicked.

> 'Do not marvel at this; for the hour is coming in which all who are in the graves will hear His voice and come forth, those who have done good, to the resurrection of life, and those who have done evil, to the resurrection of condemnation' (John 5:28–29).

Here Jesus is teaching a general resurrection in which the righteous will receive eternal life and those who have done evil will be eternally condemned.

What Jesus taught, His apostles echoed

'I have hope in God ... that there will be a resurrection of the dead, both of the just and the unjust' (Acts 24:15).

For you yourselves know perfectly that the day of the Lord so comes as a thief in the night. For when they [the wicked] say, 'Peace and safety!' then sudden destruction comes upon them, as labour pains upon a pregnant woman. And they shall not escape. But you, brethren, are not in darkness so that this day should overtake you as a thief ... For God did not appoint us to wrath, but to obtain salvation through our Lord Jesus Christ who died for us　　　　　　　(1 Thessalonians 5:2–10).

On the same day that wrath and destruction come upon the wicked, salvation will be the portion of Christians.

It is a righteous thing with God to repay with tribulation [in hell] those who trouble you, and to give you who are troubled rest [in heaven] with us, when the Lord Jesus is revealed from heaven with His mighty angels, in flaming fire taking vengeance on those who do not know God, and on those who do not obey the gospel of our Lord Jesus Christ. These shall be punished with everlasting destruction from the presence of the Lord and from the glory of His power, when He comes, in that Day to be glorified in His saints and to be admired among all those who believe

(2 Thessalonians 1:6–10).

Again, we have one coming on one day issuing in a general judgment of the just and the unjust.

Know this first of all, that in the last days mockers will come with their mocking, following after their own lusts, and saying, 'Where is the promise of His coming? For ever since the fathers fell asleep, all continues just as it was from the beginning of creation.' For when they maintain this, it escapes their notice that by the word of God the heavens existed long ago and the earth was formed out of water and by water, through which the world at that time was destroyed, being flooded with water. But the present heavens and earth by His word are being reserved for fire, kept for the day of judgment and destruction of ungodly men. But do not let this one fact escape your notice, beloved, that with the Lord one day is as a thousand years, and a thousand years as one day. The Lord is not slow about His promise, as some count slowness, but is patient toward you, not wishing for any to perish, but for all to come to repentance. But the day of the Lord will come like a thief, in which the heavens will pass away with a roar and the elements will be destroyed with intense heat, and the earth and its works burned up. Since all these things are to be destroyed in this way, what sort of people ought you to be in holy conduct and godliness, looking for and hastening the coming of the day of God, on account of which the heavens will be destroyed by burning, and the elements will melt with intense heat! But according to His promise we are looking for new heavens and a new earth, in which righteousness dwells (2 Peter 3:3–13, NASB).

Here again, Christ's return is a single coming that will be public, for the earth and the heavens are going to be renovated by fire. Moreover, His coming will be 'the day of judgment and destruction of ungodly men', but for Christians it is a day we are 'looking for' and whose coming we are 'hastening.' Is this doctrine important? Yes, very important indeed, for three reasons:

First, because the difficult and obscure passages in the book of Revelation must be interpreted in a way that is consistent with these simple and straightforward Scriptures;

Secondly, because Christians need to be prepared for persecution that is only going to get worse as the coming of Antichrist draws near. Christians are not going to be spared this time of trouble by a secret rapture;

Thirdly, because unbelievers need to know that 'now is the accepted time; behold, now is the day of salvation' (2 Corinthians 6:2). When the Bridegroom comes, the door of salvation will be shut permanently to those who foolishly have not prepared for the single event of His return

(Matthew 25:1–13).

8 God enthroned
supreme as Creator

⁴:¹After these things I looked, and behold, a door standing open in heaven. And the first voice which I heard was like a trumpet speaking with me, saying, 'Come up here, and I will show you things which must take place after this.'

²Immediately I was in the Spirit; and behold, a throne set in heaven, and One sat on the throne. ³And He who sat there was like a jasper and a sardius stone in appearance; and there was a rainbow around the throne, in appearance like an emerald. ⁴Around the throne were twenty-four thrones, and on the thrones I saw twenty-four elders sitting, clothed in white robes; and they had crowns of gold on their heads. ⁵And from the throne proceeded lightnings, thunderings, and voices. Seven lamps of fire were burning before the throne, which are the seven Spirits of God.

⁶Before the throne there was a sea of glass, like crystal. And in the midst of the throne, and around the throne, were four living creatures full of eyes in front and in back. ⁷The first living creature was like a lion, the second living creature like a calf, the third living creature had a face like a man, and the fourth living creature was like a flying eagle. ⁸The four living creatures, each having six wings, were full of eyes around and within. And they do not rest day or night, saying:

'Holy, holy, holy,
Lord God Almighty,
Who was and is and is to come!'

⁹Whenever the living creatures give glory and honor and thanks to
Him who sits on the throne, who lives forever and ever, ¹⁰the twenty-
four elders fall down before Him who sits on the throne and worship
Him who lives forever and ever, and cast their crowns before the
throne, saying:

¹¹'You are worthy, O Lord,
To receive glory and honor and power;
For You created all things,
And by Your will they exist and were created.'   (Revelation 4:1–11)

The vantage point from which we view things will determine how we
see them. A rich man's view of things will differ from the way a poor
man sees them. The same is true also of our perception of spiritual
reality, and so for the Christian nothing is more important than to see
things from God's perspective. This does not mean that Christians are
able to see as God sees. Rather, it means that God's perspective since it
is all-knowing, all-wise and all-powerful, is always the truest and best
perspective. Insofar, then, as we can bring our perspective in line with
His, we are not only submitting our mind to the mind of God, we are
also seeing things most truly as they are. A true insight into history,
past, present and future, is possible only when we view things from the
vantage point of God's throne which is mentioned twelve times in the
eleven verses of chapter 4.

Now that, of course, is part of what the study of Scripture is all
about. It is an attempt to think God's thoughts after Him; to look at
everything the way He looks at it, for He has given us His holy word
that we may know His mind. And of all the passages in the Bible that
contribute to that end, Revelation chapters 4 and 5 are a good example.
These two chapters constitute a single vision of God enthroned

supreme as Creator and of the Lamb enthroned supreme as Redeemer. Before John can be shown 'things which must take place after this' (4:1), before the tumult of the opening of the seals, and the blowing of the trumpets, and the pouring out of the bowls, there must come this great vision of God and the Lamb enthroned supreme over all. This preliminary vision was vital in order that John and his readers might be reminded that the terrible things that are about to happen on earth are under God, and will end with God. There would be no history but for God. It is He who made the world, who has set the process going and who will bring it to the end that He has predetermined.

The ineffable transcendence of God

Chapter 4 therefore begins, 'After these things [the appearance of the exalted Christ and the dictation of the seven letters] I looked, and behold, a door standing open in heaven. And the first voice, which I had heard speaking to me like a trumpet [1:10], said, "Come up here, and I will show you what must take place after this"' (ESV). Notice the divine 'must'. History has been foreordained. To quote Matthew Henry, 'Whatever is transacted on earth is first designed and settled in heaven.'[1] John then adds, 'Immediately I was in the Spirit' (v. 2a). John's experience of being 'in the Spirit' which began in chapter 1:10 now resumes, perhaps to an intensified degree that enables him to see through the open door 'a throne set in heaven, and One sat on the throne' (v. 2b).

What follows next is a symbolic portrayal of God's transcendence which is ineffable (too great for words). How can anyone describe what God looks like? We can enumerate His wonderful attributes, but God is so transcendent as to be beyond description. Other prophets also had this problem. Think of Isaiah ministering in the temple in Jerusalem, disconsolate because good king Uzziah had died, wondering no doubt what sort of inferior monarch his son Ahaz would make. Suddenly the whole place was ablaze with light as the prophet saw 'the

Lord sitting on a throne, high and lifted up, and the train of His robe filled the temple. Above it stood seraphim; each one had six wings: with two he covered his face, with two he covered his feet, and with two he flew. And one cried to another and said, "Holy, holy, holy is the LORD of hosts; the whole earth is full of His glory!'" (Isaiah 6:1–3). Or think of Ezekiel among the captives by the River Chebar in the land of the Babylonians, suddenly engulfed in a fearful storm in which he saw four living creatures. 'Above the expanse over their heads was what looked like a throne of sapphire, and high above on the throne was a figure like that of a man. I saw that from what appeared to be His waist up He looked like glowing metal, as if full of fire, and that from there down He looked like fire; and brilliant light surrounded Him. Like the appearance of a rainbow in the clouds on a rainy day, so was the radiance around Him. This was the appearance of the likeness of the glory of the LORD. When I saw it, I fell face-down' (Ezekiel 1:26–28, NIV).

It is quite clear that John sees his vision of God enthroned in heaven in similar terms. The finite human language at his disposal is incompetent to depict the infinite realities of the transcendental glory of God. So as we study what he saw, let us never forget that the heavenly reality is infinitely greater than the earthly symbol. Verse 3, 'And He who sat there [on the throne] was like a jasper and a sardius stone in appearance; and there was a rainbow around the throne, in appearance like an emerald.' The lack of precise definition from people in Bible times make an identification of precious stones rather difficult. A jasper stone in modern times is an 'opaque variety of quartz, usually red, yellow or brown.'[2] But because in Revelation 21:10–11 John describes 'the great city, the holy Jerusalem, descending out of heaven from God, having the glory of God, and her light was like a most precious stone, like a jasper stone, clear as crystal', it is best to take the jasper stone here to be a diamond. It is a symbol of the dazzling brightness of the purity and holiness of God.

It is generally agreed that the 'sardius' stone was a blood red stone named after Sardis where it was found. It is also known as 'carnelian' (ESV), and its blood red colour probably speaks of the uncompromising nature of God's justice and judgment against all evil. But just as God's just judgment in Scripture is often mentioned in conjunction with His mercy, so here in this vision John sees 'a rainbow around the throne, in appearance like an emerald' (v. 3b). The first rainbow was given to humankind as a symbol of God's covenant to be merciful and never again destroy the world by a flood (Genesis 9:16–17). In Isaiah 54:9–10 God clarifies the symbolism this way: '"For this is like the waters of Noah to Me; for as I have sworn that the waters of Noah would no longer cover the earth, so have I sworn that I would not be angry with you, nor rebuke you. For the mountains shall depart and the hills be removed, but My kindness shall not depart from you, nor My covenant of peace be removed", says the LORD, who has mercy on you.' Moreover, the rainbow described here is not multicoloured, but 'like an emerald', for green is the colour of unfading life and fruitful growth. Death and decay have no place where God reigns supreme.

On this same theme, John says something else: 'Before the throne there was a sea of glass, like crystal' (v. 6a). It is a symbol of perfect order in God's kingdom of absolute righteousness, whereas 'the wicked are like the troubled sea, when it cannot rest, whose waters cast up mire and dirt' (Isaiah 57:20). Thomas F. Torrance draws out the meaning of the symbol of the sea of glass beautifully:

> The dictators of the earth live and strut and boast as long and only as long as the Ancient of Days on the throne allows. Look wherever you will in the world today. You will see clearly a raging sea and the beasts that rise out of it, but thank God for a glimpse of the eternal Throne and the Ancient of Days. Thank God not only for Ezekiel's 'likeness as the appearance of a man', but for the Gospel of Jesus Christ in whose hand all the winds are firmly held and who in His own supernal moment will

rebuke the wind and the sea and there will be a great calm. These are *things which must be hereafter.*

That is how we are to understand this chapter in the Book of Revelation. In it we are bidden to look beyond the wild chaos of the ages. The Throne is still there and the Majesty of God upon it, but all is changed at last. The sea no longer rages; it is as smooth as glass and as clear as crystal. Once again as in Ezekiel's vision the rainbow is in the cloud. That is the sign that the fierce floods are past and gone forever. It is the sign of God's everlasting covenant with His creation.[3]

This vision in chapter 4 of the ineffable transcendence of God enthroned supreme which was given to John and the readers of his day is just as vital for us today.

The church glorified and complete in heaven

Verse 4, 'Around the throne were twenty-four thrones, and on the thrones I saw twenty-four elders sitting, clothed in white robes; and they had crowns of gold on their heads.' This is a surprise feature of God's throne, for there is no obvious parallel for them in either Isaiah's or Ezekiel's visions. Some commentators ascribe the elders to some high order of angels, but the problem with that view is that in Scripture angels are never called 'elders', and never sit on thrones in heaven with crowns of gold on their heads. The leaders of God's people in the Old Testament and the New, however, are called elders. The twelve sons of Jacob were the original elders of the tribes of Israel, and the twelve apostles the original elders of the Christian church (Leviticus 9:1; 1 Peter 5:1). So the twelve patriarchs of Israel plus the twelve apostles of Christ which make up the twenty-four elders together stand for God's true believers from both the Old and New Testament eras, or the complete church. Accordingly, they are 'clothed in white robes' which symbolizes the spotless robe of Christ's righteousness imputed to them (3:4–5,18; 7:9,14; 19:8,14).

Moreover, they have 'crowns of gold on their heads' because they 'shall reign forever and ever' with Christ (3:21; 2 Timothy 2:12; Revelation 22:5). Now those who disagree with this view quote chapter 5:8–10 as their reason why. For in the other modern versions the elders speak there in the third person, implying that they do not see themselves among the redeemed: 'You have made *them* to be a kingdom and priests to serve our God and *they* will reign on the earth' (NIV, italics mine). The King James Version, however, follows a strong manuscript tradition that reads, 'and has made us kings and priests to our God; and we shall reign on the earth.' It is surprising that the other modern versions do not include that variation in their margins, for they do include most other variant readings. If we take that alternate reading as the correct one, then the twenty-four elders are a symbol of the church glorified and complete in heaven. John, I think, is not portraying here a hierarchical order of angelic beings, but the dazzling splendour of a God who behind the troubled scenes of history sits enthroned supreme amidst the unceasing adoration of His redeemed people, glorified and complete in heaven.

Creation renewed for the glory of God

In John's vision of heaven creation also reflects the transcendence of God, not just the church. Verse 5a, 'And from the throne proceeded lightnings, thunderings, and voices.' All three metaphors are to be understood in the same way. They are awe-inspiring, terrifying manifestations of nature unleashed in a severe storm. Thunder is the voice of God in several Old Testament passages (Psalm 77:18; 81:7; 104:7). The scene is reminiscent of the giving of the law at Sinai. Moses says, 'there were thunderings and lightnings, and a thick cloud on the mountain; and the sound of the trumpet was very loud, so that all the people who were in the camp trembled' (Exodus 19:16). Exactly the same image is used of the throne of God in heaven to emphasise His distance from us.

Next, John says, 'And there were seven lamps of fire burning before the throne, which are the seven Spirits of God' (v. 5b). As we have seen above (1:4; 3:1), the seven Spirits of God stand for the Holy Spirit, seven being the number of divinity. The seven lamps of fire burning before the throne symbolize the truth that God exercises His sovereignty in the earth through the Holy Spirit in such a way that God Himself is still removed from it. Notwithstanding, however, creation must worship its Creator, as John is shown in verses 6–8: 'And in the midst of the throne, and around the throne were four living creatures full of eyes in front and in back. The first living creature was like a lion, the second living creature like a calf, the third living creature had a face like a man, and the fourth living creature was like a flying eagle. And the four living creatures, each having six wings, were full of eyes around and within. And they do not rest day or night, saying: "Holy, holy, holy, Lord God Almighty, who was and is and is to come!"'

The four living creatures have characteristics that connect them with the seraphim in Isaiah's vision. They have 'six wings' and they cry, 'Holy, holy, holy' as they worship God (v. 8; Isaiah 6:2–3). It would therefore seem that the four living creatures are members of this high order of angels chosen to represent the worship of a renewed creation. The apostle Paul hints at this in Romans 8:19–21, 'For the earnest expectation of the creation eagerly waits for the revealing of the sons of God … because the creation itself also will be delivered from the bondage of corruption into the glorious liberty of the children of God.' Even now, David says, 'The heavens declare the glory of God; and the firmament shows His handiwork' (Psalm 19:1). But in the new heaven and the new earth creation will give its Creator perfect praise. The fact that they are 'four living creatures' underscores this, for the numeral *four* is the number of creation. The Bible speaks of the four corners of the earth and the four winds of the heaven (Isaiah 11:12; Daniel 7:2). Moreover, their representation of animate creation is portrayed in their appearance, and here John's vision is like that of Ezekiel's (1:5,10).

The first is like a 'lion', the king of all wild animals; the second is like a 'calf or ox', the king of domesticated animals; the third has 'a face like a man', God's viceroy over all creation; and the fourth is like a 'flying eagle', king of the birds of the air. There is no one to represent the creatures of the deep, because Revelation 21:1 says that when 'the first earth had passed away … there was no more sea.'

Next, reminiscent of Ezekiel's vision (1:18), John tells us that 'the four living creatures were full of eyes, in front and in back … around and within.' The eyes probably speak of the ceaseless and complete attention in the world to come which creation will give both outwardly and inwardly to its praise of God; 'For now we see in a mirror, dimly, but then face to face. Now I know in part, but then I shall know just as I also am known' (1 Corinthians 13:12). John further observes that each of the four living creatures has 'six wings', like each of the seraphim of Isaiah 6:2 who 'with two he covered his face [indicating reverence], with two he covered his feet [in modesty], and with two he flew [in swift obedience to God's commands].

The unceasing worship of God in heaven

Verse 8b, 'And they do not rest day or night, saying, "Holy, holy, holy, Lord God Almighty, who was and is and is to come!"' The four living creatures worship all three persons of the blessed Trinity, Father, Son and Holy Spirit, who are Three in One and One in Three. To worship God as 'holy' is not first and foremost to worship His moral purity or separateness. In the first instance it is an acknowledgment of the Godhood of God, for holiness is the sum of all His attributes. It is because He is God that He is necessarily separate from us, and if we are to be holy we must be united to Him. The worship of God's holiness then leads to worship of His omnipotence as 'Lord God Almighty.' He has conquered all His enemies on earth, both demonic and human. Moreover, His holiness and omnipotence are from everlasting to everlasting, for He is the one God 'who was and is and is to come!' This truth is so important that it is repeated in verses 9 and 10 where God is twice designated as 'Him who lives forever and ever.' No evil can outlive God and no power is beyond His control. He alone is eternally sovereign over all. Nothing precedes Him and nothing succeeds Him.

Now although the adoration of the four living creatures represents the adoration of renewed creation in its completeness, including man who is still God's ruler over it, it is important to remember that man, made in the image of God, is above and apart from the rest of creation and therefore the worship of the twenty-four elders is seen as distinct and separate from the four living creatures. The four living creatures and the twenty-four elders are united when it comes to the worship of God as their Creator, but only the twenty-four elders can say to the Lamb, 'You have redeemed us to God by Your blood … and have made us kings and priests to our God (5:9–10). In verses 9, 10 and 11, then, the two groups worship God as their Creator: 'Whenever the living creatures give glory and honour and thanks to Him who sits on the throne, who lives forever and ever, the twenty-four elders fall down before Him who sits on the throne and worship Him who lives forever and ever, and cast their crowns before the throne, saying: "You are worthy, O Lord, to receive glory and honour and power; for You created all things, and by Your will they exist and were created."'

Do not be misled by the word 'whenever' at the beginning of verse 9. It is not a contradiction of the preceding assertion in verse 8 where we are told that the living creatures 'do not rest day or night' giving their praise to God. John is simply making the point that in the new creation the twenty-four elders will not be outdone in their worship of God by the four living creatures. Indeed, the praise of the elders differs from that of the living creatures in that it is *personal* rather than general. So in the first place they do what the four living creatures cannot do: they prostrate themselves before God and cast their crowns before His throne, acknowledging by their action that their crowns are really His.

They have nothing which they have not received as a gift from God (1 Corinthians 4:7). Therefore He alone is worthy to receive literally 'the glory and the honour and the power' for all they are and have done.

In the second place, their praise is addressed directly to God: 'You are worthy, O Lord.' These words were part of the political language of the day. Robert H. Mounce says, '"Worthy art thou" greeted the entrance of the emperor in triumphal procession, and "our Lord and God" was introduced into the cult of emperor worship by Domitian. For the Christian only the One upon the heavenly throne is worthy: the claims of all others are blasphemous.'[4] In the third place, the twenty-four elders praise God for the fact that He created all things (including the church) by His will, and providentially sustains all things by His will. They existed first in the eternal will of God and through His will came into being at His appointed time: 'You created all things, and by Your will they existed and were created' (v. 11, ESV). Moreover, God is immutable and subject to no change in His being or determinations. To quote Arthur W. Pink, 'God's purpose never alters. One of two things causes a man to change his mind and reverse his plans: want of foresight to anticipate everything, or lack of power to execute them. But as God is both omniscient and omnipotent, there is never any need for Him to revise His decrees. No, "The counsel of the LORD standeth forever, the thoughts of His heart to all generations" (Psalm 33:11). Therefore we read of "the immutability of His counsel" (Hebrews 6:17).'[5]

That is what John and his readers, present and future, need to see and never forget. In the midst of the conflict and chaos created by hostile enemies they need to be inspired by this first heavenly vision of the ineffable transcendence of the Lord God Almighty, high and lifted up on His throne of glory, bringing the good pleasure of His will to fulfilment. This vision of God enthroned supreme is a powerful assertion of our spiritual freedom in the face of tyranny. God has not abandoned His world. He created all things for His good pleasure: to bring greater glory to His name and eternal blessing to His creatures. 'John's readers must not think that evil is in control. Evil is real. But the divine purpose still stands.'[6] God is on the eternal throne supreme over all and He is able to make even the wrath of man to praise Him. Blessed are those who ever have this vision of God before their eyes.

> He hides Himself so wondrously,
>   As though there were no God;
> He is least seen when all the powers
>   Of ill are most abroad.
>
> Thrice blessed is he to whom is given
>   The instinct that can tell
> That God is on the field when He
>   Is most invisible.
>
> For right is right, since God is God;
>   And right the day must win;
> To doubt would be disloyalty,
>   To falter would be sin.
>   (F.W. Faber, 1814–63, altd.)

9 Christ enthroned supreme as Redeemer

5:1And I saw in the right hand of Him who sat on the throne a scroll written inside and on the back, sealed with seven seals. 2Then I saw a strong angel proclaiming with a loud voice, 'Who is worthy to open the scroll and to unloose its seals?' 3And no one in heaven or on the earth or under the earth was able to open the scroll, or to look at it.

4So I wept much, because no one was found worthy to open and read the scroll, or to look at it. 5But one of the elders said to me, 'Do not weep. Behold, the Lion of the tribe of Judah, the Root of David, has prevailed to open the scroll and to loose its seven seals.'

6And I looked, and behold, in the midst of the throne and of the four living creatures, and in the midst of the elders, stood a Lamb as though it had been slain, having seven horns and seven eyes, which are the seven Spirits of God sent out into all the earth. 7Then He came and took the scroll out of the right hand of Him who sat on the throne.

8Now when He had taken the scroll, the four living creatures and the twenty-four elders fell down before the Lamb, each having a harp, and golden bowls full of incense, which are the prayers of the saints.

9And they sang a new song, saying:

'You are worthy to take the scroll,
And to open its seals;
For You were slain,
And have redeemed us to God by Your blood
Out of every tongue and people and nation,
[10]And have made us kings and priests to our God;
And we shall reign on the earth.'

[11]Then I looked, and I heard the voice of many angels around the throne, the living creatures, and the elders, and the number of them was ten thousand times ten thousand, and thousands of thousands, [12]saying with a loud voice:

'Worthy is the Lamb that was slain
To receive power and riches and wisdom,
And strength and honor and glory and blessing!'

[13]And every creature which is in heaven and on the earth and under the earth and such as are in the sea, and all that are in them, I heard saying:

'Blessing and honor and glory and power
Be to Him who sits on the throne,
And to the Lamb, forever and ever!'

[14]Then the four living creatures said, 'Amen!' And the twenty-four elders fell down and worshiped Him who lives forever and ever

(Revelation 5:1–14)

Revelation chapters 4 and 5 constitute a separate, single vision of God enthroned supreme as Creator and Redeemer. They are a necessary interlude or pause before John can be shown 'things which must take place after this' (4:1). Without chapters 4 and 5 there can be no understanding of chapters 6 to 20 which portray the long but successful struggle in which 'the kingdoms of this world have become the kingdoms of our Lord and of His Christ, and He shall reign forever and ever!' (11:15). Or to put it another way, these two chapters tell us how the whole of creation currently cursed by sin can become 'the new earth and the new heaven' of Revelation 21 and 22 where we read: 'And there shall be no more curse, but the throne of God and of the Lamb shall be in it, and His servants shall serve Him. They shall see His face, and His name shall be on their foreheads' (22:3–4).

The sealed scroll in God's right hand

Wherein lies the explanation of the ultimate defeat of evil? It lies hidden in a scroll sealed with seven seals: 'And I saw in the right hand of Him who sat on the throne a scroll written inside and on the back, sealed with seven seals' (v. 1). Of course, there is no literal scroll in heaven and God being a pure spirit has no right hand. It is symbolism used to convey realities greater than human words can describe, and the key to understanding the vision is to understand what this scroll represents. By itself a scroll was simply a sheet of papyrus usually thirty feet long wound around a rod, but the scroll in this vision has writing on both sides, doubling its capacity. In most scrolls it was normal to write only on the inside, but if you had a lot to write and wanted it all on one scroll, you would write on the inside face and on the back. To read it one would have to unroll it; but unrolling this scroll was not possible because it was 'sealed with seven seals.' Seven is the number of divine appointment signifying the absolute inviolability of the scroll.

What is the content of the sealed scroll in God's right hand? Fortunately the answer is not in much doubt. To begin with, the background is once again Ezekiel where in chapter 2 the prophet is shown a scroll with 'writing on the inside and on the outside, and written on it were lamentations and mourning and woe' (v. 10). In other words, prophesies of judgment. The second thing that helps us to ascertain the contents of the scroll in Revelation 5 is to notice what happens when the seals are eventually broken: judgment falls upon the wicked. The third piece of evidence to note is the further references to such a scroll in chapter 13:8 and chapter 17:8, called 'the Book [literally scroll] of Life of the Lamb slain from the foundation of the world' in which the names of the redeemed have been written.

The scroll in chapter 5, then, is the scroll of world-destiny which contains the sum of God's purposes for the redemption of His people and the judgment of the wicked. Thomas F. Torrance elaborates on the significance of the scroll as follows:

> Here is the message of this chapter. In spite of the monstrous and demonic upheaval of the world, in spite of the fact that the whole world seems to have broken loose from God in our time, in spite of all the unbelievable disorder and ruthless sway of evil, there is a book in heaven carefully and decisively written by the hand of God about the destiny of the world. There is order behind the chaos. There is plan behind the confusion. There is a book of human destiny sealed and firm in the hand of God. God still holds the world in His hand and He will not be thwarted. His purpose will be and actually is being fulfilled here and now.
>
> … there is a book in heaven, a volume of ordered destiny and divine purpose. It is held in God's own right hand, written by the finger of love and righteousness. Heaven and earth may pass away but this Word of God will not pass away.[1]

So all of history from creation at the beginning to recreation at the end has been carefully planned and purposed by God Himself. God has left nothing to chance, but has ordained everything which comes to pass. He expressly declares: 'For I am God, and there is no other; I am God, and there is none like Me, declaring the end from the beginning, and from ancient times things that are not yet done, saying, "My counsel shall stand, and I will do all My pleasure"'; and again, 'He does according to His will in the army of heaven and among the inhabitants of the earth. No one can restrain His hand' (Isaiah 46:9–10; Daniel 4:35). Moreover, God does not make His plans as He goes along or tries to fit them in with our plans. Rather, they were decreed in eternity past: 'Known to God from eternity are all His works' (Acts

15:18); … in whom [Christ] also we have obtained an inheritance, being predestined according to the purpose of Him who works all things according to the counsel of His will' (Ephesians 1:11).

Who is worthy to open the scroll?

'I saw a strong angel proclaiming with a loud voice, "Who is worthy to open the scroll and to loose its seals?" And no one in heaven or on earth or under the earth was able to open the scroll, or to look at it. So I wept much, because no one was found worthy to open and read the scroll, or to look at it' (vv. 2–4). Here, then, in the scroll is God's plan for history decreed from the foundation of the world; His plan to judge the world and His plan to redeem a people out of the world for Himself (13:8; 17:8; 21:27). It is all there! No detail is missing. But as John looks it is still a secret and an unfilled plan. It is fully sealed with seven seals waiting to be loosed. A mighty angel with a loud voice is commissioned to issue a challenge to anyone in the whole universe who is worthy to approach God in His ineffable transcendence and open the scroll. What is required is not the authority or the right to do so, but the *virtue*.

But no angel in heaven, no human being on earth, no great hero from the past is found worthy to loosen the seals and make known the plan and purpose of God. What an extraordinary situation! Here are the eternal decrees of God and as far as creation can see they cannot be carried out. Here are the names of the elect of God in the Book of Life (17:8) and they cannot be called out. And here is the final judgment of God upon all evil and it cannot be implemented. What John is being shown here is that God's purposes for redemption and judgment cannot come to pass in the world without a worthy Mediator to carry them out.

John's response is one of intense grief: 'So I wept much, because no one was found worthy to open and read the scroll, or to look at it' (v. 4). In this regard Robert H. Mounce writes: 'All suggestions that

John wept out of disappointment for his own sake are unworthy of the Seer. He wept at the prospect of an indefinite postponement of God's final and decisive action. The universe itself was morally incapable of effecting its own destiny.'[2] John therefore portrays to us the agony of our world. We feel intuitively that there is a purpose in our being on earth, but we seem incapable of achieving that noble and glorious destiny. It remains in every age a tantalizing mirage: a hope that never seems to materialise. These tears of John, then, mirror the tears of countless millions of human beings who are sorrowful at the apparent invincibility of evil. Try as we may, Utopia never comes, and we are left with the question: Can God's eternal purpose in creating the world be stalled?

But all is not lost! John's copious tears evoke a response: 'But one of the elders said to me, "Do not weep. Behold, the Lion of the tribe of Judah, the Root of David, has prevailed to open the scroll and to loose its seven seals"' (v. 5). The fact that it is one of the elders who breaks the news to John is of no particular significance, except that he is a representative of the redeemed to whom God has revealed his secrets (Deuteronomy 29:29; Psalm 25:14; Proverbs 3:32). He appears again in chapter 7:13ff to explain to John who the great multitude clothed with white robes in heaven are. Although the expression 'the Lion of the Tribe of Judah' occurs here only in the Bible, it comes from a prophecy given by Jacob as early as Genesis 49:9–10. In his last words to his sons the patriarch calls Judah 'a lion's whelp' and says, 'the sceptre shall not depart from Judah ... until Shiloh [Messiah/Christ] comes; and to Him shall be the obedience of the people.' The tribe of Judah was the tribe of David from whom Jesus Christ came to be God's king over a kingdom which would last forever (2 Samuel 7:13,16; Isaiah 9:6–7; Luke 1:32–33). The title denotes Jesus Christ's human lineage by virtue of the incarnation.

But the One who is able to open the scroll is also called 'the Root of David' because He not only came after David but was before him. It denotes His pre-existence as the eternal Son of God (Mic. 5:2; John 1:1–14; 8:56–59). This is the One who 'has prevailed to open the scroll and to loose its seven seals.' He has met the requirements of God for the task. He has kingly authority and power to make known and bring to pass God's purposes for redemption and judgment in a fallen world. 'The Root of David' is a title that comes from a prophecy in Isaiah 11 where God's Messiah is called 'a root of Jesse' (v. 10, David's father). Moreover, 'with the breath of His lips He shall slay the wicked' (v. 4) and under His reign 'the earth shall be full of the knowledge of the LORD' (vv. 6–9). The identity of this worthy One is put beyond all doubt when our Lord says at the end of Revelation, 'I, Jesus, have sent My angel to testify to you these things in the churches. I am the Root, and the Offspring of David, the Bright and Morning Star' (22:16).

Who then can query the worthiness of this invincible, lion-like divine-human King to open the scroll and bring God's everlasting kingdom on earth? No one! So John looks around heaven to see where this Lion of the tribe of Judah is, and to his great surprise he sees not a Lion, but a Lamb. 'And I looked, and behold, in the midst of the throne and of the four living creatures, and in the midst of the elders, stood a Lamb as though it had been slain' (v. 6). In one brilliant master stroke of visual metaphor, John sees, not a mighty Lion, but a slain Lamb; a beast of weakness and innocence and sacrifice, still bearing the marks of its slaughter. This is the characteristic designation of Christ in the book of Revelation where it occurs twenty-eight times. The only other person to ascribe the title to Jesus was John the Baptist who pointed Him out to the people as 'the Lamb of God who takes away the sin of the world' (John 1:29,36).

But this Lamb is no longer lying dead on an altar. He is standing regnant 'in the midst of the throne and of the four living creatures, and in the midst of the elders' who surround the throne. He is a warrior Lamb, for He has 'seven horns', a symbol of complete power or omnipotence. Did He not announce to His followers after His resurrection, 'All authority has been given to Me in heaven and on earth' (Matthew 28:18)? He also has 'seven eyes' which signify His divine omniscience. He sees and knows everything. Nothing escapes His attention. The explanation that the seven eyes 'are the seven Spirits of God sent out into all the earth' is a reference to the promise of the Holy Spirit which the Father gave to His Son (John 15:26; Acts 1:4–5) to apply the redemption Christ accomplished at the cross for His people (Acts 1:8). The Holy Spirit, who is also called the 'Spirit of Christ' (Romans 8:9), is a missionary Spirit. He is the Spirit who performs the things that the eyes of the Lamb see need to be done to advance the kingdom of God on earth.

How comforting it must have been for John when the Lamb 'came and took the scroll out of the right hand of Him who sat on the throne' (v. 7). The scroll can now be opened and God's end-time purposes executed. All the hosts of heaven, too, are relieved and exultant, for the Lamb's action evokes a great outburst of praise and adoration from them. John says, 'Now when He had taken the scroll, the four living creatures and the twenty-four elders fell down before the Lamb, each having a harp, and golden bowls full of incense, which are the prayers of the saints. And they sang a new song …' (vv. 8,9a). This inspiring scene brought added comfort and confidence to the Apostle, for as Leon Morris points out:

> On earth the saints are despised and accounted as of no importance. In heaven their prayers are precious, being brought into the very presence of God Himself, while the bowls in which they are offered are golden. John often brings out the reversal of values in heaven from those accepted by his earthly (and earthy!) contemporaries.[3]

The 'new song' is a eulogy of the Lamb whose death and resurrection are epochal events and require a new and special song of praise. It is not simply new in point of time, but more important, it is new and distinctive in quality. No song composed prior to this song will do, and no other song will outdate or replace it, because the greatness of this salvation will never grow old or diminish in importance and wonder and awe. Its newness will last as long as the new heaven and the new earth. It will remain forever new.

The cross is central to all God's purposes

'And they sang a new song, saying, "You are worthy to take the scroll, and to open its seals."' Why? '"For You were slain, and have redeemed us to God by Your blood out of every tribe and tongue and people and nation, and have made us kings and priests to our God; and we shall reign on the earth"' (vv. 9–10). It is not because of the glorious person He is by nature as the Son of God, co-equal and co-eternal with the Father; nor is it because of the leading role He played in creation as the Word of God (John 1:1–3; Colossians 1:16–17; Hebrews 1:2–3). No! He is worthy supremely because of what He accomplished in time and history as the Lamb of God. The scroll is written and sealed. God has planned and decreed how everything is going to end. He is going to save a multi-national people who will live with Him forever in a new heaven and a new earth (21:1–5). But the fulfilment of God's purposes of redemption and judgment in history were contingent upon the death of the Lamb upon the cross of Calvary in Jerusalem AD 33. The cross was the most significant part of God's eternal plan which involved the participation of both Father and Son.

The world may see Calvary as just the martyrdom of a good man. Or they may say that the shedding of His life's blood on the cross was intended to demonstrate God's love and willingness to forgive our sin. But the Bible says it stands for something infinitely more than that. The cross was absolutely necessary in order for God to forgive sin and remain a just God. Left to themselves, no one can deal with their own sin. No one can erase their past, for no one can satisfy the just demands of God's law upon their law-breaking. The penalty of sin is eternal death and suffering in hell (Romans 6:23; Revelation 20:11–15), and to pay that penalty on behalf of an innumerable multitude of believing sinners required a sinless substitute of infinite worth. Only God in the person of His own Son could meet that requirement. Only Christ, who took our flesh in order that He might take our sin upon Himself and bear its punishment, could save us from hell.

The world is in chaos because of the curse of sin, but Jesus Christ has borne that curse. He has borne the wrath of God which the sin of every believer deserves, and therefore God can forgive their sin. Thus Paul can say, 'Christ redeemed us from the curse of the law, having become a curse for us (for it is written, "Cursed is everyone who hangs on a tree")'; and again, '[God] made Him who knew no sin to be sin for us, that we might become the righteousness of God in Him' (Galatians 3:13; 2 Corinthians 5:21). That is why Jesus Christ is described here as a slain Lamb. A slain lamb in the eyes of any Jew was an innocent animal sacrificed to God as an offering for sin. Thus Christ alone is the real sacrifice that takes away the sin of the world. All the animals slain before Him were only pointers to Him. Significantly, the perfect tense of the verb 'slain' in verse 6 signifies that the Lamb was not only slain at a point of time, but that the efficacy of His death is still present in all its power. Accordingly, Leon Morris can say, 'The Lamb continues permanently in the character of One who was slain for men. The crucifixion is not regarded simply as a happening that took place and is all over. While there is a once-for-all aspect to it, there is also the aspect which sees it as of permanent validity and continuing effect.'[4]

A more epochal event has never occurred in history. The cross is the pivotal point which has dealt with the problem of sin and changed the unchangeable. It has changed heaven and opened its doors to sinners who have been 'redeemed to God by [Christ's] blood', and now sing 'a new song.' The death of Christ has laid the foundation for the kingdom of God to be established on earth forever, embracing men, women and children 'out of every tribe and tongue and people and nation.' Moreover, it is the means whereby He purchases us 'to God', and bought us at such a great price that we are not our own. We must 'therefore glorify God in [our] body and in [our] spirit, which are God's' (1 Corinthians 6:19–20). When at last God's kingdom is consummated, 'we shall reign on earth.' That is to say, we will reign with Christ in the new heaven and the new earth' (Matthew 19:28; 2 Timothy 2:12). In the meantime we are to serve God as 'priests'. We are to be the representatives of God to the rest of humankind, proclaiming the good news of the kingdom and remission of sins in Christ's name, and praying for their salvation.

The Lamb is worshipped as God

Worship is an activity reserved for God (22:8–9). The fact that the Lamb is worshipped in verses 8 to 12 is evidence of His full deity. This is supported by the fact that He is situated 'in the midst of the throne' (v. 6). Twice in chapter 22 we read of 'the throne of God and of the Lamb' (vv. 1,3). Jesus shares God's throne and the worship of the four living creatures and the twenty-four elders who surround the throne (v. 8). In verses 11 and 12 the living creatures and the elders are joined in their worship of Christ by 'the voice of many angels around the throne … and the number of them was ten thousand times ten thousand, and thousands of thousands, saying with a loud voice: "Worthy is the Lamb who was slain to receive power and riches and wisdom and strength and honour and glory and blessing!"' It is a similar ascription of worship given to God the Creator of all in chapter 4:11 and again in chapter 7:12.

Scarcely have the angels finished their homage of praise and worship to the Lamb when the chorus is taken up afresh by the whole of creation and directed both to God the Creator of all and to His incarnate Son, the Lamb, who is God the Redeemer. Verse 13, 'And every creature which is in heaven and on the earth, and under the earth, and such as are in the sea, and all that are in them, I heard saying, "Blessing and honour and glory and power be to Him who sits on the throne, and to the Lamb, forever and ever!"' Then the four living creatures said, "Amen!"' The circle of those who worship God and the Lamb gets wider and wider until now it includes every created being. Verse 13 should not be taken too literally, otherwise 'every creature' would include every evil person and 'under the earth' would refer to demons. Rather verse 13 is a poetic way of describing the praise of God and the Lamb that comes from every quarter of the universe. The universality of Christ's accomplishment calls for a universal response. So the four living creatures who represent all creation before the throne of God are called in to endorse this universal worship with their 'Amen.' And the twenty-four elders are so overwhelmed that John says they 'fell down and worshiped Him who lives forever and ever', for it is He who gave them their Saviour.

We are not left in the slightest doubt, then, that Jesus the Lamb is to be reckoned with God as God. For if heaven adores the sovereignty of God the Creator, it wonders even more at the triumph of God the Redeemer. The world may dismiss Christ with sparse praise. They may honour Him as a great prophet, as all Muslims and Hindus do. But there is only one Jesus heaven knows, and that is Jesus the enthroned Lamb and the victorious executor of the plans and purposes of God. The question is, however: Is that the Jesus you and I know? For no one is ready to go to heaven who is not ready to worship Jesus Christ as God. If we do not believe in the deity of Christ and do not think He is worthy of the same adoration and worship that is given to the Father, then as long as we are in that condition, we will never enter the glory of heaven. For the heaven that is revealed to us here in chapter 5 and the rest of the book of Revelation is a place where every creature worships Christ as God.

Christ's sevenfold ascription of worthiness

The Lamb who was slain is now acclaimed by the choir of angels as worthy of having seven attributes that belong to God alone (vv. 11–12; cf. 1 Chronicles 29:10–12). The first four are qualities He rightfully possesses and the last three are expressions of worship that are rightly due to Him. *First*, Jesus Christ is the worthy possessor of *power*, for the indelible marks of His self-sacrifice are the proof of His love for us and the guarantee that He will never abuse that power. It is because the sceptre of universal sovereignty is in a nail-pierced hand, that we can have confidence that His rule will never degenerate into tyranny or despotism. *Secondly*, He is the worthy possessor of *riches*. Riches tend to make a man covetous. The more he gets, the more he wants. But Christ's worthiness to possess riches is seen in the fact that He was absolutely content on earth with the little He had (Matthew 8:20), for His supreme delight was to do the will of God His Father. So poor was He at His death that He hung naked on a cruel cross. Thus Paul could say, 'You know the grace of our Lord Jesus, that though He was rich, yet for your sake He became poor, so that by His poverty you might become rich' (2 Corinthians 8:9).

Thirdly, the Lamb is the worthy possessor of *wisdom*. Wisdom is more than knowledge, for it is the ability to make the right use of knowledge. Christ is the wisdom of God, the source and fount of all true wisdom (1 Corinthians 1:24). His infinite knowledge is always used for the highest and greatest good of Himself and His people. *Fourthly*, the Lamb is the worthy possessor of *strength*. There is a difference between strength and power. Samson had power but not strength. Though physically powerful, he was morally and spiritually weak. Moral strength is the highest strength. In the gospels our Lord portrays Himself as the strong man who overcame the devil and spoiled his goods (Luke 11:22). This victory was obtained by His atoning death on the cross (Colossians 2:13–15).

Fifthly, Christ is the worthy possessor of *honour*. Honour is bestowed in just recognition of service rendered or excellence attained. No one in heaven or on earth can match the achievements of the Lamb who has destroyed the power of death 'and brought immortality and life to light' (2 Timothy 1:10). *Sixthly*, Christ is the worthy possessor of *glory*.

Glory is the unfading splendour of God's perfect, infinite being. The praise we give to Christ is of the highest order, for He is 'the brightness of [God's] glory and the express image of His person' (Hebrews 1:3). *Seventhly*, Christ is the worthy possessor of *blessing*. We bless Him because He has abundantly blessed us. It is our duty and joy to return grateful praise and homage for the blessings He has conferred upon us. Although we cannot enrich the Lamb, we can please Him by blessing His name.

Revelation 5 is the most magnificent portrayal in Scripture of the worship of Jesus Christ as our God and Saviour in heaven. But it is not a duty that can wait until then. Indeed, it is in this life that men and women are recruited into the choir of heaven and trained to sing the song: 'Worthy is the Lamb that was slain.' Some join the choir early; some do not join the choir until their later years. But if we are ever going to sing in glory, we need to join this choir on earth. That is why the gospel is to be proclaimed to every nation; to tell men and women that there is a way to enter heaven through the shed blood of Christ, and that if we will put our trust in Him now to wash away our sin, He will put this new song in our mouth forever.

> Crown Him with many crowns,
>   The Lamb upon His throne;
> Hark! how the heavenly anthem drowns
>   All music but its own:
>   Awake, my soul, and sing
>   Of Him who died for thee,
> And hail Him as thy chosen King
>   Through all eternity.
>
> Crown Him the Lord of life,
>   Who triumphed o'er the grave,
> And rose victorious in the strife,
>   For those He came to save:
>   His glories now we sing,

Who died and rose on high,
Who died eternal life to bring,
    And lives that death may die.

Crown Him the Lord of heaven,
    Enthroned in worlds above;
Crown Him the King to whom is given
    The wondrous name of love:
    All hail, Redeemer, hail!
    For Thou hast died for me;
Thy praise shall never, never fail
    Throughout eternity.

(Matthew Bridges, 1800–94, Godfrey Thring, 1823–1903)

10 The Lamb opens the seals

6:1Now I saw when the Lamb opened one of the seals; and I heard one of the four living creatures saying with a voice like thunder, 'Come and see.' 2And I looked, and behold, a white horse. He who sat on it had a bow; and a crown was given to him, and he went out conquering and to conquer. 3When He opened the second seal, I heard the second living creature saying, 'Come and see.' 4Another horse, fiery red, went out. And it was granted to the one who sat on it to take peace from the earth, and that people should kill one another; and there was given to him a great sword. 5When He opened the third seal, I heard the third living creature say, 'Come and see.' So I looked, and behold, a black horse, and he who sat on it had a pair of scales in his hand. 6And I heard a voice in the midst of the four living creatures saying, 'A quart of wheat for a denarius, and three quarts of barley for a denarius; and do not harm the oil and the wine.'

7When He opened the fourth seal, I heard the voice of the fourth living creature saying, 'Come and see.' 8So I looked, and behold, a pale horse. And the name of him who sat on it was Death, and Hades followed with him. And power was given to them over a fourth of the earth, to kill with sword, with hunger, with death, and by the beasts of the earth.

9When He opened the fifth seal, I saw under the altar the souls of those who had been slain for the word of God and for the testimony which they held. [10]And they cried with a loud voice, saying, 'How long, O Lord, holy and true, until You judge and avenge our blood on those who dwell on the earth?' [11]Then a white robe was given to each of them; and it was said to them that they should rest a little while longer, until both the number of their fellow servants and their brethren, who would be killed as they were, was completed.

[12]I looked when He opened the sixth seal, and behold, there was a great earthquake; and the sun became black as sackcloth of hair, and the moon became like blood. [13]And the stars of heaven fell to the earth, as a fig tree drops its late figs when it is shaken by a mighty wind. [14]Then the sky receded as a scroll when it is rolled up, and every mountain and island was moved out of its place. [15]And the kings of the earth, the great men, the rich men, the commanders, the mighty men, every slave and every free man, hid themselves in the caves and in the rocks of the mountains, [16]and said to the mountains and rocks, 'Fall on us and hide us from the face of Him who sits on the throne and from the wrath of the Lamb! [17]For the great day of His wrath has come, and who is able to stand?'

(Revelation 6:1–17)

Revelation is supremely the unveiling of the exaltation of Jesus Christ to the right hand of God the Father from where He controls the destiny of the world. In seven main consecutive visions the apostle John is shown 'things which will/must take place after this' (1:19; 4:1). The first vision unveiled Jesus Christ as the exalted Judge superintending the affairs of His church on earth from His first coming to His second (1:9–3:22). Now, in the second vision, Jesus Christ is revealed as the exalted Redeemer who alone is worthy to open the sealed scroll of world-destiny and carry out God's original purpose for creation; namely, to redeem a people for Himself, to destroy evil, and to renovate the universe (4:1–8:1).

In Revelation 6 the apostle John sees the Lamb opening the six seals of divine judgment upon an evil world which will come to a climax in the great day of God's wrath. The seals are opened one by one, and as each seal is removed we are given a grim picture of a series of continuing judgments upon the world. They represent afflictions throughout this church age by means of which the redemptive and judicial purposes of God are being carried out. Moreover, it is important to note that the church of Jesus Christ is not exempt from this suffering. The martyrs are singled out in verses 9–11, and the innumerable company of the redeemed are sealed and spiritually preserved in chapter 7. To quote Leon Morris, 'John sees God as in control of the whole process and God is concerned for His people. So, though the apocalyptic judgments be loosed against all mankind, God's people need never be dismayed. They will be preserved no matter what the tribulation.'[1]

The first four seals are of a piece with one another; they form a unity. They portray four different coloured horses and their riders. Now in biblical times horses were not beasts of burden, but beasts of battle. They were a very potent force in warfare, because they were animals endowed with considerable speed and strength. Here is how the horse is praised in Job: 'Have you given the horse strength? Have you clothed his neck with thunder? … His majestic snorting strikes terror … he gallops into the clash of arms. He mocks at fear, and is not frightened; nor does he turn back from the sword' (39:19–22). That is the picture conveyed by these horses; a picture of power that cannot be stopped by men. They do not, however, symbolise uncontrolled power, for these horses all have a rider who directs the horse according to the instructions of the Lamb in heaven who sends them. They each come out of the scroll at Christ's command and they follow what is written of them by God the Father before the world was made. So the rider and the horse constitute one symbol and represent one facet of history. We must not look for a separate identity for the rider that is different from the horse. The *colour* of the horse is the key symbol.

The first seal opened: conquest

Verse 1, 'Now I saw when the Lamb opened one of the seals; and I heard one of the four living creatures saying with a voice like thunder, "Come and see."' The best manuscripts simply have the single command, 'Come', for the summons is addressed to the rider and not to John. Some of the early copyists unfortunately took the summons as being addressed to John, and so they added the words 'and see'. The living creature, however, is calling the rider on behalf of the Lamb to come forth from the scroll of destiny. In response to the summons we read, 'And I looked, and behold, a white horse. He who sat on it had a bow; and a crown was given to him, and he went out conquering and to conquer' (v. 2).

Many commentators seek to identify this rider on a white horse with Christ and the victorious progress of the gospel throughout the world. They connect him with the King of kings and Lord of lords in chapter 19:11–16 who returns from heaven on a white horse to destroy the nations who have rejected Him. But there is no similarity between these two riders except the colour of the horse, which is not enough to make the identification between the first horseman and Jesus Christ. The horseman in verse 2 is one of four, all 'given' power to inflict suffering and death upon 'a fourth of the earth' (v. 8). He is not bent on saving the world, but on conquering it. Conquerors in ancient times would normally ride on a white horse.

Moreover, the rider in verse 2 is given the laurel wreath (Gk., *stephanos*) awarded to victors at the Greek games and not the many royal crowns (Gk., *diademata*) given to Jesus Christ in chapter 19. Everything in chapter 6 points to the seals as unfolding a series of divine judgments. The four horsemen must surely be taken together, and therefore the first horseman represents the spirit of continuing imperialism throughout the dispensation of the church. For over 2000 years the world has seen the horror of the rise and fall of nations as they have vied with one another for international supremacy, whether it be the Romans, the Turks, the French, the British or the Germans, to name only a few. Millions upon millions have died unnaturally as a result. 'He went out conquering and to conquer.' In Matthew 24:6–8 Jesus describes this feature of the church age in these words, '"And you will hear of wars and rumours of wars. See that you are not troubled for all these things must come to pass, but the end is not yet. For nation will rise against nation, and kingdom against kingdom. And there will be famines, pestilences, and earthquakes in various places. All these are the beginning of sorrows."'

The second seal opened: revolution

Verses 3–4, 'When He opened the second seal, I heard the second living creature saying, "Come." And another horse, fiery red, went out. And it was granted to the one who sat on it to take peace from the earth, and that people should kill one another; and there was given to him a great sword.' John does not explain whom he means by 'He', but it surely refers to the Lamb who opened the first seal. This is now the pattern for the rest of the seals. So with the opening of the second seal by the Lamb, the second living creature issues the command for the second horseman to come forth, riding on a 'fiery red' horse. This seems to represent the same scourge of war as the first horseman unleashes, but the emphasis of what follows suggests that there is a difference. This rider is sent to 'take peace from the earth', whereas one of the positive benefits of imperialism was to bring peace and order to the world. The *pax Romana*, for instance, was the thing that enabled the apostles to travel the then known world in relative safety. Blood-thirsty revolutionaries and terrorists very seldom bring peace in their wake. In our day we only have to think of what happened in the Communist revolutions of Russia and China, and the genocide in Nigeria, Cambodia, Rwanda, Sudan and Bosnia. Red is an appropriate colour for revolution, as well as being the colour of blood. Humankind in our age has been robbed of much 'peace' and incalculable life as the second horseman is given power to incite 'people [to] kill [lit., slaughter] one another.'

The third seal opened: hunger

Verses 5–6, 'When he opened the third seal, I heard the third living creature say, "Come." And I looked, and behold, a black horse, and he who sat on it had a pair of scales in his hand. And I heard a voice in the midst of the four living creatures saying, "A quart of wheat for a denarius, and three quarts of barley for a denarius; and do not harm the oil and the wine."' Black symbolizes hunger produced by war or famine. In his hand the rider carries a 'pair of scales', which, in the Old Testament was usually mentioned in connection with the need to weigh out exact measures of grain, especially when food was scarce (Leviticus 26:26; Ezekiel 4:9–13; Amos 8:4–6). From the power given to the third horseman, then, it would seem that black is here a symbol of hunger. Food is barely enough to survive on and being sold at an exorbitant price. A dry 'quart of wheat' was what one man needed to live on for a day and a 'denarius' was the daily wage for a labourer. At such an inflated price he would not be able to feed his wife and children. His only option was to buy a cheaper, coarser grain like 'barley' that sold at three quarts for a day's wage. But even then the average family would have to tighten their belts to meet the costs of housing and clothing. It is a picture of economic hardship persisting right throughout the church age. The first coming of Christ and the blessing of the gospel is not going to redress the chronic inflation and economic injustices that will occur. Three-quarters of the world's population in every generation during this period have always lived in poverty, barely earning enough to make ends meet and dying at an early age. It is still true today in spite of all our technical advances.

There are limits, however, that are imposed on this rider and his black horse: 'And do not harm the oil and the wine' (v. 6). Some think that the oil and the wine are symbols of the luxuries that only the rich can afford, and who will therefore not suffer. But olive oil and cheap wine were necessary commodities in every household for cooking and for drinking. Water in the Middle East was and still is hard on the stomach (1 Timothy 5:23). It is best, therefore, to take the oil and the wine as symbols of the fact that there are limits beyond which this rider will not be allowed to go. Food will be scarce and costly, but not unobtainable. This is all in God's plan. For times of scarcity are a warning to people to see the shortness and uncertainty of life, and to turn to the Lord in repentance and believe the gospel.

The fourth seal opened: pestilence

Verses 7–8, 'When He opened the fourth seal, I heard the voice of the fourth living creature saying: "Come." So I looked, and behold a pale horse. And the name of him who sat on it was Death, and Hades followed with him. And power was given to them over a fourth of the earth to kill with sword, with hunger, with death, and by the beasts of the earth.' The colour of this horse is said to be 'pale'. The Greek word is *chloros* from which we get our word chlorine. Literally it denotes the yellowish green colour of a dead body. So it is the colour of death. And following close behind is Hades, the bodyless state to which all persons are reduced by death. To them we are told, 'power was given over a fourth of the earth to kill with the sword [through war or revolution]; with hunger; with death [lit., pestilence, as the word is often rendered]; and by the beasts of the earth.' In the Old Testament when the inhabitants of a land grew few by war or pestilence, they quickly became prey to wild beasts.

Death affecting 'a fourth of the earth' by all these factors (a symbol for a significant number, not to be understood literally), has been a feature of human history throughout this age. Here are some of the statistics confirming the prophecy. Ten-million soldiers were killed in World War I, not counting civilians. In World War II over fifty-million soldiers and civilians were killed. In the 'Black Death' pandemic

of 1347–1350 at least thirty-million people died in Europe alone,
not counting Central Asia and India and China where the plague
began, and no count was taken. In 1918 an influenza pandemic killed
more humans in a couple of months than any scourge in history: an
estimated fifty-million worldwide.[2]

The fifth seal opened: persecution

Also contributing to the unnatural termination of human life during
the church age will be anti-Christian aggression. The symbolism
now changes as the Lamb begins to open the fifth seal. There are no
more horses and their riders, and no more scenes of general unrest
and violence on earth. Instead, John is given a very moving picture of
another feature of the history of this age until the return of Christ:
namely, the persecution and martyrdom of Christians. Verses 9–11,
'When He opened the fifth seal, I saw under the altar the souls of
those who had been slain for the word of God and for the testimony
which they held. And they cried with a loud voice, saying, "How long,
O Lord, holy and true, until You judge and avenge our blood on those
who dwell on the earth?" Then a white robe was given to each of them;
and it was said to them that they should rest a little while longer, until
both the number of their fellow servants and their brethren, who
would be killed as they were, was completed.' John is clearly speaking
of those Christians who have been 'slain' (lit., slaughtered) for their
faithfulness to 'the word of God and for the testimony [of Christ]
which they held.' This is the only authentic ground for martyrdom.
A person is not a martyr because he or she is killed in a car or plane
accident on the mission field; or because they contract a deadly disease
there. A martyr is a Christian who is killed by the enemies of God for
the sole reason that he or she will not deny Christ or stop proclaiming
the gospel which is the word of God.

They are called 'souls' because although the enemies of God
were successful in killing their bodies, they were not able, as Jesus

promised, to destroy their souls (Matthew 10:28). However, they are not portrayed as standing with the rest of the church in heaven, symbolized by the twenty-four elders. Rather, John sees their souls 'under the altar'. This again is pure symbolism, for there is no temple or altar in heaven (21:22). The apostle is being shown that in martyrdom Christians are symbolically offering their lives as a sacrifice of worship to God. The scene is borrowed from the altar of sacrifice in the Mosaic system in which the blood of the animal was poured out at the base of the altar as a drink offering to God (Exodus 29:12; Leviticus 4:7). For according to the Old Testament the 'life' or soul of an animal or a human being was considered to be in the blood (Leviticus 17:11). That is the symbolism of the souls of these martyrs 'under the altar'. The apostle Paul similarly viewed his approaching martyrdom as an offering to be poured out (2 Timothy 4:6). The martyrs are never separate from the church.

Now John hears the martyrs of all ages cry out in verse 10 for God to 'judge and avenge [their] blood', not only on those who have killed them, but on all God's enemies 'who dwell on the earth.' For it is worldwide opposition to the gospel that fuels the flames of persecution and emboldens the hands of those who actually do the slaying. Their prayer is bothersome to liberal Christians who say it smacks of revenge! But that would be to misunderstand their motive. There is nothing self-centred about the prayer of these martyred souls. They are 'the spirits of just men made perfect' who are in heaven (Hebrews 12:23). They cannot sin or have unworthy motives, so they cannot be asking for personal vindication. No, in God's eyes the shedding of innocent blood always cries out for justice. When Cain murdered his brother Abel because his works were more righteous than his own, God said, 'the voice of your brother's blood cries out to Me from the ground' (Genesis 4:10). So the cry of the martyrs here is not for personal revenge, but a passionate and agonizing longing for the day when God, who is 'holy and true', will vindicate Himself and bring in His everlasting kingdom of righteousness. As long as the world continues in unbelief and persecutes His church, the holiness and truth of God will continue to be defied. Moreover, in verse 11 God does not reject their petition but answers it affirmatively in two ways. First, he receives them as His own: 'A white robe was given to each of them.' They are dressed in the absolute purity and righteousness of Christ, for sinners cannot make themselves righteous. It is God who justifies them. Secondly, they are given the assurance that their prayer has been heard and that at God's appointed time it will be answered. Providence is purposive. Nothing happens outside the will of God!

Having finished their toil for God on earth, they are now resting from their labours in heaven, where in the exhilarating and captivating worship of their glorious God, it will seem but a moment before their righteous prayer is answered. It is only being delayed because the number of their fellow believers who are yet to suffer martyrdom is not complete. God is in control, and the determination of that number is in His hands. Superficially the martyrdom of Christ's followers may seem to be in the hands of wicked men, but in reality it is in the hands of Christ who is carrying out what God has ordained in the scroll of destiny. A martyrdom may seem like a defeat for Christ's cause, but it leads only to 'the furtherance of the gospel' (Philippians 1:12). Hence the famous dictum of Tertullian (the early third century apologist): 'The blood of the martyrs is the seed of the church.' And therein God makes even the wrath of man to praise Him.

The sixth seal opened: the final judgment

Verses 12–17, 'I looked when He opened the sixth seal, and behold, there was a great earthquake; and the sun became black as sackcloth of hair, and the moon became like blood. And the stars of heaven fell to the earth, as a fig tree drops its late figs when it is shaken by a mighty wind. Then the sky receded as a scroll when it is rolled up, and every mountain and island was moved out of its place. And the kings of the earth, the great men, the rich men, the commanders, the mighty men, every slave and every free man, hid themselves in the caves and in the rocks of the mountains, and said to the mountains and rocks, "Fall on us and hide us from the face of Him who sits on the throne and from the wrath of the Lamb! For the great day of His wrath has come, and who is able to stand?"'

We have seen, so far, that the opening of the seals does not introduce cataclysms that will occur at the end of the world during the short period referred to as the 'great tribulation' (Matthew 24:21). Rather, they are divine judgments upon universal sin and unbelief which occur throughout the entire period stretching from our Lord's first coming to His second coming. Thus the seals are broken immediately after the Lamb who was slain takes His place on His Father's throne; that is, at His ascension and exaltation, forty days after His resurrection. But in the sixth and penultimate seal the scene moves beyond the mere signs leading up to the end and focuses on the very threshold of the end itself; to events which will happen on a future day which are beyond anything the world has ever known.

It is significant that in our Lord's own magisterial discourse in Matthew 24:1–31, He not only expounds the same subject, but expounds it in the same order. Nor should we be surprised, since the same Person is dealing with the same subject in each case. In Matthew our Lord is dealing with the disciples' question: 'What will be the sign of Your coming, and of the end of the age?' (24:3). Not only do the two passages conclude with a reference to the cosmic disturbances that will herald the final judgment (Revelation 6:12–17 and Matthew 24:29–31), but there is also a connection with the earlier seals. For example, in Matthew 24 Jesus says: 'And you will hear of wars and rumours of wars. See that you are not troubled; for all these things must come to pass, but the end is not yet. For nation will rise against nation, and kingdom against kingdom. And there will be famines, pestilences and earthquakes in various places. All these are the beginning of sorrows [lit., the birth pains]. Then they will deliver you up to tribulation and

kill you, and you will be hated by all nations for My name's sake' (vv.
6–9). So what 'Jesus Christ, the faithful witness', at one time had said
on earth, He now reveals from a scroll in heaven. In both places He is
unveiling something about the future.

Now although what John saw here is expressed in symbolic language
and is obviously not a scientific description of what is going to happen,
there is no reason why these cosmic events should not be taken at face
value. It is without doubt couched in metaphorical language. The 'stars
of heaven' are bigger than our planet, yet they fall to the earth 'as a fig
tree drops its late figs when it is shaken by a mighty wind.' Again, 'the
sky receded as a scroll when it is rolled up.' Nevertheless the scene has
to be taken literally because both the Old Testament and our Lord use
similar language to describe the end (Isaiah 34:4; Matthew 24:29–31).
Moreover, in 2 Peter 3:10 the apostle predicts that 'the day of the
Lord will come as a thief in the night, in which the heavens will pass
away with a great noise, and the elements will melt with fervent heat;
both the earth and the works that are in it will be burned up.' There
can be no doubt that the world will end with unimaginable cosmic
disturbances.

How terrifying that final day of history will be! From the day when
Adam and Eve sinned and hid themselves from the presence of God,
men and women have become fugitives from God. But on the last day
there will be no place to hide. The security of all unbelievers, whether
great or small, rich or poor, will be shattered, and all alike will seek
refuge to no avail. The judgment of God which is absolutely just and
impartial will be inescapable. To be crushed by mountains and rocks
will seem far preferable to facing 'the wrath of the Lamb!' Once again,
it is Thomas F. Torrance who so helpfully brings out the nuance of this
extraordinary phrase which is found only here:

The wrath of the Lamb! Who ever heard of a lamb being angry? What
a terrible thought—the gentlest of all God's creatures angry! It is the
wrath of love, the wrath of sacrificial love which, having done the absolute

utmost for us and our salvation, tells us as nothing else could the certainty with which evil awaits its doom at the hand of God ... No man survives ... the wrath of God's Lamb, the consuming passion of His holy love that wills to destroy all that is unloving and untrue. That is the Lion of the Tribe of Judah that is also the Lamb of Calvary.[3]

A question everyone must face

The utter hopelessness of wretched mortal sinners having to face God and the Lamb on their own, whether at death or the final judgment, is expressed in the despairing question: 'and who is able to stand?' What is frightening is not simply the process of dying, but the horror of experiencing the just judgment of God upon our sin. For the day of grace will be over, and it will be too late to repent and believe in the Lamb who was slain as an offering for sinners. In supreme self-sacrificial love, Jesus Christ went to the cross of Calvary and bore the wrath of God in the place of all who will trust Him for salvation, so that they may be spared from such a terrible ordeal. History is moving on; time is running out; the great day of God's wrath is near. Will we be able to stand when the storm of the final judgment causes heaven and earth to fall to pieces? Is the foundation of our life resting solidly on the rock Christ Jesus (Matthew 7:24–25)? The ultimate answer to this question: 'Who is able to stand?' will be fully given to the apostle John in Revelation 7.

The comfort of God's sovereignty

There is enough foreboding in Revelation 6 to instil fear and anxiety into even the bravest human hearts, or there would be, if we did not have the interlude of God and the Lamb enthroned supreme over the entire universe (4:1–5:14). We must constantly bear in mind that our Lord Jesus Christ is sharing the throne with His Father, and that the scroll of world-destiny is in the nail-pierced hands of 'Him who loves us and has freed us from our sins by His blood' (1:5, ESV). All the turmoil, suffering and death predicted in chapter 6 take place only when the Lamb who was slain breaks the seals and commands these judgments to come into effect.

Thus we read that 'a crown was given' to the rider of the white horse; that 'it was granted to the one who sat on [the fiery red horse] to take peace from the earth … and there was given to him a great sword'; the rider on the black horse was ordered, 'do not harm the oil and the wine'; and to Death and Hades 'power was given to them over a fourth of the earth to kill.' God is supreme! The control of human affairs remains firmly in His hands. These four agents of divine judgment exercise only the power that He gives them. Each one is, as it were, on a leash which sets limits to his activity. Even in the martyrdom of His people, God is in control. The determination as to when their number is complete is not in the hands of those who unjustly persecute them, but in His hands (v. 11). The martyrs who righteously long for God to vindicate Himself and His holy cause, must 'rest a little while longer' in the enjoyment of their blessedness, as God continues to stay His hand and to withhold His final judgment upon a wicked world. But while He waits to be gracious to humankind, He does not condone their evil.

Now this is important because there are some who say: 'I accept the fact that God is the giver of good things, but I cannot accept that God sends war and revolution and want and pestilence and persecution into the world. He allows bad things to happen, but He does not send them.' But that is not what Revelation 6 is saying. The lesson from the opening of the seals is that Christ Himself is executing these judgments upon the world. God purposes the good and the bad things in history without, by some strange mystery of His providence, being the author of evil. For in every event God works with the full and free cooperation of men. God does not make them do the evil things that they do. They are of their own doing. But more to the point and more comforting is the fact that Revelation 6 tells us that God sends everything to *benefit* the righteous and *restrain* the wicked. Take the latter first. Philip Edgcumbe Hughes rightly points out:

> Catastrophic events of the kind mentioned here [i.e. in Revelation 6], which are restrained within certain limits, should be understood as sore acts of judgment which ungodly or apostate communities bring down upon themselves, and which at the same time are warnings to repent before it is too late, and foretastes of total judgment yet to come.[4]

The words of the apostle Paul in Philippians are a testimony to the truth of the former: the *benefit* of persecution to the righteous. The apostle has been unjustly imprisoned for preaching Christ crucified and risen, and will ultimately be martyred. Yet he tells the Philippians, 'I want you to know, brethren, that the things which happened to me have actually turned out for the furtherance of the gospel' (1:12). Earlier in his ministry Paul applied this truth to all situations when he wrote to the Romans: 'And we know that all things work together for good to those who love God, to those who are called according to His purpose'; and again, 'For I am persuaded that neither death nor life, nor angels nor principalities nor powers, nor things present nor things to come, nor height nor depth, nor any created thing, shall be able to separate us from the love of God which is in Christ Jesus our Lord' (8:28, 38–39). There is no comfort to compare with the comfort of knowing that God in His sovereignty will bring good out of every evil His people have to face in the world.

> Ye fearful saints fresh courage take;
>   The clouds ye so much dread
> Are big with mercy, and shall break
>   In blessings on your head.
>
> Judge not the Lord by feeble sense,
>   But trust Him for His grace;
> Behind a frowning providence
>   He hides a smiling face.

His purposes will ripen fast,
    Unfolding every hour;
The bud may have a bitter taste,
    But sweet will be the flower.

Blind unbelief is sure to err,
    And scan His work in vain;
God is His own interpreter,
    And He will make it plain.

                        (*William Cowper, 1731–1800*)

11 The sealing, security and bliss of believers

7:1After these things I saw four angels standing at the four corners of the earth, holding the four winds of the earth, that the wind should not blow on the earth, on the sea, or on any tree. 2Then I saw another angel ascending from the east, having the seal of the living God. And he cried with a loud voice to the four angels to whom it was granted to harm the earth and the sea, 3saying, 'Do not harm the earth, the sea, or the trees till we have sealed the servants of our God on their foreheads.' 4And I heard the number of those who were sealed. One hundred and forty-four thousand of all the tribes of the children of Israel were sealed:

5of the tribe of Judah twelve thousand were sealed; of the tribe of Reuben twelve thousand were sealed; of the tribe of Gad twelve thousand were sealed;

6of the tribe of Asher twelve thousand were sealed; of the tribe of Naphtali twelve thousand were sealed; of the tribe of Manasseh twelve thousand were sealed;

7of the tribe of Simeon twelve thousand were sealed; of the tribe of Levi twelve thousand were sealed; of the tribe of Issachar twelve thousand were sealed;

8of the tribe of Zebulun twelve thousand were sealed; of the tribe of Joseph twelve thousand were sealed; of the tribe of Benjamin twelve thousand were sealed.

9After these things I looked, and behold, a great multitude which no one could number, of all nations, tribes, peoples and tongues, standing before the throne and before the Lamb, clothed with white robes, with palm branches in their hands, 10and crying out with a loud voice, saying, 'Salvation belongs to our God who sits on the throne, and to the Lamb!' 11All the angels stood around the throne and the elders and the four living creatures, and fell on their faces before the throne and worshipped God, 12saying:

'Amen! Blessing and glory and wisdom,
Thanksgiving and honor and power and might,
Be to our God forever and ever.
Amen.'

13Then one of the elders answered, saying to me, 'Who are these arrayed in white robes, and where did they come from?'

14And I said to him, 'Sir, you know.'

So he said to me, 'These are the ones who come out of the great tribulation, and washed their robes and made them white in the blood of the Lamb. 15Therefore they are before the throne of God, and serve Him day and night in His temple. And He who sits on the throne will dwell among them. 16They shall neither hunger anymore nor thirst anymore; the sun shall not strike them, nor any heat; 17for the Lamb who is in the midst of the throne will shepherd them and lead them to living fountains of waters. And God will wipe away every tear from their eyes.'

(Revelation 7:1–17)

With Revelation 6 ending with the opening of the sixth seal, we would naturally expect that Revelation 7 would begin with the opening of the seventh seal. Instead, chapter 7 serves as a critical interlude between the sixth and seventh seals. Further on there is a similar interlude between the blowing of the sixth and seventh trumpets (10:1–11:14). So, far from being unconnected to chapter 6, chapter 7 serves as a very practical and important link. It contrasts the security and blessedness which mark the redeemed people of God with the panic and fear that will grip unbelievers trying in vain to escape the final judgment. In other words, it answers the question at the end of chapter 6: 'For the great day of His [the Lamb's] wrath has come, and who is able to stand?'

The purpose of chapter 7, then, is to reassure God's servants (v. 3) that they will be kept safe and unharmed when the world is falling to pieces all around them. They can rely on their Redeemer's promise: 'Most assuredly, I say to you, he who hears My word and believes in Him who sent Me has everlasting life, and shall not come into judgment, but has passed from death into life' (John 5:24). The chapter begins, 'After these things I saw.' That tells us that chapter 7 follows chapter 6 in the order of the things John 'saw' in this second series of visions, but it does not follow the actual order of events in chapter 6. The destructive judgments that accompany the opening of the first six seals have not yet fallen on the earth (7:3). That should be obvious, for if the sealing of God's servants came after the destruction of the earth in chapter 6, it would be too late to protect them.

Chapter 7, then, is retelling the prophecy of things to come in chapter 6 from another perspective, using different symbols. 'After these things', says John, 'I saw four angels standing at the four corners of the earth, holding the four winds of the earth, that the wind should not blow on the earth, on the sea, or on any tree.' The number 'four' signifies universality and 'winds' are a natural symbol of destructive power sent by God (cf. Jeremiah 4:11–12; 49:36; 51:1). So the four winds of God's judgment in chapter 7 are like the four horsemen in chapter 6, except that the four angels are holding back these forces of destruction from harming the earth. Why? Because God has a vast company of people on earth who must be sealed and preserved from the harmful judgments He is bringing in this age on a sinful world (v. 3).

The sealing of the church militant on earth

Verses 2–3, 'Then I saw another angel ascending from the east, having the seal of the living God. And he cried with a loud voice to the four angels to whom it was granted to harm the earth and the sea, saying, "Do not harm the earth, the sea, or the trees till we have sealed the servants of our God on their foreheads."' Revelation 7 consists of two separate visions describing two human communities. In verses 1–8 we have a community on earth that is called the 144,000 who are drawn from the twelve tribes of Israel (12,000 from each of the twelve tribes). In verses 9–17 we have 'a great multitude which no one could number, of all nations, tribes, peoples and tongues, standing before the throne and before the Lamb' (v. 9). So the number of the company on earth is known, but the number of the company in heaven is not. How do we understand that mystery? Many ingenious answers have been given. Jehovah's Witnesses say that the 144,000 constitute the exact number of Jehovah's servants who have rendered exceptional service for their organization, the Watch Tower Society, and who alone will be rewarded with a place in heaven. The remaining Jehovah's Witnesses will be resuscitated from their graves at the final judgment to enjoy paradise on earth in their normal physical state.

Dispensationalists, following the view in the Schofield Reference Bible, insist that the 144,000 consist of Jews converted to Christ after the rapture of the church at the beginning of Antichrist's reign of terror. God is going to use these Jewish evangelists to convert millions of Jews and Gentiles to Christ during the seven years of the great tribulation. To quote John Walvoord, 'The second half of chapter 7 of Revelation demonstrates that not only will many be saved in Israel but also many Gentiles will come to Christ in the great tribulation … In contrast to those coming from the twelve tribes as pictured earlier in the chapter, this throng comes from all nations.'[1] This is the most popular view among evangelicals today, but as explained in chapter 4 above, history will terminate at the rapture. The day of grace will be over, the door of salvation shut forever, and all humankind will appear before God at the final judgment.

The more plausible and traditional explanation of these two communities in Revelation 7 is to view them as pictures of the same people; of all the redeemed people of God viewed from different perspectives. The first company of people are living on earth and need to be sealed before the four angels holding the four winds can harm the earth. A seal symbolized three things: it signified *ownership*, it confirmed *authenticity* and it bestowed *inviolability*. Who are these people that God does not wish to be harmed? They are called 'the servants of our God' (v. 3). There is no indication of any limit or condition to be imposed on the number of God's servants who are to be sealed. They are made up of the full number of those who through faith in Jesus Christ have been liberated from the bondage of sin and Satan to serve God. If the message of Revelation is for us (and it is, chapter 1:1), then we are God's servants and are sealed. This is confirmed by the fact that the New Testament teaches us that every Christian believer is sealed by the Holy Spirit at conversion. Thus Paul says: 'Now He who establishes us with you in Christ and has anointed us is God, who also has sealed us and given us the Spirit in our hearts as a deposit'; and again, 'In Him you also trusted, after you heard the word of truth, the gospel of your salvation, in whom also, having believed, you were sealed with the Holy Spirit of promise, who is the guarantee of our inheritance until the redemption of the purchased possession, to the praise of His glory' (2 Corinthians 1:21–22; Ephesians 1:13–14; see also Ephesians 4:30; 2 Timothy 2:19).

Now if we are told in verse 4 that the sealed servants of God number 144,000 and all Christians are 'His servants' (1:1; 19:5; 22:3; Romans 6:22; 1 Corinthians 7:22), then the figure of 144,000 must be purely

symbolic. Indeed, it is too stylized to be just a *statistic*. For twelve is
always a symbol of the church. Thus the twelve patriarchs of Israel
formed the nucleus of the Old Testament church and the twelve
apostles formed the nucleus of the New Testament church. So here
the 144,000 is twelve times twelve times one thousand. The number
one thousand conveys the notion of magnitude and completeness.
Hence in Revelation 20 Christians are said to reign with Christ in
heaven for a thousand years between His first and second comings,
and God's angels are numbered in terms of many thousands (5:11). The
number 144,000, therefore, is almost certainly a symbol of the total
church of God on earth.

But if this is so, why is John told that this first company is made
up 'of all the tribes of the children of Israel' (v. 4)? This may seem
to contradict the above, but it too is in line with what the New
Testament teaches. For although the church is made up of Jews and
Gentiles, it is sometimes referred to as 'the twelve tribes' (James 1:1; cf.
Matthew 19:28; Luke 22:30).

Paul says in Romans 2:29, 'He is not a Jew who is one outwardly
… but he is a Jew who is one inwardly.' In Galatians 3:29 he states, 'If
you are Christ's, then you are Abraham's seed.' In Galatians 6:16 he
calls his Christian readers 'the Israel of God'. And in Philippians 3:3
he says, 'For we are the circumcision who worship God in the Spirit.'
Moreover, if the 144,000 consist only of Jews, why is the tribe of Dan
omitted altogether? The twelve tribes are listed eighteen times in the
Old Testament, none of which omits Dan. Verses 4–8, then, refer not
to a truncated Jewish nation, but to the entire church on earth made
up of believing Jews and Gentiles.

To sum up verses 1–8, the 144,000 is the church militant on
earth marshalled in battle array like the twelve tribes of Israel in the
wilderness. They constitute a fixed number known only to God which
is symbolically stated as 144,000. The name of every elect member is
'written in the Lamb's Book of Life from the foundation of the world'

(17:8; 21:27). The fact that they are sealed with 'the Holy Spirit of promise' (Ephesians 1:13) does not mean that they are preserved from physical harm while they are on earth, but that they are preserved from every evil that would prevent them from enjoying eternity with God in heaven (Romans 8:33–39). They have a spiritual security which cannot be harmed by physical adversity. To quote C.H. Spurgeon: 'It is impossible that any ill should happen to the man who is beloved of the Lord; the most crushing calamities can only shorten his journey and hasten him to his reward. Ill to him is no ill, but only good in a mysterious form. Losses enrich him, sickness is his medicine, reproach is his honour, death is his gain. No evil in the strict sense of the word can happen to him, for everything is overruled for good. Happy is he who is in such a case. He is secure where others are in peril, he lives where others die.'[2]

The rejoicing of the church triumphant in heaven

Verse 9, 'After these things I looked, and behold, a great multitude which no one could number, of all nations, tribes, peoples and tongues, standing before the throne and before the Lamb, clothed with white robes, with palm branches in their hands.' In verse 4 John *hears* the number of those who are sealed. He does not see anything, but hears the angel call out the roll. In verse 9 he *looks*. The curtain of heaven is drawn aside and he sees the sealed now safe and secure in heaven, a company so vast that 'no one could number' them. He throws that in just in case any of his readers should think that the number given as 144,000 should be taken literally.

Moreover, John sees that they are a truly international community drawn from 'the four corners of the earth' against which the winds of divine judgment have been blowing. In other words, they are the fulfilment of God's promise to Abraham: 'In your seed all the nations of the earth shall be blessed'; and again, 'I will multiply your descendants as the stars of the heaven and as the sand which is on the seashore' (Genesis 22:17–18; 26:4). Furthermore, this innumerable cosmopolitan congregation, their battle over, their victory won, are 'standing before the throne and before the Lamb' enjoying the presence of their Creator and Redeemer, unlike the wicked in chapter 6 who cannot 'stand' before Him and cry to the mountains and rocks to fall on them and hide them 'from the wrath of the Lamb' (cf. 6:17 with 7:9).

Their presence in heaven is proof that God 'is able to keep you [believers] from stumbling, and to present you faultless before the presence of His glory with exceeding joy' (Jude 24). They are therefore 'clothed with white robes', a symbol that they have been justified and made righteous in the sight of God. How they have been justified will shortly be explained to John. The fact that they have 'palm branches in their hands' signifies rejoicing over the ingathering of the harvest. This took place annually at the Feast of Tabernacles when the people waved palm branches and rejoiced before the Lord (Leviticus 23:33–40). The innumerable company of the redeemed in heaven will celebrate the great ingathering of God's eternal harvest (Matthew 9:37–38; 13:30).

The song they were singing

Verse 10, 'A great multitude (v. 9) … crying out with a loud voice, saying, "Salvation belongs to our God who sits on the throne, and to the Lamb!"' John listens in rapture to the heavenly singing. Tongues previously accustomed to speaking in different languages, now sing in majestic unison a new song, and the burden of their anthem is an ascription of salvation to God and the Lamb. They have been finally and fully saved. They have been delivered completely from the penalty, power and presence of sin. They are now sinless and perfect in God's sight. And for this completed salvation they glorify God as the Author, and 'the Lamb who was slain' as the Mediator. Their gratitude and rejoicing know no bounds.

Philip Edgcumbe Hughes' comment on the content of their praise is rich:

> They claim no merit or righteousness of their own. The initiative belongs entirely to the God of grace, for, as St. Paul says, 'God shows His love for us in that while we were yet sinners Christ died for us' and in that 'while we were enemies we were reconciled to God by the death of His Son' (Romans 5:8,10). From beginning to end *salvation belongs to our God*; it is all from God (2 Corinthians 5:18,21). This is a constantly recurring theme in Scripture. Moses and the people of Israel sang after their crossing of the Red Sea: 'The Lord is my strength and my song, and He has become my salvation' (Exodus 15:2). The psalmist declared that 'the salvation of the righteous is from the Lord' (Psalm 37:39; cf. 3:8; 62:7); and through His prophet Isaiah God proclaims: 'I am the Lord and besides Me there is no saviour' (Isaiah 43:11; cf. 12:2; 45:21; Hosea 13:4; Jonah 2:9). Hence also the apostolic insistence that 'there is salvation in no one else' than Jesus Christ who, as the incarnate Son, is the Lamb of God (Acts 4:12) and 'our great God and Saviour' (Titus 2:13; cf. 3:4–7).[3]

Verse 11, 'And all the angels stood around the throne and the elders and the four living creatures, and fell on their faces before the throne and worshipped God, saying: "Amen! Blessing and glory and wisdom, thanksgiving and honour and power and might, be to our God forever and ever, Amen."' It is now the turn of all the angels in heaven to offer their praise to God. They are in a circle surrounding the twenty-four elders (representing the church) and the four living creatures (representing the renewed creation). Hearing the cry of the countless redeemed in verse 9, they respond by prostrating themselves before God in rapturous worship. 'If there is "joy before the angels of God over one sinner who repents" (Luke 15:10), how unbelievably great will be the joyful adoration of the heavenly host when all the redeemed stand before their God!'[4]

Their first response is to say, 'Amen!' They affirm what the redeemed have said about salvation belonging to God and the Lamb. 'Amen' is the Hebrew word for 'It is so' (or, it is true). They rejoice in seeing in the redeemed the glorious handiwork of the salvation of God and the Lamb, and proceed to ascribe seven qualities to God that are all preceded by the definite article, which is awkward to bring out in our English translations. They join together with one voice, saying, 'The blessing (not a blessing, but the blessing above all other blessings) and the glory and the wisdom, the thanksgiving and the honour and the power and the might (above all others), be to our God forever and ever.' And then the angels end as they began with a second 'Amen' affirming the verity of their praise. It is the same paean of praise that is addressed to the Lamb by the myriads of angels in chapter 5:12 except that 'thanksgiving' replaces 'riches'.

Here is a great truth. The life of heaven is one long continuous and jubilant celebration of the salvation of God and the Lamb who was slain. Neither the redeemed nor the holy angels will ever tire of rejoicing in 'the grace of God that brings salvation' (Titus 2:11). If we belong to the glorious company of the redeemed, we must begin now to add our voices to theirs and join in the mighty chorus. Every child of God by redemption can say with David, 'He has put a new song in my mouth—praise to our God; many will see it and fear, and will trust in the LORD' (Psalm 40:3). But that was not all that John noticed about the saints in final glory.

The robes they were wearing

In John's vision one of the elders before the throne asks him the question, 'Who are these arrayed in white robes, and where did they come from' (v. 13)? The question is asked, not because the elder desires John to give him the information which the elder already possesses, for John is not able to supply it. Rather, it is asked in order to arouse John's curiosity about the white-robed throng who stand before God's throne so resplendent and perfect in their resurrection bodies. And when John replies, 'Sir, you know', his words indicate that he desires to be informed about the identity of this 'great multitude'. The elder therefore explains, 'These are the ones who come out of the great tribulation, and washed their robes and made them white in the blood of the Lamb. Therefore they are before the throne of God' (vv. 14–15).

The angel specifies two characteristics about them. First, they have 'come out of the great tribulation' (v. 14). Our Lord, echoing the book of Daniel, taught that just before the final judgment there will be tribulation on earth 'such as has not been since the beginning of the world' (Matthew 24:21–22; Daniel 12:1). But He made it clear that this will be the climax of a persecution the church will have to endure throughout this age (Matthew 24:3–22). It is great, not just in terms of its *ferocity* but also in terms of its *duration*, for the godly have always had to suffer persecution for righteousness' sake (Matthew 5:10–12). Abel was killed by his brother Cain; David was persecuted by Saul; Jeremiah was imprisoned; Daniel was thrown to the lions; and John the Baptist and James were beheaded. Our Lord Himself was taken by wicked hands and crucified; and He warned all His disciples to expect the same treatment. 'You will be hated by all for My name's sake', He said (Matthew 10:22); and again, 'In the world you will have tribulation' (John 16:33). Paul also warned of the same thing in Acts 14:22, 'We must through many tribulations enter the kingdom of God.'

The invitation of Jesus is plain: 'If anyone desires to come after Me, let him deny himself, and take up his cross daily, and follow Me.' A cross is a place of death. Or as Dietrich Bonhoeffer put it, 'When Christ calls a man, He bids him come and die.'[5] Of course, not all Christians will suffer as martyrs, but all Christians, if they are uncomprisingly loyal to Jesus Christ, will know what it is to suffer for their loyalty; if not martyrdom, then ridicule or slander or rejection (Matthew 5:11–12). If we take our stand without compromise on the uniqueness of Jesus Christ as the only Saviour of sinners, we will be strongly opposed by those who believe in the equality of all religions. Again, to take our stand without compromise on the truth

that salvation is a free gift which cannot be earned or merited, will
offend the self-righteous. Or again, if we take our stand without
compromise on purity and self-control in a sexually permissive society,
we will create enemies and suffer for it. Through this tribulation all
the redeemed have to pass, and by their perseverance, they prove the
genuineness of their faith (Matthew 24:13).

The second characteristic about this company is that they have
'washed their robes and made them white in the blood of the Lamb.'
If this countless multitude have come through great tribulation and
been acquitted at the final judgment, how did they manage it? After
all, they were frail, sinful human creatures like every other member
of the human race. It could not be because of anything in themselves
that they owed their salvation. The only reason why they are standing
before the throne of God is that they have 'washed their robes and
made them white in the blood of the Lamb' (v. 14). Liberals are
repelled by this precious truth, but there is no need for anyone to be
offended. The imagery of the book of Revelation is symbolical, not
pictorial. Garments laundered in blood do not come out white. It is
a highly dramatic figure of speech that is not difficult to interpret.
The Lamb is not just Jesus, but the Jesus 'who was slain' as 'the Lamb
of God who takes away the sin of the world' (5:12; John 1:29). Like
the Passover lamb in the Old Testament, He has died in our place
bearing the judgment of God upon our sin for us (Exodus 12:1 23;
1 Corinthians 5:7). The 'blood of the Lamb' stands for the permanent
power and effectiveness of the once-for-all atoning death of God's Son
which 'cleanses us from all sin' (1 John 1:7). And to 'wash our robes
in the blood of the Lamb' is to appeal to Him in faith to have mercy
on us and make us clean and fit for His presence. There is no other
way, for in God's sight even our 'righteousnesses are like filthy rags'
(Isaiah 64:6).

The bliss they were enjoying

The elder in vv. 15–16 unfolds both the positive and negative characteristics of the bliss that the blessed ones enjoy in heaven. It consists of the perfect enjoyment of what they had already begun to enjoy in part, and what they had always longed to enjoy more fully while on earth. First, 'they are before the throne of God.' Their experience of the presence of God which had once been fitful and spasmodic, is now continuous and permanent. They who had sought while on earth to draw near to the throne of grace, are now never absent from the throne of grace. Nothing stands between them and the enjoyment of the presence of the Triune God: no sin, no fears, no doubts, no lack of love or misunderstanding. 'They are before the throne of God.' There is no room for purgatory here. To suppose that one has to languish miserably in the dingy cells of purgatory, is derogatory to the finished work of Jesus Christ. 'His blood can make the foulest clean.' Indeed, so effective and adequate is the cleansing obtained by Christ's penal, substitutionary death, that we are immediately fitted for God's holy presence at death.

Secondly, 'they serve Him day and night in His temple.' Each of them when on earth had sought to know God better, to love Him more dearly and to serve Him more fully. Now in heaven they render unceasing worship in undivided allegiance to Him who lives and reigns forever and ever. They never tire of singing the praises of Him who died to redeem them. Thirdly, 'He who sits upon the throne will shelter them with His presence.' These blood-bought children of God are now eternally sheltered in the absolute security that only God's presence can provide.

Equally wonderful are the negative blessings. The physical instincts that drive men on earth to toil and sweat in order to satisfy their physical needs, will no longer plague them. The saints 'shall hunger no more.' The scorching heat of the midday sun or the flames of martyrdom have no more power to harm them, for 'the sun shall not strike upon them, nor any heat.' The endless search for pure water (so difficult to find in the parched lands of the Mid-East) is now over, for they shall not 'thirst anymore.' And the reason why, is that the Lamb of God whose sacrifice has reopened the gates of Paradise, will (by a daring mixed metaphor) become their Shepherd who will 'guide them to springs of living water' (v. 17, ESV; Isaiah 49:10; John 4:14; 6:35). The reference to 'springs of living water' tells us that the absence of thirst in verse 16 does not mean the *absence of desire*, for the redeemed will always thirst for God. The difference, however, is that in heaven their thirst will always be satisfied.

Lastly, and surely one of the most beautiful touches of all in this sublime revelation of the saints in final glory: 'God will wipe away every tear from their eyes.' There will be no more sorrow, because there will be no more sin or suffering to spoil this final and perfect salvation (this vision of God which is the reward of the blessed). But it is only in heaven, and only in the case of those who have been redeemed by the blood of the Lamb, that tears will be wiped away forever from human eyes. By and large this world is, and always will be, a vale of tears. Discoveries of medical science may indeed deaden, but they will never wholly eliminate the physical and mental pain of men and women on earth. Only in God and in the redemption offered to us in Jesus Christ, can our final happiness be found. And only in heaven will He wipe away every tear from our eyes.

Such is the glorious destiny of the redeemed people of God. And while we rejoice for those who have gone before, we must not forget that the seeds of the destiny we shall reap then, are being sown now. If we want to stand before the throne of God then, we must have our robes washed now. If we want to worship God day and night in His temple then, we must start singing His praises now. If we want to drink at the perennial fountain then, we must begin to find our satisfaction in the Lord Jesus now. More simply, if we would sing that song and enjoy that bliss, we must wear those robes. By faith we must wash our robes and make them white in the blood of the Lamb now. Nothing less and nothing else than the atoning blood of Jesus can render us fit to share in the inheritance of the saints in final glory.

What will it be to dwell above,
    And with the Lord of glory reign,
Since the sweet earnest of His love
    So brightens all this dreary plain?
No heart can think, so tongue explain
What joy 'twill be with Christ to reign.

When sin no more obstructs our sight,
    When sorrow pains the heart no more,
When we shall see the Prince of light,
    And all His works of grace explore,
What heights and depths of love divine
Will there through endless ages shine!

Our God has fixed the happy day
    When the last tear shall dim our eyes,
When He will wipe all tears away,
    And fill our hearts with glad surprise,
To hear His voice, to see His face,
And know the riches of His grace.

This is the joy we seek to know,
    For this with patience we would wait,
Till called from earth and all below,
    We rise, our gracious Lord to meet;
To wave our palm, our crown to wear,
And praise the love that brought us there.   (*Joseph Swain, 1761–1796*)

12 God's trumpet blasts of warning

8:1When he opened the seventh seal, there was silence in heaven for about half an hour. 2And I saw the seven angels who stand before God, and to them were given seven trumpets. 3Then another angel, having a golden censer, came and stood at the altar. He was given much incense, that he should offer it with the prayers of all the saints upon the golden altar which was before the throne. 4And the smoke of the incense, with the prayers of the saints, ascended before God from the angel's hand. 5Then the angel took the censer, filled it with fire from the altar, and threw it to the earth. And there were noises, thundering, lightnings, and an earthquake.

6So the seven angels who had the seven trumpets prepared themselves to sound.

7The first angel sounded: And hail and fire followed, mingled with blood, and they were thrown to the earth. And a third of the trees were burned up, and all green grass was burned up.

8Then the second angel sounded: And something like a great mountain burning with fire was thrown into the sea, and a third of the sea became blood. [9]And a third of the living creatures in the sea died, and a third of the ships were destroyed.

[10]Then the third angel sounded: And a great star fell from heaven, burning like a torch, and it fell on a third of the rivers and on the springs of water. [11]The name of the star is Wormwood. A third of the waters became wormwood, and many men died from the water, because it was made bitter.

[12]Then the fourth angel sounded: And a third of the sun was struck, a third of the moon, and a third of the stars, so that a third of them were darkened. A third of the day did not shine, and likewise the night.

[13]And I looked, and I heard an angel flying through the midst of heaven, saying with a loud voice, 'Woe, woe, woe to the inhabitants of the earth, because of the remaining blasts of the trumpet of the three angels who are about to sound.' 9:[1]Then the fifth angel sounded: And I saw a star fallen from heaven to the earth. To him was given the key to the bottomless pit. [2]And he opened the bottomless pit, and smoke arose out of the pit like the smoke of a great furnace. So the sun and the air were darkened because of the smoke of the pit. [3]Then out of the smoke locusts came upon the earth. And to them was given power, as the scorpions of the earth have power. [4]They were commanded not to harm the grass of the earth, or any green thing, or any tree, but only those men who do not have the seal of God on their foreheads. [5]And they were not given authority to kill them, but to torment them for five months. Their torment was like the torment of a scorpion when it strikes a man. [6]In those days men will seek death and will not find it; they will desire to die, and death will flee from them.

[7]The shape of the locusts was like horses prepared for battle. On their heads were crowns of something like gold, and their faces were like the faces of men. [8]They had hair like women's hair, and their teeth were like lions' teeth. [9]And they had breastplates like breastplates of iron, and the sound of their wings was like the sound of chariots with many horses

running into battle. ¹⁰They had tails like scorpions, and there were stings in their tails. Their power was to hurt men five months. ¹¹And they had as king over them the angel of the bottomless pit, whose name in Hebrew is Abaddon, but in Greek he has the name Apollyon.

¹²One woe is past. Behold, still two more woes are coming after these things.

¹³Then the sixth angel sounded: And I heard a voice from the four horns of the golden altar which is before God, ¹⁴saying to the sixth angel who had the trumpet, 'Release the four angels who are bound at the great river Euphrates.' ¹⁵So the four angels, who had been prepared for the hour and day and month and year, were released to kill a third of mankind. ¹⁶Now the number of the army of the horsemen was two hundred million; I heard the number of them. ¹⁷And thus I saw the horses in the vision: those who sat on them had breastplates of fiery red, hyacinth blue, and sulphur yellow; and the heads of the horses were like the heads of lions; and out of their mouths came fire, smoke, and brimstone. ¹⁸By these three plagues a third of mankind was killed—by the fire and the smoke and the brimstone which came out of their mouths. ¹⁹For their power is in their mouth and in their tails; for their tails are like serpents, having heads; and with them they do harm.

²⁰But the rest of mankind, who were not killed by these plagues, did not repent of the works of their hands, that they should not worship demons, and idols of gold, silver, brass, stone, and wood, which can neither see nor hear nor walk. ²¹And they did not repent of their murders or their sorceries or their sexual immorality or their thefts.　(Revelation 8:1–9:21)

As we come to Revelation 8, the apostle John's vision of the opening of the seven seals is followed by a third major vision in which he sees and hears seven angels blowing seven trumpets (8:2). This is a little perplexing, because the opening of the sixth seal revealed the total disintegration of the universe that will mark the end of the world and the return of our Lord Jesus Christ (Matthew 24:29–31; 2 Peter 3:10–

13). What more is there to unveil with the opening of the seventh seal than the final judgment of the living and the dead before the throne of God and the creation of a new heaven and a new earth (20:11–22:4)? But to our great surprise that is not what happens in chapter 8 when the seventh seal is opened. Instead, we read that when the Lamb 'opened the seventh seal, there was silence in heaven for about half an hour' (v. 1). And then when the silence is broken and John catches his breath, as it were, he is given this third vision of seven trumpet-blowing angels. In biblical times trumpets were mainly used to give warning of an imminent invasion by enemy forces (Jeremiah 4:5–6; Ezekiel 33:1–6; 1 Corinthians 14:8).

The relation between the seals and the trumpets

It is important to note that just as the seven seals were opened in sequence and not all at once, so the trumpets are sounded in sequence, not in unison. Moreover, distressing things happen on the earth as each trumpet is blown. It is as if we are being transported back again to chapter 6 and the alarming events of the first six seals. And then to confuse matters even more, the seven trumpets are followed by the seven bowls of God's wrath that are poured out on the earth (16:1–21). Each sequence of seven seems to end with Jesus Christ on the point of returning to earth. We are faced here with the critical question of the structure of the book of Revelation which we dealt with in the introduction: Do the seals and the trumpets and the bowls follow a *linear* pattern or a *cyclical* one? That is to say, do the events unveiled in these three visions run in a straight line of strict chronological succession with each event following on after the other? Or do they follow a cyclical pattern in which the events unveiled in the first six seals are repeated again in the first six trumpet blasts and yet again in the outpouring of the bowls of wrath?

To my mind the latter answer is the better way to understand and explain these three sequences of seven symbols in which each series ends with Christ's return and the final judgment (11:15–18; 16:17–21; 19:11–21). For John is simply going back over the same ground each time, so that the seals, the trumpets and the bowls recapitulate what the other has unveiled with added detail and intensity. For the purpose of the unveiling we are being given through them is not to provide us with a precise timetable of the events leading up to the end of the world. Rather, their purpose is to reveal to us the way in which history from the time of Christ's ascension to His return will move through cycles of increasingly intense tribulation and calamity. This is the best way to harmonize the sixth seal with the fourth trumpet. For if the sun and the moon and the stars are extinguished in chapter 6:12–14 when the sixth seal is opened, how can their light be darkened by 'a third' in chapter 8:12 when the fourth trumpet is sounded? We can only conclude that though the trumpets come after the seven seals in sequence, they do not follow them in chronological order.

So the seals and the trumpets are alike in that they both cover the same period of history that now spans 2000 years. They confirm the truth that history repeats itself. The events that will characterize the last dark moments before Christ's return will have been foreshadowed again and again in the experience of the church all through history. They are unlike in that whereas the *fifth seal* shows Christians suffering persecution at the hands of unbelievers (6:9–11), the *fifth trumpet* shows unbelievers suffering torment at the hand of God (9:4–6), because they disregard His warnings and refuse to repent of their sin and believe the gospel (9:20–21). Michael Wilcock says, 'This difference between the two scenes [the seals and the trumpets] actually confirms their unity. They are the two sides of the same coin.'[1]

Silence in heaven for about half an hour

Chapter 8:1, 'When He [the Lamb] opened the seventh seal, there was silence in heaven for about half an hour.' There has been a great deal of speculation about the significance of this half-hour of silence, but the immediate context makes it clear that this silence in heaven is connected with the offering of 'the prayers of all the saints' on earth (vv. 3–6). 'Saints', of course, is one of the New Testament's descriptions for Christians (Romans 1:7; 1 Corinthians 1:2; 2 Corinthians 1:1; Ephesians 1:1), and prayer should occupy a central place in every Christian's life. It is a precious privilege bought at enormous cost through the suffering and death of our Lord Jesus Christ on the cross as an atonement for our sin. Without the merits of His shed blood which 'cleanses us from all sin' (1 John 1:7) we could not have access into God's holy presence to pray.

> O wondrous love, to bleed and die,
> To bear the cross and shame,
> That guilty sinners, such as I,
> Might plead Thy gracious name!　　　　*(John Newton, 1725–1807)*

The world may dismiss God's saints as irrelevant, but in God's sight they are important. The seven angels are about to sound their trumpets of judgment in turn and each blast will be followed by great cosmic cataclysms. But first there is an intervention by another angel who is charged with bringing the prayers of the saints before God. The praises of the angelic hosts in heaven now give way to a momentary silence so that 'the prayers of all the saints' may be offered to God. Verses 3–4, 'Then another angel, having a golden censer, came and stood at the altar. And he was given much incense, that he should offer it with the prayers of all the saints upon the golden altar which was before the throne. And the smoke of the incense, with the prayers of the saints, ascended before God from the angel's hand.' The symbolism of this scene has its origin in the worship of the Old Testament conducted in the tabernacle and the temple. Every day after the morning and evening sacrifice one of the priests took some red hot coals from the brazen altar of sacrifice and put them in a golden censer that was a pan suspended on a chain. Those burning coals were then taken from the outer court of the priests into the Holy Place and put on the golden altar of incense that stood just before the thick veil that surrounded the Ark of the Covenant. The priest would then sprinkle incense on the fiery coals, thus creating a cloud of fragrant smoke which symbolized God's pleasure in accepting the prayers of His people.

Prayer possible only through Christ crucified

Moreover, the prayers of the saints are only accepted by God because they are offered 'upon the golden altar which was before the throne.' Incense does not emit a fragrance without fire; and the golden altar in the tabernacle had no fire. The fire had to be brought in from the brazen altar in the outer court where the sacrifices were offered: 'For without the shedding of blood there is no forgiveness of sins' (Hebrews 9:22, RSV), and without the forgiveness of their sins, the prayers of the Israelites symbolized by the burning incense could not be offered to God. What we are therefore being taught in verses 3 and 4 is that it is only through the shedding of Christ's blood on the altar of the cross at Calvary that effectual prayer can be made by the saints of God.

Thus Scripture says, 'But now in Christ Jesus you who once were far off have been brought near by the blood of Christ. For He Himself is our peace ... for through Him we ... have access by one Spirit to the Father' (Ephesians 2:13–17); and again, 'Having boldness to enter the Holiest by the blood of Jesus ... let us draw near with a true heart in full assurance of faith, having our hearts sprinkled from an evil conscience' (Hebrews 10:19,22). That is what the Bible teaches. There can be no prayer acceptable to God but prayer that is made at the altar of the cross where Christ's blood was shed as an atonement for sin. And it is a truism that the more we really believe in Christ crucified, the more we will truly pray. The less we understand this, the less we will appreciate the privilege of prayer.

Prayer and the purposes of God

The prayers of the saints were heard and answered by God, with the result that verse 5 says: 'Then the angel took the censer, filled it with fire from the altar, and threw it to the earth. And there were noises, thundering, lightnings, and an earthquake.' These forces of destruction, are symbols of divine judgment. The very censer used to convey our prayers to God is now used to cast fire on the earth. This surely means that the prayers of God's people play a necessary part in ushering in the judgments of God to follow. Our Lord Himself said, 'I came to cast fire on the earth' (Luke 12:49). Psalm 97:3–7 expresses the same truth: 'A fire goes before Him, and burns up His enemies round about. His lightnings light the world; the earth sees and trembles. The mountains melt like wax at the presence of the Lord ... Let all be put to shame who serve carved images, who boast of idols.'

The church does not pray in vain. In verse 1 the seventh seal is opened and we are told that the prayers of God's saints are vital to the course of history; that their prayers are ordained of God for the fulfilment of His purposes in this world. They pave the way for God's blessing to come to those who believe the gospel and God's judgment to fall on those who will not believe. Now if God acts through prayer, it is because He is not only the Appointer of prayer, but the Inspirer as well. Prayer is the means God has ordained to accomplish His plans on earth. In Ezekiel 36:36–37 when God says that He will restore His people to their land and rebuild the ruined places, He adds: 'I will also let the house of Israel inquire of Me to do this for them' (cf. Isaiah 45:11). We see the same thing in Acts 1. God had promised in Joel 2 that He would pour out the Holy Spirit in blessing upon His people, but He also inspired them to pray for it for ten days, after which the Holy Spirit came upon them at Pentecost. Again, we read in Acts 12 that after King Herod killed the apostle James, 'Peter was therefore kept in prison; but constant prayer was offered to God for him by the church' (v. 5). And in answer to their prayers an angel was sent by God to miraculously rescue Peter from prison. Later we read that an angel of the Lord struck Herod dead, 'but the word of God grew and multiplied' (vv. 23–24). Judgment and blessing came in answer to prayer. What a most humbling and comforting truth about prayer is being taught here.

The first trumpet: the vegetation stricken

Now as the half-hour of silence ends, the seven angels who had the seven trumpets prepared themselves to sound. 'The first angel sounded: and hail and fire followed, mingled with blood, and they were thrown to the earth. And a third of the trees were burned up, and all green grass was burned up' (v. 7). Human wickedness does not go unnoticed by God who has His own way and His own time of dealing with it. This judgment speaks of destruction brought upon the vegetation of the earth by hail and fire (lightning) and blood (or war). But they are all inflicted by God from heaven and restricted to 'a third', because they are partial or provisional judgments, not the final judgment. They affect a significant proportion but not all of the earth. The fraction 'a third' occurs twelve times in verses 7–12. Even the statement, 'all green grass was burned up' refers only to the green grass on a third of the earth, for in chapter 9:4 the locusts are prohibited from harming the rest of the grass on the earth.

Hail and fire recall the seventh plague that was sent upon Egypt when God sent 'fire mingled with hail' upon the land (Exodus 9:24). The situations are similar, for as divine plagues preceded the exodus of the children of Israel from their Egyptian oppressors, so also will divine plagues precede the rapture of the church from a hostile world at the return of Christ as the Judge of all the earth (1 Thessalonians 4:13–18; 2 Thessalonians 1:6–10). So the purpose of the trumpet judgments is to warn the inhabitants of the earth that the full wrath of God is yet to come, and in doing so to bring them to repentance. To that end, please note that God's judgments are being increased in their effect from 'a fourth of the earth' under the seals (6:8) to 'a third' under the trumpets. As God's judgments progress during the church age they get worse.

The second trumpet: the sea stricken

Verses 8–9, 'Then the second angel sounded: and something like a great mountain burning with fire was thrown into the sea, and a third of the sea became blood, and a third of the living creatures in the sea died, and a third of the ships were destroyed.' Once again, God's judgment affects man's environment, only this time it is the sea. There is also an affinity between this partial judgment and the first Egyptian plague in which the Nile and other waterways in Egypt were turned to blood, killing the fish and making the water undrinkable (Exodus 7:20–21). The symbol of 'something like a great mountain burning with fire' is not to be taken literally as a reference to a massive volcanic eruption, for volcanoes hurl rocks and lava into the sea, but do not themselves fall into the sea. It is simply a picture of divine destruction affecting a third of the sea when totalled up over 2000 years, whether the source is volcanoes, hurricanes, earthquakes causing tsunamis, or naval battles, or over-kill by fishing with massive nets. And the destruction will involve 'blood', because of the loss of both marine and human life. Again, the judgment is partial. It affects but a third of the sea, its life and commerce, because its purpose is to warn and lead sinners to repentance. When totalled up, the loss of all life to disasters on the sea worldwide over twenty centuries could well amount to a third. That is to say, to a significant amount. The human race will be hurt by the effect of this judgment.

The third trumpet: the rivers stricken

Verses 10–11, 'Then the third angel sounded: and a great star fell from heaven, burning like a torch, and it fell on a third of the rivers and on the springs of water; and the name of the star is Wormwood; and a third of the waters became wormwood, and many men died from the water, because it was made bitter.' The judgments of God in this gospel age will affect not only the waters of the sea, but also the waters of the land. Many men will die from the pollution of one-third of the earth's drinking water. The star that is the cause of this pollution is a symbol pointing to the fact that once again this is a judgment that comes from God who rules the earth from heaven. John speaks of 'a great star' falling from heaven on a third of the rivers and springs of water. But even a very tiny star would smash the earth to smithereens. His description is not to be taken literally.

Moreover, the star is named for the effect it has on the fresh waters. It is called 'Wormwood' after the strong bitter taste of the plant of that name (Proverbs 5:3–4; Jeremiah 23:15). It is a graphic way of saying that this judgment is going to be a bitter pill to swallow, because it too will result in men dying. How this comes about is not spelt out beyond the fact that it is sent by God as a punishment upon ungodly men. To live men need fresh water. So anything that robs them of drinking water is a judgment of God. It may come about through droughts that dry up rivers and fountains. Perhaps that is why the star that fell on the waters is described as 'burning like a torch.' At such times men have fought over fresh water, and those tribes driven into desert areas have suffered great loss of life from the fighting and from being deprived of water by their fellow men. We must also include people who die from illnesses caused by industrial pollution. And who knows how many will die if terrorists are ever successful in poisoning municipal water?

The fourth trumpet: the luminaries stricken

Verse 12, 'Then the fourth angel sounded: and a third of the sun was struck, a third of the moon, and a third of the stars, so that a third of them were darkened; and a third of the day did not shine, and likewise the night.' The scene recalls the ninth plague with which God smote Egypt with total darkness for three days, except that what John perceives here is a partial darkness caused by a third of the luminaries being darkened. In other words, there was a total absence of light for a third part of both day and night. Darkness is a symbol of judgment throughout Scripture (Joel 2:1–2; 3:14–15; Amos 5:18; 8:9; Matthew 24:29). How this darkness will come about is not easy to explain, but as Michael Wilcock points out: 'The supernatural events of the Bible are concerned not with "How?" but with "Who?" and "Why?" Trumpet four again points us back to the book of Exodus, where the importance of the plagues which struck Egypt was precisely that men could not understand how they happened, and had to admit that God was at work (Exodus 8:7,16–19) … the trumpets are sounding not doom, but warning.'[2]

If unbelievers, however, persist in ignoring God's warnings to repent through these judgments on the environment that affect them indirectly, the remaining trumpets will now affect them directly and spiritually. Verse 13: 'And I looked, and I heard an angel flying through the midst of heaven, saying with a loud voice: "Woe, woe, woe to the inhabitants of the earth, because of the remaining blasts of the trumpet of the three angels who are about to sound!"' The King James Version speaks here of an 'angel', not an 'eagle' (ESV, NASB, NIV), pronouncing the three woes, which seems to me to fit the context best, for this is a scene where angels predominate, and it would seem more appropriate for yet another angel to pronounce the next three woes rather than an 'eagle'.

The fifth trumpet: demonic torment

Chapter 9:1, 'Then the fifth angel sounded: And I saw a star fallen from heaven to earth. And to him was given the key to the bottomless pit.' This star is not a heavenly body but a heavenly being. Stars are also symbols of angels (1:20), and he is the same angel who locks Satan up in the bottomless pit in Revelation 20:1–8 and then after a thousand years releases him from his prison 'to deceive the nations which are in the four corners of the earth.' The two scenes are too similar to be speaking of two different events. The fifth trumpet is warning the earth that sometime near the end of this age, Satan and his hordes of demons will be released to exercise his full tyranny upon all the inhabitants of the earth. In verse 11 Satan is called 'Apollyon' (meaning Destroyer) and described as the 'king' of the demons. The bottomless pit is not hell as Hendriksen suggests. Hell is a place of torment from which no man or demon can be released, and Satan and his followers will be cast into hell only at the final judgment (20:10). A better interpretation is to see 'the bottomless pit' as a symbol of the spiritual restrictions which God in His sovereignty placed on Satan and his angelic followers after their expulsion from heaven. They cannot do anything without God's permission. They are spiritually restrained or contained.

Now to operate at maximum capacity, Satan and his minions are allowed to rise 'out of the pit like the smoke of a great furnace' (vv. 2–3). In other words, they will bring great spiritual darkness to society in general (to 'those men who do not have the seal of God on their foreheads', v. 4). They are described aptly as 'locusts' (destroyers) who are armed like 'scorpions' (which can hurt but not kill), shaped like 'horses' (powerful), with the 'faces of men' (intelligence), with 'women's hair' (gentleness), lions' teeth (ferociousness), 'breastplates of iron' (well-protected), flying 'like the sound of chariots' (frightening), and charged not to harm any vegetation 'but only those men who do not have the seal of God on their foreheads' (vv. 3–11). Furthermore, their power to hurt unbelievers was limited to 'five months' (the normal lifespan of a locust). The figure is symbolic, the equivalent to Satan being 'released for a little while' in Revelation 20:3. No one knows the exact length of time but God who in His sovereignty has decreed 'the hour and day and month and year' (v. 15) for its beginning and end. As always God is in total control (Job 1:12: 2:6) ensuring spiritual light and blessing for those who have His seal (2 Timothy 2:19), and spiritual darkness and torment for those who do not.

The sixth trumpet: the final warning

Verse 12, 'One woe is past. Behold, still two more woes are coming after these things.' If the fifth trumpet blast unleashed the first 'woe', then the second woe will be unleashed by the sixth trumpet blast and the third woe by the seventh trumpet blast (11:15). Chapter 9:13, 'Then the sixth angel sounded: and I heard a voice from the four horns of the golden altar which is before God.' It was the prayers of the saints offered from this altar of incense in chapter 8 that called forth these trumpet judgments, and it is probably the voice of Christ, our great High Priest, that comes from the golden altar before God in response to the prayers of His church. John hears the voice 'saying to the sixth angel who had the trumpet, "Release the four angels who are bound at the great river Euphrates."' The angels here are fallen angels or demons who have been restrained until now. In Scripture God's good angels are never represented as bound. These bad angels are stationed 'at the great river Euphrates', the eastern border of the promised land, or just outside 'the camp of the saints' (20:9). These demons of destruction, with an army of two hundred million horsemen, cannot harm the sealed of God.

John is told they have been 'prepared for the hour and day and month and year ... to kill a third of mankind' (v. 15). The precise moment of this judgment had been set by God's calendar, not just for the year and the month and the day, but for the very *hour* in which God's will is to be done. Every single death inflicted upon the ungodly in this final warning will happen exactly as and when God has purposed it. It would seem, however, to refer to a time just preceding Christ's return, for the very next trumpet is the 'last trumpet' which announces the consummation of Christ's kingdom and the final judgment (11:15–19; Matthew 24:30–31; 1 Corinthians 15:52; 1 Thessalonians 4:16–17). As in the case of the other trumpet judgments, the reference to a 'third of mankind' being killed simply means a large number, but not the majority. The judgment is partial, for only at the final judgment will all sinners be destroyed.

Verse 17 is meant to convey the spiritual power of this army of soul-destroying demons: 'And thus I saw the horses in the vision, those who sat on them had breastplates of fiery red, hyacinth blue, and sulphur yellow; and the heads of the horses were like the heads of lions; and out of their mouths came fire, smoke and brimstone.' None of this can be taken literally. Demons do not ride horses; and horses do not have heads like lions and do not breathe out fire, smoke and brimstone. The whole purpose of this scene is to highlight the intimidating presence of this horde of demons upon the earth. In verse 18, 'the fire and the smoke and the brimstone' which are descriptive of the very nature of hell, are now said to be 'three plagues'. And it is these plagues that come out of the horses' mouths that kill men.

The conflict is spiritual and not military as William Hendricksen suggests: 'These are not ordinary horses. They clearly symbolize war-engines, war-tools of every description. Think of tanks, cannons, battleships, etc. All this terrible death-dealing war-machinery, causing destruction on every side, verse 19, is included in the symbolism of these "horses". They kill one-third of mankind.'[3] Whereas the judgments of the first four trumpets are all physical, the last three trumpets all have to do with the spiritual realm. And so verse 19 clarifies the picture by saying, 'For their power is in their mouth.' John is witnessing the spiritual destruction by false teaching of a large number of people who when they die go to hell. 'Their tails are like serpent heads' identifies these agents with demons. The judgment of the sixth trumpet is about spiritual warfare, not military warfare.

Lessons from the trumpet judgments

God's warnings will intensify towards the end
As the church age progresses, the effect of the judgments gets worse.

After the sounding of the first four trumpets in chapter 8 which affect humankind physically, an angel gives a triple warning of greater 'woe' to come (8:13). As the final judgment nears the fifth and sixth trumpet blasts unleash horrific demonic torment upon unbelievers worldwide which afflict men and women spiritually. Physical affliction is easier to cope with than spiritual affliction. 'In those days men will seek death and will not find it; they will desire to die, and death will flee [lit. keep running] from them' (9:6). Increasing ungodliness through demonic influence will produce of itself an intensification of woe from which men will not escape. If unbelievers are determined to serve the devil, God will increasingly make them feel the awful tyranny of his dominion. Philip Edgcumbe Hughes has a helpful note on verse 6:

> The harsh pain from which escape is sought results from the infecting of the lives of men and women with the venom of the inhumanity which is engendered by ungodliness, involving the corruption and brutalization of society, the terror of frustration and violence, and the senselessness of existence which has been robbed of meaning and purpose. Dying will seem preferable to living, in the false hope that it will be self-obliteration; but the godless will find no way of escape from the judgment they have brought upon themselves.[4]

Suicide is the deception of demons because for the wicked it will be an escape from torment on earth to the inescapable torment of hell, the 'second death' (20:14–15). The remedy does not lie in the death of the body. It lies in 'the seal of God': in the Holy Spirit and His power of regeneration.

The hardness of human hearts

What the history of the last two thousand years has shown is that in spite of God's judgments there comes a time in each generation when men are beyond repentance, and when the word of God only seems to harden them in sin. Verses 20–21, 'But the rest of mankind, who were not killed by these plagues, did not repent of the works of their hands, that they should not worship demons, and idols of gold, silver, brass, stone, and wood, which can neither see nor hear nor walk. And they did not repent of their murders or their sorceries or their sexual immorality or their thefts.' Many people are perplexed at how a good God allows tragedy and suffering to afflict the earth, but the severity of God's judgments is not what puzzles John here. What astounds him is the continued wickedness of those who are not moved by these divine judgments to repent of their sins and turn to God for mercy. God's judgments upon the world have a loving purpose.

As C.S. Lewis so characteristically put it: '... we can ignore even pleasure. But pain insists upon being attended to. God whispers to us in our pleasures, speaks in our conscience, but shouts in our pains: it is His megaphone to rouse a deaf world ... No doubt Pain as God's megaphone is a terrible instrument; it may lead to final and unrepented rebellion. But it gives the only opportunity the bad man can have for amendment. It removes the veil; it plants the flag of truth within the fortress of a rebel soul.'[5]

What God repeatedly says to the impenitent is: Beware, the seventh trumpet is going to sound soon and usher in the final judgment which will be worse than all the judgments that have gone before. Paul warns us of this in Romans 2:5–6 when he says, 'In accordance with your hardness and your impenitent heart, you are treasuring up for yourself wrath in the day of wrath and revelation of the righteous judgment of God, who will render to each one according to his deeds.'

God's patience is not unlimited

Revelation 8 and 9 is all about God's warnings to a wicked and recalcitrant world. It is not a picture of God smiling at impenitent sinners. He is frowning at them. But behind that frown is a heart of love and compassion that has no pleasure in the death of the wicked, but patiently waits, longing for them to repent and be saved before it is too late (Ezekiel 33:11; Romans 10:21; 1 Timothy 2:3–4; 2 Peter 3:9). God's judgments are really kindnesses, but His patience is not without its limits. For to be patient with sinners indefinitely would mean that

God is indifferent to their sin, and that He can never be. Sinners may obtain a moratorium for their sins now by God's grace, but they will never obtain a permanent amnesty. When at last God's patience runs out, the end will come. The seventh trumpet will sound and while the wicked will be cast into hell, God's saints will be united forever with Jesus Christ in a new heaven and a new earth.

According to the Bible there are only two places where God can punish our sins. One is hell, where impenitent sinners experience for ever the just penalty their sins deserve. The other is the cross of Calvary, where Jesus Christ, the Lamb of God, in His own sinless, divine-human person, bore the damnation of hell on behalf of all who believe in His name and receive Him as their Saviour and Lord (John 1:11–13). 'Believe in the Lord Jesus Christ, and you will be saved' is God's command to all unbelieving sinners.

13 The little book and the two witnesses

¹⁰:¹I saw still another mighty angel coming down from heaven, clothed with a cloud. And a rainbow was on his head, his face was like the sun, and his feet like pillars of fire. ²He had a little book open in his hand. And he set his right foot on the sea and his left foot on the land, ³and cried with a loud voice, as when a lion roars. When he cried out, seven thunders uttered their voices. ⁴Now when the seven thunders uttered their voices, I was about to write; but I heard a voice from heaven saying to me, 'Seal up the things which the seven thunders uttered, and do not write them.'

⁵The angel whom I saw standing on the sea and on the land, raised up his hand to heaven ⁶and swore by Him who lives forever and ever, who created heaven and the things that are in it, the earth and the things that are in it, and the sea and the things that are in it, that there should be delay no longer, ⁷but in the days of the sounding of the seventh angel, when he is about to sound, the mystery of God would be finished, as He declared to His servants the prophets.

⁸Then the voice which I heard from heaven spoke to me again and said, 'Go, take the little book which is open in the hand of the angel who stands on the sea and on the earth.'

⁹So I went to the angel and said to him, 'Give me the little book.' And he said to me, 'Take and eat it; and it will make your stomach bitter, but it will be as sweet as honey in your mouth.'

¹⁰Then I took the little book out of the angel's hand and ate it, and it was as sweet as honey in my mouth. But when I had eaten it, my stomach became bitter. ¹¹And he said to me, 'You must prophesy again about many peoples, nations, tongues, and kings.'

¹¹:¹Then I was given a reed like a measuring rod. And the angel stood, saying, 'Rise and measure the temple of God, the altar, and those who worship there. ²But leave out the court which is outside the temple, and do not measure it, for it has been given to the Gentiles. And they will tread the holy city under foot for forty-two months. ³And I will give power to my two witnesses, and they will prophesy one thousand two hundred and sixty days, clothed in sackcloth.'

⁴These are the two olive trees and the two lampstands standing before the God of the earth. ⁵And if anyone wants to harm them, fire proceeds from their mouth and devours their enemies. And if anyone wants to harm them, he must be killed in this manner. ⁶These have power to shut heaven, so that no rain falls in the days of their prophecy; and they have power over waters to turn them to blood, and to strike the earth with all plagues, as often as they desire.

⁷When they finish their testimony, the beast that ascends out of the bottomless pit will make war against them, overcome them, and kill them. ⁸And their dead bodies will lie in the street of the great city which spiritually is called Sodom and Egypt, where also our Lord was crucified. ⁹Then those from the peoples, tribes, tongues, and nations will see their dead bodies three-and–a-half days, and not allow their dead bodies to be put into graves. ¹⁰And those who dwell on the earth will rejoice over them, make merry, and send gifts to one another, because these two prophets tormented those who dwell on the earth.

¹¹Now after the three-and-a-half days the breath of life from God entered

them, and they stood on their feet, and great fear fell on those who saw them. [12] And they heard a loud voice from heaven saying to them, 'Come up here.' And they ascended to heaven in a cloud, and their enemies saw them. [13] In the same hour there was a great earthquake, and a tenth of the city fell. In the earthquake seven thousand people were killed, and the rest were afraid and gave glory to the God of heaven.

[14] The second woe is past. Behold, the third woe is coming quickly.

(Revelation 10:1–11:14)

Between the opening of the sixth and seventh seals there was an interlude or pause consisting of two related visions in which the one hundred and forty-four thousand are sealed from spiritual harm (7:1–8) and the countless multitude of the redeemed are found in heaven praising God (7:9–17). Now with the close of chapter 9 when six of the seven trumpets have sounded, there is another interlude of two related visions concerning a little open scroll (10:1–11) and two witnesses (11:1–14). The seventh trumpet will herald the end of the world and the consummation of the kingdom of God and His Christ (11:15–19). In the midst of all the judgments that will afflict the wicked during trumpets one to six, what will be the fate of the church? John is shown here that it has a message to deliver and consequent opposition to endure (10:1–11:14) before it is caught up to glory. There will be no similar interlude between the pouring out of the sixth and seventh bowls of divine wrath (16:1–21), for by then all warnings will have been exhausted and the final judgment set in motion.

The gospel is God's final word to the world

'I saw still another mighty angel coming down from heaven, clothed with a cloud. And a rainbow was on his head, his face was like the sun, and his feet like pillars of fire.' Mighty or strong angels are mentioned three times in Revelation (5:2; 10:1; 18:21), and from their appearance and accomplishments they may well be archangels. Some commentators even suggest that this mighty angel is Jesus Christ who elsewhere in Revelation has been described as 'coming with clouds' (1:7), His feet 'like fine brass, as if refined in a furnace', His countenance 'like the sun shining in its strength' (1:15–16), and 'a rainbow around [His] throne' (4:3). This, however, cannot be, because as God incarnate our Lord would not have to swear by God as this angel does in verse 6, and John does not fall down and worship this mighty angel when he approaches him in verse 10. Rather, the imagery clearly conveys the truth that he speaks on behalf of the divine Christ. His voice is as loud 'as when a lion roars' (v. 3; cf. Amos 3:8), and he is unimaginably gigantic in size, spanning land and sea with his legs astride. Everything about this angel is designed to provoke in us a sense of irresistible power. What else do we learn about him? 'And he had a little book [lit. scroll] open in his hand' (v.2).

What an amazing contrast! The Greek word is a diminutive twice over for a normal scroll. Leon Morris says, 'If the present word has diminutive force the significance will be that the *little book* contained part only of the revelation of God's purpose.'[1] It represents, as we will see below, the gospel of the grace of God or the New Testament which is less than one-third the volume of the Old Testament. It also lies fully open in the palm of the angel's hand. Indeed, the Greek word conveys the idea that the little book will stay permanently open, for no one can prevent its contents from being made known (11:1–13). The angel's feet straddling land and sea proclaims the universality of its message (cf. 10:11), and the rainbow on his head is a symbol that it is the word of a gracious, covenant-keeping God (Genesis 9:8–17).

The permanent openness of the gospel of Christ is further emphasised in verses 3 and 4: 'and cried with a loud voice as when a lion roars. And when he cried out, seven thunders uttered their voices. Now when the seven thunders uttered their voices, I was about to write; but I heard a voice from heaven saying to me, "Seal up the things which the seven thunders uttered, and do not write them."' Six times in the Old Testament the prophets speak of God roaring like a lion

(Isaiah 31:4; Jeremiah 25:30–31; Hosea 11:10; Joel 3:16; Amos 1:2, 3:8). Here the angel speaks with the roar of the lion of the tribe of Judah (5:5). The mighty roar of supernatural power is immediately followed by the sounding of 'the seven thunders' which are not just inarticulate atmospheric noises, but intelligent voices that John heard and was able to understand what God was communicating. To his amazement he is forbidden to write the revelation down and pass it on to the churches.

Why should the 'little book' remain open while the vision of 'the seven thunders' is to remain secret? They both contain words that come from God Himself! Moses, under the inspiration of the Holy Spirit, gives us the answer: 'The secret things belong to the LORD our God, but those things which are revealed belong to us and to our children forever, that we may do all the words of this law' (Deuteronomy 29:29). God has revealed everything we need to know about the way and purpose of salvation in His little, open book of the gospel, but in His wisdom He has seen fit to keep certain things about the future hidden until the actual events transpire. And our response to these 'secret things' should not be one of speculation or complaint, but of faith and love.

The gospel is a timely message from God

'And the angel whom I saw standing on the sea and on the land lifted up his hand to heaven and swore by Him who lives forever and ever, who created heaven and the things that are in it, the earth and the things that are in it, and the sea and the things that are in it, that there should be delay no longer, but in the days of the sounding of the seventh angel, when he is about to sound, the mystery of God would be finished [fulfilled, ESV], as He declared to His servants the prophets' (vv. 5–7). The angel swears by God 'because he could swear by no one greater' (Hebrews 6:13), and says, in effect, that with the coming of the gospel 'there would be no more delay' (ESV) in the process of 'the mystery of God [being] fulfilled' through the salvation of all the elect and the final judgment of all the wicked. Both events are dependent upon the first coming of Jesus Christ to provide a way for God to be 'just and the justifier of the one who has faith in Jesus' (Romans 3:21–28, cf. Acts 17:30–31).

This truth is confirmed by the fact that the mighty angel goes on in verse 7 to say, 'when he [the seventh angel] is about to sound, the mystery of God would be finished [or fulfilled], as He declared to His servants the prophets.' The word translated 'mystery' is a common New Testament term for the gospel (God's good news of salvation) which remained hidden in Old Testament times until our Lord Jesus Christ came to earth to accomplish redemption and unveil it to His apostles by the Holy Spirit. Thus Paul can speak of 'my gospel and the preaching of Jesus Christ, according to the revelation of the mystery which was kept secret since the world began but now has been made manifest, and by the prophetic Scriptures has been made known to all nations, according to the commandment of the everlasting God, for obedience to the faith' (Romans 16:25–26; cf. Ephesians 3:1–6; 6:18–19). A further clue is found in the verb 'declared [lit. gospel led or told the good news] to His servants the prophets' (v. 7).

What, then, does the mighty angel mean when he says that at the sound of the seventh trumpet 'the mystery of God would be finished'? Leon Morris gives the answer as follows:

> God has one purpose through the ages and it reaches its climax at this point [the seventh trumpet]. From the very beginning God has planned to bring His people to salvation, and thus His whole purpose is coming to its culmination. It involves the judgment of evil, but also the deliverance and vindication of the people of God. John's readers are to reflect that the mighty world forces they saw, far from being triumphant, are about to be overthrown decisively. A purpose that God has planned before the world and has matured throughout all ages will not lightly be jettisoned. *The mystery of God* will indeed be finished.[2]

The church is to believe the gospel and pass it on

The unidentified voice which John heard from heaven, perhaps the voice of Jesus Christ Himself, now says to him in verse 8, "'Go, take the little book which is open in the hand of the angel who stands on the sea and on the earth." And I went to the angel and said to him, "Give me the little book." And he said to me, "Take and eat it"' (lit. "devour it" or "eat it down", v. 9). In other words: Take it into your innermost being and make its contents thoroughly your own. A mere intellectual acquaintance with the gospel will not do (James 1:22; Colossians 3:16). The voice from heaven goes on, "'And it will make your stomach bitter, but it will be as sweet as honey in your mouth." And I took the little book out of the angel's hand and ate it, and it was as sweet as honey in my mouth. But when I had eaten it, my stomach became bitter' (vv. 9–10). Every Jew would know from the Old Testament what this symbolized. In Ezekiel 3:1–7 God says to the prophet, "'Son of man … eat this scroll, and go, speak to the house of Israel" … So I ate, and it was in my mouth like honey in sweetness. And He said to me, "Son of man, go to the house of Israel and speak with My words to them … But the house of Israel will not listen to you, because they will not listen to Me"' (cf. Psalm 119:103; Jeremiah 15:16). Because the gospel promises salvation to all who believe in Jesus Christ as their Saviour, it is necessarily sweet to their souls. To have the assurance of sins forgiven and to receive the gift of the Holy Spirit as our Helper is 'joy inexpressible and full of glory' to every believer's soul (Ephesians 1:7; John 14:16; Acts 2:38; 1 Peter 1:8).

But the same gospel that is so sweet to the believer also has a bitter after-effect: 'But when I had eaten it, my stomach became bitter.' The bitterness is felt both internally and externally in the case of both John and every believer. The gospel is indeed good news, but the fact that it also contains severe warnings of eternal punishment for those who refuse to repent and believe in Christ, does not make it pleasant to deliver. Hell should always be preached with tears and heartfelt sorrow for the impenitent, as our Lord exemplified (Luke 19:41–44). Moreover, like his Saviour, John found that preaching the gospel is also a bitter experience *externally*. That is why he is in exile on the island of Patmos (1:9); but not even banishment can curtail his ministry.

Verse 11, 'And he [the voice from heaven, the Head of the church who reserves the right to commission His people to take the gospel to every creature] said to me, "You must prophesy *again* about [concerning, NASB] many peoples, nations, tongues and kings."' This is not a new commission, for John was commissioned by Christ 60 years before this. Rather, his commission is renewed here. That is the force of the word 'again'. With the new revelation he is receiving in these visions from God on the island of Patmos, John's commission is being renewed with an added dimension. He, as the last surviving apostle, has been privileged to receive what can only be called the culmination of all predictive prophecy. And so the book of Revelation is actually a part of the 'little book' from heaven that John is commanded to eat, for it will complete the New Testament. Revelation 10 is a beautiful vision couched in beautiful symbolism that is fairly easy to understand. Our task is to accept its message and play our part in the fulfilling of our Lord's great commission (Matthew 28:18–20).

God will preserve His church in the world

Revelation 11:1–13 continues the interlude which began in chapter 10 between the sounding of the sixth and seventh trumpets. In chapter 11 the purpose of the vision of the 'two witnesses' (v. 3) is to encourage the church in its divinely given commission to prophesy 'about [concerning God's salvation to] many peoples, nations, tongues, and kings' (10:11). It is a must. The task cannot be neglected, even though the opposition is formidable. Verse 1, 'Then I was given a measuring rod. And the angel stood, saying, "Rise and measure the temple of God, the altar [of incense previously mentioned in 8:3 and 9:13], and those who worship there.'" In Scripture measuring is often a symbol of God's gracious protection and provision for His people (cf. a new city and a new temple that will supersede the old order, Ezekiel 40:48). Although the King James Version says an 'angel' gave the measuring rod to John, it is clear from the context that the command came from Christ Himself who in verse 3 speaks of 'My two witnesses.'

The 'temple of God' that John is to measure cannot be the temple in Jerusalem for two reasons. First, the temple in Jerusalem was destroyed by the Romans 25 years before John saw this vision and it will not be rebuilt, because Christ's death has brought an end to the Aaronic priesthood and animal sacrifices forever. Secondly, in the New Testament God's temple is no longer a physical building in Jerusalem, but a spiritual dwelling place in the hearts of Christians collectively and individually all over the world (1 Corinthians 3:16–17; 2 Corinthians 6:16; Ephesians 2:19–22; 1 Peter 2:5). Moreover, John is told to measure 'those who worship there', which tells us that this has nothing to do with a physical building, for you cannot measure the number of people in a place with a measuring rod. The whole picture is a spiritual one, for the purpose of measuring these worshippers is to mark out those who are to be protected from the enemies of God who hate the little open book. This measuring corresponds to the sealing of God's people in chapter 7:1–8, which does not protect them from physical harm, but guarantees a safe passage to heaven (John 10:27–30).

But that will not apply to those who are outside the true church. Verse 2, 'But leave out the court which is outside the temple, and do not measure it, for it is given to the Gentiles' (or heathen nations). The temple in Jerusalem housed a shrine or building made up of two compartments: the Holy Place and the Holy of Holies. This sanctuary was further surrounded by a large outside court consisting of the court of the priests where the animals were sacrificed on the brazen altar; the court of Israel where only Jewish men were admitted; and then the court of the women. It is the entire outside court that John is commanded not to measure, 'for it has been given to the Gentiles. And they will tread the holy city underfoot for forty-two months' (v. 2). Here the symbolism is not as clear as in verse 1, but we are given a clue in the word 'tread' (lit. trample). For Jesus predicted that 'Jerusalem will be trampled by Gentiles until the times of the Gentiles are fulfilled' (Luke 21:24). These two verses have to be referring to the same thing; to Jerusalem as apostate Judaism. In Revelation 11:2 Jerusalem is called the 'holy city' simply to identify it with what it used to be in God's eyes before it turned apostate and crucified our Lord (11:8).

So what John is being shown in verse 2 is the truth that because the Jewish nation has rejected Christ it is not part of 'the temple of God' that is going to be divinely protected. The 'holy city' destroyed by Rome in AD 70 will continue to be oppressed by the heathen nations of the world until the 'times' allocated for Gentile supremacy have run their course. That time is fixed and its limit is symbolically portrayed as 'forty-two months' (three-and-a-half years). It is the same amount of time (one thousand two hundred and sixty days, v. 3) allocated to the church to preach the gospel to the world; to the woman (who is a symbol of the church, 12:6) to be protected from the dragon in the wilderness; and that is given to the 'beast' who is Satan's agent to spread all his 'blasphemies' in the world (13:5). In other words, forty-two months or one thousand two hundred and sixty days is a symbol for the whole period from Christ's ascension to His return during which the church will be preserved by God.

The church will be empowered by the Holy Spirit

These particular numbers have been chosen to symbolize Satan's efforts to oppose God's plan to save many people through the church's efforts to evangelize the world. Forty-two months (or three-and-a-half years) is a way of saying that Satan is not going to succeed, for three-and-a-half falls hopelessly short of the number seven which stands for the completion of a task (i.e. creation). Verse 3, 'And I will give power to My two witnesses, and they will prophesy one thousand two hundred and sixty days, clothed in sackcloth.' Dispensationalists like John MacArthur think that these two witnesses who have great prophetic and miracle-working powers, are Moses and Elijah returned to the earth.[3] But because the church will be in the world until the last day, it does not need Moses and Elijah to come back to the earth to do its work. Besides Jesus clearly identified John the Baptist as the fulfilment of the promise in Malachi 4:5, 'Behold, I will send you Elijah the prophet before the coming of the great and dreadful day of the Lord' (see Matthew 12:13–14).

So who are the 'two witnesses'? The traditional view has been to see them as a symbol of the church witnessing to Christ in the world, for Jesus sent His disciples out two by two to preach the gospel (Mark 6:7; Luke 10:1). Two is the number for reliable witness (Deuteronomy 19:15; Matthew 18:16; John 8:17–18; 1 Timothy 5:19). Notice too that the witnesses are 'clothed in sackcloth', because sackcloth is the symbol of repentance and mourning over sin (Neh. 9:1; Isaiah 32:11; Jonah 3:5; Matthew 11:21). The church can only bear a powerful witness when it is a penitent church. A self-righteous, complacent church has no power to stir the world either to repentance or to opposition.

But something even more important is needed, and so the two witnesses are also portrayed as 'the two olive trees and the two lampstands standing before the God of the earth' (v. 4). They are depicted as 'two lampstands', because in chapters 1 and 2 our Lord refers six times to the seven churches as lampstands. The witnesses, symbolizing the church, are bearers of light (Matthew 5:14–16). But lampstands need oil if they are going to burn and shed light. So John in his vision sees the two witnesses also as 'two olive trees' that have the oil for the two lampstands to bear light. The oil, of course, is a symbol of the Holy Spirit. For in a similar vision in Zechariah 4:6 Zerubbabel and Joshua are portrayed as two olive trees feeding oil to a single lampstand. And when the vision is explained to Zechariah, he is told, 'This is the word of the LORD to Zerubbabel: "Not by might nor by power, but by My Spirit', says the LORD of hosts.' If the church is to succeed in witnessing to Christ in the world, it must preach the gospel not 'in word only, but also in power and in the Holy Spirit and with full conviction' (1 Thessalonians 1:5, NASB).

Their Spirit-filled ministry will arouse opposition: 'And if anyone wants to harm them, fire proceeds from their mouth and devours their enemies. And if anyone wants to harm them, he must be killed in this manner' (v. 5). The Lord's witnesses may be hated and even put to death, but they cannot be harmed in a spiritual or eternal sense (Matthew 10:28). Those who try to harm them succeed only in bringing eternal destruction upon themselves. The fire that comes out of their mouths and consumes their enemies is not literal as John MacArthur suggests,[4] but is the gospel of Christ whose word saves the penitent and destroys the impenitent. The phrase 'must be killed' shows that the 'fire' of hell is certain for those who reject their witness. Verse 6, 'These have power to shut heaven, so that no rain falls in the days of their prophecy; and they have power over waters to turn them to blood, and to strike the earth with all plagues, as often as they desire.' The imagery here expresses the truth that the gospel is not impotent. Christ's servants in the age of the New Testament have just as much power to back up their word as Moses and Elijah had in the Old Testament era. The big difference, however, is that the gospel has power to bring spiritual plagues as well as physical ones on those who seek to destroy its witness, as outlined in chapters 6 and 9.

The church's light will sometimes be eclipsed

Verse 7, 'Now when they finish their testimony, the beast that ascends out of the bottomless pit will make war against them, overcome them, and kill them' (cf. Revelation 20:7–9). Notice again God's control of this situation. The human enemies who hate the gospel and the demons from the bottomless pit can only silence the church when its God-given task is finished; namely, to call out by their testimony a people for God from the world (Romans 8:28–30; 1 Corinthians 1:2). The Greek literally says, 'Whenever they finish their testimony.' Their assignment is not cut short. Only when their task is accomplished does the beast come out of the pit where Satan is held (9:11; 20:1–3,7–10). Verse 7 does not speak of *a* beast, but *the* beast, an evil being who is prominent from chapters 13 to 19, and is known as the final Antichrist (for many antichrists have arisen throughout church history, Matthew 24:24; 1 John 4:1–4). The two witnesses are regarded not as individuals but as a multitude against which the beast 'will make war' (v. 7).

Moreover, in this war the beast will be successful, just as in Daniel 7 he is pictured as 'making war with the saints, and prevailing against them' (v. 21). Revelation 11:7 is specifically a reference to the final great tribulation (Matthew 24:21–22; Revelation 20:7–10) which will be experienced by the church near the very end of this age. However, because there are many lesser antichrists, the sequel is repeated to a lesser extent throughout church history. The church's light has at times been almost extinguished, as in the Dark Ages (AD 500–1100).

Verse 8, 'And their dead bodies will lie in the street of the great city which spiritually is called Sodom and Egypt, where also our Lord was crucified.' The Greek literally says, 'the corpse of them.' They are seen as a single entity, the church. And the place where the corpse lies is called first 'the great city', for it represents not just one city, but the whole world that is opposed to Christ and His church. Thus John says that 'those from the peoples, tribes, tongues and nations will see the corpse of them' (v. 9). Accordingly, the great city is 'spiritually called Sodom and Egypt', for Sodom was a city renowned for wickedness, and Egypt a country renowned for its oppression of God's people. And then just to cap the spiritual allegory, the great city is also called the place 'where our Lord was crucified', for the church suffers physically the same fate as her Lord suffered in the world. The great world-city is not our home, but only the sphere of our witness: 'Here we have no continuing city, but we seek the city which is to come' (Hebrews 13:14).

The death of the church here has got to be interpreted figuratively, for the church cannot die or be destroyed (Matthew 16:18). It only appears to the world to be dead because its witness has been temporarily silenced. One only has to think of the Middle Ages (c. AD 800–1600) when the gospel was not preached until God raised up men like Wycliffe, Hus, Savonarola, Tyndale, Luther, Calvin and other reformers. Notice the world's hatred of the church: 'Then those from the peoples, tribes, tongues and nations will see their corpse three and a half days, and not allow their corpses to be put into graves' (v. 9). That is the worst indignity you can inflict upon any person in the Middle East where a person's corpse is to be buried within twenty-four hours of death. But so great is the world's hatred of the church that its corpse has to suffer the shame of being exposed to the gloating ridicule of onlookers via mass media.

The number three-and-a-half days is a symbol deliberately chosen to show that under Antichrist it will be a very short time in comparison with the length of the whole church age which is measured in terms of three-and-a-half years. The celebrations of the citizens of the great world-city will be short-lived, because theirs is a hollow victory as we will see from verse 11. But witness their great jubilation! Verse 10, 'And those who dwell on the earth will rejoice over them, make merry, and send gifts to one another, because these two prophets tormented those who dwell on the earth.' The world loves a party, and none more so than one thrown to celebrate the destruction of the church that is the voice of its conscience. The faithful preaching of the gospel is always disturbing to the world (1 Kings. 18:17; Acts 24:25), and so the silencing of that voice has always been a priority for the ungodly. Up till now, success in this regard has only been spasmodic and confined to a country here or there. But at the end of this age, the final Antichrist will publicly silence the church's voice worldwide (Daniel 7:24–25; Matthew 24:21–24; 2 Thessalonians 2:1–12).

The church will triumph in the end

Verse 11, 'Now after the three-and-a-half days the breath of life from God entered them, and they stood on their feet, and great fear fell on those who saw them.' In the previous verses John has been speaking in the future tense, but in verses 11–13 he changes to the past tense because these events are so certain that he can speak of them as already having taken place. And what he sees as so absolutely certain is the visible return of Christ accompanied by the visible rapture of the church and the destruction of the wicked. Verse 11 speaks of the visible rapture of the church that strikes great fear into the hearts of the wicked who see that the church has not been destroyed because the church belongs to God. In verse 12 Christ cries out with a loud voice that unfailingly affects what it speaks: 'Come up here' (cf. John 11:43–44; Hebrews 1:3). And John says, 'They ascended to heaven in a cloud, and their enemies saw them.' There is no secret rapture here. Both in verse 11 and verse 12 John says their enemies 'saw them.' And the cloud in which the church ascends to heaven is not just any cloud. John speaks of *the* cloud (NASB), because it is the cloud of Christ's shekinah glory with which He Himself ascended into heaven and with which He will return (Acts 1:9–11; Mark 13:26–27).

Thus the Lord's witnesses who have suffered and died over the millennia will be at no disadvantage when He comes for His own at the end of the age. For as Paul says in 1 Thessalonians 4:16–17, 'The dead in Christ will rise first. Then we who are alive and remain shall be caught up together with them in the clouds to meet the Lord in the air. And thus we shall always be with the Lord.' It is no wonder (v. 11) that 'great fear fell on those who saw' the rising and ascending of those they sought to destroy. For it is now only too clear to them that all that remains is for them to face the judgment of Almighty God. Verse 13,

'In the same hour', says John. There is no time interval between these final events. They all happen at once. 'In the same hour there was a great earthquake, and a tenth of the city fell.'

This is the most difficult verse in the book of Revelation. But it would seem that the 'earthquake' here at the sounding of the sixth trumpet corresponds with the earthquake in chapter 6:12 when the sixth seal was opened. It is a symbol of the divine shaking of the universe that will herald Christ's return, the resurrection of all the dead, and the final judgment (Isaiah 2:12,19; Haggai 2:6–7; Matthew 24:29; Hebrews 12:26). In chapter 6 it produced fear that led men to hide from the wrath of the Lamb, but here the wicked are compelled by fear to begrudgingly give 'glory to the God of heaven' (cf. Philippians 2:9–11).

When verse 13 says 'a tenth of the city fell', we must not forget that this is not just any city, but 'the great city' (a worldwide community organized against God). The 'tenth' equals 'seven thousand people'. And if we interpret John's numerical symbols consistently, then ten (and multiples of ten like one thousand) is a symbol of magnitude, the vastness of which is known only to God. When it is multiplied again by seven, the number of divine appointment, it signifies that all humankind not caught up to be with Christ on that day will have to face the final judgment described in verses 15–19. This will be the 'third woe', heralded by the seventh trumpet, which is 'coming quickly' (v.14).

There is much to encourage Christians in these twin visions of the apostle John in chapters 10 and 11, the chief lesson of which is well summed up by Thomas F. Torrance:

The Word of God towers over land and sea, and dominates the ages … If there is no wormwood, are we really in touch with the Word of God? If our message is not disturbing and even sometimes tormenting, may we not wonder whether we have really eaten God's holy Word? This chapter [10] tells us quite plainly that we cannot partake of God's Word in this world without bitterness. Why does the Church of Jesus Christ sit so easy to her surroundings? Why do Christian people live such comfortable and such undisturbed lives in this evil and disturbed world? Surely it is because we are not true to the Word of God ...

The Apostle's vision goes on to show how much the world hates the truth [chapter 11], for the Word of God is a torment to them. It disturbs them in every aspect of their life. When the Christian Church bears faithful witness to God, there is no department in human life that does not feel its penetrating challenge, no region of human experience that is not disturbed and does not suffer upheaval. True it is that the Word of God is always a Word of salvation and peace, but so long as the world is unrepentant, the Word of God can only be a torment to it ... Is it any wonder that whole regions of the earth have tried to stamp out the fire of God and have tried to silence His voice? ...

Let us listen to what this chapter has to say to us. No matter what the world does, the Word of God cannot be silenced. The world indeed may kill the witness-bearers and ravage the Church of Jesus Christ, and there may be much congratulation and rejoicing over that, but God will resurrect His Church wherever she is laid low, and great fear shall fall upon all that see her. God's Word is a living Word. It will not be silenced. It will always accomplish that whereunto it has been sent. It will march through tribulation and through the valley of the shadow of death and come out triumphant and rejoicing on the other side.[5]

14 War in heaven and on earth

^{11:15}Then the seventh angel sounded: And there were loud voices in heaven, saying, 'The kingdoms of this world have become the kingdoms of our Lord and of His Christ, and He shall reign forever and ever!' ¹⁶And the twenty-four elders who sat before God on their thrones fell on their faces and worshiped God, ¹⁷saying:

'We give You thanks, O Lord God Almighty,
The One who is and who was and who is to come,
Because You have taken Your great power and reigned.
¹⁸The nations were angry, and Your wrath has come,
And the time of the dead, that they should be judged,
And that You should reward Your servants the prophets and the saints,
And those who fear Your name, small and great,
And should destroy those who destroy the earth.'

¹⁹Then the temple of God was opened in heaven, and the ark of His covenant was seen in His temple. And there were lightnings, noises, thundering, an earthquake, and great hail.

^{12:1}Now a great sign appeared in heaven: a woman clothed with the sun, with the moon under her feet, and on her head a garland of twelve stars. ²Then being with child, she cried out in labour and in pain to give birth.

³And another sign appeared in heaven: behold, a great fiery red dragon

having seven heads and ten horns, and seven diadems on his heads. 4His tail drew a third of the stars of heaven and threw them to the earth. And the dragon stood before the woman who was ready to give birth, to devour her Child as soon as it was born. 5She bore a male Child who was to rule all nations with a rod of iron. And her Child was caught up to God and to His throne. 6Then the woman fled into the wilderness, where she has a place prepared by God, that they should feed her there one thousand two hundred and sixty days.

7And war broke out in heaven: Michael and his angels fought with the dragon, and the dragon and his angels fought, 8but they did not prevail, nor was a place found for them in heaven any longer. 9So the great dragon was cast out, that serpent of old, called the Devil and Satan, who deceives the whole world; he was cast to the earth, and his angels were cast out with him.

10Then I heard a loud voice saying in heaven, 'Now salvation, and strength, and the kingdom of our God, and the power of His Christ have come, for the accuser of our brethren, who accused them before our God day and night, has been cast down. 11And they overcame him by the blood of the Lamb and by the word of their testimony, and they did not love their lives to the death. 12Therefore rejoice, O heavens, and you who dwell in them! Woe to the inhabitants of the earth and the sea! For the devil has come down to you, having great wrath, because he knows that he has a short time.'

13Now when the dragon saw that he had been cast to the earth, he persecuted the woman who gave birth to the male Child. 14But the woman was given two wings of a great eagle, that she might fly into the wilderness to her place, where she is nourished for a time and times and half a time, from the presence of the serpent. 15So the serpent spewed water out of his mouth like a flood after the woman, that he might cause her to be carried away by the flood. 16But the earth helped the woman, and the earth opened its mouth and swallowed up the flood which the dragon had spewed out of his mouth. 17And the dragon was enraged with the woman, and he went to make war with the rest of her offspring, who keep the commandments of God and have the testimony of Jesus Christ.

(Revelation 11:15–12:17)

Just as the seven trumpets followed right after the opening of the seventh seal (8:1–6), so we have another series of seven visions following immediately after the blowing of the seventh trumpet (11:15–14:20), which we may call *'seven signs of cosmic conflict.'* This new series of visions contain a group of seven signs (12:1) designed to help beleaguered Christians understand the malevolent nature and power of the invisible forces which are bent on their destruction. And as in the three visions that have preceded it, vision four covers the same ground of Church history from our Lord Jesus Christ's first coming to His second.

The ultimate outcome of the conflict

Salvation is more than an individual experience in which our sins are forgiven and we receive the gift of eternal life through the death and resurrection of Jesus Christ (John 1:29; 3:16). Salvation also involves becoming a citizen of God's kingdom by Christ's gift of the Holy Spirit to permanently reside in our lives. By that gift we are spiritually reborn and brought under the rule of God (John 3:5; 14:16–17; 1 Corinthians 6:19,20). When Adam and Eve succumbed to sin the human race fell under the sway of a false god and a false ruler (Matthew 4:8–10; John 12:31; 14:30; 2 Corinthians 4:4). But through Christ's work of redemption on the cross, human lives are being brought back to the place where God has their true allegiance. It is in this sense that the loud voices in heaven exclaim, 'The kingdoms of this world have become the kingdoms of our Lord and of His Christ, and He shall reign forever and ever' (v. 15).

The word 'kingdoms' should be singular, not only because many other manuscripts have it as a singular noun, but also because Satan's kingdom is a worldwide kingdom. The verb is in the past tense ('have become'), because the event is certain. Although the consummation of God's kingdom is still future, heaven can speak of it as having already occurred. Moreover, the fact that it is 'the kingdom of our Lord [the Father] and of His Christ' does not mean that it has two kings, for God is one. Thus verse 15 says, 'And He [not 'they'] shall reign forever and ever.' For when all Christ's enemies have been subdued at His return (Psalm 110:1; Acts 2:34), 'then comes the end', says Paul, 'when He delivers the kingdom to God the Father … that God may be all in all' (1 Corinthians 15:22–28) and rule as the Trinitarian God.

The coming of this eternal kingdom of God was clearly predicted in Daniel 7:14, 'Then to Him [the Son of Man] was given dominion and glory and a kingdom, that all peoples, nations and languages should serve Him. His dominion is an everlasting dominion, which shall not pass away, and His kingdom the one which shall not be destroyed' (cf. Daniel 2:44). And when our Lord Jesus Christ was born the prophecy was repeated by the angel Gabriel to Mary: 'And behold, you will conceive in your womb and bring forth a Son, and you shall call His name Jesus. He will be great, and will be called the Son of the Highest; and the Lord God will give Him the throne of His father David. And He will reign over the house of Jacob forever, and of His kingdom there will be no end' (Luke 1:31–33). That is what God decreed before the world was made, and that is what Jesus said we must regularly pray for: 'Your kingdom come. Your will be done on earth as it is in heaven' (Matthew 6:10).

Although normally seated, the twenty-four elders 'fell on their faces and worshipped God' in the singing of a hymn of thanksgiving for this anticipated victory. Verse 17, 'We give You thanks, O Lord God Almighty, the One who is and who was and who is to come, because You have taken Your great power and reigned.' The elders are not implying that God has not been all-powerful through the ages past, but pointing to the arrival of the great consummating moment in which God overthrows all His enemies. He could have stopped the devil in his tracks in the Garden of Eden, but instead He has restrained His power in mercy and longsuffering in order to save a countless multitude of sinners for Himself (7:9–10; 2 Peter 3:8–9). The Lord God Almighty is able to accomplish in His perfect time all that He has determined to do. Thus the elders rejoice that the hour of reckoning has at last arrived when the defiance of humankind is brought to account at the final judgment, when both the living and the dead will receive their just reward. To die is not to escape final judgment (Hebrews 9:27). All the dead throughout the whole period of human history, as well as those who are alive at the time, will appear before God. Verse 18, 'The nations were angry, and Your wrath has come, and the time of the dead, that they should be judged.'

The hostility of the wicked is utterly futile and self-destructive, as Psalm 2 so vividly portrays: 'Why do the nations rage, and the people plot a vain thing? The kings of the earth set themselves, and the rulers take counsel together against the LORD and against His Anointed, saying, "Let us break Their bonds in pieces and cast away Their cords from us." He who sits in the heavens shall laugh; the LORD shall hold them in derision … You shall break them with a rod of iron; you shall dash them to pieces like a potter's vessel … Kiss the Son, lest He be angry, and you perish in the way, when His wrath is kindled but a little. Blessed are all those who put their trust in Him' (vv. 2–4,9,12). Their anger deserves His anger. The punishment fits the crime. God's wrath is not irrational, but the fitting reaction to the conduct of *the nations*.'[1] It is the time when God 'should destroy those who destroy the earth' (v. 18e).

The day of final judgment, however, will not be a day of terror for believers, for their sins have already been judged at the cross of Calvary when Christ died for their sins (John 5:24; 2 Corinthians 5:21; Galatians 3:13; 1 Peter 3:18). Instead, it will be a day for the rewarding of God's servants: 'And that You should reward Your servants the prophets and the saints, and those who fear Your name, small and great' (v. 18cd). The saints are the lesser lights among God's people who are not called to high office, but all alike are further described as 'those who fear Your name, small and great.' None will be forgotten whatever their position in the church, and all will be rewarded for their faithfulness and perseverance, not because of any merit in themselves. For they have nothing that they did not receive in the first place as a gift of grace (1 Corinthians 4:7) and all that they have been able to accomplish has only been possible by the enabling power of Jesus Christ (John 15:5; Romans 8:37; Philippians 4:13).

Verse 19, 'Then the temple of God was opened in heaven, and the ark of His covenant was seen in His temple. And there were lightnings, noises, thundering, an earthquake, and great hail.' In the Old Testament the ark of the covenant was a symbol of the abiding presence of God, for it was housed in the inner sanctuary of the temple known as 'the Holy of Holies.' Nobody could go beyond the thick veil that separated the ark of the covenant from the rest of the temple, except the High Priest, and then only once a year on the Day of Atonement with the blood of the covenant. The ark of the covenant was simply a gold-covered rectangular chest which housed the Ten Commandments. The top of the chest was called the 'mercy seat' which acted as a place of mediation between the law of God inside the ark and the glory of God's presence above the mercy seat on which the blood of atonement was sprinkled. So what verse 19 is saying is that by the reconciling death of Jesus, whose blood is now called 'the blood of the everlasting covenant' (Hebrews 13:20), that restriction no longer applies. The way into God's presence in heaven is eternally open to those whose law-breaking has been atoned for by the blood of Jesus Christ (Hebrews 9:11–15; 10:19–22). This was God's purpose when He designed and decreed the plan of salvation before the world was made, and now as the consummation of God's kingdom is anticipated, the blessing is disclosed. Not surprisingly, as with the giving of the law at Mount Sinai (Exodus 20:16–18), it is heralded by awesome signs from heaven to attest that God has indeed done something great and marvellous. 'And there were lightnings, noises, thundering, an earthquake, and great hail' (v. 19).

The key players in the conflict (the sign of the woman, her male child, and the dragon)

Revelation 12:1–2, 'Now a great sign appeared in heaven: a woman clothed with the sun, with the moon under her feet, and on her head a garland of twelve stars. Then being with child, she cried out in labour and in pain to give birth.' Notice the word 'sign'. The important thing about a sign is what it points to rather than what it says, and in calling what he now sees 'a great sign', John is emphasising its exceptional significance. For this is no ordinary woman. She is the mother of our Lord Jesus Christ, God's incarnate Son, the Saviour of the world (v. 5). But at the same time she is not just one particular woman like Eve to whom the promise was given that through her seed the head of the serpent would be bruised (Genesis 3:15). Nor is she simply the virgin Mary who actually gave birth to Christ, for the symbolism surrounding her clearly points to the church of God in the Old and New Testaments of which she was an individual member.

The people of God are one throughout all redemptive history and depicted as a woman God has taken to wife (Isaiah 54:5–6; 62:5; Jeremiah 3:14,20; 31:31–32; 2 Corinthians 11:2; Revelation 19:7–8; 21:2). 'Just as Zion or Jerusalem is the mother of the people of God in the Old Testament, so in the New Testament the Jerusalem above is our mother (Galatians 4:26). The Messiah comes out of this messianic community … This becomes obvious when you get down to the end of the chapter, for the offspring of the woman are those who keep God's commands and hold fast their testimony about Jesus … So this is a reference to the church, the church of the living God which is the ongoing messianic community.'[2]

John further tells us that the woman is 'clothed with the sun, with the moon under her feet.' These symbols come from Joseph's dream in which his father and mother and eleven brothers are likened to the sun, moon and eleven stars (Genesis 37:9–11). Joseph was the twelfth star before whom his father and mother and his brothers bowed down. Her being 'clothed with the sun' indicates the church's resplendent beauty (Ephesians 5:25–27) and 'the moon under her feet' is a sign of her heavenly authority. The 'garland [or wreath] of twelve stars' is a symbol of the church. Our Lord Himself links the twelve apostles with the twelve tribes as representative of the church from the old and new covenants (Matthew 19:28; Luke 22:28–30). One further clue that the woman is God's church and not just an individual, is the fact that in verse 6 after Christ's ascension, she continues to 'be fed or nourished for one thousand two hundred and sixty days' (11:3, the entire church age which has now lasted two thousand years).

Verse 3, 'And another *sign* appeared in heaven: behold, a great, fiery red dragon having seven heads, and ten horns and seven diadems on his heads' (italics added). There is no doubt about the identity of the dragon, for in verse 9 he is identified as 'that serpent of old, the Devil and Satan, who deceives the whole world.' He is described as 'great', for he is formidable and terribly intimidating. He is 'fiery red', because red is the colour of blood, and the devil is a murderer (John 8:44). He is a spiritually deadly foe to all on earth. His 'seven heads' signify his God-given longevity. He is hard to kill. You may cut off one head, but he can still function normally with the other heads still in place. He has 'ten horns' (a symbol of magnitude), for his power to do evil is greater than any other creature of God which at the most may have only two horns (cf. 13:1; 17:3). We must never underestimate the adversary of God and man's soul. He is an evil power to be reckoned with. Those who do not take his threats seriously will quickly become his victims. Verse 4, 'his tail drew a third of the stars of heaven and threw them to the earth.' This is a reference to the angels (the stars of heaven) who rebelled with Satan against God and were thrown out of heaven, out of the presence of God. A 'third' denotes a considerable proportion, but not a majority. They and their king cannot assault

God in heaven, so they seek to foil His plans on earth: 'And the dragon stood before the woman who was ready to give birth, to devour her Child as soon as it was born.'

God had told Satan in the Garden of Eden (Genesis 3:15): 'I will put enmity between you and the woman, and between your seed [followers] and her Seed [Christ]; He shall bruise your head [a fatal blow], and you shall bruise His heel' (a minor blow). That was Satan's death warrant. He did not know which woman it would be or which Child. So from the time Adam and Eve had their first child, Satan was on the lookout for his Nemesis and had Cain murder his righteous brother Abel. The godly line, however, continued through Seth. Right through history you can trace his efforts to find and devour the Christ-Child, and it all builds up to a climax in Herod's brutal slaughter of the innocents and our Lord's eventual crucifixion and burial (Matthew 2:16–18; 26:1–5; 27:32–66). But Satan's efforts were defeated by Christ's resurrection and ascension to heaven (Matthew 28; Acts 1:1–11). Verse 5, 'And she bore a male Child who was to rule [lit. shepherd] all nations with a rod of iron. And her Child was caught up to God and to His throne.' Satan tried hard to destroy Jesus Christ, but failed. The Son of God, as we shall see below, won a decisive victory. The serpent's head was fatally bruised.

The crucial battle of the conflict (the sign of Satan cast out of heaven)

Verse 6, 'Then the woman fled into the wilderness, where she has a place prepared by God, that they should feed her there one thousand two hundred and sixty days.' Now that her Son, the God-man has been exalted to the throne of God, the woman has to bear the full brunt of the dragon's hostility, but she is not to fear. God has prepared a place for her in the wilderness where she can find spiritual refuge and nourishment for one thousand two hundred and sixty days. The wilderness is not meant to be taken as a literal place, but simply as a symbol of the fact that in God the church has a refuge where she can be protected from the devil's attacks (Exodus 16:1–17:7; 1 Kings 17). The period of one thousand two hundred and sixty days is the same period in chapter 11:3 in which the church is able to witness to the world and fulfil the great commission given to her by her exalted Head. It is also defined in verse 14 as 'a time and times and half a time', and in 13:5 as 'forty-two months'. If we divide one thousand two hundred and sixty days by thirty which is the symbol for a month, we get forty-two months, or three-and-a-half years, which is the same as 'a time (one year), and times (two more) and half a time.' What does this symbolize? The answer is to remember that seven is the number of divine appointment and that three-and-a-half is half of seven. If seven years denotes the period of human history necessary to complete God's plan of redemption, then three-and-a-half years symbolizes the period of Old Testament history and the other three-and-a-half years is the period of New Testament history from the first coming to the second coming of Christ.

So the message of verse 6 is that the church is not to fear the attacks of the devil, for God will protect and nourish her during the entire time that she must bear witness to Christ before the world (11:2–3; 12:6,14; 13:5). Having been assured of that, John is reminded that the mopping-up operations after the decisive battle of Calvary must not be taken lightly. The devil is not going to take defeat easily. He is, after all, a dragon, and is intent on utterly destroying the church Christ came to save.

Verse 7, 'And war broke out in heaven.' In Scripture there are three heavens. There is the heaven where the birds fly, the heaven of invisible spiritual conflict (Ephesians 6:12); the heaven where God dwells with His saints and the angels (2 Corinthians 12:2). The heaven spoken of in verses 7–9 is the heaven of invisible spiritual conflict: 'And war broke out in heaven: Michael and his angels fought against the dragon; and the dragon and his angels fought, but they did not prevail, nor was a place found for them in heaven any longer. So the great dragon was cast out, that serpent of old, called the Devil and Satan, who deceives the whole world; he was cast to the earth, and his angels were cast out with him.' Satan and his forces had exercised their evil influence on earth right from the Fall (Genesis 3), but by the incarnation, atoning death and heavenly ascension of God's Son (12:1–5), Satan was cast out of heaven as the accuser of God's people. In other words, Satan's authority was not broken because of the strength of Michael and the good angels, but because of Christ's victory over him at the cross. For the angels had been locked in unresolved conflict from the beginning of time, but then something happened in history that resolved the age-old conflict. 'Christ died for our sins … was buried, and … rose again the third day according to the Scriptures' (1 Corinthians 15:3–4).

Verse 10, 'Then I heard a loud voice saying in heaven, "Now salvation, and strength, and the kingdom of our God, and the power of His Christ have come, for the accuser of our brethren, who accused them before our God day and night, has been cast down."' What does this mean? It means that Satan's previous authority in the spiritual realm was one of legal, not military power. Up and until Calvary he was the self-appointed prosecutor of God's people. The term 'Devil' means 'slanderer' and the name 'Satan' means 'adversary' or 'accuser'. Thus, for example, he slanderously accused Job before God saying, 'Does Job fear God for nothing? … You have blessed the work of his hands, and his possessions have increased in the land. But now, stretch out Your hand and touch all that he has, and he will surely curse You to Your face!' (Job 1:9–11). Satan also found fault with Joshua the high priest, but was rebuked by God (Zechariah 3:1–5). That was Satan's strategy all through the ages. He tried to turn God's justice into a weapon against His people.

Now sheer power or omnipotence was not enough on its own to win this legal battle against Satan's vicious defamation campaign. To redeem His people, God had to provide a way to 'be just and the justifier of the one who has faith in Jesus (Romans 3:21–26). He had to put the reputation of Himself and His saints beyond question. He had to lawfully and righteously silence Satan's accusations. And that, from one point of view, is exactly what God's plan of salvation was all about. What Christ achieved on the cross at Calvary was the justification of God's people. By dying in their place, Christ paid the penalty for their sin (Romans 6:23) and satisfied the just demands of God's law which they had broken. There is now no possible way that they can be condemned again. Thus Paul can fearlessly throw out the challenge, 'Who shall bring a charge against God's elect? It is God who justifies. Who is he who condemns? It is Christ who died, and furthermore is also risen, who is even at the right hand of God, who makes intercession for us' (Romans 8:33–34).

So it is not Michael who has won the victory over Satan, but the woman's male Child. What John describes here pictorially, Paul explains theologically in Colossians 2:13–15, 'And you, who were dead in your trespasses ... God made alive together with Him, having forgiven us all our trespasses, by cancelling the record of debt that stood against us with its legal demands. This He set aside, nailing it to the cross. He disarmed the rulers and authorities [i.e. demonic] and put them to open shame, by triumphing over them in Him' (mg. or in it, i.e. the cross, ESV). Christ's atoning blood robbed Satan's accusations against God's people of all semblance of justice, and as a consequence, Michael and his angels were able to throw Satan and his demons out of the heavenly court altogether. Moreover, the brethren whom he slanders are also able to overcome him: 'And they overcame him by the blood of the Lamb and by the word of their testimony, and they did not love their lives to the death' (v. 11). That is to say, Satan has no power to destroy them, because Christ's blood cleanses them from all sin and enables the Holy Spirit to come into their lives and deliver them from evil.

Indeed, more than that, free from condemnation and empowered by the Holy Spirit, they are not only able to overcome Satan in their personal lives, but also in the world. Through their 'testimony' to Christ, even to the point of laying down their lives for His sake, they who are Christ's brethren ('the rest of the woman's offspring') drive Satan out of one stronghold after another (2 Corinthians 10:3–5). Verse 12, 'Therefore rejoice, O heavens, and you who dwell in them! Woe to the inhabitants of the earth and the sea [meaning, the islands of the sea]! For the devil has come down to you, having great wrath, because he knows that he has a short time.' That is, before he is finally cast into hell to suffer eternal torment. But such is his great hatred of God and His saints, that though he has already been defeated in heaven and will soon be overcome on earth, he is going to go on opposing God's work of rescuing the lost (Matthew 18:11; Luke 15:1–7; 19:10).

The unbridled rage of Satan (the sign of a persecuted church)

Tyrants, of whom Satan is chief, go down fighting to the end, determined to wreak as much damage and injury as possible upon their conquerors. Not being able to vent his spleen on Jesus Christ Himself, who has ascended to the throne of God in heaven, the devil's fury is turned upon 'the woman who gave birth to the male Child' (v. 13) and to 'the rest of her offspring' (v. 17), as opposed to Jesus. Although he cannot destroy Christ's church (the messianic community), he will make them suffer physical and spiritual trials (Matthew 16:18; Romans 8:31–39; 1 Corinthians 4:11; 2 Corinthians 12:7). Satan is pure malice. He inflicts pain even when he stands to gain no advantage from it (Matthew 13:24–30; 36–43).

Moreover, his rage is fuelled by three inescapable factors. First, Satan knows that he has but 'a short time' (v. 12). He does not have the millennia he had before Christ's birth and ascension. He knows that Christ is 'coming quickly' and that his destruction 'must shortly take place' (Revelation 1:1–2; 22:20), and so he is determined to do all the harm he can while he can. Secondly, he is angry because the sphere and power of his activity has been restricted. He has been cast out of heaven, and deprived of his authority as 'the accuser of our brethren' (v. 10). Also, while he can deceive individual human beings, he cannot 'deceive the nations' (20:3). Christ has even given His brethren power over the devil. After their preaching and healing assignment, Luke says: 'Then the seventy returned with joy, saying, "Lord, even the demons are subject to us in Your name." And He said to them, "I saw Satan fall like lightning from heaven"' (10:17–18).

Thirdly, try as hard as he might, all his efforts to destroy the woman and her offspring are to no avail. He may kill the body of a believer, but he cannot kill their soul. He may rob them of life on earth, but not life hereafter in heaven which is eternal (Matthew 10:28; 16:24–28). This is essentially the message of verses 13–17: 'Now when the dragon saw that he had been cast to the earth, he persecuted the woman who gave birth to the male Child. But the woman was given two wings of a great eagle, that she might fly into the wilderness to her place, where she is nourished for a time and times and half a time, from the presence of the serpent. So the serpent spewed water out of his mouth like a flood after the woman, that he might cause her to be carried away by the flood. But the earth helped the woman, and the earth opened its mouth and swallowed up the flood which the dragon had spewed out of his mouth. And the dragon was enraged with the woman, and he went to make war with the rest of her offspring [Christ's brethren], who keep the commandments of God and have the testimony of Jesus Christ.'

The wings of a great eagle, the place prepared in the desert, and the earth opening its mouth to swallow the river that flowed out of the dragon's mouth are all symbols that underline the security of the church. The same metaphor of 'eagles' wings' was used of God's deliverance of His people from the pursuing Egyptians. For in Exodus

19:4 God says, 'You have seen what I did to the Egyptians, and how I bore you on eagles' wings and brought you to Myself.' Christians have nothing to fear. They have God's word on it. They will not only be delivered 'from the presence of the serpent' (v. 14), but they will also be brought safely into the presence of God Himself.

How Christians overcome the devil

First, we must take the devil seriously. C.S. Lewis says, 'There are two equal opposite errors into which our race can fall about devils. One is to disbelieve in their existence. The other is to believe, and to feel an excessive and unhealthy interest in them. They themselves are equally pleased by both errors.'[3] The devil and his fellow workers are no laughing matter. If we are wise and well-instructed Christians, we will take the reality and hostility of the forces of evil very seriously indeed. It is not for nothing that the apostle sees him as 'a great fiery red dragon' raging against Christ's followers. He is no myth, as liberal theologians would have us believe. Hence Peter's warning to his Christian readers: 'Be sober, be vigilant; because your adversary walks about like a roaring lion, seeking whom he may devour. Resist him steadfast in the faith, knowing that the same sufferings [you are experiencing] are experienced by your brotherhood in the world' (1 Peter 5:8–9). Revelation 12 should help us to get Satan in perspective. He is a real and powerful foe.

Secondly, John says, 'And they overcame Him by the blood of the Lamb' (v. 11). There are some who erroneously believe that if you pronounce the blood of Jesus over a person or object, you can set them free from Satan's power. The Greek word translated 'by', however, does not mean 'by means of', as if Christians are to use the words 'the blood of the Lamb' as a mantra; as some sort of magic formula that protects us. To quote A.T. Robertson, 'The blood of Christ is here presented by *dia* as the ground for the victory and not the means … *dia* with the accusative gives only the reason.'[4] This means that no matter how often

Christians sin they do not fall from grace, because 'the blood of Jesus Christ His Son cleanses us from all sin' (1 John 1:7). Satan has no claim on any Christian, not because we do not sin, but because Jesus Christ has paid the penalty for all our sins in His penal, substitutionary death for us on the cross (Romans 5:8; 2 Corinthians 5:21; Hebrews 10:12–14; 1 Peter 3:18). All the blessings that are ours in Jesus Christ, the forgiveness of our sins, the gift of the Holy Spirit, the hope of eternal life, stem from His atoning death on the cross. 'They overcame him because of the blood of the Lamb.'

Thirdly, 'And they overcame him ... by [because of] the word of their testimony.' This refers to our testimony to Jesus Christ and the good news of salvation through His death and resurrection. The 'gospel of Christ ... is the power of God to salvation for everyone who believes' (Romans 1:16). The gospel is the light that Jesus brought to the world which 'shines in the darkness, and the darkness has not overcome it' (John 1:4–5, ESV). There is no other way to overcome Satan and liberate those he holds captive in sin, than by preaching the gospel and testifying to Christ's saving power. To keep silent may save our skins, but it will spell momentary defeat.

Fourthly, 'they overcame him because ... they did not love their lives to death.' It is very hard to stop the spread of the gospel of Christ when His followers are prepared to die for Him rather than keep silent. After all, there is nothing else the devil can do to them after that! He cannot prevent the souls of Christian martyrs from immediately entering the presence of God in heaven where there 'are pleasures for evermore' and they will be free of sin and Satan forever (Psalm 16:11; Revelation 6:9–11; 20:10; 21:3–4; 22:3). When Paul was in prison awaiting execution for preaching the gospel, he could say, 'For me to live is Christ, and to die is gain. But if I live on in the flesh, this will mean fruit for my labour; yet what I shall choose I cannot tell. For I am hard pressed between the two, having a desire to depart and be with Christ, which is far better. Nevertheless to remain in the flesh is more needful for you' (Philippians 1:21–24). However it comes, Christians have nothing to lose in death, and everything to gain.

That is the way, the only way, the kingdom of this world will become the kingdom of our Lord and of His Christ: when Christians overcome the devil on the grounds of the blood of the Lamb and the word of their testimony and their readiness for martyrdom. We are witnesses of this very phenomenon. There has been more missionary progress in the last one hundred years than in all the previous centuries combined: more people converted, more Bible translations done and more missionaries sent to the ends of the earth. But it is also true that more Christians have been martyred in these last one hundred years than in all the previous centuries combined.[5]

On 11th May, 1685 two Scottish Covenanter women, Margaret Wilson and Margaret McLauchlan were chained to stakes in the Solway Firth, Southwest Scotland, and drowned. They were martyred for refusing to swear an oath declaring James VII as head of the church in Scotland and give up attending prayer meetings and worship services in open-air field assemblies. The older woman, Margaret McLauchlan, was situated near the mouth of the estuary, and as the tide came in, she drowned first. Margaret Wilson was only eighteen years old and a little further back, but she was not intimidated into denying her faith. As the water was sweeping over her fellow-martyr she was tauntingly asked, 'What do you see?' Margaret Wilson replied, 'What do I see but Christ wrestling there. Think you that we are the sufferers? No, it is Christ in us who suffers.' Then she sang the 25th Psalm and recited the 8th chapter to the Romans. She died unafraid.[6]

15 Satan's agents in his war on the church

13:1Then I stood on the sand of the sea. And I saw a beast rising up out of the sea, having seven heads and ten horns, and on his horns ten crowns, and on his heads a blasphemous name. 2Now the beast which I saw was like a leopard, his feet were like the feet of a bear, and his mouth like the mouth of a lion. The dragon gave him his power, his throne, and great authority. 3And I saw one of his heads as if it had been mortally wounded, and his deadly wound was healed. And all the world marvelled and followed the beast. 4So they worshipped the dragon who gave authority to the beast; and they worshipped the beast, saying, 'Who is like the beast? Who is able to make war with him?'

5And he was given a mouth speaking great things and blasphemies, and he was given authority to continue for forty-two months. 6Then he opened his mouth in blasphemy against God, to blaspheme His name, His tabernacle, and those who dwell in heaven. 7It was granted to him to make war with the saints and to overcome them. And authority was given him over every tribe, tongue and nation. 8All who dwell on the earth will worship him, whose names have not been written in the Book of Life of the Lamb slain from the foundation of the world.

9If anyone has an ear, let him hear. 10He who leads into captivity shall go into captivity; he who kills with the sword must be killed with the sword. Here is the patience and the faith of the saints.

[11]Then I saw another beast coming up out of the earth, and he had two horns like a lamb and spoke like a dragon. [12]And he exercises all the authority of the first beast in his presence, and causes the earth and those who dwell in it to worship the first beast, whose deadly wound was healed. [13]He performs great signs, so that he even makes fire come down from heaven on the earth in the sight of men. [14]And he deceives those who dwell on the earth by those signs which he was granted to do in the sight of the beast, telling those who dwell on the earth to make an image to the beast who was wounded by the sword and lived. [15]He was granted power to give breath to the image of the beast, that the image of the beast should both speak and cause as many as would not worship the image of the beast to be killed. [16]He causes all, both small and great, rich and poor, free and slave, to receive a mark on their right hand or on their foreheads, [17]and that no one may buy or sell except one who has the mark or the name of the beast, or the number of his name.

[18]Here is wisdom. Let him who has understanding calculate the number of the beast, for it is the number of a man: His number is 666.

(Revelation 13:1–18)

Revelation 13 continues the fourth vision of seven signs of cosmic conflict given to help beleaguered Christians understand the malevolent nature and power of the invisible forces bent on their destruction. In the previous chapter we considered Revelation 12 and the sign of the dragon's (Satan's) murderous hatred of Christ; the sign of Satan cast out of heaven; and the sign of Satan's persecution of the church. Revelation 13 continues the vision of the seven signs of cosmic conflict by unveiling the two main henchmen the devil uses to do his dirty work; namely, Antichrist and the false prophet. Satan, as a fallen spirit being, cannot work in isolation or apart from human agents. So Revelation 12 and 13 belong together, for the beast from the sea (Antichrist) and the beast from the earth (the false prophet) work hand-in-glove with the dragon in his rage against Christ's church.

The beast from the sea (the sign of Antichrist)

'And the dragon was enraged with the woman [the messianic community], and he went to make war with the rest of her offspring [as opposed to Jesus], who keep the commandments of God and have the testimony of Jesus Christ. Then I stood on the sand of the sea. And I saw a beast rising up out of the sea' (12:17–13:1a). The words 'I stood' actually refer to the dragon and not to John. 'The textual evidence is strongly in favour of the RSV reading, "he stood."'[1] The Greek verb literally means '"he stopped" on his way to war with the rest of the woman's seed'[2] to get help from the 'sea'. The restless waters of the sea are often likened to the troubled masses of the ungodly: 'But the wicked are like the troubled sea, when it cannot rest, whose waters cast up mire and dirt. "There is no peace", says My God, "for the wicked"' (Isaiah 57:21); and again, 'The waters which you saw, where the harlot sits, are peoples, multitudes, nations and tongues' (Revelation 17:15). It is a suitable symbol, for who can tell what exists in the turbulent depths of the sea? The dragon obviously has a formidable ally in mind, for John now says: 'And I saw a beast rising up out of the sea, having seven heads and ten horns, and on the horns ten crowns, and on his heads a blasphemous name' (v. 1). Notice, the beast has the same 'seven heads and ten horns' that the dragon has, for 'The dragon gave him his power, his throne and great authority' (v. 2b). Chapter 13 says very little about the dragon, but he is there all the time working behind the scenes through his chosen instruments.

Thus although the beast has ten crowns on his ten horns (power of great magnitude), Satan has seven crowns on his seven heads (divinely-permitted authority, 12:3). In other words, although Satan gives his power to the beast, it is he who calls the shots. The crowns on the dragon's heads symbolize the brains behind the beast's rule.

It is Satan's plans that are being carried out by the beast through the formidable power Satan has given him. Moreover, the strategy behind all Satan's plans is to blaspheme God in the greatest possible way, by demanding that he (incarnate in the beast) be worshipped as God. That is the significance of the fact that on each of the seven heads of the beast there is 'a blasphemous name'. Seven is the number of divine appointment. The beast's blasphemy is a claim of absolute deity.

The beast is the Antichrist of Scripture

Now from the earliest times readers of the book of Revelation have identified the beast from the sea as various antichrists persecuting the church through some form of totalitarian government. John's readers probably saw him in the Emperor Domitian who was persecuting Christians in their day and went so far as to demand that men address him as *Dominus et Deus noster* (our Lord and God). Later some Christians saw antichrist in Mohammed, or an assortment of popes, Napoleon, Kaizer Wilhelm, Hitler, Stalin and Mao Tse-Tung, to name a few. And they were correct, because the spirit of antichrist has manifested itself right from the beginning of the Christian era. Thus John says elsewhere, 'Little children, it is the last hour; and as you have heard that the Antichrist is coming, even now many antichrists have come, by which we know that it is the last hour' (1 John 2:18). This final age which has now gone on for two thousand years, is the 'last hour' during which Satan, working through various antichrists, has been and still is present and active on earth, warring against the church. To quote John again, 'Every spirit that does not confess that Jesus Christ has come in the flesh is not of God. And this is the spirit of the Antichrist, which you have heard was coming, and is now already in the world' (1 John 4:3). What was true then, is no less true now.

Of course, his final and fiercest appearance will come right at the end of this present age and precipitate the ultimate climax of all history: the return of Christ, the resurrection and the final judgment. Paul speaks of this in 2 Thessalonians 2:3–4 when he says, 'for that Day [Christ's return] will not come unless the falling away [the apostasy] comes first, and the man of sin [Antichrist] is revealed, the son of perdition, who opposes and exalts himself above all that is called God or that is worshipped, so that he sits as God in the temple of God showing himself that he is God.' It is probably this that John is signifying when he ascribes to the beast from the sea in Revelation 13 the main features that are found in the four beasts that come up out of the sea in Daniel 7. So in verse 2, John's beast from the sea 'was like a leopard' (as was Daniel's third beast); 'his feet were like the feet of a bear' (Daniel's second beast); his mouth was 'like the mouth of a lion' (Daniel's first beast); and he had 'ten horns' (just like Daniel's fourth beast that is also described as 'dreadful and terrible, exceedingly strong'). In other words, John's beast ultimately stands for a final worldwide dictatorship in which all the frightful evil of its predecessors will be combined in one composite anti-God monster.

The spirit of antichrist keeps resurging

Verse 3, 'And I saw one of his heads as if it had been mortally wounded, and his deadly wound was healed. And all the world marvelled and followed the beast.' The symbolism here is saying that the spirit of antichrist will seem to Christians throughout the age to be *invincible.* The beast is smitten only to recover. Thus the Christians lost Nero only to gain a worse persecutor in Domitian. They lost one pope only to gain a worse one. They lost the Czar only to gain Lenin and Stalin. The beast cannot be removed from the world by force of arms. He keeps reappearing, uglier and nastier than ever.

But the prophecy in verse 3 has a deeper significance than that, for its ultimate fulfilment will be in the person of the Antichrist who appears at the end of this age to launch Satan's final assault on God's people. But during his brief reign somebody will kill him. The phrase, 'as if it had been mortally wounded' literally reads 'as having been slain to death' and is used of the Lamb slain in chapter 5:6. The beast's resuscitation from the dead, however, is not explained to John. Only

God can raise the dead, and God would certainly not raise Antichrist from the dead. It is plausible, therefore, that the person who will be slain is not Antichrist but a stand-in (a look-alike) that dictators often employ to survive assassination attempts. Whatever the explanation, this is one of several features about the life of the real Christ that this false christ is pictured as parodying. If Jesus can survive death, so can he. It's no wonder, then, that John goes on to say, 'And all the world marvelled and followed the beast.' Like the assassination of President Kennedy it will be replayed again and again to the whole world. And then the world will see him alive again. Seeing is believing and within no time the clever deceit of Antichrist will evoke worldwide admiration and allegiance.

The reign of Antichrist will be hugely popular

Verse 4, 'So they worshipped the dragon who gave authority to the beast; and they worshipped the beast, saying, "Who is like the beast? Who is able to make war with him?"' Democracy will not protect the world against this dictatorship. People are not as smart as our confidence in democracy would have us believe. When the end comes, the world will overwhelmingly vote the beast into power just as Germany voted Hitler into power. The fact is that people admire might more than they admire righteousness. As fallen creatures humankind will gladly worship the beast and the dragon that is behind his power.

The reign of Antichrist will be totalitarian

Verses 5–7, 'And he was given a mouth speaking great things and blasphemies, and he was given authority to continue for forty-two months. Then he opened his mouth in blasphemy against God to blaspheme His name, His tabernacle, and those who dwell in heaven. And it was granted to him to make war with the saints and to overcome them. And authority was given him over every tribe, tongue and nation.' As with previous antichrists, so the final Antichrist will demand total obedience (physical, mental and spiritual) from all his citizens. Indeed, his rule will be the most tyrannical ever, demanding universal worship of himself (2 Thessalonians 2:3–4). So he commits the ultimate blasphemy. He 'speaks great things', claiming to be the one true God and dismissing the God of the Bible as a myth. He blasphemes God's 'name', ridiculing and defaming all He stands for: His holiness, His omnipotence, His omniscience, His omnipresence and His grace and goodness. He also blasphemes God's 'tabernacle' which is the company of the redeemed in whom God dwells. The church is God's temple (1 Corinthians 3:16–17). These people are further identified as 'those who dwell in heaven', for every Christian's true home and citizenship is not here on earth where they are hated and treated as foreigners, but in heaven. Unbelievers, on the other hand, are described four times in Revelation 13 as 'those who dwell on the earth' (vv. 8,12,14). They see the earth as their only home and place of delight.

Moreover, Antichrist will be permitted to wage all-out war against God's saints, and to all outward appearances 'to overcome them' (cf. Daniel 7:25). They will universally be arrested and imprisoned and some martyred. This period of persecution will not be isolated to a few countries, for 'authority was given him over every tribe, tongue, and nation' (v. 7). But the beast's victory is more apparent than real; it is temporary, not permanent. For God has only given him authority to make war with the saints for 'forty-two months' (half of seven years), the symbol of an incomplete reign. God cuts it short before Satan and his henchmen can complete their objective. It is the same period of time in which the woman in chapter 12 finds refuge in the desert from the attacks of the dragon, and the two witnesses in chapter 11 have to preach. It has lasted two thousand years now, but it is nonetheless a broken reign. God's saints can draw courage from the fact that the duration of their suffering is determined by God, not the beast. The verb 'was given' occurs four times in verses 5–7 and stresses the beast's subordinate position before Almighty God.

But there is another reason why the beast's power is limited; namely, he may destroy the bodies of God's saints, but not their souls (Matthew 10:28). John tells us that 'nothing unclean will ever enter [heaven] … but only those who are written in the Lamb's book of life' (21:27, ESV), whereas 'all who dwell on earth will worship [the beast], everyone whose name has not been written before the foundation of the world in the book of life of the Lamb who was slain' (13:8, ESV). Here we have the ultimate division of all humankind. The fact that the names of God's elect were written in the Lamb's book of life from the foundation of the world testifies to the infallibility of His purpose in creation. What tremendous consolation this has brought to persecuted Christians, not only in John's day, but throughout these past two thousand years. And it will do the same for God's saints in the final reign of Antichrist. Leon Morris writes, 'John wants his little handful of persecuted Christians to see that the thing that matters is the sovereignty of God, not the power of evil. When a man's name is written in the book of life he will not be forgotten. His place is secure.'[3]

The Christian response to persecution

'If anyone has an ear, let him hear. He who leads into captivity shall go into captivity; he who kills with the sword must be killed with the sword. Here is the patience and the faith of the saints' (vv. 9–10). We must be careful here, because there are some textual difficulties. On the one hand we can take both couplets in verse 10 as referring to those who persecute Christians, and therefore as saying that what the wicked do to God's people will eventually be done to them (KJV). On the other hand we can regard both couplets in verse 10 as referring to Christians (ESV). In other words, Christians must not resist persecution physically. The first half of the couplet states that if it is the will of God that a Christian should be imprisoned, then to prison he will definitely go. The second half of the couplet warns of the consequences of not submitting to the providence of God. The man who resists arrest by using the sword will die by the sword. The latter interpretation seems more probable. Our Lord issued the same warning to Peter when he tried to use a sword to resist the soldiers who came to arrest Him in the garden of Gethsemane: 'Jesus said to him, "Put your sword in its place, for all who take the sword will perish by the sword. Or do you think that I cannot now pray to My Father, and He will provide Me with more than twelve legions of angels?"' (Matthew 26:52–53). This is always how Christians are to respond to the persecution of the beast and the dragon that empowers him, for 'If we endure, we shall also reign with Him' (2 Timothy 2:12). If, however, we take the sword to fight the enemies of Christ we will fail, for the kingdom of God cannot be established by force of arms. We will ultimately perish with the sword.

To quote William Barclay, 'Here is the truth—and it is still true—that the right can never be defended by doing wrong; that, when Christianity begins to defend itself by force, it ceases to be Christianity; that it is an intolerable paradox to defend the gospel of the love of God by using the violence of man.'[4] So verse 10 is not teaching *fatalism*. It is not saying whatever will be, will be, and there's nothing we can do about it. To suffer is just our fate. Rather, it is teaching *faith*. It is telling us to trust in the sovereignty of God who uses even the suffering of His people for Christ's sake to work out His good and perfect will. To confess steadfastly that 'Jesus Christ is Lord' is a spiritual witness that publicly exposes the illegitimacy and blasphemy of the beast, whether he appears in the form of a Roman emperor or as the final reality. It speaks to men's consciences, and reminds them of what they really know, that there is only One who rightly deserves their worship and that is Jesus Christ, God incarnate. Of course, when nearly everyone is worshipping the beast, it takes faith to stand up for God and confess that 'Jesus is Lord' (Romans 10:9; 1 Corinthians 12:3). So verse 10 ends with the words, 'Here is the patience and the faith of the saints.' 'Patience' is steadfast endurance of persecution for the sake of Jesus Christ our Lord. 'Faith' is that firm trust that knows 'that all things work together for good to those who love God, to those who are the called according to His purpose'

(Romans 8:28). The acceptance of persecution gives proof of the genuineness of our faith and the unshakability of our hope in Christ.

But how does the rest of humankind accept the reign of any antichrist, especially the final Antichrist? That is the answer we want. Surely such a tyrannical system of government can only be maintained by the most repressive coercion. John, however, tells us that the world will voluntarily submit to the beast's authority. How is it done? What is his secret?

The beast from the earth (the sign of the false prophet)

Verses 11–12, 'Then I saw another beast coming up out of the earth, and he had two horns like a lamb and spoke like a dragon. And he exercises all the authority of the first beast in his presence, and causes the earth and those who dwell in it to worship the first beast, whose deadly wound was healed.' The primary function of the second beast is to promote the worship of the first beast by all the inhabitants of the earth. In the final analysis he is the head of Antichrist's state church and propaganda machine. In Revelation 19:20 this beast is called 'the false prophet' (cf. 16:13; 20:10).

To John's contemporaries, no doubt, the false prophet was manifested in the propaganda of the cult of emperor worship with its impressive priesthood and magical trappings. Throughout the Middle Ages Protestant martyrs would identify the false prophet as Roman Catholicism which gave the Papacy unparalleled political power. Today we would see the false prophet in the godless religions which have appeared *incognito* in the form of Fascism, Marxism, Humanism, Socialism, Capitalism and radical Islam. These systems of propaganda may not use normal religious terminology, but they fulfil religious functions to win over the masses to their form of totalitarianism and anti-Christianity.

The false prophet is a specialist in deception

Deception is his chief weapon because he wants to appear as an authentic prophet, not as a false one. So he masquerades as a 'lamb' with 'two horns'. But in reality he is the Public Relations Officer of the dragon and Antichrist. He is the front man who looks as harmless and innocent as a *lamb* on the outside, but speaks with deadly power like a *dragon*. For, says John, 'he exercises all the authority of the first beast', and he does so 'in his presence' (i.e. under his watchful eye and direction). Behind every false prophet in every generation is an antichrist, and behind every antichrist who has ever appeared is Satan himself.

Now pretending to be one thing but in reality being something very different, is one of Satan's cleverest wiles. He is the great impersonator, the master of disguises. In John 8:44 our Lord called Satan 'a liar and the father of lies', and warned His disciples, saying: 'Beware of false prophets, who come to you in sheep's clothing, but inwardly they are ravenous wolves' (Matthew 7:15). Expanding on this, Paul says, 'Satan himself transforms himself into an angel of light. Therefore it is no great thing if his ministers also transform themselves into ministers of righteousness' (2 Corinthians 11:14–15). The repetition of the fact that the first beast's 'deadly wound was healed' (v. 12) shows that his resuscitation from apparent death is going to make a tremendous impression on the world at the end of the age. Indeed, it is the foundation on which the ultimate false prophet is going to use other 'great signs' to build his case as to why the earth should worship Antichrist.

Verses 13–14, 'He performs great signs, so that he even makes fire come down from heaven on the earth in the sight of men. And he deceives those who dwell on the earth by those signs which he was granted to do in the sight of the beast, telling those who dwell on the earth to make an image to the beast who was wounded by the sword and lived.' Here we have further evidence of the unholy trinity of

Satan, Antichrist and the false prophet parodying Christ. If Christ confirmed the authenticity of His teaching by miracles, so can the false prophet. But because the false prophet gets his power from Antichrist and Satan, these are not genuine signs but *counterfeits*. Using demonic power, sophisticated magic and modern technology, he will convince the public at large that Antichrist is the real incarnation of God, not Jesus Christ. They must make him the leader of the world, because he alone has the power to quell terrorism, revive the economy of the world with an even distribution of wealth, and bring all religions together into one faith.

The earth's confidence, however, is going to be sadly misplaced, for the 'great signs' of any false prophet are deceptive. Speaking of the end of the age, our Lord said: 'Then if anyone says to you, "Look, here is the Christ!" or "There!" do not believe it. For false christs and false prophets will rise and show great signs and wonders to deceive, if possible, even the elect. See, I have told you beforehand' (Matthew 24:23–24). The apostle Paul also warned of the same thing: 'The coming of the lawless one [the Antichrist] is according to the working of Satan, with all power, signs, and lying wonders, and with all unrighteous deception among those who perish, because they did not receive the love of the truth, that they might be saved' (2 Thessalonians 2:9–10). 'Love of the truth (it is implied) was offered to them, but they refused it. Behind the great deception there lay the great refusal.'[5] It is comforting to know that both our Saviour and Paul assure us that only unbelievers will be deceived. God's elect will not be taken in by the great signs of the false prophet.

The false prophet will demand conformity

Christians will rather die than worship the beast or his image. Verse 15, 'And there was given to him to give breath to the image of the beast, that the image of the beast might even speak' (NASB). Because Satan is not God he has no power to give breath to inanimate objects. This can only mean that he enables the false prophet to deceive people into thinking the image can speak. Robert H. Mounce says, 'Belief in statues which spoke and performed miracles is widely attested in ancient literature … Ventriloquism was practised by the priests of Oriental Cults, and sorcery had found a place in the official circles of Rome. Apelles of Ascalon was at home in the court of Caligula, and Apollonius was a friend of several Roman emperors.'[6] The end of verse 15 presents a problem because an image cannot kill people. The subject in all these verses (11–17) is the false prophet, and so it is logical to understand verse 15 as saying that it is he who not only appears to give breath to the image, but also causes the death of those who refuse to worship the image of the first beast or Antichrist.

The martyrdom of the saints, however, will be a last resort, for Satan only wins if all are compliant and not if all are killed. So he will resort to starving them into submission. Verses 16–17, 'And he [the false prophet] causes all, both small and great, rich and poor, free and slave, to receive a mark on their right hand or on their foreheads, and that no one may buy or sell except one who has the mark or the name of the beast, or the number of his name.' The more our society is locked into computers, Social Security numbers and plastic money, the more frighteningly real the possibility of this kind of control over every individual becomes. The mark may be literal or symbolical. Most likely the reference is *symbolical* and will be tied up in the system under Antichrist. It will control access to work (symbolized by the 'right hand') as well as communication via modern means (symbolized by the 'forehead'). Any anti-Christian government that controls work and media, controls everyone. This is not a once-upon-a-time story! It is a divinely inspired prophecy that will come to pass one way or another just as certainly as the prophecies about Christ's first coming came to pass. The details of *when* and *how* it will take place are not clear, but as to *what* will happen when it does take place, there is no doubt. Everyone will have to be identified as a worshipper of the beast or suffer the consequences.

A clue to identifying Antichrist when he appears

Verse 18, 'Here is wisdom. Let him who has understanding calculate the number of the beast, for it is the number of a man: his number is 666.' Much fanciful speculation has been written about the number 666 and any clue it may give to identifying the Antichrist when he comes on the scene. But they are just that: fanciful! Because the Greek letters of the alphabet stood for numbers as well as vowels and consonants, some believe that Antichrist's name can be discovered by adding up the numerical value of the letters by which his name is spelt. But depending on each individual's ingenuity and credulity, the number 666 can be worked out to mean almost anything one wishes. The best way to understand this number is to treat it like all the other numbers in Revelation. We must recognise what the numbers symbolize. The only clue John gives us here is that he says, 'It is the number of a man'; not some particular man, but of man in general. We also know from our study of Revelation that seven is the number of divinity. Whatever it is associated with has reference to God. Thus the Holy Spirit is called 'the seven Spirits of God' (1:4; 3:1; 5:6). Antichrist, however, is not like Christ who is God incarnate. Antichrist is only a mere man, so his number is 6 because man was created on the sixth day and man is imperfect as a result of his fall into sin. He falls short of the number 7.

But why is Antichrist's number 666? It is 666 because in everything he is and does, he repeatedly falls short of the perfection and completeness of Christ, the God-Man. He is a false christ, a false prophet, a false miracle-worker, and a false god. Those who calculate the number of the beast as a symbol of imperfection, says John, will have 'wisdom' and 'understanding' because they will not be deceived. No matter how great his signs and powers may appear, God's elect will know that Antichrist is not omnipotent. He will be seen as a mere man whose number is 666, and as a fake who will be destroyed by Christ.

Every Christian needs to understand this and be assured by God's words through John. There is only one man who can claim to be God, and that is Jesus Christ. And because He is fully God and fully Man, He, and He alone, is to be worshipped as 'our God and Saviour' (Titus 2:13; 2 Peter 1:1). Those who worship Antichrist will bear the number of his name. They will bear his false image and be cast with him and the false prophet and the devil 'into the lake of fire and brimstone', into the place God has prepared for them (20:10). Those who worship Christ, on the other hand, will bear His image, which is 'the express image of God' (Hebrews 1:1–3), and they will go with Him at His return to the place He has prepared for them (John 14:1–3; 1 Thessalonians 4:16–17). 'God's firm foundation stands, bearing this seal: "The Lord knows those who are His," and, "Let everyone who names the name of the Lord depart from iniquity"' (2 Timothy 2:19).

16 The Lamb, the 144,000 and the harvest

14:1Then I looked, and behold, a Lamb standing on Mount Zion, and with Him one hundred and forty-four thousand, having His Father's name written on their foreheads. 2And I heard a voice from heaven, like the voice of many waters, and like the voice of loud thunder. And I heard the sound of harpists playing their harps. 3They sang as it were a new song before the throne, before the four living creatures, and the elders; and no one could learn that song except the hundred and forty-four thousand who were redeemed from the earth. 4These are the ones who were not defiled with women, for they are virgins. These are the ones who follow the Lamb wherever He goes. These were redeemed from among men, being firstfruits to God and to the Lamb. 5And in their mouth was found no deceit, for they are without fault before the throne of God.

6Then I saw another angel flying in the midst of heaven, having the everlasting gospel to preach to those who dwell on the earth—to every nation, tribe, tongue, and people—7saying with a loud voice, 'Fear God and give glory to Him, for the hour of His judgment has come; and worship Him who made heaven and earth, the sea and springs of water.'

8And another angel followed, saying, 'Babylon is fallen, is fallen, that great city, because she has made all nations drink of the wine of the wrath of her fornication.'

9Then a third angel followed them, saying with a loud voice, 'If anyone worships the beast and his image, and receives his mark on his forehead or on his hand, 10he himself shall also drink of the wine of the wrath of God, which is poured out full strength into the cup of His indignation. He shall be tormented with fire and brimstone in the presence of the holy angels and in the presence of the Lamb. 11And the smoke of their torment ascends forever and ever; and they have no rest day or night, who worship the beast and his image, and whoever receives the mark of his name.'

12Here is the patience of the saints; here are those who keep the commandments of God and the faith of Jesus.

13Then I heard a voice from heaven saying to me, 'Write: "Blessed are the dead who die in the Lord from now on."'

'Yes,' says the Spirit, 'that they may rest from their labours, and their works follow them.'

14Then I looked, and behold, a white cloud, and on the cloud sat One like the Son of Man, having on His head a golden crown, and in His hand a sharp sickle. 15And another angel came out of the temple, crying with a loud voice to Him who sat on the cloud, 'Thrust in Your sickle and reap, for the time has come for You to reap, for the harvest of the earth is ripe.' 16So He who sat on the cloud thrust in His sickle on the earth, and the earth was reaped.

17Then another angel came out of the temple which is in heaven, he also having a sharp sickle.

18And another angel came out from the altar, who had power over fire, and he cried with a loud cry to him who had the sharp sickle, saying, 'Thrust in your sharp sickle and gather the clusters of the vine of the earth, for her grapes are fully ripe.' 19So the angel thrust his sickle into the earth and gathered the vine of the earth, and threw it into the great winepress of the wrath of God. [20]And the winepress was trampled outside the city, and blood came out of the winepress, up to the horses' bridles, for one thousand six hundred furlongs.   (Revelation 14:1–20)

The apocalyptic books of the Bible like Daniel and Revelation focus on the triumphant end of the purpose of God in human history. We cannot understand the present unless we look at it from the vantage point of the end that God has decreed. Thus Thomas Torrance writes:

> With this chapter [Revelation 14] the vision changes sharply. Instead of gazing down upon the murky expanse of a restless sea, the apostle looks upward and sees and hears things very different. Although he is allowed to penetrate into the mystery of iniquity and to discern the black secrets of evil [Revelation 13], St. John is not allowed to dwell upon them, for there can be an unhealthy morbid preoccupation with disease and tribulation and sin. That is perhaps why the scenes of the Apocalypse change so quickly from time to time, for again and again as we look into the horrifying depths of the pit an angel breaks in upon our contemplation and bids us look upward, and what a reward there is in that heavenward look![1]

Revelation 14 contains the last two of seven signs of cosmic conflict that make up the fourth major vision in the Apocalypse: the sign of the Lamb on Mount Zion (vv. 1–5), and the sign of the reaping of earth's harvest (vv. 6–20). And just as the first three main visions end with Christ's return or the final judgment or both, so does the fourth vision of the seven signs of cosmic conflict. Revelation was written to Christians all over the Roman Empire who were being severely persecuted at the end of the first century, and God is assuring them through John that Christ's victory over Satan at Calvary guarantees that in the end the righteous will be with Christ in glory, and the wicked will be with Satan in hell. The message is timeless. Christians of every generation have turned to the book of Revelation for their deepest comfort in times of severe persecution.

The Lamb on Mount Zion with the 144,000 (the sign of the redeemed)

Verse 1, 'Then I looked, and behold, a Lamb was standing on Mount Zion, and with Him one hundred and forty-four thousand, having His Father's name written on their foreheads.' Mount Zion can refer to the actual site on which the earthly city of Jerusalem still stands, and there are many scholars who take this reference in that literal sense. They say that this is a picture of Christ at the beginning of His millennial reign on earth joining with the one hundred and forty-four thousand Jewish evangelists who, because they were 'sealed', have come through the terror of the great tribulation without a single casualty. But the chief objection to this view is that the one hundred and forty-four thousand do not refer to a distinct group of Jewish evangelists, but to the whole church which we encountered in Revelation 7:4–8, who are also described as the great multitude of the redeemed which no man can number (7:9). Moreover, there are not two communities of saved people in the New Testament but one, which is the church of Christ made up of Jewish and Gentile believers without distinction (Galatians 3:26–29; Ephesians 2:11–18).

The other objection is that this is a scene that takes place in heaven and not on earth, and it follows rather than precedes the final judgment which ends this fourth vision in verses 6–20. Mount Zion in both the Old Testament and the New is more often a symbol of God's church than of the earthly city of Jerusalem and that is how the term should be interpreted here. Psalm 125:1 says, 'Those who trust in the Lord are like Mount Zion which cannot be moved, but abides forever' (cf. Joel 2:32). It is not Mount Zion itself which abides forever, but God's people whom it symbolizes. Mount Zion stands for God's dwelling place and therefore for God's church (1 Corinthians 3:16; Revelation 21:2–3). In the New Testament believers are given the assurance that they 'have come to Mount Zion and to the city of the living God, the heavenly Jerusalem … to the general assembly and church of the firstborn who are registered in heaven' (Hebrews 12:22–24).

So Mount Zion and the one hundred and forty-four thousand are symbols of the people of Christ whom John says (according to the better manuscripts) have 'His name and the name of His Father written on their foreheads.' This is corroborated in Revelation 3:12 where our Lord says to His church, 'He who overcomes, I will make him a pillar in the temple of My God, and he shall go out no more. I will write on him the name of My God and the name of the city of My God, the new Jerusalem, which comes down out of heaven from My God. And I will write on him My new name.' The 'city of My God' is one with Mount Zion where the church is standing with the Lamb in heaven. Verse 1, then, is speaking of the whole church; of all Christian overcomers who have refused to be marked with the name of the beast (13:16–17), and have now entered into the full blessing of their eternal citizenship in heaven (Philippians 3:20). As the roll is called up yonder not one is missing. Symbolically one hundred and forty-four thousand were sealed on earth by the Holy Spirit at their conversion and now there are one hundred and forty-four thousand in heaven. It is just as Jesus promised, 'This is the will of My Father who sent Me, that of all He has given Me, I should lose nothing' (John 6:39).

What the redeemed are doing in heaven

Verse 2, 'And I heard a voice from heaven, like the voice of many waters, and like the voice of loud thunder. And I heard the sound of harpists playing their harps.' What is this sound that is so thunderous and majestic, and yet accompanied by the sweet music of harps? Verse 3 tells us that it is the song of the one hundred and forty-four thousand in heaven: 'And they sang as it were a new song before the throne, before the four living creatures, and the elders; and no one could learn that song except the hundred and forty-four thousand who were redeemed from the earth.' The saints who have overcome Satan on earth are jubilant with song. They have been 'redeemed from the earth'; from the tyranny of evil on the earth. They are now enjoying the 'new heavens and a new earth in which righteousness dwells' (2 Peter 3:13), and the whole universe reverberates with the strongest and sweetest song of praise that the throne of God has ever heard. William Cowper's hymn captures the spirit well:

> There is a fountain filled with blood
> Drawn from Immanuel's veins,
> And sinners plunged beneath that flood
> Lose all their guilty stains.
>
> Dear dying Lamb, Thy precious blood
> Shall never lose its power,
> Till all the ransomed Church of God
> Be saved to sin no more.
>
> E'er since by faith I saw the stream
> Thy flowing wounds supply,
> Redeeming love has been my theme
> And shall be till I die.
>
> When this poor lisping, stamm'ring tongue
> Lies silent in the grave,
> Then in a nobler, sweeter song
> I'll sing Thy power to save.   (*William Cowper, 1731–1800*)

It is a song that only those who have been redeemed from a wicked world can sing; the song of those who were once enslaved, but are now gloriously free from sin's presence and power. It is a 'new song' because although the angels sang about it in Revelation 5:8–10, they cannot sing it from personal experience. This is a song that has never before been heard in heaven, because up till now the redeemed in glory have only been half saved. They had worshipped God as 'the spirits of just men made perfect' (Hebrews 12:23). But now with resurrected glorified bodies their praise reaches a glorious climax as they stand before the Lamb who is heaven itself. 'As good Rutherford said, "Heaven and

Christ are the same. To be with Christ is to be in heaven, and to be in heaven is to be with Christ. Oh my Lord Christ, if I were in heaven without You, it would be a hell. And if I were in hell with You it would be a heaven, for You are all the heaven I want.'"[2]

The chief characteristics of the redeemed in heaven

The one hundred and forty-four thousand are now described in four different ways. First, they have been faithful to God. Verse 4, 'These are the ones who were not defiled with women, for they are virgins.' Here again we have spiritual truth conveyed in symbolic language. For the New Testament does not regard sexual relations between married people as defiling: 'Marriage is honourable among all, and the bed undefiled; but fornicators and adulterers God will judge' (Hebrews 13:4). Indeed, in Revelation 21 the church is called 'the Bride, the Lamb's wife.' God the Holy Spirit would never speak of Christ being married to His church if there was anything morally inferior about marriage. Again, it is unthinkable to conclude that Peter and the other apostles who were married (Mark 1:30; 1 Corinthians 9:5) are for that reason to be excluded from the company of the one hundred and forty-four thousand and the new song they alone can sing.

To understand verse 4 we have to remember that in the Old Testament as well as the New, God uses the marriage metaphor to describe His relationship with His redeemed people. On many occasions in the Old Testament Israel is spoken of as a 'virgin' (2 Kings 19:21; Lamentations 2:13; Amos 5:2). But when she lapsed into idolatry, she is said to have 'played the harlot' (Jeremiah 3:6; Hosea 2:5). In Deuteronomy 31:16 God says to Moses, 'Behold, you will rest with your fathers; and this people will rise up and play the harlot with the gods of the foreigners of the land where they go … and they will forsake Me and break My covenant which I made with them.'

This accusation is made seventeen times in the Old Testament, and it is the same fear that lies behind Paul's words to the Corinthians, 'For I am jealous for you with godly jealousy. For I have betrothed you to one husband, that I may present you as a chaste virgin to Christ. But I fear, lest somehow, as the serpent deceived Eve by his craftiness, so your minds may be corrupted from the simplicity that is in Christ' (2 Corinthians 11:2–3). The purity in question, then, is that of spiritual fidelity, and John is simply saying that the one hundred and forty-four thousand are those who have not been unfaithful to God or the Lamb. They are still spiritual virgins as they wait for 'the marriage supper of the Lamb' (19:9).

Secondly, the one hundred and forty-four thousand have been obedient to the commands of Jesus Christ: 'These are they who follow the Lamb wherever He goes' (v. 4b). As the Good Shepherd, our Lord goes before His sheep and they have dutifully followed Him on earth. They have not gone their own way.

Thirdly, the redeemed have been totally dedicated to God: 'These were redeemed from among men, being firstfruits to God and to the Lamb.' In the Old Testament God commanded that the first ears of corn that ripened belonged solely to Him. The rest of the harvest could be kept by men. That is the sense in which the redeemed are here called 'firstfruits to God and to the Lamb.' They are those who by the mercies of God presented their 'bodies a living sacrifice, holy, acceptable to God' (Romans 12:1–2). The same thought is found in Jeremiah 2:2–3, 'Thus says the Lord: "I remember you, the kindness of your youth, the love of your betrothal, when you went after Me in the wilderness in a land not sown. Israel was holiness to the Lord, the firstfruits of His increase."' It is in this sense also that this term is used of Christians in James 1:18, 'Of His own will [God] brought us forth by the word of truth, that we might be a kind of firstfruits of His creatures.' The term 'firstfruits' is used in all three places (Revelation, Jeremiah and James) as a metaphor of consecration and not of harvest. John is not suggesting that the one hundred and forty-four thousand are a special group of believers whose resurrection in the final great tribulation is going to be followed by the full harvest of the redeemed at the end of the world. Rather, the one hundred and forty-four thousand are a symbol of all the redeemed from both the Old and New Testament eras, and John is simply using the metaphor of the firstfruits to describe them as God's own special possession. They belong solely to Him.

Fourthly, the redeemed in heaven are those who are characterized as being utterly sincere in their profession of faith and love toward God: 'And in their mouth was found no deceit, for they are without fault before the throne of God' (v. 5). Contrast this with the way those outside heaven are described: 'But outside are dogs and sorcerers and sexually immoral and murderers and idolaters, and whoever loves and practises a lie' (22:15).

The warnings of three angels (the sign of final judgment)

In verses 6–13 God sends three angels to give notice of the final judgment that precedes the heavenly scene of final glory in verses 1–5: 'Then I saw another angel flying in the midst of heaven, having the everlasting gospel to preach to those who dwell on the earth—to every nation, tribe, tongue, and people—saying with a loud voice, "Fear God and give glory to Him, for the hour of His judgment has come; and worship Him who made heaven and earth, the sea and springs of water"' (vv. 6–7).

The warning of the first angel to repent

Verses 6–7 are difficult, to say the least, and there are four things to note before we even try to interpret them. First, it is an angel who does the preaching and not the church. Secondly, he proclaims his gospel in midair and not on the earth. Thirdly, what he proclaims is an everlasting gospel for humankind to be ready for the final judgment. And fourthly, it is an everlasting gospel because its message has eternal consequences. What can all this possibly mean?

We begin with the fact that it is an angel who preaches this good

news. Now an angel can bring good news to individuals like Mary and
Joseph and the shepherds, but God does not send angels to evangelize
the world. That is the task of the church (Matthew 28:18–20; Luke
24:46–49; Acts 1:8). These three angels symbolize three important
warnings that 'those who dwell on the earth' must hear, now that 'the
hour of [God's] judgment has come.' The first angel stands for God's
call for universal repentance which comes through general or natural
revelation. For all human beings are constantly made aware of the fact
that the God who created 'heaven and earth, the sea and springs of
water' is Someone who must be feared and worshipped. Failure to seek
Him and 'give glory to Him' will incur His just judgment (Romans
1:18–32). The everlasting gospel contains good news and bad news. For
we first have to feel the weight of the bad news that we are sinners in
the hands of an angry God, before we can cry to Him to have mercy
upon us. The good news is that those who seek Him will find Him
(Deuteronomy 4:29; 1 Chronicles 28:9; 2 Chronicles 15:2,15; Isaiah
55:6–7; Jeremiah 29:13).

The second angel heralds the downfall of paganism

Verse 8, 'And another angel followed, saying, "Babylon is fallen, is
fallen, that great city; because she has made all nations drink of the
wine of the wrath of her fornication."' The city of Babylon, of course,
had already been destroyed by Cyrus in 539 BC. John is referring to it
as a symbol of godless humanism and pride (Daniel 4:29–31; Jeremiah
51:7). The first mention of the city is in Genesis 11:1–9 where after the
flood the human race said to one another, 'Come, let us build ourselves
a city, and a tower whose top is in the heavens; let us make a name
for ourselves, lest we be scattered abroad over the face of the whole
earth.' It was in defiance of God's command, 'Be fruitful and multiply;
fill the earth and subdue it' (Genesis 1:28). The city was 'called Babel'
(of which Babylon is a variant). Thus Babylon became the symbol of
society puffed up with self-absorption and self-assertive pride against
God. But, as the angel proclaims, the citadels of paganism will all
ultimately fall to pieces because of their corrupting influence. Babylon

'made all nations drink of the wine of the wrath of her fornication.' That is to say, the wine of her godlessness that brings down the wrath of God upon her.

The third angel warns of torment for those who worship the beast

Verses 9–10, 'Then a third angel followed them, saying with a loud voice, "If anyone worships the beast and his image, and receives his mark on his forehead or on his hand, he himself shall also drink of the wine of the wrath of God, which is poured out full strength into the cup of His indignation."' This angel too has a warning for the whole earth, hence his 'loud voice'; and it is this: As the day of final judgment approaches, men will increasingly be faced with one choice: Fear God and give Him glory, or worship Antichrist; obey your conscience or follow the crowd.

Here and now God's wrath is mixed with mercy. There is still time to repent and be saved. But on the Day of Judgment the 'full strength' of God's wrath will be poured out on all who choose the beast and Babylon. This 'full strength' (literally 'undiluted') wrath of God will mean that the wicked 'shall be tormented with fire and brimstone [sulphur].' Although John is speaking symbolically, the picture is to be taken seriously, for, as always, the reality behind the symbol is much greater than the symbol itself. Moreover, the burning never ceases. The fire is 'unquenchable' and 'eternal' (Matthew 3:12; 25:41). So John says, 'And the smoke of their torment ascends forever and ever; and they have no rest day or night, who worship the beast and his image, and whoever receives the mark of his name' (v. 11).

Such language is intended to communicate to us what a horrible and terrifying place hell is, and those who are wise will take it seriously and seek God in repentance. Of course, there are some who are offended by the whole idea of hell. They say: How can you talk about a God of love and at the same time attribute to Him a revolting spectre like this? The only answer the Bible gives is that we deserve hell. It is not cruel and unusual punishment, but justice. Jesus was not embarrassed by the judgment of impenitent sinners in hell. He spoke of hell more often than anyone else in the Bible. Indeed, Jesus and the angels oversee the execution of justice in hell (v. 10b). The Lamb is divinely omnipresent and His sovereign control of all things includes hell. Just as the presence of the Lamb's favour makes heaven a place of everlasting happiness, so the presence of the Lamb's wrath will make hell a place of everlasting torment. Nothing exists by itself. Everything has been created by Him, and if it is to continue to exist it must be sustained by Him (Colossians 1:16–17), even the fire or torment of hell (cf. 19:15).

The redeemed will enjoy eternal rest and reward

Now the warning of this third angel concerning the final judgment of God is meant not only to bring reluctant sinners to repentance, but also to encourage persecuted believers to persevere in doing the will of God: 'Here is the patience [endurance, ESV] of the saints; here are those who keep the commandments of God and the faith of Jesus' (v. 12). It is in the certainty of the final judgment and the triumph of justice, that the saints find 'patience' to endure the persecution of the ungodly, and strength to 'keep the commandments of God and the faith of Jesus.' For the natural tendency of men is to think of blessedness only in terms of this life, but persecuted Christians who keep believing in Jesus have assurance of an even greater blessedness in the life to come.

Verse 13, 'Then I heard a voice from heaven saying to me: "Write: 'Blessed are the dead who die in the Lord from now on.'" "Yes", says the Spirit, "that they may rest from their labours, and their works follow them."' God's people may be unjustly treated and even put to death, but it is they, and not their persecutors, who remain forever blessed. Contrary to what is often said, death is not the great equalizer. For the destiny of those who die in the Lord and those who die in their sin could not be greater. Death has no terrors for those who die in the Lord. Death for them is but a gateway to heaven (Romans 8:31–39;

1 Corinthians 15:51–57; 2 Corinthians 5:1–8; Philippians 1:21–23).
Whatever trials or persecutions they have had to endure for Christ's
sake will end when through death they 'rest from their labours.'
Moreover, 'their works follow them.' The good they have done will
last. It will continue to bring glory to God hereafter. This is not wishful
thinking, for it is confirmed by the emphatic '"Yes", says the Spirit' (see
1 Corinthians 15:58).

A twofold picture of the final judgment

The moment has now arrived for Christ to return with His angels, 'for
the harvest of the earth is ripe' (Matthew 13:36–43; 47–50). Verses
14–16, 'And I looked, and behold, a white cloud, and on the cloud sat
One like the Son of Man, having on His head a golden crown, and in
His hand a sharp sickle. And another angel came out of the temple,
crying with a loud voice to Him who sat on the cloud, "Thrust in
Your sickle and reap, for the time has come for You to reap, for the
harvest of the earth is ripe." So He who sat on the cloud thrust in
His sickle on the earth, and the earth was reaped.' As the visions of
the seven seals and the seven trumpets have each ended with the final
judgment (6:12–17; 11:15–19), so the fourth vision ends on this note of
dramatic finality, even though we are only about two-thirds of the way
through the book.

The final judgment pictured as a grain harvest

This picture portrays the inevitability of the final judgment. It will take
place when 'the harvest of the earth is ripe' (v. 15). The One seated on
the cloud 'like the Son of Man' is our Lord Jesus Christ Himself. The
background is Daniel 7:13–14 in which the prophet sees 'One like the
Son of Man coming with the clouds of heaven' to whom 'was given
dominion and glory and a kingdom ... which shall not be destroyed.'
He is also the same Christ referred to in Matthew 24:30–31, 'Then the
sign of the Son of Man will appear in heaven, and then all the tribes of
the earth will mourn, and they will see the Son of Man coming on the

clouds of heaven with power and great glory. And He will send His angels with a great sound of a trumpet, and they will gather together His elect from the four winds, from one end of heaven to the other.'

This is the reaping described in verse 16. Our Lord gives us the same picture in the parable of the wheat and the tares. He says, 'the harvest is the end of the age, and the reapers are the angels' (Matthew 13:39). The harvest of mankind is a twofold reaping. There is the reaping of the wheat and the reaping of the tares; the reaping of the righteous to glory, and the reaping of the wicked to condemnation. The language is once again drawn from the Old Testament: 'Put in the sickle, for the harvest is ripe ... for their wickedness is great' (Joel 3:13).

There is a right time to harvest, and when that time arrives there can be no delay. The sickle is thrust in and the grain reaped. That is why the actual harvest is so briefly described at the end of verse 16: 'and the earth was reaped.' So the angel is not telling our Lord what to do, but simply announcing that the time for reaping has arrived. It is the Father who determines the 'day and hour' of the final judgment (Matthew 24:36), and in John's vision the Father announces it through an angel. The 'golden crown' on Christ's head removes all doubt as to His absolute sovereignty. He acts on His Father's authority and not on the command of an angel (John 5:25–30).

The final judgment pictured as the winepress of God's wrath

Verses 17–20 give us a second agricultural picture in which John is shown the final judgment in terms of grapes which are 'fully ripe' and need to be 'trampled'. 'Then another angel came out of the temple which is in heaven, he also having a sharp sickle. And another angel came out from the altar [from which the prayers of the saints are offered to God to avenge their blood; for the final judgment is God's final answer to their prayers, 6:9–11], who had power over fire, and he cried out with a loud cry to him who had the sharp sickle, saying, "Thrust in your sharp sickle and gather the clusters of the vine of the earth, for her grapes are fully ripe." So the angel thrust his sickle into the earth and gathered the vine of the earth, and threw it into the great winepress of the wrath of God. And the winepress was trampled outside the city, and blood came out of the winepress, up to the horses' bridles, for one thousand six hundred furlongs' (about 184 miles).[3]

The number (1,600 furlongs), like all the numbers in this book, is symbolic. It signifies a destruction that is worldwide and of great magnitude. Thus the number is computed of multiples of 4 and 10 (4 times 4 times 10 times 10). *Four* as we know is the number of the universe, and *ten* is the number of magnitude the size of which is known only to God. The city outside which the winepress is trodden is not earthly Jerusalem, for the destruction is worldwide. Rather, it is 'the holy city, New Jerusalem', 'the Jerusalem above', 'the heavenly Jerusalem' which is the church (21:2; Galatians 4:26; Hebrews 12:22–24).

In other words, final destruction affects everyone outside Christ's church. For having rejected the grace that flows from His cross, they must suffer the wrath of the Lamb that will fall upon all who have rejected His offer of salvation; who are not standing with Him on Mount Zion, but are 'trampled outside the city'. The imagery of the treading of the winepress of divine wrath is found in Isaiah 63:1–6, a passage of graphic intensity in which the Lord whose will has been disregarded and whose mercy has been spurned is asked the question, 'Why is Your apparel red, and Your garments like one who treads in the wine press?' And the Lord answers by saying, 'I have trodden the wine press alone, and from the peoples no one was with Me. For I have trodden them in My anger, and trampled them in My fury; their blood is sprinkled upon My garments, and I have stained all My robes. For the day of vengeance is in My heart, and the year of My redeemed has come … I have trodden down the peoples in My anger, made them drunk in My fury, and brought down their strength to the earth.'

Julia Ward Howe (1819–1910) wrote what is regarded as one of America's finest national hymns, *The Battle Hymn of the Republic.*

She was a recognised poet and vehemently opposed to slavery. At the beginning of the tragic civil war between the northern and southern states, 'day after day Mrs. Howe watched the troops go by as they marched off to war and heard them singing the strains of *John Brown's Body* named for a self-styled abolitionist who was hanged for his efforts to have the slaves freed. One day, while witnessing a parade of soldiers singing this catchy tune, a visiting friend … turned to Mrs. Howe and said, "Why don't you write some decent words for that tune?" "I will", answered Mrs. Howe, and the words came to her that same evening.'[4]
Its stirring lines resonate with the closing theme of Revelation 14:

> Mine eyes have seen the glory of the coming of the Lord,
> He is trampling out the vintage where the grapes of wrath are stored;
> He hath loosed the fateful lightning of His terrible swift sword—
> His truth is marching on.
>
> He has sounded forth the trumpet that shall never sound retreat,
> He is sifting out the hearts of men before His judgment seat;
> O be swift, my soul, to answer Him! be jubilant, my feet!
> Our God is marching on.

17 The seven bowls of God's wrath

15:¹Then I saw another sign in heaven, great and marvellous: seven angels having the seven last plagues, for in them the wrath of God is complete.

²And I saw something like a sea of glass mingled with fire, and those who have the victory over the beast, over his image and over his mark and over the number of his name, standing on the sea of glass, having harps of God. ³They sing the song of Moses, the servant of God, and the song of the Lamb, saying:

'Great and marvellous are Your works,
Lord God Almighty!
Just and true are Your ways,
O King of the saints!
⁴Who shall not fear You, O Lord, and glorify Your name?
For You alone are holy.
For all nations shall come and worship before You,
For Your judgments have been manifested.'

⁵After these things I looked, and behold, the temple of the tabernacle of the testimony in heaven was opened. ⁶And out of the temple came the seven angels having the seven plagues, clothed in pure bright linen, and

having their chests girded with golden bands. [7]Then one of the four living creatures gave to the seven angels seven golden bowls full of the wrath of God who lives forever and ever. [8]The temple was filled with smoke from the glory of God and from His power, and no one was able to enter the temple till the seven plagues of the seven angels were completed.

[16:1]Then I heard a loud voice from the temple saying to the seven angels, 'Go and pour out the bowls of the wrath of God on the earth.'

[2]So the first went and poured out his bowl upon the earth, and a foul and loathsome sore came upon the men who had the mark of the beast and those who worshiped his image.

[3]Then the second angel poured out his bowl on the sea, and it became blood as of a dead man; and every living creature in the sea died.

[4]Then the third angel poured out his bowl on the rivers and springs of water, and they became blood. [5]And I heard the angel of the waters saying:

'You are righteous, O Lord,
The One who is and who was and who is to be,
Because You have judged these things.
[6]For they have shed the blood of saints and prophets,
And you have given them blood to drink.
For it is their just due.'

[7]And I heard another from the altar saying, 'Even so, Lord God Almighty, true and righteous are Your judgments.'

[8]Then the fourth angel poured out his bowl on the sun, and power was given to him to scorch men with fire. [9]And men were scorched with great heat, and they blasphemed the name of God who has power over these plagues; and they did not repent and give Him glory.

[10]Then the fifth angel poured out his bowl on the throne of the beast, and his kingdom became full of darkness; and they gnawed their tongues

because of the pain. [11]They blasphemed the God of heaven because of their pains and their sores, and did not repent of their deeds.

[12]Then the sixth angel poured out his bowl on the great river Euphrates, and its water was dried up, so that the way of the kings from the east might be prepared. [13]And I saw three unclean spirits like frogs coming out of the mouth of the dragon, out of the mouth of the beast, and out of the mouth of the false prophet. [14]For they are spirits of demons, performing signs, which go out to the kings of the earth and of the whole world, to gather them to the battle of that great day of God Almighty.

[15]'Behold, I am coming as a thief. Blessed is he who watches, and keeps his garments, lest he walk naked and they see his shame.'

[16]And they gathered them together to the place called in Hebrew, Armageddon.

[17]Then the seventh angel poured out his bowl into the air, and a loud voice came out of the temple of heaven, from the throne, saying, 'It is done!' [18]And there were noises and thundering and lightnings; and there was a great earthquake, such a mighty and great earthquake as had not occurred since men were on the earth. [19]Now the great city was divided into three parts, and the cities of the nations fell. And great Babylon was remembered before God, to give her the cup of the wine of the fierceness of His wrath. [20]Then every island fled away, and the mountains were not found. [21]And great hail from heaven fell upon men, each hailstone about the weight of a talent. Men blasphemed God because of the plague of the hail, since that plague was exceedingly great.   (Revelation 15:1–16:21)

Revelation 15 and 16 contain the fifth of seven major visions that our Lord Jesus Christ revealed to His servant, the apostle John, on the island of Patmos. Each of these visions reveals something of God's dealings with the church and the world during the interval between Christ's first and second comings. Again and again God's purpose has been to preserve the church and prosper its witness while at the same time bringing judgments upon the world that are designed to lead sinners to repentance. These judgments increase with intensity as the world comes nearer to the end of the age, so that in symbolical terms 'a fourth of the earth' is affected under the seals and 'a third' under the trumpets (6:8; 8:7–12). The intensification of divine judgment reaches its climax in the fifth vision of the bowls containing 'the seven last plagues; for in them the wrath of God is complete' (15:1).

Now there are two things that need to be clarified in order for us to understand what this means. Firstly, the plagues in chapters 15 and 16 complete the warnings that God seeks to bring to men on the earth through His temporal judgments. If the wicked fail to heed His warnings and continue to harden their hearts, they will have to face Him at the final judgment on the last day. Secondly, although the bowl judgments speak specifically to the situation on earth at the end of this age, that does not mean that they have had no relevance to people throughout the past two thousand years. For this fifth vision is simply saying that when God brings death to any impenitent sinner in this life, he or she will still have to wait in torment, in a disembodied state, for the final judgment when they will be publicly sentenced to suffer body and soul in hell forever (20:11–15). And if that is true of individual unbelievers throughout the church age, it will be even more true of them collectively at the end of the world. These plagues are the 'last' earth will know, for 'in them the wrath of God is complete' (literally, is 'filled up'; it has reached its goal). 'His justice is satisfied and all is ready for the new heaven and earth, the renewed creation that is free from sin and its consequences and therefore free from wrath.'[1]

Perhaps we should pause here to explain what the Bible means by 'the wrath of God'. God's wrath is His settled, implacable hostility to sin which some believe is an attribute that is not worthy of Him, for 'God is love' (1 John 4:8). But as J.I. Packer explains: 'God's wrath in the Bible is never the capricious, self-indulgent, irritable, morally ignoble thing that human anger so often is. It is, instead, a right and necessary reaction to objective moral evil. God is only angry where anger is called for. Even among men, there is such a thing as *righteous* indignation, though it is, perhaps, rarely found. But all God's indignation is righteous. Would a God who took as much pleasure in evil as He did in good be a good God? Would a God who did not react adversely to evil in His world be morally perfect? Surely not. But it is precisely this adverse reaction to evil, which is a necessary part of moral perfection, that the Bible has in view when it speaks of God's wrath.'[2]

The song of Moses and the Lamb

Before our Lord unveils to John the outpouring of the bowls of wrath on earth in chapter 16, He shows him something in chapter 15 that puts these final earthly judgments in their proper perspective. Just as there was a prelude before the opening of the seven seals (5:1–14) and another before the sounding of the seven trumpets (7:1–8:5), so here in chapter 15 we have a prelude to the outpouring of the seven bowls of wrath. Clearly, the song is to be related to the bowl judgments.

These last plagues are going to mirror the plagues that God brought upon Egypt in order to deliver His people in the Old Testament from those who oppressed and persecuted them. Ten is the number that signifies a magnitude determined by God, and the ten plagues on Egypt brought a great deliverance for the Israelites from their earthly enemies. In this sense the plagues that fell on the Egyptians anticipate the final and severest judgments of God upon the world which will only be met with blasphemy by men whose hearts, like that of Pharaoh, are hardened against the Almighty (Exodus 7:13; 8:15,19,32; Revelation 16:9,11,21). In addition, Christians will be completely delivered from their enemies, for seven is the number divine judgment. Thus 'the sign in heaven, great and marvellous' which John sees is 'seven angels having seven plagues, which are the last, because in them the wrath of God is complete' (15:1, NASB). When they are poured out there will be no more enemies left on earth to oppress and

persecute God's people. Both God's judgment upon their enemies and
His deliverance of His people will be complete.

The redeemed rejoicing in the victory of God

'And I saw something like a sea of glass mingled with fire, and those
who have the victory over the beast, over his image and over his mark
and over the number of his name, standing on the sea of glass, having
harps of God' (v. 2). God's great and marvellous deliverance of His
people from the oppression of Egypt is cited again and again in the Old
Testament as proof of His saving power (Psalm 78:12–13; 106:9–12;
Isaiah 63:11–14). And as Moses stood on the edge of the Red Sea
and saw the destruction of the enemies of God and of His people, he
was inspired to sing a song of praise in Exodus 15. 'I will sing to the
LORD', he says, 'for He has triumphed gloriously! The horse and its
rider He has thrown into the sea! ... (v. 6) Your right hand, O LORD,
has become glorious in power; Your right hand, O LORD, has dashed
the enemy in pieces ... (v. 11) 'Who is like You, O LORD, among the
gods? Who is like You, glorious in holiness, fearful in praises, doing
wonders?' That is the scene that is being repeated here as the saints,
pictured as safe in heaven, look back and rejoice in the victory Christ
has given them over Satan and the beast. They are 'standing beside the
sea of glass' (ESV) in heaven symbolizing the majesty and holiness of
God (4:6). This time, however, it is 'mingled with fire' to reflect God's
burning justice. And they, too, sing a song of victory on harps supplied
by God, for God delights in their praises.

Verse 3, 'They sing the song of Moses, the servant of God, and
the song of the Lamb.' The phrase 'of Moses' is a subjective genitive
inferring that Moses is the singer. The song is being led by Moses who
is part of the redeemed church, and the song they are singing is 'the
song of the Lamb.' Here the Greek uses an objective genitive to tell
us that the theme of the song is the Lamb. 'Great and marvellous are
Your works, Lord God Almighty! Just and true are Your ways, O King

of the nations' (v. 3b, ESV). The word 'nations' is to be preferred to 'King of the saints', for Christ is 'King of kings and Lord of lords.' The world marvelled at the lying wonders of the beast, but as the redeemed in heaven look back at these last seven plagues and the overthrow of the beast, they can see whose works are truly 'great and marvellous.' They are also 'just' in punishing the wicked as they deserve, and 'true' in following through on what God has promised in His word He would do to save His people from their persecutors (16:5:6).

Verse 4, 'Who shall not fear You, O Lord, and glorify your name? For You alone are holy.' Notice the conjunction 'for'. It occurs three times at the end of this song to explain the praise of God's saints in glory. For the only ground on which the redeemed can 'fear' (i.e. reverence) and 'glorify' God is that He alone is holy. He is a God of absolute purity. He never acts with impure or unjust motives. And one day a countless multitude will bear witness to this, 'for all nations shall come and worship before You.' This does not mean that everybody is going to be saved, but that God in His holiness will gather a people from all nations who will gratefully praise Him for His salvation. And they will have good cause to do so, 'for Your judgments have been manifested.' The word 'judgments' means God's 'righteous acts' have been made plain to all. The redeemed will have nothing to boast of, because they are only in heaven by the mercy of God. Likewise the wicked will have nothing to complain of, because they spurned God's mercy and remained impenitent.

Please notice the purity of this praise by God's saints. There is no mention of themselves in it. It is all about God and how great and marvellous His works are. To quote William Barclay, 'From beginning to end the whole song is a lyric outburst on the greatness of God. Heaven is a place where men forget themselves, forget their own achievements, and remember only God … In heaven a man will see the greatness of God fully displayed, and at last he will remember that nothing matters except God. Heaven is heaven because in it at last all self, and self-importance, are lost in the presence of the greatness and the glory of God.'[3]

The seven avenging angels from heaven

'After these things I looked, and behold, the temple of the tabernacle of the testimony in heaven was opened' (v.5). When the Jews left Egypt, God commanded them to build the tabernacle. It was a large rectangular tent that served two purposes. It was first a 'temple', the holy of holies where God's presence was manifested (Numbers 9:15). But it was also a 'tent of testimony/witness' (Numbers 17:7) because inside the holy of holies was the ark or chest containing 'the two tablets of testimony' on which God had written the ten commandments, the essence of the Law (Exodus 32:15; Deuteronomy 10:5). The top of the chest was called the mercy seat upon which once a year the high priest sprinkled the blood of the atonement for the forgiveness of the people's sins (Leviticus 16:14–16). So from the true sanctuary of God's presence in heaven where His requirements for righteousness are laid down, His avenging angels emerge to bring His wrath on those who have transgressed His Law and not sought His forgiveness. It echoes John's teaching in his Gospel that to reject the grace of salvation is to incur the judgment of condemnation upon oneself (John 3:14–19).

The seven angels with the seven last plagues are 'clothed in pure bright linen, and having their chests girded with golden bands' (v. 6; cf. Matthew 28:3; Mark 16:5). These plagues come with the fullest endorsement of God, for the angels are bright with the radiance of being in God's presence, and they have the golden band of a judge around their chests. These are all symbols to show the purity of God's wrath that the angels are about to pour on the earth. It is free of all unjustified, irrational and uncontrolled anger. 'Then one of the four living creatures gave to the seven angels seven golden bowls full of the wrath of God who lives forever and ever' (v. 7). The fact that one of the four living creatures who represent creation gives the bowls of wrath to the seven angels speaks of creation's endorsement of God's judgment upon those who have been destroying the earth (11:18). For the Fall not only brought the curse of sin upon humankind, but also upon the rest of creation which 'was subjected to futility, not willingly, but because of Him who subjected it in hope' (Romans 8:20–21).

Verse 8, 'The temple was filled with smoke from the glory of God and from His power, and no one was able to enter the temple till the seven plagues of the seven angels were completed.' Why? Because God's patience has reached its limit. God in His wrath has shut up His tender mercies. The time of final judgment has come and none can stay His hand. The time for intercession is past. Nothing can be done to halt the execution of divine justice, until it has completed its purpose.

The seven bowls of God's wrath poured out

'Then I heard a loud voice from the temple saying to the seven angels, "Go and pour out the bowls of the wrath of God on the earth"' (16:1). The loud voice can only be the voice of God, for no one else is in the temple. God is in control. Even though the angels have already received their bowls, they have to wait for the command of God before they pour out their plagues.

The first bowl
'So the first went and poured out his bowl upon the earth, and a foul and loathsome sore ['harmful and painful sores', ESV] came upon the men who had the mark of the beast and those who worshipped his image' (v. 2). The saints are not afflicted. The deliverance of God's people from Egypt and the deliverance of Christians from the judgments of God upon Antichrist's regime at the end of the world bear a resemblance as we have already seen. Thus the sixth plague inflicted painful boils on the Egyptians only (Exodus 9:8–11). But while no personal suffering was inflicted on men by the first five plagues on Egypt, the followers of Antichrist are attacked from the beginning of the bowl judgments.

The second bowl

It is also clear from chapter 16 that the plagues are described more
concisely than the judgments under the seals and the trumpets: 'Then
the second angel poured out his bowl on the sea, and it became blood
as of a dead man; and every living creature in the sea died' (v. 3). The
deprivation of this vital food supply, of course, will again afflict the
followers of the beast who alone have the mark to 'buy or sell' (13:16–
17). The effect, once more, is universal. It will kill 'every living creature
in the sea', not just a 'third' (8:8–9). There is a finality about the bowl
judgments that will afflict the beast and all his followers worldwide.
They are not partial and precursory, but total and final. They are
bringing us to the completion of God's overthrow of evil (15:1,8).

The third bowl

'Then the third angel poured out his bowl on the rivers and springs of
water, and they became as blood' (v. 4). This plague is very similar to
the first Egyptian plague (Exodus 7:20ff) as well as the third trumpet
which heralded the poisoning of a third of the rivers and springs of
waters, causing the death of many (8:10–11). 'It is true that it is not
said here that men died, but that presumably is only because other
judgments followed so swiftly. Without water to drink there is no
future for man.'[4]

How close it will be to Christ's return we do not know, but,
once again, the effect is total, not partial, for this is a plague of final
judgment, not just a warning. Society at the time will surely find fault,
as always. But the angel who has poured out this third plague is quick
to affirm here the rightness and appropriateness of this judgment of
God. 'And I heard the angel of the waters saying: "You are righteous,
O Lord, the One who is and who was and who is to be, because You
have judged these things. For they have shed the blood of saints and
prophets, and You have given them blood to drink. For it is their just
due"' (vv. 5–6). Since the persecutors of the church have religiously
shed the blood of God's servants, it is fitting that they should now

drink blood. It is what they deserve. And to this the saints in glory add their Amen, for the altar in verse 7 is the altar from which their prayers have ascended to God (6:9–11), and the Greek literally says: 'And I heard the altar saying, "Yes, Lord God the Almighty, true and just are Your judgments!"' (ESV)

The fourth bowl

'Then the fourth angel poured out his bowl on the sun, and power was given to him to scorch men with fire. And men were scorched with great heat, and they blasphemed the name of God who has power over these plagues; and they did not repent and give Him glory' (vv. 8–9). At the sounding of the fourth trumpet a third of the sun's light was darkened. Its heat was decreased. Here, with the pouring out of the fourth bowl, the sun's heat is greatly intensified so that the followers of Antichrist are severely burned and blaspheme 'the name of God who has power over these plagues.' Of course, the scientists will put it down to natural causes. But in their hearts the wicked will know that it has come from Almighty God, and their refusal to repent and give glory to God is 'a sin unto death' (1 John 5:16, AV) by which they bring final judgment on themselves.

The fifth bowl

'Then the fifth angel poured out his bowl on the throne of the beast, and his kingdom became full of darkness; and they gnawed their tongues because of the pain. They blasphemed the God of heaven because of their pains and their sores, and did not repent of their deeds' (vv. 10–11). The fifth of the last plagues is similar to the ninth plague God poured out on Egypt by which the land was afflicted with a darkness that could be 'felt' (Exodus 10:21–23). There is also a significant correspondence between the judgments of the fifth trumpet and the fifth bowl in that the action moves from the physical world to the spiritual world. The fifth trumpet unlocks 'the bottomless pit' releasing smoke, darkness and demonic activity that torments 'only those men who do not have the seal of God on their foreheads', causing them to 'seek death' to no avail (9:1–11).

Likewise, when the fifth bowl is poured out, we are not told what caused the darkness or the accompanying pain. It would seem to be a spiritual darkness because it is poured out 'on the throne of the beast, and his kingdom became full of darkness.' Elsewhere in the New Testament Satan's kingdom is defined in terms of spiritual darkness (Matthew 4:16; Acts 26:18; Ephesians 5:8; 1 Thessalonians 5:5; 1 Peter 2:9; 1 John 2:11). So the fifth bowl will throw the evil empire into the darkness of total confusion as they become painfully aware that their godless Utopia is falling to pieces and about to be destroyed forever. Their pain, however, does not lead them to repentance. Rather, they remain implacable in their hostility and blaspheme 'the God of heaven'. Great pains have always accompanied the fall of anti-God regimes like Egypt, Rome, Nazi Germany and the Soviet Union, to name a few. But none of these pains will compare with the pain experienced by those who have sold their souls to the greatest anti-God regime ever, the throne of the beast who has received his power directly from Satan (13:2).

The sixth bowl

'Then the sixth angel poured out his bowl on the great river Euphrates, and its water was dried up, so that the way of the kings from the east might be prepared' (v. 12). Here we have another connection between the bowl and the trumpet judgments which was the signal for the 'release [of] the four angels who are bound at the great river Euphrates … to kill a third of mankind' (9:14–15). Geographically, the Euphrates River formed a barrier one thousand eight hundred miles long, three thousand six hundred feet wide and an average of thirty feet deep, that protected Israel from their greatest enemies in the east.

The drying up of this great barrier is a symbol of the fact that at the end of the world God is going to prepare the way for Antichrist to stir up a worldwide war against the church with the help of demons. 'And I saw three unclean spirits like frogs coming out of the mouth of the dragon, out of the mouth of the beast, and out of the mouth of the false prophet. For they are spirits of demons, performing signs, which go out to the kings of the earth and of the whole world, to gather them to the battle of that great day of God Almighty' (vv. 13–14). Satan, Antichrist and the false prophet are pictured here as a trinity of evil all collaborating to seduce the rulers and the people of the world into joining forces to eliminate all Christ's followers on earth. These unclean spirits are enabled by Satan to perform counterfeit miracles as our Lord and Paul have forewarned us (Matthew 24:24; 2 Thessalonians 2:9–10). The frenzied hostility that stirred up the people to put Christ to death, will reach its peak at the end of the church age on what Satan thinks will be his great day, but to his consternation it will be the 'great day of God Almighty' (16:14).

Verse 15, 'Behold, I am coming as a thief. Blessed is he who watches, and keeps his garments, lest he walk naked and they see his shame.' With all 'the kings of the earth' committed to destroy His church in their domain, our Lord interrupts the vision of the bowls of wrath. The forces of the beast will seem invincible, but the saints must not despair. For the King of kings and Lord of lords will come at the right time to rescue His people and destroy their enemies. The command to watch for His coming is one that our Lord often made, for it is evidence of our faith in His promise to return (Matthew 24:42–44; 25:1–13; Luke 12:35–40). Those who do not watch will have their hypocrisy exposed and be seen for what they really are. Their garments will be spotted by the world (James 1:27; Matthew 7:21–23).

Verse 16, 'And they gathered them together to the place called in Hebrew, Armageddon.' The Old Testament also contains prophecies of the last day when anti-God nations will seek to destroy the people of God and, instead, are routed with great carnage and dominion is given to the saints of the Most High (Ezekiel 38,39; Daniel 7; Zechariah 14). It is this same final battle that the apostle John envisions here as the unclean spirits gather their worldwide anti-Christian coalition to a place called Armageddon which means 'the mountain of Megiddo.' Actually, Megiddo was a town situated in the north of Palestine in the valley of Jezreel, between the Sea of Galilee and the Mediterranean, and was built on a mound. The road from the east to Egypt in the south passed through here and it was the scene of some famous battles. But our Lord is not predicting a battle here between Jews and Arabs, or between East and West. This is a battle in which the whole world wages war against Christ's church wherever it can be found. Armageddon, therefore, is simply being used here as a symbol of the final battle between the world and the church, between Antichrist and Jesus Christ, the mother of all battles.

The seventh bowl

'Then the seventh angel poured out his bowl into the air, and a loud voice came out of the temple, from the throne, saying, "It is done"' (v. 17). The last plague affects the *air* (the second heaven) in which Satan operates. It is the realm of spiritual conflict. In Ephesians 2:2 he is called 'the prince of the power of the air who now works in the sons of disobedience.' So when he and the demons are taken out of the battle, there is no more fight in their human allies. God's judgment of evil on earth is 'done'. All that remains is for Satan, the beast, the false prophet and all their human followers to be cast forever into hell, which is the final judgment (20:7–15). Verse 18, 'And there were noises and thunderings and lightnings; and there was a great earthquake, such a mighty and great earthquake as had not occurred since men were on the earth.' The Bible often describes the world coming to an end by means of a great earthquake in which God shakes not only the earth but also heaven (6:12–17; cf. Ezekiel 38:18–20; Hag. 2:6; Matthew 24:21,29; Hebrews 12:26–27).

This is what John envisions when the seventh of the last plagues is poured out: 'Now the great city [i.e. the worldwide community of the enemies of God] was divided into three parts, and the cities of the nations fell. And great Babylon [the name of the great world-city, 17:1,2,5,18] was remembered before God, to give her the cup of the wine of the fierceness of His wrath. Then every island fled away, and the mountains were not found. And great hail from heaven fell upon men, each hailstone about the weight of a talent' (vv. 19–21a). A talent 'varied in weight among different peoples and at various times. The range seems to be from about sixty pounds to something over a hundred.'[5] You would think that such a cataclysmic judgment on the last of the last days would be more than enough to put the fear of God into any person and drive them to repentance. But like Pharaoh during the plagues on Egypt, the people who have the mark of the beast and worship his image have hardened their hearts beyond the point of return. So John says, 'And men [i.e. the ungodly] blasphemed God because of the plague of hail, since that plague was exceedingly great' (v. 21b). Only the free and sovereign grace of God can melt a sinner's heart and bring him or her to repentance of sin and faith in Jesus Christ (Acts 5:31; 11:18; Ephesians 2:8; Philippians 1:29). When God says, 'It is done', the door of salvation will be permanently shut and all the elect safely gathered into His everlasting arms.

Revelation 15 and 16 are hair-raising chapters, but for the true Christian they hold no terror. For our eyes are not focused on the last plagues but on our returning Lord, His overwhelming victory over evil and our being with Him in glory forever. With that fair prospect we can truthfully sing:

The King there, in His beauty,
    Without a veil is seen;
It were a well-spent journey,
    Though seven deaths lay between;
The Lamb with His fair army
    Doth on Mount Zion stand,
And glory, glory dwelleth
    In Immanuel's land.   (*Anne Ross Cousin, 1824–1906*)

'Amen. Even so, come, Lord Jesus!' (22:20)

18 The mystery of Babylon the great

17:1Then one of the seven angels who had the seven bowls came and talked with me, saying to me, 'Come, I will show you the judgment of the great harlot who sits on many waters, 2with whom the kings of the earth committed fornication, and the inhabitants of the earth were made drunk with the wine of her fornication.'

3So he carried me away in the Spirit into the wilderness. And I saw a woman sitting on a scarlet beast which was full of names of blasphemy, having seven heads and ten horns. 4The woman was arrayed in purple and scarlet, and adorned with gold and precious stones and pearls, having in her hand a golden cup full of abominations and the filthiness of her fornication. 5And on her forehead a name was written:

MYSTERY,

BABYLON THE GREAT,

THE MOTHER OF HARLOTS AND OF THE ABOMINATIONS OF THE EARTH.

6I saw the woman, drunk with the blood of the saints and with the blood of the martyrs of Jesus. And when I saw her, I marvelled with great amazement.

7But the angel said to me, 'Why did you marvel? I will tell you the mystery of the woman and of the beast that carries her, which has the seven heads and the ten horns. [8]The beast that you saw was, and is not, and will ascend out of the bottomless pit and go to perdition. And those who dwell on the earth will marvel, whose names are not written in the Book of Life from the foundation of the world, when they see the beast that was, and is not, and yet is.

[9]'Here is the mind which has wisdom: The seven heads are seven mountains on which the woman sits. [10]There are also seven kings. Five have fallen, one is, and the other has not yet come. And when he comes, he must continue a short time. [11]The beast that was, and is not, is himself also the eighth, and is of the seven, and is going to perdition.

[12]'The ten horns which you saw are ten kings who have received no kingdom

as yet, but they receive authority for one hour as kings with the beast. [13]These are of one mind, and they will give their power and authority to the beast. [14]These will make war with the Lamb, and the Lamb will overcome them, for He is Lord of lords, and King of kings; and those who are with Him are called, chosen, and faithful.'

[15]Then he said to me, 'The waters which you saw, where the harlot sits, are peoples, multitudes, nations, and tongues. [16]And the ten horns which you saw on the beast, these will hate the harlot, make her desolate and naked, eat her flesh and burn her with fire. [17]For God has put it into their hearts to fulfil His purpose, to be of one mind, and to give their kingdom to the beast, until the words of God are fulfilled. [18]And the woman whom you saw is that great city which reigns over the kings of the earth.'

(Revelation 17:1–18)

Revelation 17 is the beginning of vision six, the second last major division of the prophecy that our Lord Jesus Christ gave to 'His servant John.' Up till this point John has been shown the formidable power and the intense hostility of our Lord's five main enemies in the cosmic conflict between good and evil. These enemies in order of greatness are the 'dragon' (Satan and his fellow demons), the 'beast out of the sea' (Antichrist), the 'beast out of the earth' (the false prophet), 'great Babylon' (the seductions of the world), and 'the men who have the mark of the beast' (the followers of Antichrist). Now in vision six *the mighty triumph of God over all His enemies* is unveiled. In chapters 17–18 the great whore is destroyed; in chapter 19 the two beasts are destroyed; and in chapter 20 Satan and his followers (human and demonic) are destroyed.

The seductiveness of the great harlot

'Then one of the seven angels who had the seven bowls came and talked with me, saying to me, "Come, I will show you the judgment of the great harlot who sits on many waters."' (v. 1). It is appropriate that one of the angels connected with the pouring out of the bowls of God's final wrath on a godless world is chosen to show John how each of God's enemies is totally destroyed. It is also fitting that in chapter 21:9 we read, 'Then one of the seven angels who had the seven bowls filled with the seven last plagues came to me and talked with me, saying, "Come, I will show you the bride, the Lamb's wife."' For God's final judgment has a single purpose that embodies not only the destruction of His enemies, but also the salvation of His people who will live forever with Him in a new heaven and a new earth.

In chapter 17 the angel first describes for John the characteristics of 'the great harlot' and how she operates, before he goes on in chapter 18 to unveil her actual judgment and destruction. The great harlot, who is also called 'Babylon the great' (v. 5), stands for the spirit of worldliness that motivates godless society all over the world. Thus she 'is seated on many waters' (v. 1) which the angel later explains 'are peoples, multitudes, nations, and tongues' (v. 15). The great harlot plies her trade all over the world, for (v. 2) she is the one 'with whom the kings of the earth committed fornication, and the inhabitants of the earth were made drunk with the wine of her fornication.' The angel, of course, is speaking here primarily of fornication in a spiritual sense. He is speaking of idolatry; of the unfaithfulness of men and women to God as their Creator in every form, whether it is the worship of images or creaturely comforts. It is the putting of riches, pleasure, power or any other thing above the worship of God. Elsewhere John defines it this way: 'Do not love the world or the things in the world [i.e. do not love them more than God]. If anyone loves the world, the love of the Father is not in him. For all that is in the world—the lust of the flesh, the lust of the eyes, and the pride of life—is not of the Father but is of the world. And the world is passing away, and the lust of it; but he who does the will of God abides forever' (1 John 2:15–17).

This is what the great harlot (or Babylon) stands for: the spirit of worldliness which Satan uses to entice men and women to fix their affections supremely on creaturely things, both good and bad. Its form may change through the centuries from worshipping images, to worshipping money or sex or drugs or sport or success; indeed, idolizing anything rather than giving supreme place to our Creator, the one true living God (Romans 1:25). 'So', says John, 'he carried me away in the Spirit into the wilderness' (v. 3). 'In the Spirit' means in a spiritual state of mind by means of which John could visualize the great harlot. He is carried metaphorically, not literally, 'into the wilderness', which is the place in chapter 12 where the church finds refuge from the attacks of the dragon, and, separated from the glitter of the world, can see things with spiritual objectivity. 'And I saw a woman sitting on a scarlet beast which was full of names of blasphemy, having seven heads and ten horns' (v. 3b). The beast here is the same beast from the sea in chapter 13 who is 'the spirit of the antichrist,' (1 John 4:3; cf. 1 John 2:18; 2 John 7), Satan's henchman who has persecuted the church throughout this age. He is 'scarlet' because red is the colour of the dragon who is Satan (12:3) as well as the colour of sin (Isaiah 1:18). Moreover, the scarlet beast was 'full of names of blasphemy' because throughout the ages the spirit of the Antichrist has brazenly opposed God and defamed His all-glorious name.

Again, he has 'seven heads and ten horns' because his master, the dragon, has seven heads and ten horns (12:3). The 'seven heads' symbolize divinely-given power over the forces of evil. He is commander-in-chief over all Satan's minions as well as the false prophet and the great harlot, for 'the dragon gave him his power, his throne, and great authority' (13:2). A horn is a symbol of strength, and so 'ten horns' signify strength of great power, for ten is the symbol of magnitude predetermined by God. The fact that the great harlot is sitting on the scarlet beast indicates that it is by his power that she is able to seduce kings and nations (vv. 2,18). In addition she is also attractive: 'The woman was arrayed in purple and scarlet, and adorned with gold and precious stones and pearls, having in her hand a golden cup full of abominations and the filthiness of her fornication' (v. 4). As a seducer the woman is appropriately attired in purple and scarlet which were garments only worn by the wealthy, since the dyes producing them were difficult to extract and very expensive. Ordinary people wore brown or off-white, the colour of wool. She is also liberally adorned with precious jewels to impress and attract her victims. The 'golden cup' in her hand deceives people into thinking that only the best drink can be worthy of such a costly receptacle, when in fact it is 'full of abominations', a word particularly associated with idolatry in the Old Testament (Ezekiel 20:7,8,30).

The repulsiveness of the great harlot

'And on her forehead a name was written: MYSTERY, BABYLON THE GREAT, THE MOTHER OF HARLOTS AND OF THE ABOMINATIONS OF THE EARTH' (v. 5). The harlot's name is a 'mystery' because its meaning can only be known by divine revelation. The ungodly do not know it, but the angel makes it known to John and through John we know it. First, she is identified with 'Babylon' because in the Bible Babylon is the epitome of universal secularism characterised by prevailing idolatry, extravagant luxury and unbridled pleasures (see comments on 14:8 and 16:19). Secondly, she is the 'mother of harlots' because she spawns every 'abomination of the earth' (everything that takes the place of God and is therefore detestable in His sight). All this is hidden from the rest of the world who do not know God or His Word. All they can see is the attractiveness of her costly attire and the tempting pleasures of her golden cup.

Now some think the great harlot is the apostate church in general, or the Roman Catholic Church in particular, but that is to fail to understand the mystery. The woman is a harlot or a prostitute. She is not an unfaithful wife. She has no connection with God and does not claim any. People who profess to know God but are unfaithful to Him are not called harlots, but adulteresses. Thus Jesus called the Jews of His day 'an evil and adulterous generation' (Matthew 12:39; 16:4). James chides worldly church members in his day saying, 'Adulterers and adulteresses! Do you not know that friendship with the world is enmity with God? Whoever therefore wants to be a friend of the world makes himself an enemy of God' (4:4). The name of 'Babylon the Great, the Mother of Harlots' is written on the forehead of all worldly enticements.

Verse 6, 'I saw the woman, drunk with the blood of the saints and with the blood of the martyrs of Jesus. And when I saw her, I marvelled with great amazement.' The metaphor of being 'drunk' shows that the harlot had shed blood freely and enjoyed the experience. The verse, however, is not easy to interpret, for people who are spiritually drunk with the worship of things are not an organized group who actively pursue the death of Christians. What is probably being referred to here is the way the spirit of worldliness has at times influenced movements or leaders to go after Christians. Rulers besotted with power like Pharaoh, Antiochus Epiphanes, Nero, Domitian, Hitler, Stalin, Chairman Mao and now Abu Bakr al-Baghdadi, have shed the blood of untold millions of believers across the centuries. Nor is apostate Christendom without its share of guilt, as the history of the church has demonstrated. But what has been true in the past will surely reach its zenith only during the rise of the final Antichrist, the most power-hungry, bloodthirsty dictator ever.

The words 'saints' and 'martyrs' are not to be distinguished, for the word 'martyrs' literally means 'witnesses'. It is therefore a specific reference to those who are witnesses of Jesus. The word 'saints' refers to the witness of all believers from the beginning of time that has been borne in a life that is consistently separated from the world for the service of God. 'And when I saw her', says John, 'I marvelled with great amazement', not only because the spectacle of a drunken harlot lavishly adorned and seated on a beast with seven heads and ten horns was so extraordinary, but also because the meaning of the vision was so puzzling to him. The angel had invited him in verse 1 to see 'the judgment of the great harlot'. Instead he sees her drunk with success in her antichrist endeavours. John, however, is not left long in the dark: 'But the angel said to me, "Why did you marvel? I will tell you the mystery of the woman and of the beast that carries her, which has seven heads and ten horns"' (v. 7).

The mystery of the harlot and the beast

'The beast that you saw was, and is not, and will ascend out of the bottomless pit and go to perdition. And those who dwell on the earth will marvel, whose names are not written in the Book of Life from the foundation of the world, when they see the beast that was, and is not, and yet is' (v. 8). The beast is the more important of the two and so the explanation begins with him. In chapter 13:1 he comes up out of the 'sea', which is a symbol of the restless multitude of unregenerate humanity. He is the spirit of antichrist who has been embodied in various forms throughout history, but the essence of his being has always been the same. For his real habitat is not the sea or unregenerate mankind, but 'the bottomless pit'. He is an incarnation of Satan of sorts. And invested with Satan's power and authority he does his master's work in different ways at different times. He appears and disappears and then reappears as the enemy of God and His people. His ultimate destiny, however, is to 'go to perdition' with the devil and the false prophet (20:10). That is the meaning of the assertion that he 'was, and is not, and will ascend out of the bottomless pit and go to perdition.' And so for Christians there is no uncertainty regarding the final overthrow of Antichrist.

The ungodly, however, 'whose names are not written in the Book of Life from the foundation of the world', do not have this assurance. They 'marvel' at the beast's resilience who 'was, and is not, and yet is'. They think he is divinely invincible. In verses 9–14 the angel gives John some further clues to the identity of the scarlet beast. 'Here is the mind which has wisdom: The seven heads are seven mountains on which the woman sits. There are also seven kings. Five have fallen, one is, and the other has not yet come. And when he comes, he must continue a short time' (vv. 9–10). The 'seven heads' are now said to be 'seven mountains'. This identifies the beast with Rome which has always been called the city on seven hills; but the reference is not just to the city, but to the empire of Rome. Leon Morris says, 'In the first century, Rome was a striking embodiment of what John means by Babylon. In Rome as nowhere else men could see the city of man bent on its own blasphemous way, opposing with all its might the things of God.'[1] So the harlot, sitting on the seven mountains, plies her trade on the back of the greatest and longest-running worldwide kingdom humankind had seen so far. Never before did so many people all over the known world enjoy riches and pleasures and power and peace in such great measure.

Verse 10, however, makes it clear that Rome does not exhaust the identity of the beast, for the angel goes on to tell John that the 'seven mountains' are also 'seven kings' (or kingdoms, Daniel 7:17,23). It is important to remember that these seven kingdoms are all a manifestation of the beast. They are anti-God kingdoms in that they have defied His laws and persecuted His people throughout history.

So John says, 'Five have fallen.' They are no longer a threat to God's church. And who are these five kings? I do not think the angel is speaking of a sequence of seven Roman emperors followed hundreds of years later by an eighth ruler who will head up a revived Roman Empire at the end of this age.[2] A better explanation is to take the seven kings as a succession of world empires; namely, Egypt, Assyria, Babylon, Persia, and Greece. These five 'have fallen'. Rome is the sixth: 'one is'. It was the empire in which John was living and was infamous for burning Christians at the stake and feeding them to wild animals. 'And the other [the seventh] has not yet come. And when he comes, he must continue a short time.' We cannot understand this prophecy unless we see its connection with verse 11: 'And the beast that was [i.e. foreshadowed in the first six], and is not [i.e. he has not yet appeared in John's time], is himself also the eighth, and is of the seven, and is going to perdition.' This prophecy was made nearly two thousand years ago, and the question is: Has the seventh worldwide anti-God kingdom come? And the answer is 'No'. Rulers like Charlemagne, Napoleon, Hitler and Stalin did not govern worldwide empires. To whom then can this seventh kingdom belong?

John's answer is that we do not know, because it has not yet appeared on the stage of world history: 'and the other has not yet come' (v. 10). For the next worldwide, anti-God kingdom (the seventh) will be ruled by the beast himself who is the final, ultimate Antichrist. The previous six kingdoms were not ruled by him, but by his surrogates. His kingdom, however, will be more worldwide than any other before him, and it will be the most anti-Christian and anti-God of them all. So it is the seventh kingdom in that it comes sometime after the previous six, but at the same time he is 'also the eighth', because he is not really one of them (solely human), but a satanic incarnation never seen before. That makes him different and therefore even greater than they ever were. His being 'also the eighth' probably refers as well to the fact that during the brief reign of Antichrist he will recover from a deadly wound to the amazement of the world (13:3).

Now there are two clues in verses 10–11 that seem to confirm the interpretation above. The first is the phrase 'and is going to perdition' or damnation. That connects verse 11 with verse 8 where we are told that this same beast that 'was, and is not ... will ascend out of the bottomless pit and go to perdition.' Both verses are talking about Antichrist who after continuing 'a short time' (v. 10) 'is going to perdition.' The beast in verse 8 is the eighth king in verse 11 who 'is of the seven'. The other clue is found in verse 10 where we read, 'And when he comes, he must continue a short time.' Antichrist's reign will be very short indeed. It is the same 'little while' assigned to Satan in chapter 20:3, for the beast's career is intertwined with that of the dragon's and of the same duration ('a short time', 12:12). Consequently, their eternal destiny is the same: 'And the devil, who deceived them [the nations], was cast into the lake of fire and brimstone where the beast and the false prophet are. And they will be tormented day and night forever and ever' (20:10). Chapter 20 and chapter 17 are speaking of the same event; Satan's last and fiercest effort to exterminate Christ's church that will take place under this seventh king and end with his utter destruction in hell (17:13–14; 20:7–9).

So much for verse 11, but we are not out of the woods yet: 'The ten horns which you saw are ten kings who have received no kingdom as yet, but they receive authority for one hour as kings with the beast. These are of one mind, and they will give their power and authority to the beast' (vv. 12–13). Here the angel is giving John a bit more light on Antichrist's final assault on the followers of the Lamb. Antichrist is going to need the assistance and cooperation of all the rulers of the world. The number ten is the Bible's symbol for many, the exact amount of which is known only to God who has decreed what it shall be. Moreover, these many rulers all over the world are under the authority of Antichrist and therefore it can be said that they 'have received no kingdom as yet.' It seems that Antichrist's agreement with them is that once they have helped him to rid the earth of the scourge of the church, he will apportion to each a trouble-free kingdom. It is a lie, of course, but they have been deceived. Fortunately, however, God, in His sovereignty, will rescue His saints when the axis of evil has only come together for 'one hour' (i.e. before they can accomplish anything; 'For in one hour your judgment has come', 18:10).

Verse 14, 'These will make war with the Lamb, and the Lamb will overcome them, for He is Lord of lords, and King of kings; and those who are with Him are called, chosen, and faithful.' This is a clear reference to the return of Christ and, once again, it is accompanied by the resurrection (the saints are with Him) and the final judgment. The assault of all these kings on Christ's church is, of course, an assault on Christ, the Lamb of God who purchased the church with His own blood (Acts 20:28). He told Saul of Tarsus that to persecute Christians is to persecute Him (22:7–8). But this worldwide army of persecutors is no threat to His almighty power. As Lord of lords and King of kings, His lordship is absolute and His sovereignty invincible. Their destruction is a foregone conclusion. His church will be safe and secure under His protection. Not only that, Christians will share in their Saviour's victory. Verse 14 says that they 'are with Him' (1 Thessalonians 4:14,17). To quote Leon Morris again, 'These are His retinue, not His resources. They represent no independent source of aid, for He needs none. Indeed, the very qualities named show that they depend on Him.'[3] First, they are 'called' by Him with an effectual calling. Their response was dependent upon His call to them to follow Him (Romans 1:7; 1 Corinthians 1:1–2). Secondly, they have been 'chosen' by Him not because of any merit in themselves, but because in His infinite grace He set His love on them before the world was made (John 15:16; Ephesians 1:3–6; 2 Thessalonians 2:13). And thirdly, they are 'faithful' to Him because He is faithful to keep them faithful to Himself (1 Corinthians 1:8–9; Philippians 1:6; 1 Peter 1:5).

The manner of Babylon's approaching destruction

'And he said to me, "The waters which you saw, where the harlot sits, are peoples, multitudes, nations, and tongues'" (v. 15). The fact that in this vision the angel portrays the harlot as sitting on many waters (v. 1), and then on a scarlet beast (v. 3), and then on the beast's seven heads which are seven mountains (v. 9), is not a sign of inconsistency. The angel is simply using a variety of symbols to show John and his readers how universal and demonic and powerful is the harlot's influence upon the world. She commands a great following, but her position is not inviolable: 'And the ten horns which you saw on the beast, these will hate the harlot, make her desolate and naked, eat her flesh and burn her with fire' (v. 16). This is a very difficult verse to explain by any measure. Some commentators think that verse 16 is saying that at the end of the world the forces of Antichrist will become divided and destroy one another. Leon Morris says, 'There is no cohesion in evil. Wicked men are not just one happy band of brothers. Being wicked, they give way to jealousy and hatred. At the climax their mutual hatreds will result in mutual destruction.'[4] The trouble with this view is that the ten kings remain loyal to Antichrist to the very end.

The explanation of Philip Edgcumbe Hughes is that worldliness sows the seeds of its own destruction: 'The euphoria of being drunken with the wine of the harlot's fornication (verse 2) turns to disgust and hatred. The mad addiction to luxury and licentiousness of her citizens destroyed the grandeur of Rome, the "great Babylon" of their day ... The fate of the harlot is to be hated ... and to be destroyed by the lovers who have wanted unending existence for her.'[5]

According to verse 16, however, the harlot does not destroy herself. Rather, it seems that she is the victim of a plot hatched by Antichrist to accomplish his goal of worldwide dominion. The first part of his plan is to use the harlot to turn the worship of the world away from God to things. When he has generally achieved that end, his final and ultimate objective will be to turn the worship of all humankind to himself. Regarding this moment in history, Michael Wilcock says: 'It is the time of the great rebellion, when Satan's power will be finally unmasked. The beast repudiates his former ally, the woman, discarding persuasion in order to rely on naked power.'[6]

In other words, people who love luxury and a life of ease are only concerned about themselves. They are not the stuff of dictatorships. The people Antichrist will want to help him rid the world of Christianity will have to be fanatics for the cause; people who have the same hatred for Christianity as he has. Together, he and they will bring about an abrupt end to the whole independent self-centred system of capitalism and gross consumerism in the world: 'these will hate the harlot, make her desolate and naked, eat her flesh and burn her with fire.' Antichrist and his anti-God coalition may feel proud of their initial success, and think that the battle is all but over. Soon there will be no church to frustrate his desire for universal homage and allegiance. Little do they realize, however, that they have merely succeeded in doing God's will: 'For God has put it into their hearts to fulfil His purpose, to be of one mind, and to give their kingdom to the beast, until the words of God are fulfilled' (v. 17). These are of one mind (v. 13) because this is the way God has decreed the world will end; in a futile, all-out, universal attempt to destroy the Lamb and His little flock (v. 14). God's purpose will not be frustrated, but actually advanced, though unwillingly and unwittingly by Antichrist and his allies.

Satan exercises no power independently of God. Nothing happens without God willing it to happen before the world was made. So, as Robert H. Mounce points out, 'In the final analysis the powers of evil serve the purposes of God. The coalition between the beast and his allies will continue until the words of God—the prophecies leading up to the overthrow of Antichrist—are fulfilled.'[7] It is a perfect example of the truth of Psalm 76:10, 'Surely the wrath of man shall praise You.'

In verse 18 the angel ends his explanation of the vision of the great harlot by reminding John that her influence is worldwide. She is the 'great city which reigns over the kings of the earth.' Cities are places of bright lights, fancy food, sinful pleasures and comfortable living. They are sinful man's attempt to replicate the good life of heaven on earth. Let Christians beware 'that great city' and its sinful charms. Flirting with the world and its enticements is the beginning of backsliding. Men succumb in private long before they fall in public. Let us heed the simple yet profound exhortation of our beloved Lord: 'Do not lay up for yourselves treasures on earth, where moth and rust destroy and where thieves break in and steal; but lay up for yourselves treasures in heaven, where neither moth nor rust destroys and where thieves do not break in and steal. For where your treasure is, there your heart will be also' (Matthew 6:19–21; cf. Colossians 3:1–3).

So, says Thomas Guthrie (1803–1873), Scottish minister and social reformer, 'If you find yourself loving any pleasure more than your prayers, any book better than the Bible, any house better than the house of the Lord, any table better than the Lord's table, any persons better than Christ, or any indulgence better than the hope of heaven— be alarmed.'[8]

19 The destruction of Babylon the great

18:1After these things I saw another angel coming down from heaven, having great authority, and the earth was illuminated with his glory. 2And he cried mightily with a loud voice, saying, 'Babylon the great is fallen, is fallen, and has become a dwelling place of demons, a prison for every foul spirit, and a cage for every unclean and hated bird! 3For all the nations have drunk of the wine of the wrath of her fornication, the kings of the earth have committed fornication with her, and the merchants of the earth have become rich through the abundance of her luxury.'

4And I heard another voice from heaven saying, 'Come out of her, my people, lest you share in her sins, and lest you receive of her plagues. 5For her sins have reached to heaven, and God has remembered her iniquities. 6Render to her just as she rendered to you, and repay her double according to her works; in the cup which she has mixed, mix double for her. 7In the measure that she glorified herself and lived luxuriously, in the same measure give her torment and sorrow; for she says in her heart, "I sit as queen, and am no widow, and will not see sorrow." 8Therefore her plagues will come in one day—death and mourning and famine. And she will be utterly burned with fire, for strong is the Lord God who judges her.

9"The kings of the earth who committed fornication and lived luxuriously with her will weep and lament for her, when they see the smoke of her burning, 10standing at a distance for fear of her torment, saying, "Alas, alas, that great city Babylon, that mighty city! For in one hour your judgment has come."

11"And the merchants of the earth will weep and mourn over her, for no one buys their merchandise anymore: 12merchandise of gold and silver, precious stones and pearls, fine linen and purple, silk and scarlet, every kind of citron wood, every kind of object of ivory, every kind of object of most precious wood, bronze, iron, and marble; 13and cinnamon and incense, fragrant oil and frankincense, wine and oil, fine flour and wheat, cattle and sheep, horses and chariots, and bodies and souls of men. 14The fruit that your soul longed for has gone from you, and all the things which are rich and splendid have gone from you, and you shall find them no more at all. 15The merchants of these things, who became rich by her, will stand at a distance for fear of her torment, weeping and wailing, 16and saying, "Alas, alas, that great city that was clothed in fine linen, purple, and scarlet, and adorned with gold and precious stones and pearls!

17For in one hour such great riches came to nothing." Every shipmaster, all who travel by ship, sailors, and as many as trade on the sea, stood at a distance 18and cried out when they saw the smoke of her burning, saying, "What is like this great city?"

19"They threw dust on their heads and cried out, weeping and wailing, and saying, "Alas, alas, that great city, in which all who had ships on the sea became rich by her wealth! For in one hour she is made desolate."

20"Rejoice over her, O heaven, and you holy apostles and prophets, for God has avenged you on her!'

21Then a mighty angel took up a stone like a great millstone and threw it into the sea, saying, 'Thus with violence the great city Babylon shall be thrown down, and shall not be found any more. 22The sound of harpists, musicians, flutists, and trumpeters shall not be heard in you anymore. No craftsman of any craft shall be found in you anymore, and the sound of a millstone shall not be heard in you anymore. ²³The light of a lamp shall not shine in you anymore, and the voice of bridegroom and bride shall not be heard in you anymore. For your merchants were the great men of the earth, for by your sorcery all the nations were deceived. ²⁴And in her was found the blood of prophets and saints, and of all who were slain on the earth.'

¹⁹:¹After these things I heard a loud voice of a great multitude in heaven, saying, 'Alleluia! Salvation and glory and honour and power belong to the Lord our God! ²For true and righteous are His judgments, because He has judged the great harlot who corrupted the earth with her fornication; and He has avenged on her the blood of His servants shed by her.' ³Again they said, 'Alleluia! Her smoke rises up forever and ever!' ⁴And the twenty-four elders and the four living creatures fell down and worshiped God who sat on the throne, saying, 'Amen! Alleluia!' ⁵Then a voice came from the throne, saying, 'Praise our God, all you His servants and those who fear Him, both small and great!'   (Revelation 18:1–19:5)

Revelation 18 contains John's horrific description of God's destruction of Babylon the Great which the angel forecast in chapter 17:16–17: 'And the ten horns [kings] which you saw on the beast [Antichrist], these will hate the harlot [Babylon], make her desolate and naked, eat her flesh and burn her with fire. For God has put it into their hearts to fulfil His purpose, to be of one mind, and to give their kingdom to the beast, until the words of God are fulfilled.' It is important to keep this in mind as we study chapter 18. The destruction of 'the great city' which begins in Revelation 17 and is completed in Revelation 18 is one and the same. Babylon's super-prosperous worldwide and anti-Christian economic empire, whether it is run on a Capitalist or Socialist system, ultimately will be destroyed by God Almighty Himself (18:20; 19:2). It begins with Antichrist because he must first dominate the market place before he can dominate the church. So a major part of his strategy is to force 'all, both small and great, rich and poor, free and slave, to receive a mark on their right hand or on their foreheads, and that no one may buy or sell except one who has the mark or the name of the beast, or the number of his name' (13:16–17). The final destruction of Babylon, however, will occur simultaneously with that of Antichrist and the devil at the end of the world (20:10).

Something else to keep in mind is the fact that the Holy Spirit gives us more details on the destruction of Babylon than He does on the destruction of Antichrist and Satan. There are forty-seven verses devoted to the fall of Babylon (17:1–19:5) and only sixteen to the destruction of Antichrist (19:6–21), and fourteen to the destruction of Satan (20:1–15). Why? Because Christians face greater danger from the *seduction* of the world than from the *persecution* of Antichrist. Satan works through both, but it is generally agreed that he has more success with the attractions of the world than with the threats of prison or death. To quote Andrew Murray (1828–1917), a South African Dutch Reformed Church leader, 'There is nothing the Christian life suffers more from than the subtle and indescribable worldliness that comes from the cares or the possessions of this life.'[1]

Of course, another consideration is the truth that whereas worldliness does great harm to the church's life and witness, 'the blood of the martyrs is the seed of the church' as Tertullian (c. 160/70–c. 215/20, African apologist and theologian) so rightly pointed out. The church is always strongest and purest in times of persecution than in times of prosperity and complacency. Thus Babylon is an enemy more to be feared than she is.

The suddenness of Babylon's fall (vv. 1–8)

The world, under God's direction, is heading towards a totalitarian regime under Antichrist that is going to rid the world of a self-indulgent, independent consumerism, and demand absolute worship of and obedience to its new leader. The spirit of worldliness as men have always known it, will be greatly subdued before its end. The marketplace in every shape and form will be ruthlessly controlled. So the next angel who appears in chapter 18 does not deal with the manner of the harlot's destruction as predicted in chapter 17:15–18. Rather, his focus is on the suddenness of the great harlot's end at the hand of God and the different reactions of earth and heaven to it.

John says, 'After these things I saw another angel coming down from heaven, having great authority, and the earth was illuminated with his glory. And he cried mightily with a loud voice, saying, "Babylon the great is fallen, is fallen, and has become a habitation of demons, a prison for every foul spirit, and a cage for every unclean and hated bird!' (18:1–2). The final end of Babylon is still future, but it is so certain that the angel can say she is already 'fallen.' And this forecast is so important that God gives the angel a kind of divine glory that lights up the whole earth to impress on all men and women the great truth that worldliness, because it is ungodliness, is doomed. Thank God the Christian can sing:

> Saviour, since of Zion's city,
> I, through grace, a member am,
> Let the world deride or pity,
> I will glory in Thy name:
> Fading is the worldling's pleasure,
> All his boasted pomp and show;
> Solid joys and lasting treasure
> None but Zion's children know.
> 　　　　　　　　　　　　　　　　(*John Newton, 1725–1807*)

The absolute destruction of Babylon

To bring this further home, the angel describes the great world-city's desolation in three ways. He says first, that it has become 'a habitation of demons.' Everyone who loves the things of the world more than God will only have demons as their companions in eternity. Secondly, Babylon will become 'a prison for every foul spirit.' That is to say, the worldling will not only have demons as his companions, but will himself be just as foul and evil as they are. Thirdly, Babylon will become 'a cage for every unclean and hated bird.' The birds the angel has in mind are vultures and bats that commonly haunted the deserted remains of ruined cities. The language used here is very similar to the prophecies against physical Babylon in Isaiah 13:19–22 and Jeremiah 50:39–40. Decadent societies have perished only to rise again. But at the end of the world Babylon the great will be destroyed, never to rise again. Its ruins, figuratively speaking, will be haunted forever by ugly and repulsive creatures. What a dreadful end lies in store for the lovers and worshippers of riches and pleasures..

The angel then goes on to state that the reason for Babylon's irretrievable fall is her sin in corrupting all levels of human society: 'For all the nations have drunk of the wine of the wrath of her fornication (unfaithfulness to God, v. 3). Babylon has seduced countless millions of souls into worshipping things instead of God, and they must now drink 'the wine of the fierceness of His wrath' (16:19). Thus the angel goes on, 'the kings of the earth have committed fornication with her, and the merchants of the earth have become rich through the abundance of her luxury' (v. 3). In other words, multitudes have become wealthy through their worship of goods and trade. But these riches, however great, are fleeting. Someday will be payday (Matthew 16:26; 1 Timothy 6:17–19).

Worldliness must be shunned by God's people

Christians, of course, can also be taken in by the so-called good life of wealth and ease that the world has to offer. Indeed, we are living in a day when health and wealth are proclaimed by some as the birthright of every believer. It is called the 'prosperity gospel' and it has a fast-growing following all over the world. But God's people need to see the attractions of the world for what they are, and not be sucked in. Worldliness and Christianity are incompatible. To quote Billy Sunday, 'You might as well talk about a heavenly devil as talk about a worldly

Christian.'[2] Verse 4, 'And I heard another voice from heaven saying, "Come out of her, My people, lest you share in her sins, and lest you receive of her plagues."' God's call to His people to separate themselves from the evil ways of the world is repeated many times in Scripture. To His people held captive in Babylon, He said, 'Depart! Depart! Go out from there, touch no unclean thing; go out from the midst of her, be clean, you who bear the vessels of the LORD' (Isaiah 52:11). In 2 Corinthians 6:14–16 the apostle Paul applies this call to Christians: 'Do not be unequally yoked together with unbelievers. For what fellowship has righteousness with lawlessness? And what communion has light with darkness? And what accord has Christ with Belial? Or what part has a believer with an unbeliever? And what agreement has the temple of God with idols? For you are the temple of the living God. As God has said, "Come out from among them and be separate, says the Lord. Do not touch what is unclean."'

Now we must be careful here. This is not a command to withdraw physically from the world. That would be practically impossible. Nor is God ordering believers to have no social contact with worldlings or unbelievers. Rather, it is a command to keep ourselves separate from the wickedness of the world; to not be spiritually conformed to the world (Romans 12:1–2). Thus our Lord Jesus petitioned His Father, 'I do not pray that You should take them out of the world, but that You should keep them from the evil one' (John 17:15). The Christian must live in the world but not let the world live in him.

Babylon's many sins deserve just retribution
'For her sins have reached [or piled up] to heaven, and God has remembered her iniquities' (v. 5). By virtue of the fact that 'Christ died for our sins according to the Scriptures' (1 Corinthians 15:3), sinners who repent and believe in Him may receive the promise in Jeremiah 31:34, 'For I will forgive their iniquity, and their sin I will remember no more.' But when the world keeps rejecting God's grace and piling sin upon sin, God's patience will run out and He will punish men for the

sins He has accurately remembered (v. 5). Nothing is more dangerous for worldlings than to interpret God's patience and longsuffering as forgetfulness. God's purpose to purge His creation entirely of evil is firm and cannot fail. So the voice from heaven turns from speaking to God's people and addresses the angels who are assigned to minister God's justice (Matthew 13:41–42,49–50). The punishment demanded is a just retribution: 'Render to her just as she rendered to you, and repay her double according to her works; in the cup which she has mixed, mix double for her' (v. 6). It is similar to the pronouncement of divine judgment on the ancient city of Babylon in Jeremiah 50:29, 'Repay her according to her work; according to all she has done, do to her; for she has been proud against the LORD, against the Holy One of Israel.'

The cry that God should 'repay her double' does not mean that God should repay the great world-city twice as much punishment as her sins deserve. The term 'double' here does not mean a double amount, but the exact equivalent of what she has done to God. Just as a person who looks exactly like someone else is said to be his double, so the measure of God's retribution is going to be a duplicate of the measure of the harlot's sins. Likewise, when the voice from heaven requests that God's agents of justice 'mix for her double', it means to mix the exact equivalent in God's cup of wrath that she has mixed in 'the wine of … her fornication' (v. 3). This understanding of verse 6 is confirmed in verse 7 where the voice from heaven says, 'In the measure that she glorified herself and lived luxuriously, in the same measure give her torment and sorrow; for she says in her heart, "I sit as queen, and am no widow, and will not see sorrow."' The heart is the centre of one's being where one's attitudes and actions are determined. Wealth and power and pleasure tend to make worldlings believe what they want to believe: that these things exalt them to a position of supremacy where they are immune to disaster and sorrow. That is the attitude of the wicked in Psalm 10, 'The wicked boasts of his heart's desire: he blesses the greedy and renounces the LORD. His ways are always prospering …

he has said in his heart, "God has forgotten … He will never see it … You will not require an account"' (vv. 3,11,13).

But just as Babylon the great proudly imagines herself to be permanently enthroned as 'queen' above all loss and the sorrow that accompanies it, she will receive in 'one day' (the day of the Lord) what is her due: 'Therefore her plagues will come in one day—death and mourning and famine. And she will be utterly burned with fire, for strong is the Lord God who judges her' (v. 8). On the day of final judgment, the world that has lived luxuriously in its pursuit of things rather than God, will come to a sudden end together with the end of the devil's other two allies and himself. The forces of evil are not going to be destroyed in dribs and drabs. The final judgment of Babylon in chapter 18, and the judgment of the false prophet and Antichrist in chapter 19, and the judgment of the devil in chapter 20, will all occur within the relatively brief period known in Scripture as 'the day of the Lord' (Acts 2:20; 1 Thessalonians 5:2; 2 Peter 3:10). We can depend on it, 'for strong is the Lord God who judges her' (v. 8).

The wailing of the wicked over Babylon's fall

The fact that John sees various categories of people mourning the fall of Babylon does not mean that they survive her destruction. They are her devotees who have totally supported her idolatrous and wicked ways. A worldly belief-system without followers is nothing. It is just an ideology and you cannot punish and 'torment' a false belief, only those who in rebellion against God believe in it and practise it. Verses 9–20 are simply a picturesque way of showing how sad sinners are going to be when God brings an abrupt and complete end to their life of earthly luxury and pleasure. For their sinful lifestyle will pass away with the passing away of this world as we know it (2 Peter 3:10–11; 1 John 2:17). This truth is emphasised in this passage three times: 'no one buys their merchandise anymore' (v. 11); 'all the things which are rich and splendid … you shall find them no more' (v. 14); 'the great city Babylon

... shall not be found anymore' (v. 21). After the destruction of Babylon
life on earth is no more.

Three main beneficiaries are chosen to express their lamentation:
namely, the kings, the merchants and the mariners of the earth. And in
each case their sorrow is chiefly over their loss, not their sin. Moreover,
their sorrow is twofold. First, as those who gained the world but in the
process lost their souls, these worldlings are now suffering the worst
form of buyer's remorse possible. For 'what shall a man give in return
for his soul?' (Matthew 16:26, ESV). Everything they built their hopes
on for themselves and their children has gone up in smoke (vv. 9,18).
They are literally left with nothing in the next life, and that in itself is a
bitter enough pill for them to swallow. But that is only half the story,
for they have not only lost everything in this life that they thought
was worth having, but they must now face God's eternal wrath for the
ultimate heinous sin of worshipping things rather than Him (20:15).

The wailing of the rulers of the earth

'The kings of the earth who committed fornication and lived
luxuriously with her will weep and lament [lit. to wail, to beat and
cut oneself, Revelation 1:7] over her, when they see the smoke of her
burning, standing at a distance for fear of her torment, saying, "Alas,
alas, that great city Babylon, that mighty city! For in one hour your
judgment has come"' (vv. 9–10). It is a picture meant to convey a
solemn truth. The world's rulers stand afar because they fear the same
fate, as well they might, for their guilt is no less than hers. They are
partners in crime, as are the merchants and the mariners. To quote
Richard Brooks, 'All the kings, princes, rulers, governments, statesmen
and politicians who, having received power and responsibility from
God, have used it for their own ends and to exalt themselves—all
those who for the price of "votes" have abandoned or relaxed various
laws or moral standards and allowed an ever-increasing range of vile
and permissive practices—will mourn and lament. Included here is
the whole miserable business of the "state church" and the Roman

Catholic/Vatican State tie-up.'[3] In verse 8 the suddenness of Babylon's destruction is described as coming in 'one day'. This is now speeded up as her judgment is said to have come in 'one hour' (v. 10). The word 'judgment' shows that the rulers recognise the justice of Babylon's punishment.

The wailing of the merchants of the earth

'And the merchants of the earth will weep and mourn over her, for no one buys her merchandise anymore: merchandise of gold and silver, precious stones and pearls, fine linen and purple, silk and scarlet, every kind of citron wood, every kind of object of ivory, every kind of object of most precious wood, bronze, iron and marble; and cinnamon and incense, fragrant oil and frankincense, wine and oil, fine flour and wheat, cattle and sheep, horses and chariots, and bodies and souls of men' (vv. 11–13). Here we are given a list of just some of the things worldlings have always treasured, and for which they have been prepared to exchange their immortal souls. The trading, however, is not merely in things but also in persons ('bodies and souls of men'), whom the merchants have treated without any compunction as commodities to be bought and sold. They have bought and sold slaves. Verse 14 is addressed directly to the great world-city of Babylon, 'the fruit that your soul longed for [lit. lusted for] has gone from you, and all the things which are rich and splendid have gone from you, and you shall find them no more.' They have been burned up in a cosmic conflagration (vv. 8–9,18; 2 Peter 3:10).

Both the merchants and their goods will be 'gone' from the earth. No wonder they will be given to much weeping and wailing: 'The merchants of these things, who became rich by her, will stand at a distance for fear of her torment, weeping and wailing, and saying, "Alas, alas, that great city that was clothed in fine linen, purple, and scarlet, and adorned with gold and precious stones and pearls. For in one hour such great riches came to nothing' (vv. 15–17). The weeping and wailing of the merchants of the earth matches that of the kings of the earth. In 'one hour' all they have worked for has come to nothing.

The wailing of the mariners

'And every shipmaster, all who travel by ship, sailors, and as many as trade on the sea, stood at a distance and cried out when they saw the smoke of her burning, saying, "What is like this great city?" They threw dust on their heads and cried out, weeping and wailing, and saying, "Alas, alas, that great city, in which all, who had ships on the sea became rich by her wealth! For in one hour she is made desolate"' (vv. 17–19). For the third time the suddenness and completeness of Babylon's destruction in the final judgment is announced amidst the weeping and wailing of those who, having grown wealthy through Babylon's markets, are now 'desolate'.

Verse 20 now turns to the response of God's people to the judgment of Babylon. Their citizenship is in heaven and not on earth, so they are not to share the grief of the kings and the merchants and the mariners of the earth. Rather, they are to rejoice in it, for it vindicates the justice of Almighty God. He has rendered to Babylon exactly what she has rendered to His saints. The exhortation of verse 20 is addressed to the church as a whole, and so the better manuscripts read: 'Rejoice over her, O heaven, and you saints and apostles and prophets' (ESV). And they are to rejoice, the voice says, 'for God has avenged you on her!' This is not a vindictive charge. It is heaven's desire that justice be done, for Christians have been robbed, raped and enslaved by the devotees of Babylon, and these wrongs must be requited.

The end of Babylon

'Then a mighty angel took up a stone like a great millstone and threw it into the sea, saying, "Thus with violence the great city of Babylon shall be thrown down, and shall not be found anymore"' (v. 21). The throwing of a great millstone into the sea is heaven's final picture of the total and irrevocable destruction of Babylon the Great. It is a striking symbolic act patterned after another acted parable. In Jeremiah 51:60–64 we read that 'Jeremiah wrote in a book all the evil that would come upon Babylon [the ancient city] … and Jeremiah said to Seraiah, "When you arrive in Babylon … and read all these words … that you shall tie a stone to it and throw it into the Euphrates. Then you shall say, Thus Babylon shall sink and not rise from the catastrophe that I [the Lord] will bring upon her."'

Likewise, John is now shown that the world as a means of seducing men away from the sole worship of the true and living God is coming to an instant end. Six times the phrase 'shall not be found/heard in you anymore' occurs: 'Thus with violence the great city Babylon shall be thrown down, and shall not be found anymore' (v. 21). It will be irretrievably lost. 'The sound of harpists, musicians, flutists, and trumpeters shall not be heard in you anymore' (v. 22). All music and entertainment that is not glorifying to God will cease forever. There will be music and harps and choirs in heaven, all joyfully engaged in the worship and praise of God, but no music or singing of any kind in hell. Again, 'No craftsman of any craft shall be found in you anymore, and the sound of a millstone shall not be heard in you anymore' (v. 22). The creation of all those things that have made life on earth more comfortable and efficient and beautiful will come to an end: no more furniture, tools, modes of transport or paintings or sculptures, etc.

Verse 23, 'And the light of a lamp shall not shine in you anymore.' There will be total darkness in hell (Matthew 22:13; 25:30). 'And the voice of bridegroom and bride shall not be heard in you anymore.' Even marital bliss will be absent in hell, for there will be no love in hell, only hate. Verse 23 again, 'For your merchants were the great men of the earth, for by your sorcery all the nations were deceived.' That is to say, the rich men of the earth took the place of God as everyone imitated them. The luxury of their lifestyle bewitched whole nations like a bird mesmerized by the spell of a snake, and only the end of worldly things will end the spell of worldliness.

The supreme reason for Babylon's fall, however, is given in verse 24: 'And in her was found the blood of prophets and saints, and of all who were slain on the earth.' The loss of all life from unnatural causes can be traced to worldliness (17:6). Whether it is due to the lust for power or money or sexual pleasure or drugs or the desire to get rid of unwanted critics (prophets and saints), murder and war are the seductions of the secular world. This sin caps all Babylon's sins, for to take the life of another human being is to contemptuously disregard their creation in the image of God and usurp the power of God who alone has the prerogative to end a person's life (Genesis 1:27; 4:8–10).

The exultation in heaven over Babylon's fall

In chapter 19:1–5 heaven now responds to the exhortation to rejoice over the fall of Babylon, 'for God has avenged you of her!' (18:20). First, the angels join in a mighty thanksgiving: 'After these things I heard a loud voice of a great multitude in heaven saying, "Alleluia! Salvation and glory and honour and power belong to the Lord our God!"' (v. 1). It is a song of praise and thanksgiving. It begins with a Hebrew word of praise that is transliterated into the Greek text as well as our English New Testament. The word 'Alleluia' (Hallelujah, ESV) means 'Praise JAH [or JEHOVAH]'. It is always translated in the Old Testament as 'Praise the LORD', and occurs 24 times in the book of Psalms. The Hebrew word 'Alleluia', however, is found only here (vv. 1,3,4,6) in the English Bible. It shows that its use was carried over into Christian worship.

The reason for the praise is to assert that 'Salvation and glory and honour and power' belong to God and not the world-city of Babylon that men have worshipped: 'For true and righteous are His judgments, because He has judged the great harlot who corrupted the earth with her fornication [unfaithfulness to God]; and He has avenged on her the blood of His servants shed by her' (v. 2). The judgments of God are no less to be praised than His salvation, for the two belong together.

First, there can be no salvation for sinners unless God in His great love endures through His incarnate Son the judgment deserved by those sinners who by faith trust Christ for salvation and righteousness. 'Salvation is of the LORD' (Jonah 2:9; 2 Corinthians 5:18–21). Secondly, God's judgment is His righteous act of punishing impenitent sinners, and removing both them and the devil as the source of all the discord and destruction that has plagued His universe. So God's judgment is a part of His salvation.

Verse 3, 'Again they said, "Alleluia! Her smoke rises up forever and ever!"' The great harlot's destruction in hell is eternal. Never again will human beings worship created things. The worship of the angels is joined by the redeemed: 'And the twenty-four elders and the four living creatures fell down and worshipped God who sat on the throne, saying, "Amen! Alleluia!"' (v. 4). The twenty-four elders represent all the redeemed of mankind and the four living creatures the whole of God's renewed creation, and together they praise God for His just judgment of evil. Their 'Amen' expresses their agreement with the angel's praise of God. It is another Hebrew word transliterated straight into our Greek and English New Testament meaning, 'Let it be so.' And their 'Alleluia' takes up the Alleluia of the angels. For all who are in heaven, whether great or small, are there by the grace of God alone, and have need therefore to praise God for His so great salvation: 'Then a voice came from the throne, saying, "Praise our God, all you His servants and those who fear Him, both small and great!"' (v. 5). They are to praise Him without exception or discrimination, for all have received the same great salvation whether prophets, apostles or saints.

That is the glory of heaven! All distinctions are lost sight of as angels and archangels, saints and apostles count themselves blessed to be God's servants and revere Him in sheer gratitude. May you and I be numbered among that happy throng, because by God's grace we have obeyed the injunction in 1 John 5:21, 'Little children, keep yourselves from idols.' For 'nothing is more contrary to a heavenly hope than an earthly heart.'[4]

20 The church's Bridegroom and Victor Emmanuel

19:6And I heard, as it were, the voice of a great multitude, as the sound of many waters and as the sound of mighty thunderings, saying, 'Alleluia! For the Lord God Omnipotent reigns! 7Let us be glad and rejoice and give Him glory, for the marriage of the Lamb has come, and His wife has made herself ready.' 8And to her it was granted to be arrayed in fine linen, clean and bright, for the fine linen is the righteous acts of the saints.

9Then he said to me, 'Write: "Blessed are those who are called to the marriage supper of the Lamb!"' And he said to me, 'These are the true sayings of God.' 10And I fell at his feet to worship him. But he said to me, 'See that you do not do that! I am your fellow servant, and of your brethren who have the testimony of Jesus. Worship God! For the testimony of Jesus is the spirit of prophecy.'

11Now I saw heaven opened, and behold, a white horse. And He who sat on him was called Faithful and True, and in righteousness He judges and makes war. 12His eyes were like a flame of fire, and on His head were many crowns. He had a name written that no one knew except Himself. 13He was clothed with a robe dipped in blood, and His name is called The Word of God. 14And the armies in heaven, clothed in fine linen, white and clean, followed Him on white horses. 15Now out of His mouth goes a sharp sword, that with it He should strike the nations. And He Himself will rule them with a rod of iron. He Himself treads the winepress of the fierceness and wrath of Almighty God. [16]And He has on His robe and on His thigh a name written:

KING OF KINGS

AND LORD OF LORDS.

[17]Then I saw an angel standing in the sun; and he cried with a loud voice, saying to all the birds that fly in the midst of heaven, 'Come and gather together for the supper of the great God, [18]that you may eat the flesh of kings, the flesh of captains, the flesh of mighty men, the flesh of horses and of those who sit on them, and the flesh of all people, free and slave, both small and great.'

[19]And I saw the beast, the kings of the earth, and their armies, gathered together to make war against Him who sat on the horse and against His army. [20]Then the beast was captured, and with him the false prophet who worked signs in his presence, by which he deceived those who received the mark of the beast and those who worshiped his image. These two were cast alive into the lake of fire burning with brimstone. [21]And the rest were killed with the sword which proceeded from the mouth of Him who sat on the horse. And all the birds were filled with their flesh.

(Revelation 19:6–21)

We are still studying the sixth major vision in the book of Revelation (chapters 17 to 20). These four chapters unveil the final destruction of all Christ's enemies. So far we have looked at the destruction of 'Babylon the great, the mother of harlots', the world-city that seduces 'all the nations' into giving their worship to creaturely things rather than to their Creator (17:1–19:5). God's people will never again be tempted by worldliness ('the lust of the flesh, the lust of the eyes, and the pride of life', 1 John 2:16).

In chapter 19:6–21 we come to the destruction of Satan's two main allies: the beast from the sea who is Antichrist, and the beast from the land who is the false prophet. It is a passage containing two contrasting pictures. The first picture is of a wedding, and the second is of a war. There may be some cynics who will say that they do not see any difference at all between the two, but in this instance there very definitely is. This is the greatest wedding feast of all time, celebrating a marriage of perfect love and purity between Christ and His church which will last forever. The war described here is the greatest battle of all time, ridding God's universe forever of all those powers, seen and unseen, that have brought nothing but ruin and discord to His creation. The marriage supper of the Lamb and the Lamb's war against the armies of hell are both part of God's eternal purpose of grace that we now see moving to its final phase.

The marriage supper of the Lamb

'And I heard, as it were, the voice of a great multitude' (v. 6). Previously, all the angels in heaven had sung their Alleluia chorus to God celebrating the righteousness and finality of God's judgment of 'the great harlot who corrupted the earth with her fornication', for 'He has avenged on her the blood of His servants shed by her … and her smoke rises up forever and ever!' (19:1–3). But now John hears the voice of someone not identified (presumably an angel who speaks of 'our God') calling on the redeemed in heaven to join in: 'Then a voice came from the throne, saying, "Praise our God, all you His servants and those who fear Him, both small and great!"' (v. 5). Together, the 'great multitude' of angels and the 'great multitude' of the redeemed (7:9) continue the anthem of praise to God. And so great is their combined volume that the apostle struggles to find suitable metaphors to convey the extremely powerful but musical sound. All he can say is, 'And I heard as it were the voice of a great multitude, as the sound of many waters, and as the sound of mighty thunderings' (v. 6).

Praise for the sovereign grace of God

As with the three previous 'Alleluias', the stanza begins in verse 6 with

another 'Alleluia' which brings this mighty original Hallelujah Chorus
to a stupendous climax: 'Alleluia! For the Lord God Omnipotent
reigns!' God has been ruling over affairs on earth from the beginning,
they say. Though He has permitted evil, He has always been in
complete control of world affairs. He has been working out His
purpose to redeem creation from the curse of sin: to gather out an
innumerable number of people for Himself, and to restore the earth to
an even greater splendour than it originally had. Heaven's Hallelujah
Chorus, therefore, has two stanzas separated by the short interjection
of verse 5. The main stanza in verses 2–4 does not celebrate God's
mercy but His judgment; His destruction of the forces of evil which
seek to counter His good purpose for creation. The judgment of evil,
therefore, is not something for which heaven feels the least sympathy
or embarrassment. To quote Derek Thomas, 'The sights and sounds of
God's wrath upon Babylon bring forth joyful strains of worship from
the hosts of heaven. It is an indication of how far removed we often
are from the biblical testimony to the character of God that we can
so often recoil in horror at the graphic portrayals of God's wrath. But
heavenly saints see things differently.'[1] Indeed, to the eyes of heaven,
evil is something repulsively ugly, outrageously insolent and fully
deserving of divine punishment.

On the other hand, our Lord said, 'There is joy in the presence of
the angels of God over one sinner who repents' (Luke 15:10). So, with
good reason, the second stanza of heaven's Hallelujah Chorus turns
from praise for God's climactic act of damnation (v. 3) to His grand,
climactic act of salvation: the marriage in heaven of the church to her
Saviour, which will coincide with His creation of 'a new heaven and a
new earth' to be their perfect eternal home (21:1–2). It is truly a cause
for great celebration: 'Let us be glad and rejoice and give Him glory,
for the marriage of the Lamb has come, and His wife has made herself
ready (v. 7).

The preparation of the bride

The Lamb, of course, is Jesus Christ, 'the Lamb of God who takes away the sin of the world' (John 1:29). And the Bridegroom is called 'the Lamb', because He offered His life on the cross as an atoning sacrifice to ransom His bride from the slave-market of sin, thereby awakening within our forlorn hearts a responsive and grateful love to Him (1 John 4:9–10,19). Now to fully appreciate this imagery we need to remind ourselves of the three stages a Jewish couple had to observe before their marriage could be consummated. The first stage was the *betrothal* which was much more binding than engagement is with us. In the betrothal ceremony the terms of the marriage contract were accepted by the couple and they were legally pronounced husband and wife (Matthew 1:18–19). Under that analogy Paul tells the Corinthians, 'I have betrothed you to one husband, that I may present you as a chaste virgin to Christ' (2 Corinthians 11:2). At conversion they were spiritually married to Christ in God's eyes.

The betrothal ceremony was then followed by a *period of separation* during which the bridegroom was given time to pay the wedding dowry to the father of the bride and get everything ready for his bride to move into their new home. You remember that Jacob, because he was penniless, had to serve Laban seven years before he could have the hand of his daughter Rachel in marriage. That is how he paid the dowry owing to her father. Only when the dowry was paid could the bridegroom come to his father-in-law's house and escort his bride to her new home for the *wedding feast* and their life-long union under one roof (Genesis 24:51–53; 29:18–21). This was the third stage of the process of getting married in the Middle East, and that is the symbolism behind the words in verses 7 and 9. The time has come for the Lamb's wife to be taken to the Bridegroom's home to begin the celebration of 'the marriage supper of the Lamb' (v. 9). The dowry has been paid by God to God. Thus Paul can speak of Christians as 'the church of God which He purchased with His own blood' (Acts 20:28). Marriage is a common metaphor used in Scripture to describe

God's relationship with His redeemed people (Isaiah 54:5; Hosea
2:19f; Matthew 25:1–13; Mark 2:18–20; John 3:29; 2 Corinthians 11:2;
Ephesians 5:25–32). Moreover, the celebration will last forever, for it
will be a union of everlasting love and perfection in which Jesus Christ
and His bride will find ever-increasing joy in each other.

Naturally, for this great event the church wants to be as attractive
and as pleasing to the eye of her Saviour as she can be. So as she waits
on earth for His return, she makes 'herself ready' (v. 7). But for the
church this is not something she can achieve by herself. She needs
divine help. So verse 8 says, 'And to her it was *granted* to be arrayed
in fine linen, clean and bright, for the fine linen is the righteous acts
of the saints' (italics added). As elsewhere in Scripture, the work of
sanctification or being made holy is a process in which God's people,
in cooperation with Him, are enabled to 'put to death the deeds of the
body' (Romans 8:13). In Philippians 2:12–13 Paul exhorts Christians
to 'work out your own salvation with fear and trembling; for it is God
who works in you both to will and to do for His good pleasure.' So
though these 'righteous acts' are performed by the saints they do not
constitute a gown of self-righteousness; they do not contribute to
their justification. The saints are justified (i.e. declared righteous with
Christ's imputed righteousness) by faith alone, but the faith which
justifies is never alone; it is always followed by righteous acts made
possible by God's Spirit. The perfect righteousness of Jesus Christ
which is graciously reckoned to us in our justification by faith should
be increasingly manifested through the sanctifying work of the Holy
Spirit who transforms us 'into the same image [of Christ] from glory to
glory' (2 Corinthians 3:18).

The blessedness of the marriage supper of the Lamb
'Then he [the angel] said to me, "Write: Blessed are those who are
called to the marriage supper of the Lamb!" And he said to me, "These
are the true sayings of God"' (v. 9). The bride (or church) of Christ is
made up of those whom God has effectually 'called' and have therefore

responded by coming to Christ and believing in His name. They are 'the called, chosen and faithful' ones in chapter 17:14 who are with the Lamb when He returns to earth and overcomes the harlot, the beast, the false prophet and the devil (1 Thessalonians 4:13–18; Revelation 19:14,20; 20:10). And the blessing described here is the blessing that will be theirs when at last they are with Christ in glory, never to be separated from His visible presence again. How wonderful it will be when we see Him face to face and begin to taste the endless delights of being in His presence, and enjoying the intimacy of His love and the beauty of His holiness. On that day and forever afterwards we will be taken up with our Beloved. We will have eyes only for Him, 'chief among ten thousand' (Songs 5:10).

No one captures the experience better than C.H. Spurgeon: 'We dare not say that our Lord will love us more than He loves us now, but He will indulge His love for us more; He will manifest it more, we shall see more of it, we shall understand it better … This marriage feast will be the feast, the triumph of love … The provisions made by Him for our enjoyment will astonish us … It will have delights for us, of which we have no conception; and the pleasures we anticipate in it will be far higher and more abundant than our highest expectations have ever gone. We shall have a provision made for us which will befit, not our rank and condition, but the rank and condition, the greatness, the magnificence of a glorious God.'[2] The fact that the angel goes on to say, 'These are the true sayings of God' may at first seem unnecessary. But a church under persecution needs to be sure that this blessedness can be relied on, because these are the words of God who cannot lie (Numbers 23:19).

As Christians we need to ponder this far more than we do. We think of heaven, but we seldom picture it as the unending, joyful wedding feast of Christ and His church. Perhaps we have brushed it aside as being more sensual than spiritual. But it is something that the saints of God have looked forward to centuries before Christ came: 'I will

greatly rejoice in the LORD, my soul shall be joyful in my God; for
He has clothed me with the garments of salvation, He has covered
me with the robe of righteousness ... as a bride adorns herself with
jewels' (Isaiah 61:10). Our Lord Himself attached importance to it
by beginning His public ministry and performing His first miracle
at a wedding feast in Cana of Galilee (John 2:1–11). He referred to it
again when he said, 'I tell you, many will come from east and west
and recline at table with Abraham, Isaac and Jacob in the kingdom of
heaven' (Matthew 8:11); and then again at the institution of the Lord's
Supper when at the end He said, 'I will not drink of this fruit of the
vine from now on until that day when I drink it new with you in My
Father's kingdom' (Matthew 26:29). That heavenly wine will be endless
heavenly joy.

Worship is due solely to God

John is totally overawed at the thought. So much so, that he
momentarily forgets that it is only an angel who has just spoken to
him. True, the words are the words of God; but the speaker is only
an angel. John, however, is so overcome with the prospect of being at
the marriage supper of the Lamb, that he confesses, 'And I fell at his
feet to worship him' (v. 10). These are heady experiences, and John is
going to make the same mistake again for the same reason in chapter
22:8–9. But both here and there the angel immediately reproves him,
saying, 'See that you do not do that! I am your fellow servant, and of
your brethren who have the testimony of Jesus. Worship God! For the
testimony of Jesus is the spirit of prophecy' (v. 10). 'Prophecy' here is
the declaration of the message that God has entrusted to His servants,
and the spirit or heart of all prophecy is to witness to Jesus and His
power to save sinners. So whether the servant is an angel or a man,
his job is to declare the message of Christ that God has entrusted to
him, and not call attention to himself. Any attempt to glorify a servant
of God who is a mere creature, is totally inconsistent with the spirit
of prophecy, which is to witness to Jesus. False worship is a grave sin

which should be firmly resisted as exemplified by our Lord and Peter and Paul and Barnabas (Matthew 4:8–10; Acts 10:25–26; 14:11–18).

Henry Martyn (1781–1812) was a missionary to India and Persia with outstanding linguistic gifts. Within seven years he translated the New Testament into Hindustani and Persian. He longed that the name of Jesus should be honoured by all, and we are told that he was 'cut to the quick by any insult to Jesus. Someone said that Prince Abbas Mirza of Persia had killed so many Russian Christians that Christ from the fourth heaven reached up and took hold of Mohammed's skirt to entreat him to desist. "I was cut to the soul at this blasphemy", said Martyn. When asked what it was that was so offensive, he replied: "I could not endure existence if Jesus was not glorified; it would be hell to me, if He were to be always thus dishonoured." When the hearers were astonished and Martyn was again asked why, he continued: "If anyone pluck out your eyes, there is no saying why you feel pain; it is feeling. It is because I am one with Christ that I am thus dreadfully wounded."'[3]

Victor Emmanuel riding forth to war

'Now I saw heaven opened, and behold, a white horse. And He who sat on him was called Faithful and True' (v. 11). What John now sees is a picture of Christ returning to earth to destroy His enemies. Almost everything that is said of Christ in verses 11–16 can be found elsewhere in Scripture except the symbol of Him riding on a 'white horse'. The usual picture is of Jesus returning on the clouds of heaven (1:7; Matthew 24:30). But here the symbolism changes to a white horse to accentuate the triumph of His return, for a horse in Scripture is not a beast of burden, but an animal of war, and 'white' is the colour of victory.

The Rider's first name is Faithful and True
John's attention is quickly diverted away from the horse to its rider who is now described under four names. The first name is 'Faithful and True' (cf. 3:14). Our Lord is called 'Faithful' because He fulfils

every promise He has made to His people. Accordingly Paul can say, 'The Son of God, Jesus Christ, who was preached among you by us … was not Yes and No, but in Him was Yes. For all the promises of God in Him are Yes, and in Him Amen' (2 Corinthians 1:19–20). There is nothing vacillating about Jesus Christ. No matter how many promises God has made they are, or will be, fulfilled in Christ. He is faithful. We can rely absolutely on Him to bring God's purposes to pass.

And He is called 'True', because He is always true to His righteous character. So John goes on to say, 'and in righteousness He judges and makes war' (v. 11). There is no lust for power or spirit of vindictiveness in dealing with His enemies (see Isaiah 11:4). The basis of our Lord's righteous and just judgments is grounded in the fact that 'His eyes were like a flame of fire, and on His head were many crowns' (v. 12; cf. 1:14; 2:18). The eyes of fire probe to the innermost depths of every human being to make sure no one is destroyed in error. Nothing can be hidden from Him. The many 'diadems' on His head are a symbol of His unassailable, universal sovereignty that is now about to be exercised in the final judgment that overthrows all the wicked on earth.

The Rider's second name is unknown

'He had a name written that no one knew except Himself' (v. 12). A person's name stands for who he is. The fact, then, that Jesus has an unknown name in addition to the many He already has, means that there is something about Him that has *not yet been fully revealed*. So however much we may humbly claim to know about Jesus Christ, this name is telling us that there is something that has yet to be revealed to us by Him. Thus our Lord's return is called in the New Testament not only 'His coming' but 'His revelation' in which new depths of His person and work will be unveiled to us on that day (2 Thessalonians 1:7; 1 Peter 4:13). Only He knows the fullness and the greatness of His own person, and so it is only on the last day when He comes back to earth and we all see Him as He is, that we shall know Him as fully as a finite being can know Him (1 John 3:2–3). This is a hope that should make us eagerly look forward to the day when Jesus Christ returns and fully reveals Himself to us.

The Rider's third name is The Word of God

'He was clothed with a robe dipped in blood, and His name is called The Word of God' (v. 13). It is the only place in Scripture where the full title 'The Word of God' is given to Jesus. At the beginning of John's Gospel He is called 'the Word' and we are told that 'the Word was God', but only here is He called 'The Word of God' explicitly. And by this name Jesus is being identified as the One who is the full and final revelation of God. Just as we reveal who we are by speaking, so God has revealed who He is by speaking to us through Christ, the 'Word [who] became flesh and dwelt among us … full of grace and truth' (John 1:14). Not everything has been revealed about God in nature and Scripture, but what has been revealed has come to its fullness in the incarnation of God in Jesus Christ. He has nothing more to say to us until He returns. To quote Philip Edgcumbe Hughes, 'As the Word of God the Son is both the revealer of the divine mind and also the agent of the divine will. Since the word of God never fails to effect what it decrees (cf. Isaiah 55:11), it is through Him who is the eternal Word that the will of God is brought to pass not only in creation but also in re-creation (2 Corinthians 4:6) and in judgment (Acts 17:31).'[4]

The Word of God never fails to bring about what He commands. This is further elaborated on in verse 15: 'Now out of His mouth goes a sharp sword, that with it He should strike the nations. And He Himself will rule them with a rod of iron.' When Jesus our Victor Emmanuel returns there is not going to be a protracted battle with the enemies of God. Instead the prophecy in Isaiah 11:4 concerning Him will come to pass: 'He shall strike the earth with the rod of His mouth, and with the breath of His lips He shall slay the wicked.' Paul says the same thing in 2 Thessalonians 2:8, 'Then the lawless one will be revealed, whom the Lord will consume with the breath of His mouth and destroy with the brightness of His coming.' In fulfilment of the messianic promise in Psalm 2:9, 'You shall break them with a rod of iron: You shall dash them in pieces like a potter's vessel', Christ will slay Antichrist and the 'nations' who follow him with a word from His mouth.

The theme of the wicked's final and utter destruction continues: 'He Himself treads the winepress of the fierceness and wrath of Almighty God' (v. 15). This picture of Christ is the explanation of the first half of verse 13, 'He was clothed with a robe dipped in blood', and returns to the picture of 'the vine of the earth [being thrown] into the great winepress of the wrath of God' given in chapter 14:17–20. Here, however, our Lord Jesus Christ is said to be the One who treads and crushes the grapes of the earth which are 'fully ripe' with wickedness. As a result the robe of The Word of God is soaked with the blood of His enemies and not with His own blood which He shed for penitent sinners on the cross, as some commentators suggest. It is blood splattered on His robe from treading 'the winepress of the fierceness and wrath of Almighty God.' He is the same person predicted in Isaiah 63:2–6 who is asked, 'Why is Your apparel red, and Your garments like one who treads in the winepress?' And His response is, 'I have trodden the winepress alone ... I have trodden them in My anger, and trampled them in My fury; their blood is sprinkled upon My garments, and I have stained all My robes. For the day of vengeance is in My heart, and the year of My redeemed has come.' Once again, as seen repeatedly in Scripture, the Day of the Lord when Christ comes as a thief in the night, will be the day on which judgment and salvation coincide (Matthew 13:40–43,49–50; 2 Thessalonians 1:6–10).

Verse 14, 'And the armies in heaven, clothed in fine linen, white and clean, followed Him on white horses.' These are the followers of The Word of God, and their linen is 'white and clean', because He has delivered them from sin (Philippians 3:20–21; 2 Thessalonians 1:10; 1 John 3:2). They are sinless, and they ride on 'white horses' like His because they are riding with Him to victory over the international forces of Antichrist. Notice, they have no weapons and their robes are not bloodied. The battle is won solely by Christ with the sharp sword that proceeds out of His mouth (vv. 15,21).

His fourth name is King of kings and Lord of lords

'And He has on His robe and on His thigh a name written' (v. 16). The name is not written on His thigh itself, but on that part of His robe that hangs over His thigh. And the name on His robe is 'King of kings and Lord of lords.' This name has already been mentioned in chapter 17:14 and it declares that Christ's lordship is absolute and His sovereignty invincible. The doom of His enemies is inescapable as the rest of the chapter now makes clear. Antichrist has had his hour on the world's stage, but the time has now come for his eternal destruction. 'Then I saw an angel standing in the sun [i.e. at the highest point in the heavens]; and he cried with a loud voice, saying to all the birds that fly in the midst of heaven, "Come and gather together for the supper of the great God, that you may eat the flesh of kings, the flesh of captains, the flesh of mighty men, the flesh of horses and of those who sit on them, and the flesh of all people, free and slave, both small and great"' (vv. 17–18). The language here embraces every living ungodly person in the world on the last day of history. As Isaiah foretold 'with the breath of His mouth He shall slay the wicked' (11:4). The scene John saw is one of worldwide carnage in which all who have despised God's law and rejected His mercy in Christ will perish on the last day, the leaders as well as their followers. Figuratively speaking, the corpses and the carcasses of all the vanquished will make a great banquet provided by God for birds of prey. This is not to be taken literally, for everything will be burnt up in the conflagration that takes place at the end of the world (2 Peter 3:7,10–13).

Our Lord used this same figure of speech when He predicted this mass slaughter of the wicked at His return: 'Two men will be in the field: the one will be taken [like Lot's wife and destroyed] and the other left [he will survive like Lot]. And they answered and said to Him, "Where Lord?" [when Jesus returns, where should they expect Him to appear? Would it be in Galilee or Jerusalem or where?] So He said to them, "Wherever the body is there the eagles will be gathered together"' (Luke 17:36–37; Matthew 24:28). In other words, it will be a worldwide event. 'Every eye' (1:7) will see the returning Christ destroying the wicked and saving the righteous. Ezekiel 39:17–20 also depicts the final destruction of God's enemies as a worldwide battle in which the flesh of the wicked is given to birds and beasts to devour.

The beast, the false prophet and their allies destroyed

Verses 19–20 now describe the battle itself. 'And I saw the beast, the kings of the earth, and their armies, gathered together to make war against Him who sat on the horse and against His army. Then the beast was captured, and with him the false prophet who worked signs in his presence, by which he deceived those who received the mark of the beast and those who worshipped his image. These two were cast alive into the lake of fire burning with brimstone.' This is another picture of the battle of Armageddon that brings the world to an end (16:16). Preceding that battle, we were told that demons went forth from the mouth of the beast and the false prophet to gather the kings of the earth and their armies together 'to the battle of that great day of God Almighty' (16:13–14). Antichrist and the false prophet, as demon-possessed agents of Satan, will be cast into hell straightaway without a trial, for they have already received their sentence at our Lord's first coming (John 12:31; 16:11). That is the meaning behind their being 'cast alive into the lake of fire burning with brimstone.'

That will not be the case for their human followers: 'And the rest were killed with the sword that proceeded from the mouth of Him who sat on the horse. And all the birds were filled with their flesh.' In other words, the wicked who are alive at Christ's return will first have to suffer the anguish of physical death, and then be resurrected in a body of shame to stand before God and answer for all their sins, before they are sentenced to everlasting torment (20:11–14). One by one, the King of kings and Lord of lords is portrayed as destroying the forces of evil in fulfilment of His promise to grant eternal life and rest to His people (Matthew 11:28–30; John 10:26–30). Only the devil is left, and his destruction at the same time as the beast and the false prophet will be described in chapter 20:1–10. For all three and their allies it will be 'everlasting destruction' (2 Thessalonians 1:9; Revelation 19:3).

Once more, under the inspiration of the Spirit of truth, John has shown us how real and terrifying is the final destiny of those who do not know God and do not obey the gospel of our Lord Jesus Christ (2 Thessalonians 1:8–9). The God whose mercy endures forever is also the God whose wrath burns forever. Thus Robert H. Mounce says, 'The two nouns translated "wrath" or "anger" are found thirteen times in chapters 6 through 19. Any view of God which eliminates judgment and His hatred of sin in the interest of an emasculated doctrine of sentimental affection finds no support in the strong and virile realism of the Apocalypse.'[5]

The good news, however, is that men and women do not have to personally bear the just punishment their sins deserve. God has offered a way out by sending His only Son to bear the guilt and punishment of our sins if we will believe in Jesus and receive Him as our Lord and Saviour. Jesus Christ, on the cross, took the place of every penitent believer and endured the burning wrath of God's judgment against their sin (2 Corinthians 5:18–21; Galatians 3:13; 1 Peter 1:18–19; 3:18). For God to be just, sin must be punished; either in Jesus Christ, God's innocent sin-bearer, or in us if we remain impenitent sinners. God is holy love. It is only when sinners refuse God's forgiveness that they must bear the penalty for their wickedness.

Come to Jesus Christ in repentance and faith while there is still time to do so (Isaiah 55:6–7; 2 Corinthians 6:2). Do not procrastinate if you are not part of Christ's bride, the church. The road to hell is paved with good intentions. Why be an offering at 'the supper of the

great God' when you can be a participant in the 'marriage supper of
the Lamb'?

Lo! He comes, with clouds descending,
  Once for favoured sinners slain:
Thousand thousand saints attending
  Swell the triumph of His train:
    Hallelujah!
  Jesus now shall ever reign.

Every eye shall now behold Him
  Robed in dreadful majesty;
Those who set at nought and sold Him,
  Pierced, and nailed Him to the tree,
    Deeply wailing,
  Shall the true Messiah see.

Every island, sea, and mountain,
  Heaven and earth, shall flee away;
All who hate Him must, confounded,
  Hear the trump proclaim the day:
    Come to judgment!
  Come to judgment! come away!

Yea, amen! Let all adore Thee,
  High on Thine eternal throne:
Saviour, take the power and glory,
  Claim the Kingdom for Thine own:
    O come quickly,
  Hallelujah! Come, Lord, come!   (*Charles Wesley, 1707–88*).

21 Satan bound for a thousand years[1]

^{20:1}Then I saw an angel coming down from heaven, having the key to the bottomless pit and a great chain in his hand. ²He laid hold of the dragon, that serpent of old, who is the Devil and Satan, and bound him for a thousand years; ³and he cast him into the bottomless pit, and shut him up, and set a seal on him, so that he should deceive the nations no more till the thousand years were finished. But after these things he must be released for a little while.

⁴And I saw thrones, and they sat on them, and judgment was committed to them. Then I saw the souls of those who had been beheaded for their witness to Jesus and for the word of God, who had not worshiped the beast or his image, and had not received his mark on their foreheads or on their hands. And they lived and reigned with Christ for a thousand years. ⁵But the rest of the dead did not live again until the thousand years were finished. This is the first resurrection. ⁶Blessed and holy is he who has part in the first resurrection. Over such the second death has no power, but they shall be priests of God and of Christ, and shall reign with Him a thousand years. (Revelation 20:1–6)

Chapter 20:1–6 is undoubtedly the most difficult and most disputed passage to interpret in the book of Revelation. The whole chapter ends

the sixth main vision given to the aged apostle John which unveils
the destruction of all God's enemies. It began in chapters 17–18 with
the destruction of Babylon the great, the spirit of worldliness, the
activity of demons who seduce the world into worshipping created
things instead of God. In chapter 19 the destruction of Antichrist
and the false prophet is foretold, and now in chapter 20 John is given
a glimpse of the destruction of Satan as well as all his followers, both
the living and the dead (vv. 10–15). Although depicted separately, the
destruction of these various agents of evil will occur simultaneously at
the return of our Lord Jesus Christ who 'will consume [them] with the
breath of His mouth and destroy with the brightness of His coming'
(2 Thessalonians 2:8; see also Isaiah 11:4; Revelation 2:16; 19:15). Now
while all evangelicals agree with the fact that the final destiny of
Satan foretold in Revelation 20 is to be 'cast into the lake of fire and
brimstone' (v. 10), there is much disagreement about his situation
during the period of 'a thousand years' which is referred to six times in
verses 2–7.

The major views of the millennium

Our English term 'millennium', meaning 'a thousand years', is made
up of two Latin words: *mille*, a thousand, and *annum*, a year. Not
surprisingly, the major views of Revelation 20 are defined by an
appropriate prefix attached to the term. Basically there are four
major views of the millennium, but for the sake of simplicity they
may be reduced to two: those who believe that our Lord will return
before the millennium (historic premillennialism and dispensational
premillennialism), and those who believe that He will return after the
millennium (the postmillennial and amillennial views).

Historic and dispensational premillennialism

Historic premillennialism believes that the second coming of Christ
will be a single event after the church has gone through the great

tribulation. Dispensational premillennialism holds to a two-stage return of Jesus Christ, the first of which is to take the church out of the world before the great tribulation. Except for this difference the two views are much the same. Both teach that when the great final tribulation draws to a close, Jesus Christ will return to the world to destroy Antichrist and reign with His redeemed people (Jews and Gentiles) for literally one thousand years. Jerusalem will be His capital city and a restored temple the central place of worship for the world. During His reign the earth will experience a period of peace and prosperity predicted in the Old Testament: men will beat their swords into ploughshares, and their spears into pruning hooks; the desert will blossom as the rose, and the wolf and the lamb will feed together (Isaiah 2:4; 35:1; 65:25). Many Jews in our Lord's day expected that Jesus, as the Messiah, would usher in a 'kingdom' in which Gentile domination of the Jews would be reversed and they would experience the peace and prosperity which the prophets had predicted (Acts 1:6; Mark 10:35–37). There is no evidence in the New Testament, however, that Jesus and His apostles endorsed this misguided hope. Even Revelation 20, as we shall see below, does not describe a literal one-thousand year reign of Christ on earth from Jerusalem.

After the apostolic era, in the first half of the second century there are only two writers to whom we may point with any certainty as being premillennialists: Papias (c. 60-c. 130), Bishop of Hierapolis, who writes in extravagant language of the ten thousand-fold fruitfulness of the earth during the millennium,[2] and Justin Martyr (c. 100–165), a Christian apologist (see below). In the second half of the second century, Irenaeus (c. 175-c. 195), Bishop of Lyons, taught an earthly millennium whose benefits were exclusively for the saved, and it was through the influence of Papias, according to the historian Eusebius, that Irenaeus and many others were carried away by the same opinion. Perhaps the clearest expression of premillennial doctrine (though not necessarily the most orthodox) comes from the pen of Lactantius (c. 240-c. 320), a Christian apologist and historian. At the close of the second century and the beginning of the third the Montanists, one of the wildest sects, enthusiastically proclaimed the near approach of the millennial reign, and Tertullian (c. 160-c. 215) was the most prominent exponent of their teaching.[3]

Postmillennialism and Amillennialism

Whatever differences may distinguish these two views, the main feature that sets them apart from the two premillennial views is the fundamental conviction that Christ's second coming will occur after the millennium when He comes to judge the world and usher in a new heaven and a new earth, in which His resurrected, glorified saints will live forever. What, then, are the differences? Briefly, postmillennialism envisages the millennium as a period of history just prior to the return of Jesus when the preaching of the gospel will be widely accepted and bring about 'the conversion of the nations and the preponderance of the human race'.[4] This golden age, though not literally one thousand years long, will be a significant period of time characterised by unprecedented spiritual and material prosperity on earth. At its close Satan will be released for a little while to turn the nations against God, but the rebellion will be short-lived. Our Lord will return to destroy His enemies; raise the just and the unjust for the final judgment, and then consummate His kingdom in a new heaven and a new earth.

Postmillennialism, however, seems to run counter to the witness of the New Testament that the end-times will not see a decrease but an increase in the spread of evil and apostasy and opposition to the gospel (Matthew 24:9–13,21–22; 2 Thessalonians 2:3–4; 1 Timothy 4:1–2; Revelation 13; 20:7–9). Not only that, but if Satan's final rebellion is to be preceded by a period of worldwide revival and mass conversions, this would seem to nullify what the New Testament teaches about the imminence of the second coming. For this period of unprecedented spiritual and physical blessing has yet to come, before we can expect our Lord to return. Of course, the fact that the world will get spiritually worse as the end draws near, does not mean that the true church cannot grow stronger both numerically and spiritually at the same time. Indeed, we see it happening today in China where in spite of oppression the church is growing faster than anywhere else! Revival has always come in the darkest of times.

What, then, is the view of amillennialism? The term itself is a bit misleading, because the prefix 'a' does not mean that amillennialists do not believe in any millennium at all, but only the idea that it is a reign of Christ that takes place on earth at His return and will last a literal one thousand years. Amillennialists believe that we are living *now* in the millennium, which began with Christ's first coming and will last until His second coming. They believe that it refers to the present reign of the souls of departed Christians with Christ in heaven who by their prayers are working with Him to 'put all enemies under His feet' (1 Corinthians 15:25; Psalm 110:1). This will culminate when Christ returns to destroy Antichrist and death (2 Thessalonians 2:8; 1 Corinthians 15:26), raise both the just and the unjust for the final judgment (Acts 24:15; 10:42), and create new heavens and a new earth as the eternal abode for God and all His people (2 Peter 3:10–13; Revelation 21:1–22:4).

Amillennialism also has a long history that goes back to the apostolic era. Neither our Lord nor His apostles make any mention of the Jews returning to Jerusalem after its destruction forecast in Matthew 24; nor of the rebuilding of the temple; nor of a golden age of spiritual and material prosperity just prior to or after the second coming. Their emphases are the same as amillennialism. Turning to the early church fathers, the first Epistle of Clement (sometimes dated as early as AD 90, but not later than AD 97) mentions the return of Christ and a general resurrection, but not a word about a millennial kingdom on earth. Polycarp (c. 70–155/160), bishop of Smyrna, champion of apostolic tradition and pillar of orthodoxy, writes of a general judgment at Christ's second coming, but nothing about His reigning on earth for a thousand years.

Justin Martyr (c. 100–165) confirms the evidence above: "'I and others, who are right-minded Christians on all points, are assured that there will be a resurrection of the dead and a thousand years in Jerusalem, which will then be built, adorned and enlarged, as the prophets Ezekiel and Isaiah and others declare"; but in the same place he asserts that "many who belong to the pure and pious faith and are true Christians think otherwise" (Dialogue with Trypho, 80f)'.[5] In the third century Origen (c. 185–c. 254) argued against an earthly millennium and at length his arguments were generally accepted. It was, however, the great theologian, Augustine (AD 354–430), who made the case for Amillennialism so effectively that for centuries the subject was practically ignored. Last, but not least, the historic creeds of the church, the Apostles' Creed (AD 250) and the Nicene Creed (AD 325) both affirm 'He shall come to judge the quick and the dead', leaving no room for a millennium in between.

When does the millennium begin?

John says nothing in these first six verses of Revelation 20 to indicate when the millennium will take place. Premillennialists believe that it begins immediately after the second stage of the return of Jesus Christ described in Revelation 19:11–21. Because they interpret the book of Revelation as an unveiling of end-time events in chronological order, the millennium in chapter 20 must follow the second coming at the end of chapter 19. The problem for premillennialists, however, is that John's visions are not to be read in sequence, but as parallel accounts repeating the same period of history stretching from our Lord's first coming to His second coming and the final judgment (6:12–17; 11:15,18; 14:14–16; 16:14–21; 17:14; 19:11–16,19–21; 20:7–15). In all these depictions of the final judgment the world as we know it comes to a complete end: the saints are rewarded and the wicked have to endure God's wrath; Satan, Antichrist and the false prophet are destroyed; the sky recedes and every mountain and island is removed from its place.

All that remains is for God to create a new heaven and a new earth to be the perfect eternal home for His redeemed people (21:1–22:5).

All seven divisions of the book, then, deal with the main events between Christ's first and second coming, but each vision gives us more detail than the one before. As Anthony A. Hoekema points out, 'Although the final judgment has already been briefly described in 6:12–17, it is not set forth in full detail until we come to 20:11–15. Though the final joy of the redeemed in the life to come has been hinted at in 7:15–17, it is not until we reach chapter 21 that we find a detailed and elaborate description of the blessedness of life on the new earth (21:1–22:5).'[6] If this is so, and I do not see how it can be refuted, then chapter 20 does not follow chapter 19 in chronological order, and therefore the millennium does not succeed our Lord's second coming.

In addition, the premillennialist has some further obstacles to explain. If Christ returns to destroy all the nations gathered against His church, what nations will remain who will need protection from Satan's deception (19:17–21; 20:1–3)? Again, the final battle between good and evil in Revelation 19:17–21 is the same battle predicted in Ezekiel 39:17–20 in which God in both instances summons the birds of prey to come and feast on the slain. In Ezekiel 38:2 and 39:1 it is also called the battle of Gog and Magog, identifying it with the final battle at the end of the millennium, in which fire comes down from God to devour His enemies (Revelation 20:8–9; Ezekiel 39:6). The final battle in Revelation 19, then, is the same battle described in Revelation 20. It makes no sense to separate them by one thousand years! They are parallel accounts of the same event at the end of the age. 'The order is not chronological but theological.'[7]

One further feature of Christ's return and the final judgment that ties Revelation 20 with the previous accounts of this same event in the book, is in the cosmic shakings that accompany it (Revelation 6:12–17; 16:17–21; 20:11). All these passages speak of a single, terminal return of Jesus Christ. Moreover, according to Hebrews 12:25–29, when the earth and heaven are shaken, the things that have been made will be removed, 'that the things which cannot be shaken may remain'. Since what remains can never be shaken again, the fleeing of the earth and the heaven in Revelation 20:11 must take place at our Lord's return described in Revelation 19:11–21, and not one thousand years later.

All the above considerations lead us to believe that the millennium of Revelation 20 is the period we are now living in, which commenced with Christ's ascension and will conclude with His return.

Are the one thousand years literal or symbolical?

Given the repeated symbolic use of numbers in the book of Revelation (4, 7, 10, 12, 666, 12,000 and 144,000) it is more than likely that 'the thousand years' of Revelation 20 is also used in a symbolic sense. What, then, is the significance of this number? Since the number ten signifies a great number determined by God and known only to Him, the number one thousand, being a perfect cube of ten, signifies perfect completeness or a completeness that is all-inclusive. So, for instance, when God says, 'every beast of the forest is Mine, and the cattle on a thousand hills' (Psalm 50:10), He means every hill in the world, not just a thousand. Again, when the Psalmist says, 'For a day in Your courts is better than a thousand', he means better than any amount of time anywhere else (Psalm 84:10; cf. also 90:4 and 2 Peter 3:8). There is ample evidence in Scripture, then, to take the 'thousand years' in Revelation 20 figuratively as meaning the period of time between the first and second coming of Jesus Christ which God has determined as sufficient to complete the building of His church. We are therefore living in this millennial period of time.

The binding of Satan

> Then I saw an angel coming down from heaven, having the key to the bottomless pit and a great chain in his hand. And he laid hold of the dragon, that ancient serpent of old, who is the Devil and Satan, and

bound him for a thousand years; and he cast him into the bottomless pit, and shut him up, and set a seal on him, so that he should deceive the nations no more till the thousand years were finished. But after these things he must be released for a little while.   (Revelation 20:1–3)

The events portrayed in this vision in the form of images and symbols can hardly be interpreted literally. The 'dragon' is interpreted for us as being 'the Devil and Satan' who is a spirit being that cannot be literally chained. Only physical beings can be restrained by a literal chain. Nor can a spirit being be confined to any kind of pit, bottomless or not. The language is clearly figurative and must be interpreted figuratively of some kind of spiritual restriction and confinement imposed by God on the devil for this period of history. It is a bottomless pit in which he keeps falling. He is unable to reverse course and get out. This is further enforced by the fact that once thrown into the pit the angel 'shut it and sealed it over him' (v. 3, ESV), as well as the fact that he is bound with 'a great chain' from which not even he, one of the most powerful of God's creatures, can break free.

The purpose of this restraint of the devil is fortunately also disclosed to us. It is for the sole purpose 'that he should deceive the nations no more.' Before the thousand-year period, that was precisely what Satan was doing. Thus in chapter 12, when the 'male Child, one who is to rule all the nations with a rod of iron [till He has put all enemies under His feet] … was caught up to God and to His throne' [our Lord's ascension to reign from heaven], John says, 'the great dragon was thrown down, that serpent of old, called the devil and Satan, the deceiver of the whole world' (vv. 5,9, ESV). In other words, the birth, death, resurrection and ascension of Christ brought about a change in Satan's relationship with the nations. He is now no longer 'the deceiver of the whole world.' Prior to the incarnation, Satan kept the Gentiles in spiritual darkness by deceiving them universally with the falsehoods of idolatry and witchcraft (Psalm 107:10–11). Gentile converts like Rahab and Ruth were infrequent. Israel alone had been entrusted with 'the oracles of

God' (Romans 3:2), so that when Christ came He, through them, should be 'a light to bring revelation to the Gentiles', for it is 'they which testify of [Him]' (Luke 2:32; John 5:39). Since that time, the darkness of Satan's deception has been and still is being dispelled by Jesus who said, 'I am the light of the world, He who follows Me shall not walk in darkness, but have the light of life' (John 8:12). Elsewhere Scripture says that since Christ's first coming, 'The light shines in the darkness, and the darkness has not overcome it' (John 1:5, ESV).

So, the first coming of Christ and the binding of Satan are interconnected. Thus, when the scribes claimed that Jesus cast out demons by the power of 'Beelzebub, the ruler of demons', He countered by saying that 'if Satan casts out Satan, he is divided against himself. How then will his kingdom stand?' (Matthew 12:26). And then He gave them the correct explanation: 'No one can enter a strong man's house and plunder his goods, unless he first binds the strong man, and then he will plunder his house' (Mark 3:27). The word 'binds' is the same word translated 'bound' in Revelation 20:2. Our Lord's casting out of demons was proof that Satan had been bound. Moreover, that is why, when the seventy whom He had sent on a preaching mission came back rejoicing that even the demons were subject to them in His name, He could say to them: 'I saw Satan fall like lightning from heaven. Behold, I have given you authority … over all the power of the enemy' (Luke 10:17–19, ESV).

It is also why, as He approached the agony and victory of the cross, Jesus said, 'Now is the judgment of this world; now will the ruler of this world be cast out. And I, when I am lifted up from the earth, will draw all people to Myself' (John 12:31–32, ESV). Again, the word 'cast out' has the same root as the word 'cast into' in Revelation 20:3. Accordingly, it is in the light of this important truth that the Great Commission is possible. It is because Satan is being prevented from keeping the nations in spiritual darkness that the church can 'go and make disciples of all the nations'. While Satan can still deceive individuals (Luke 22:31; Acts 5:3; Ephesians 6:11–12), he cannot stop the gospel from spreading throughout the world. Every nation in this church age will have the opportunity to hear the gospel, and many of their people will by God's grace believe in Christ and be saved.

Reigning with Christ for 1000 years

> And I saw thrones, and they sat on them, and judgment was committed to them. And I saw the souls of those who had been beheaded for their witness to Jesus and for the word of God, who had not worshiped the beast or his image, and had not received his mark on their foreheads or on their hands. And they lived and reigned with Christ for a thousand years
>
> (Revelation 20:4).

The principle of interpreting Scripture by Scripture, and texts which are obscure in meaning by texts where the sense is clear, leads us to the conclusion that the binding of Satan and the millennium are a present reality stretching from the first advent of Christ to the second. We may also safely assume that the binding of Satan for a thousand years (vv. 1–3) and the reigning of the saints with Christ for a thousand years (vv. 4–6) are interconnected. The latter view, however, is even more controversial and difficult to explain than the former. So we need to proceed carefully.

Are these saints reigning with Christ in heaven or on earth?

For several reasons I am convinced that they are reigning with Christ in heaven. To begin with, since His ascension, Jesus Christ has been reigning from the throne of God (Psalm 110:1; 1 Corinthians 15:25; Hebrews 1:3; 8:1; 10:12–13). Secondly, if Christ is reigning from heaven, the saints whom John says 'lived and reigned with Christ for a thousand years' must also be seated on thrones in heaven (v. 4). Thirdly, the twenty-four elders who represent the church in heaven are seated on thrones (4:4; 11:16). Fourthly, in the book of Revelation, the word 'throne' occurs forty-seven times in all, forty-four of which are located in heaven. Fifthly, John describes them as 'souls' (i.e. as disembodied spirits) and as those who 'came to life' (i.e. who went to heaven), unlike 'the rest of the dead [who] did not come to life [i.e. who went to hell, the place of eternal death] until the thousand years were ended' (vv. 4–5, ESV). Sixthly, this reigning in heaven is precisely what Jesus promises to every Christian who is faithful to Him until death: 'To him who overcomes I will grant to sit with Me on My throne, as I also overcame and sat down with My Father on His throne' (3:21).

Is John referring only to martyrs?

The answer is, 'No'. John is not speaking exclusively of those who have suffered martyrdom, for the souls seated on the thrones in heaven are classified in two categories. Firstly, verse 4 begins with a general reference to believers who have died and are seated on thrones. Further on in verse 4 they are described as those 'who had not worshipped the beast or his image, and had not received his mark on their foreheads or on their hands'; in other words, every believer who has been faithful to Jesus whether they died a martyr's death or not. Secondly, John then singles out for special mention 'the souls of those who had been beheaded for their witness to Jesus and for the word of God.' Thus the English Standard Version translates verse 4: 'Then I saw thrones, and seated on them were those to whom the authority to judge was committed; *also* I saw the souls of those who had been beheaded for the testimony of Jesus and for the word of God, and those who had not worshiped the beast …' (italics added). John is repeating the distinction made in Revelation 17:6 when 'Babylon the great' becomes 'drunk with the blood of the saints and with the blood of the martyrs of Jesus.' The deaths of both groups were precious in Christ's sight, just as the deaths of the brothers James and John were. The former was the first of the apostles to be martyred (Acts 12:1–2), while the latter died in old age off the island of Patmos. But of both groups Scripture says: 'Blessed are the dead who die in the Lord from now on'; and 'Precious in the sight of the Lord is the death of His saints' (Revelation 14:13; Psalm 116:15).

What John sees, then, is that during the millennium every Christian who dies and goes to heaven is enjoying the wonderful privilege of reigning with Christ who has 'given [them] authority to judge' (v. 4, NIV). The nature of the judgment they exercise, John does not disclose. However, because the reign of Jesus involves the judgment of His enemies whom He is putting under His feet, we may assume that the saints are sharing in that judgment through their prayers; for in chapter 6:9–10 John says, 'I saw under the altar the souls of those who had been slain for the word of God and for the testimony which they held. And they cried out with a loud voice, saying, "How long, O Lord, holy and true, until You judge and avenge our blood on those who dwell on the earth?"' Again, in chapter 8:3–5 we read that the prayers of all the saints in heaven are offered to God before the seven trumpets of divine judgment are sounded. For the very censer that the angel used to bring their prayers to God, was then filled with the fire of His judgment and thrown to the earth. There is a vital connection between the prayers of our Lord and His saints in heaven and the overthrow of His enemies on earth.

These are the same 'souls' seen in Revelation 20:4, and they pray for the execution of judgment not merely on those who killed them but also 'on those who dwell on the earth' and rejoice at the suppression of the gospel (11:10), because it is the world's hatred of Christ and His church that fuels the flames of persecution (John 15:18–21; 17:14). The saints are not vengeful, as though concerned for themselves, but filled with godly zeal. Since evil and falsehood are a rebellious affront to their 'Sovereign Lord, holy and true' (ESV), they long for Him to purge the earth of the ungodliness and bloodshed by which it is being defiled. Moreover, though delayed for good reason, their prayers will be answered when all the elect are saved and Jesus Christ returns to judge the unbelieving world with fire (2 Peter 3:7–9; Revelation 20:15).

These words of reassurance are meant to bring great encouragement to Christians still on earth who are suffering persecution of all sorts.

What is meant by the first resurrection?

> But the rest of the dead did not live again until the thousand years were finished. This is the first resurrection. Blessed and holy is he who has part in the first resurrection. Over such the second death has no power, but they shall be priests of God and of Christ, and shall reign with Him a thousand years.   (vv. 5–6)

The term 'resurrection' is a purely physical one. Only the human body can be resurrected, not the human spirit. It is true that our Lord characterized conversion as having 'passed from death into life' (John 5:24) and Paul described it as being 'made alive … even when we were dead in trespasses' (Ephesians 2:1,5). But it is incorrect to spiritualize John's statement about 'the first resurrection' in this way. In the New Testament there is only one resurrection that qualifies to be called 'the first', and that is the bodily resurrection of our Lord Jesus Christ. Thus He is described as 'the firstfruits' (1 Corinthians 15:23). Others who died and were brought to life again, before and after Christ, were merely resuscitated and had to do their dying all over again. Jesus of Nazareth alone was resurrected with a glorified, immortal body with which He ascended into heaven.

The only other bodily resurrection of the dead that the Bible speaks about is the resurrection of all humankind, the good and the wicked, for the final judgment at Christ's return. Thus in Daniel 12:2 we read that at the end of the world 'those who sleep in the dust of the earth shall awake, some to everlasting life, some to shame and everlasting contempt.' Our Lord also spoke of a general resurrection in John 5:28–29, 'Do not marvel at this; for the hour is coming in which all who are in the graves will hear His voice and come forth—those who have done good, to the resurrection of life, and those who have done evil, to the resurrection of condemnation.' This is one resurrection involving two groups, the good and the evil, issuing in a twofold outcome, life with God or life in hell (see also Matthew 25:31–46; Acts 24:15). So although John does not mention a second resurrection, we may conclude that if our Lord's bodily resurrection is called 'the first', the second resurrection must be the general bodily resurrection of all human beings, which for some will be blessing because they have 'part in the first resurrection' (v. 6), but for others cursing (the second death).

Christian believers participate in the blessing of 'the first resurrection' when on earth, through faith and by God's grace, they become one with Christ their Bridegroom in a union that is so intimate that His destiny becomes their destiny. His rising is the pledge of, and the power behind, their resurrection. Yet even now, as they await this great and ultimate transformation, when the nakedness of being a disembodied spirit ceases and they are clothed with a spiritual body 'conformed' to Christ's glorious resurrection body (Philippians 3:20–21), they are said to share in the benefits of the first resurrection: 'Blessed and holy is he who has part in the first resurrection' (v. 6). First, because the Christian believer whose spirit was made alive at conversion, continues to live with Christ in heaven after death, no longer plagued with sin but as a spirit 'made perfect' or 'holy' (Hebrews 12:23; 2 Corinthians 5:6–8; Philippians 1:21–23). Second, our Christian dead are 'blessed' because they are reigning in heaven with Christ in His work of subduing His enemies. And thirdly, they are blessed because they are looking forward to receiving a resurrection body like His: 'Over such the second death has no power' (v. 6). The second death is the eternal destruction of body and soul in 'the lake of fire' after the final judgment (Matthew 10:28; Revelation 20:13–15; 21:8).

As far as the 'rest of the dead' (v. 5) are concerned (the unbelieving dead), they will also be resurrected at the return of Christ, but they will not have part in the first resurrection. Because they die in their

sins unforgiven, their spirits will remain spiritually dead when they
are sent to hell (Luke 16:19–31) to await in torment the second death
(of body and soul) after the millennium and the return of Christ and
the final judgment. They will not receive a body of glory, but a body of
ignominy (Isaiah 66:24; Daniel 12:2; Mark 9:42–48).

Further problems for a literal millennium

Besides the detailed interpretation given above that shows that
Revelation 20:1–6 does not support a literal one-thousand year reign
of Christ on the earth at His second coming, there are several other
difficulties in the way of accepting the premillennial view that need
to be considered before we conclude. *First*, it is impossible to imagine
how glorified and sinless saints, prepared for the perfection of heaven,
will be able to reign with Christ over people on earth who still have
sinful natures capable of rebelling against His rule (20:7–9). *Secondly*,
to say that those who survive the second coming and live to enjoy
the millennium will have the opportunity to repent and be saved,
and worship Christ at Jerusalem, is contrary to the New Testament
teaching that when the Bridegroom comes the door of salvation
will be permanently shut (Matthew 7:21–23; 25:1–13; Luke 13:22–28;
2 Corinthians 6:1–2; 2 Thessalonians 1:5–10).

Thirdly, God does not have two chosen people (the Jews and
Christians) but one people made up of believers from the Old
Testament and the New, who are Abraham's seed by faith and not by
blood (Romans 2:28–29; 4:11–12; 9:6; Philippians 3:3), and therefore
the only heirs of God's promises to him which are ultimately fulfilled
in heaven (Galatians 3:26–29; Hebrews 11:13–16). *Fourthly*, when all
believers have been glorified at Christ's return and made sinlessly
perfect in body and soul to enter the place He has gone to prepare
for them, what good reason can there be to delay their enjoyment of
it for one thousand years? John gives no rationale for it, and the rest
of the New Testament does not even mention it. *Fifthly*, the New

Testament divides time into two ages only, not three: namely, into 'this age' and 'the age to come' (Matthew 12:32; Mark 10:30; Luke 20:34–35; Ephesians 1:21). There is no in-between age of one thousand years.

Sixthly, our Lord's return will be followed immediately, not by a one-thousand year reign on earth, but by a general resurrection and a general judgment (Daniel 12:1–3; Matthew 13:36–43,47–50; 25:31–46; John 5:28–29; Acts 10:42; 17:30–31; 24:15). This final judgment will clear the way for the creation of 'a new heaven and a new earth' from which sin, imperfection and death are finally banished for evermore (2 Peter 3:10–13; Revelation 20:11–21:1). *Seventhly*, the expectation that in the millennium the Jewish temple will be rebuilt in Jerusalem and the Levitical sacrifices reinstituted would be a return to Judaism; a system that had served its God-given purpose and was set aside two thousand years ago. To assert that these blood sacrifices will be commemorative of the one perfect sacrifice of Jesus is unsatisfactory, for nothing could be a better memorial than the Lord's Supper which He Himself instituted.

Let each reader, seeking the help of the Holy Spirit, be persuaded in their own mind as to which view of the millennium is more consistent with 'the whole counsel of God', and most glorifying to our Saviour.

22 Satan destroyed and the last judgment

20:7Now when the thousand years have expired, Satan will be released from his prison 8and will go out to deceive the nations which are in the four corners of the earth, Gog and Magog, to gather them together to battle, whose number is as the sand of the sea. 9They went up on the breadth of the earth and surrounded the camp of the saints and the beloved city. And fire came down from God out of heaven and devoured them. 10The devil, who deceived them, was cast into the lake of fire and brimstone where the beast and the false prophet are. And they will be tormented day and night forever and ever.

11Then I saw a great white throne and Him who sat on it, from whose face the earth and the heaven fled away. And there was found no place for them. 12And I saw the dead, small and great, standing before God, and books were opened. And another book was opened, which is the Book of Life. And the dead were judged according to their works, by the things which were written in the books. 13The sea gave up the dead who were in it, and Death and Hades delivered up the dead who were in them. And they were judged, each one according to his works. 14Then Death and Hades were cast into the lake of fire. This is the second death. 15And anyone not found written in the Book of Life was cast into the lake of fire.

(Revelation 20:7–15)

As mentioned above, Revelation 20 concludes the sixth main vision of the book by portraying the activity of Satan during the current church age and his impending doom at its close. All the enemies of our Lord Jesus Christ will be simultaneously destroyed by Him when He returns as 'King of kings and Lord of lords' (6:12–17; 14:14–20; 16:12–21; 17:14; 19:11–21; Matthew 24:29–31; 2 Thessalonians 2:8). His archenemy, however, is the devil, for there can be no end to sin and death, and no final judgment until the tempter himself is cast into hell forever.

Satan released for a little while

In verses 7–10 John comes back to a truth he has emphasised several times, namely the marshalling of all the forces of evil at the end of the age to wipe God's church off the face of the earth. In chapter 16:13–16 he speaks of three unclean spirits like frogs coming out of the mouths of the dragon, the beast and the false prophet 'performing signs, which go out to the kings of the earth and of the whole world, to gather them to the battle of that great day of God Almighty … to the place called in Hebrew, Armageddon.' He mentions it again in chapter 19:19–20, 'And I saw the beast, the kings of the earth, and their armies, gathered together to make war against Him who sat on the horse and against His army. Then the beast was captured and with him the false prophet … These two were cast alive into the lake of fire burning with brimstone.' Now in chapter 20:7–10 John gives us further insight into this battle to end all battles, and he says it can only happen when, after the millennium, God releases Satan from the bottomless pit 'for a little while' (v. 3).

As can be expected neither the rebellious designs of Satan nor the enmity of humankind towards God will be changed by the restrictions they have had to endure for a thousand years. Once he is released from 'prison' the devil will revert to his old tricks and immediately set about deceiving the nations with a vengeance. He will use Antichrist, the false prophet and all the demons at his command to convince the world with lying wonders to put aside their racial, religious and political differences in a united effort to set up a universal kingdom free from the inhibiting influences of Christianity. 'Now when the thousand years have expired, Satan will be released from his prison and will go out to deceive the nations which are in the four corners of the earth, Gog and Magog, to gather them together to battle, whose number is as the sand of the sea. They went up on the breadth of the earth and surrounded the camp of the saints and the beloved city' (vv. 7–9a).

It is the same final effort to annihilate the church that John has been shown before. This time, however, the Holy Spirit uses a prophecy from Ezekiel 38–39 to confirm what John sees. Magog is 'the land of Gog' who is presented as the enemy of God (38:2). But as in the scenes in Revelation, so in Ezekiel God is in complete control of this coming onslaught. For God says to Gog, 'After many days [cf. 'Now when the thousand years have expired'] you will be summoned; in the latter years [the end times] you will come into the land … to the mountains of Israel (38:8) … you will come like a storm … you and all your troops, and many peoples with you (v. 9) … and you will come up against My people Israel like a cloud to cover the land. It will come about in the last days [the end times] that I shall bring you against My land … O Gog (v. 16) … and with pestilence and with blood I shall enter into judgment with him; and I shall rain on him, and on his troops, and on the many peoples who are with him, a torrential rain, with hailstones, fire and brimstone' (v. 22, NASB). At the end of the battle God says to Ezekiel, 'Speak to every kind of bird and to every beast of the field, "Assemble and come … to My sacrifice … on the mountains of Israel, that you may eat flesh and drink blood. You shall eat the flesh of mighty men, and drink the blood of the princes of the earth"' (39:17–18, NASB).

John and Ezekiel predict the same final battle with 'Gog and Magog' which ends metaphorically with all the birds feasting on the slain (Revelation 19:17–18; 20:7–10). John, however, also connects this battle with Jesus Christ's return (19:11–16) and the casting of Antichrist, the false prophet and Satan into the lake of fire (19:20; 20:7–10). There is, therefore, no literal one-thousand year reign of Jesus Christ between His return and Satan's destruction.

Satan cast into hell forever

The similarity between this battle and the final battle in Revelation 19 and 20 is too striking to miss. Indeed, Revelation 19 and 20 tells us that Ezekiel 38 and 39 will only be ultimately fulfilled at the end of history in the battle of Armageddon. John's description of the end in chapter 20 is terse: 'They went up on the breadth of the earth and surrounded the camp of the saints and the beloved city. And fire came down from God out of heaven and devoured them' (v. 9). The conflict is worldwide and the defeat of Satan's forces is sudden and dramatic. It is important to notice again that the final battle is not between Jews and Arabs, or East and West, but between a satanic-inspired world and Christ's church. The whole world is involved in this all-out attempt to eradicate the church which is first described as 'the camp of the saints' to identify Christians with believers in the Old Testament and their encampments in their wilderness journey to the Promised Land. We are the spiritual descendants of those believing Jews. It is a picture of defenceless, pacifist tent dwellers who to all human appearance are easy prey for the mighty armies of the rulers of the earth. Compare this with Gog's depiction of God's people in Ezekiel 38:11, 'I will go up against a land of unwalled villages; I will go to a peaceful people.'

The church is also described as 'the beloved *city*' to remind us that though it is passing through this temporary scene in tents, it is a 'city' that has permanent foundations in heaven. Thus Hebrews 11:9–10 says, 'By faith (Abraham) dwelt in the land of promise as in a foreign country, dwelling in tents with Isaac and Jacob, the heirs with him of the same promise; for he waited for the city which has foundations, whose builder and maker is God.' And Hebrews 12:22 says that Christians 'have come to Mount Zion and to the city of the living God, the heavenly Jerusalem.' So when the hosts of Gog and Magog pick on the church, they are picking on the wrong people, 'for the Lord's portion is His people … He found him in a desert land … He kept him as the apple of His eye' (Deuteronomy 32:9–10). Instead of a great battle ensuing, it is an instant rout. As portrayed in Ezekiel 38:22, the human armies here in Revelation 20 are also destroyed by 'fire' which John says 'came down from God out of heaven and devoured them' (cf. 2 Thessalonians 1:7).

'And the devil, who deceived them, was cast into the lake of fire and brimstone, where the beast and the false prophet are.' We are not meant to understand here that Satan goes into hell one thousand years after his evil cohorts. On the contrary, they are all cast into hell together at the return of Jesus Christ. All John has been doing in chapters 18, 19 and 20 is to give three separate descriptions of the destruction of all evil, including the evil one (John 17:15), on the last day of history. 'And they will be tormented day and night forever and ever' (v. 10b). The eternal confinement and punishment of the devil and his agents will be sudden and irreversible in fulfilment of our Lord's promise: 'The Son of Man will send out His angels, and they will gather out of His kingdom all things that offend, and those who practise lawlessness, and will cast them into the furnace of fire' (Matthew 13:41–42).

The last judgment

The fact that one day all human beings will be judged by God is a most unwelcome prospect. None of us wants our lives to be subject to divine examination and assessment, but it is a fact to be reckoned with. Though we may close our minds, and try to forget it, we will not be able to avoid it. Thus John Blanchard says, 'Anyone who does not find this sobering is not being serious. The fact that we have an inescapable appointment with our Maker means that trying to avoid Him is both foolish and futile. Trying to run away from God is as ridiculous as trying to run away from death, because every moment spent doing so brings us closer to the moment we are trying to avoid. The Bible spells out the only sensible response: "Prepare to meet your God" (Amos 4:12).'[1]

The last judgment is last for two reasons. Previously, while God's judgments here on earth may have been hidden, or partial, or delayed, on the last day of history God's judgment will be *final*. There will be no retrial or any higher court of appeal. The verdict cannot be overturned because the evidence is complete and conclusive. There is no possibility of being misjudged. The other reason why it is termed the last judgment is the fact that it will be *decisive*. It is not merely the last in a line of temporal judgments. It will determine the destiny of each and every person forever.

The being and character of the Judge

'Then I saw a great white throne and Him who sat on it' (v. 11a). The One on this throne is God, the only Sovereign of the universe, who is infinite and eternal in His Being, power, holiness, love, justice, wisdom and glory. It is a 'great' throne because it surpasses every other throne in grandeur and majesty, and because of the universal scope of its jurisdiction. It is also described as a 'white' throne because of the absolute purity and justice of the judgments that are pronounced from it. No one will be able to find fault with the Judge's verdicts, whether His condemnations or acquittals. As Abraham affirmed, 'Far be it from You ... to slay the righteous with the wicked ... Shall not the Judge of all the earth do right?' (Genesis 18:25). Indeed, so great and awesome and glorious is the God who sits on the 'great white throne' that John goes on to say: 'from whose face the earth and the heaven fled away. And there was found no place for them' (v. 11b). The second coming of Jesus Christ will not only destroy the human and demonic forces that brought the curse of sin upon the earth, it will also have cataclysmic consequences for the whole universe itself. The cosmos, however, will not be entirely destroyed, only the effects of the curse of sin upon it.

Our Lord spoke of it as 'the regeneration, when the Son of Man sits on the throne of His glory' (Matthew 19:28). In Acts 3:21 Peter speaks of 'Jesus Christ … whom heaven must receive until the time for restoring all the things about which God spoke by the mouth of His holy prophets long ago' (ESV). In Romans 8:21 Paul says, 'the creation itself will be set free from its bondage to corruption and obtain the freedom of the glory of the children of God' (ESV). Peter describes it as a renovation by fire: 'But the day of the Lord will come as a thief in the night, in which the heavens will pass away with a great noise, and the elements will melt with fervent heat; both the earth and the works that are in it will be burned up' (2 Peter 3:10). This will all be done to prepare a new heaven and a new earth for God's saints to live in forever, and enjoy a paradise far superior to the original creation.

God will judge the world by His incarnate Son

Several Scriptures speak of God the Father as the supreme Judge: 'The Father, who without partiality judges according to each one's works' (1 Peter 1:17; see also Romans 14:10; 2 Thessalonians 1:5; 1 Peter 2:23). In the fuller light of the New Testament it is revealed that the God who judges everything is God the Son. Our Lord Himself said by way of explanation: 'For the Father judges no one, but has committed all judgment to the Son, that all should honour the Son just as they honour the Father' (John 5:22). The apostle Paul echoed his Master's teaching: 'God … now commands all men everywhere to repent, because He has appointed a day on which He will judge the world in righteousness by the Man whom He has ordained. He has given assurance of this to all, by raising Him from the dead' (Acts 17:30–31). And in 2 Corinthians 5:10 he writes: 'For we must all appear before the judgment seat of Christ, that each one may receive the things done in the body, according to what He has done, whether good or bad' (cf. Matthew 25:31–32; John 5:27; Acts 10:42; Romans 14:10; 2 Timothy 4:1).

The Judge at the last judgment will not be an unfeeling spirit, but a divine-human being who walked in our shoes and knows what it is to live sinlessly in a sinful world. Thus Anthony Hoekema says, "It is indeed most appropriate that Christ should be the judge in the final judgment. He is the one who became incarnate, died, and rose again for the salvation of His people. Those who believe on Him are saved through Him, hence it is most fitting that He should be their judge. Those who have rejected Him, on the other hand, have sinned against Him; hence it is appropriate that the One whom they have rejected should be their judge. The work of judging, moreover, will be Christ's final exaltation and highest triumph. While on earth He was condemned by earthly rulers; now He will sit in judgment over all earthly authorities. Christ will now carry out to its completion His saving work for His people. The judgment will mean the total subjugation of all His enemies, and the completion of His kingdom, after which He will deliver the kingdom to God the Father (1 Corinthians 15:24).'[2]

The universality of the last judgment

'And I saw the dead, small and great, standing before God … The sea gave up the dead who were in it, and Death and Hades delivered up the dead who were in them' (v. 12a and 13a). When Jesus Christ returns to bring a fitting, God-glorifying end to history, all human beings of all ages will be raised and summoned for judgment, and they will take their place before His judgment seat. Everyone who has ever lived will be there. No one will be missing. It will include princes and peasants, rich and poor, the famous and the unknown—none will be so important as to make judgment inappropriate. It does not matter where or how they died, on land or in the sea, they will all be raised for judgment. The event is unimaginable, but human imagination is no barrier to what God has determined and can do.

The Bible confirms the universality of the last judgment in several other places. Jesus said that when He sits 'on the throne of His glory, all the nations will be gathered before Him, and He will separate them one from another' (Matthew 25:31–32). Paul says that 'He will judge the world in righteousness' (Acts 17:31) and that this will include 'the living and the dead' (2 Timothy 4:1). This must, of course, include all believers from Old and New Testament eras. Paul includes himself when he says, 'We must all appear before the judgment seat of Christ' (2 Corinthians 5:10; cf. James 3:1; 1 Peter 4:17). Even the most holy and faithful of believers will have to 'give an account of himself to God' (Romans 14:12; cf. Hebrews 4:13). The last judgment will be personal and individual for everyone, Christian or non-Christian.

The basis of the last judgment

John tells us that it will be a judgment based on works: '… and books were opened. And another book was opened which is the Book of Life. And the dead were judged according to their works, by the things which were written in the books … And they were judged, each one according to his works' (vv. 12b, 13b). Everybody will be judged on the basis of everything they have done, which has been meticulously and accurately recorded by God in the record books of heaven. Of course there will be no literal books there. This is just a figurative way of saying that every bit of incontrovertible evidence of how we have lived our lives is actually stored in the omniscient mind of God, the divine Judge. It also assures us that the last judgment will not be an investigative trial in which evidence is sought and witnesses questioned. No evidence will be needed, for all the facts of each case are already fully known to God, and no witnesses will be needed either, for the all-seeing, all-knowing God Himself will be the sole supreme witness necessary (Matthew 6:4; Luke 12:2; Romans 2:16; Hebrews 4:13). The last judgment will simply be a public unveiling of the irrefutable evidence God has, accompanied by a public declaration of the just sentence He has determined (Romans 2:5; 1 Corinthians 4:5).

The last judgment, of course, will also concern itself with the words people have spoken. Jesus warned, 'But I say to you that every idle word men may speak, they will give account of it in the day of judgment. For by your words you will be justified, and by your words you will be condemned' (Matthew12:36–37). Even the hidden thoughts and motives of men will be judged: 'Therefore judge nothing before the time, until the Lord comes, who will both bring to light the hidden things of darkness and reveal the counsels [motives, NIV] of the heart' (1 Corinthians 4:5; see also Luke 12:3). A person's thoughts, words and deeds are a sure indication of the nature and bent of their life. The evidence presented will be complete. No one will escape condemnation because their motives were not disclosed. But—and this is equally important—in addition to the comprehensiveness and the absolute reliability of the evidence revealed at the last judgment is the total commitment on the part of the Judge to do what is right by every person (Genesis 18:25). J.I. Dagg, the nineteenth-century American theologian, makes the point forcefully when he says, 'Every one will be brought to judgment as if he were the only creature present, and every one will give account of himself, and receive sentence for himself, with as much discrimination and perfection of justice as if the Judge were wholly absorbed in the consideration of his single cause.'[3]

How, then, will the sins of believers be judged? Their sins, all of them, will be revealed at the last judgment as *forgiven sins*. For 'the Lamb of God who takes away the sins of the world' (John 1:29) by making 'His soul an offering for sin' on the cross (Isaiah 53:10; 1 Corinthians 15:3), has paid the penalty of their sins in full (1 Peter 1:18; 3:18). They have now been acquitted in the sight of God, and having been justified freely by His grace through faith, they 'have peace with God' (Romans 3:24; 5:1). So John says, 'And another book was opened, which is the Book of Life' (v. 12b). Elsewhere it is called 'the

Lamb's Book of Life', or 'the Book of Life of the Lamb slain from the foundation of the world' (21:27; 13:8). Moreover, we are told that those 'whose names … are written in the Book of Life from the foundation of the world' are the only ones who will enter heaven (17:8; 21:27).

In other words, the names written in the Lamb's Book of Life are the names of those whom Christ has purchased with His own blood from the slave-market of sin (Acts 20:28; 1 Peter 1:18–19). For God 'chose us in Him before the foundation of the world, that we should be holy and without blame before Him in love, having predestined us to adoption as sons by Jesus Christ to Himself, according to the good pleasure of His will, to the praise of the glory of His grace, by which He made us accepted in the Beloved. In Him we have redemption through His blood, the forgiveness of sins, according to the riches of His grace' (Ephesians 1:4–7). To quote Anthony A. Hoekema again, 'Believers have nothing to fear from the [final] judgment—though the realization that they will have to give an account of everything they have done, said and thought should be for them a constant incentive to diligent fighting against sin, conscientious Christian service and consecrated living.'[4]

The necessity of the last judgment

It is sometimes argued that a judgment at the end of the world is unnecessary because the eternal destiny of every person is settled at death. When a person dies believing in Jesus Christ as their Saviour they immediately go to be with Him in glory. When they die impenitent in their sins they immediately go to hell. Why, then, is the last judgment necessary? There are several reasons, two of which are given by John in our text. The first reason has to do with the full apportionment of their final estate, whether for weal or woe. A bodyless spirit is only half a human being and therefore incapable of fully experiencing the bliss or torment that is to be their final lot. For this to happen, everyone has to wait for the general resurrection at the end of the world when they will receive a body of glory or a body of shame. This is what John is referring to in verse 14: 'Then Death and Hades were thrown into the lake of fire. This is the second death, the lake of fire' (ESV). Death is the power that separates the body from the spirit, and Hades is the power that keeps the spirit in a bodyless state. But when at the general resurrection Death and Hades have no further part to play in God's purposes they will be discarded forever in the lake of fire which is also called 'the second death', the final abode of the wicked (v. 15; 21:8). Henry Alford defines the term (the second death) well: 'As there is a second and higher life, so there is also a second and deeper death. And as after that life there is no more death (ch. xxi. 4), so after that death there is no more life.'[5]

The second reason for the last judgment is cosmological. For until sin is universally judged and the devil and his demons and his human followers are destroyed forever, God Almighty cannot create 'new heavens and a new earth in which righteousness dwells' (20:10,15; 2 Peter 3:10). Accordingly, this is the next vision that John is shown (21:1–22:6).

The supreme necessity for the last judgment, however, is His glory. It is the glory of God to judge justly and for His judgments to be seen to be just beyond all question. Up to the last judgment the final destiny of each person, human and demonic has been hidden. Now that destiny, along with the deeds each one did, will be publicly revealed in a way that God's grace will be magnified in the salvation of the elect, and His justice in the damnation of the wicked. The last judgment will be God's final self-vindication against every charge that He has not ruled the world in righteousness and justice (Psalm 50:16–21; Revelation 6:10; 16:5–7; 19:1–6).

The last judgment is a difficult and dreadful subject for anyone with any sensitivity to write or think about. C.S. Lewis wrote, 'There is no doctrine which I would more willingly remove from Christianity than this, if it lay in my power. But it has the full support of Scripture and, especially, of our Lord's own words … I would pay any price to be able to say truthfully, "All will be saved."'[6] It is true that 'anyone not found written in the Book of Life was cast into the lake of fire' (v. 15). But if the rest of Scripture is to be our guide, our destiny is not a matter of *fate*, but of *faith*. Eternal life is to be received by *believing in Jesus Christ* (John 3:14–19,36). So being cast into the lake of fire is not an arbitrary infliction. It is rather a constant, conscious choosing of the state in which one wants to be. As J.I. Packer so plainly states: The unbeliever has preferred to be by himself, without God, defying God, having God against him, and he shall have his preference. Nobody stands under the wrath of God save those who have chosen to do so. The essence of God's action in wrath is to *give men what they choose*, in all its implications: nothing more, and equally nothing less. God's readiness to respect human choice to this extent may appear disconcerting and even terrifying, but it is plain that His attitude here is supremely just, and poles apart from the wanton and irresponsible inflicting of pain which is what we mean by cruelty.'[7]

'What shall we do?' (Acts 2:37). Though we cannot look at the Book of Life to see if our name is written there, we can do what God commands and that is to repent; to turn from our rebellious ways and put our faith in Jesus Christ for pardon and eternal life (Mark 1:15; Acts 17:30–31; 20:21; John 3:16,36). 'Knowledge of future judgment is always a summons to present repentance. Only the penitent will be prepared for judgment when it comes.'[8]

> Day of judgment! Day of wonders!
> Hark! The trumpet's aweful sound,
> Louder than a thousand thunders,
> Shakes the vast creation round:
> How the summons, How the summons
> Will the sinner's heart confound!
>
> See, the Judge, our nature wearing,
> Clothed in majesty divine;
> Ye who long for His appearing

Then shall say, 'This God is mine!'
Gracious Saviour, Gracious Saviour,
Own me in that day for Thine.

At His call the dead awaken,
Rise to life from earth and sea;
All the pow'rs of nature shaken
By His look, prepare to flee;
Careless sinner, Careless sinner,
What will then become of Thee?

But to those who have confessed,
Loved and served the Lord below,
He will say, 'Come near, ye blessed,
See the kingdom I bestow;
You forever, You forever
Shall My love and glory know.'   *(John Newton, 1725–1807)*

23 A new heaven and a new earth[1]

²¹:¹Now I saw a new heaven and a new earth, for the first heaven and the first earth had passed away. Also there was no more sea. ²Then I, John, saw the holy city, New Jerusalem, coming down out of heaven from God, prepared as a bride adorned for her husband. ³And I heard a loud voice from heaven saying, 'Behold, the tabernacle of God is with men, and He will dwell with them, and they shall be His people. God Himself will be with them and be their God. ⁴And God will wipe away every tear from their eyes; there shall be no more death, nor sorrow, nor crying. There shall be no more pain, for the former things have passed away.'

⁵Then He who sat on the throne said, 'Behold, I make all things new.' And He said to me, 'Write, for these words are true and faithful.'

⁶And He said to me, 'It is done! I am the Alpha and the Omega, the Beginning and the End. I will give of the fountain of the water of life freely to him who thirsts. ⁷He who overcomes shall inherit all things, and I will be his God and he shall be My son. ⁸But the cowardly, unbelieving, abominable, murderers, sexually immoral, sorcerers, idolaters, and all liars shall have their part in the lake which burns with fire and brimstone, which is the second death.'

⁹Then one of the seven angels who had the seven bowls filled with the seven last plagues came to me and talked with me, saying, 'Come, I will

show you the bride, the Lamb's wife.' [10]And he carried me away in the Spirit to a great and high mountain, and showed me the great city, the holy Jerusalem, descending out of heaven from God, [11]having the glory of God. Her light was like a most precious stone, like a jasper stone, clear as crystal. [12]Also she had a great and high wall with twelve gates, and twelve angels at the gates, and names written on them, which are the names of the twelve tribes of the children of Israel: [13]three gates on the east, three gates on the north, three gates on the south, and three gates on the west.

[14]Now the wall of the city had twelve foundations, and on them were the names of the twelve apostles of the Lamb. [15]And he who talked with me had a gold reed to measure the city, its gates, and its wall. [16]The city is laid out as a square; its length is as great as its breadth. And he measured the city with the reed: twelve thousand furlongs. Its length, breadth, and height are equal. [17]Then he measured its wall: one hundred and forty-four cubits, according to the measure of a man, that is, of an angel. [18]The construction of its wall was of jasper, and the city was pure gold, like clear glass. [19]The foundations of the wall of the city were adorned with all kinds of precious stones: the first foundation was jasper, the second sapphire, the third chalcedony, the fourth emerald, [20]the fifth sardonyx, the sixth sardius, the seventh chrysolite, the eighth beryl, the ninth topaz, the tenth chrysoprase, the eleventh jacinth, and the twelfth amethyst. [21]The twelve gates were twelve pearls: each individual gate was of one pearl. And the street of the city was pure gold, like transparent glass.

[22]But I saw no temple in it, for the Lord God Almighty and the Lamb are its temple. [23]The city had no need of the sun or of the moon to shine in it, for the glory of God illuminated it. The Lamb is its light. [24]And the nations of those who are saved shall walk in its light, and the kings of the earth bring their glory and honour into it. [25]Its gates shall not be shut at all by day (there shall be no night there). [26]And they shall bring the glory and the honour of the nations into it. [27]But there shall by no means enter it anything that defiles, or causes an abomination or a lie, but only those who are written in the Lamb's Book of Life.

22:1And he showed me a pure river of water of life, clear as crystal, proceeding from the throne of God and of the Lamb. 2In the middle of its street, and on either side of the river, was the tree of life, which bore twelve fruits, each tree yielding its fruit every month. The leaves of the tree were for the healing of the nations. 3And there shall be no more curse, but the throne of God and of the Lamb shall be in it, and His servants shall serve Him. 4They shall see His face, and His name shall be on their foreheads. 5There shall be no night there: They need no lamp nor light of the sun, for the Lord God gives them light. And they shall reign forever and ever.   (Revelation 21:1–22:5)

Revelation 21 and 22 record the seventh and final major vision which our Lord Jesus Christ gave to John, the last of His apostles on earth. With the final judgment and the casting of Satan and all the ungodly into hell forever (20:7–15), the way is now clear for God to create 'new heavens and a new earth in which righteousness dwells' (2 Peter 3:13). It is something that God promised through Isaiah He would do: '"For behold, I create new heavens and a new earth; and the former shall not be remembered or come to mind. But be glad and rejoice forever in what I create; for behold, I create Jerusalem as a rejoicing, and her people a joy … For as the heavens and the new earth which I will make shall remain before Me," says the Lord, "so shall your descendants and your name remain"' (65:17–18; 66:22). God's plan of redemption, designed before the world began, will not stop with the spiritual perfection of Christ's church. It will include the whole of physical creation which the apostle Paul says, 'eagerly waits for the revealing [the glorification] of the sons of God … because the creation itself also will be delivered from the bondage of corruption into the glorious liberty of the children of God' (Romans 8:19,21). Moreover, because God is immutable (unchanging), we can be sure that all that He has committed Himself in Scripture to do, will infallibly be done. Though, in His inscrutable wisdom, God permitted the devil to oppose and seemingly hinder His plans, no power in heaven or on earth can stop

His purposes from being carried out to perfection in His appointed time (Psalm 33:10–11; Isaiah 46:9–10).

Revelation 21 and 22, then, is a wonderful and detailed picture of what the renewing of creation will mean for God's believing people. It is a vision calculated to excite our expectation and kindle our hope as we look forward to our Lord's return to purge the world and 'make all things new' (21:6). But once again we need to approach this final vision with the same caution needed for interpreting the previous visions in the Revelation, for like them it is crammed full with vivid and dramatic images. In each scene unveiled to John in these last two chapters of the Bible, the Holy Spirit is emphasising a different and important aspect of the age to come. The first scene is contained in verses 1–8.

The continuity between the old and new creation

Then I saw a great white throne and Him who sat on it, from whose face the earth and the heaven fled away. And there was found no place for them … Now I saw a new heaven and a new earth, for the first heaven and the first earth had passed away (20:11; 21:1).

This does not mean that the former heaven and earth will be obliterated without a trace, and replaced by a totally new creation. What God begins He completes, whether in the spiritual or the material realm (Philippians 1:6; Revelation 21 and 22). If Satan could force God to give up something He started, it would signify a victory over God, and then God would no longer be God. In the spiritual realm, although by nature we are born 'dead in trespasses and sins', in Christ we are 'made alive' and become 'a new creation; old things are passed away; behold, all things have become new' (Ephesians 2:1,5; 2 Corinthians 5:17). In the process of conversion our spirit is regenerated by God, not annihilated. In the physical realm, God does not let the believer's body return to dust forever, but resurrects it as a new and gloried body which is connected to the old body in a similar way as a flower is to its seed (1 Corinthians 15:37–38). So

Cornelis Venema says, 'just as the resurrected body represents the transformation of the present body of the believer, so the new creation represents the transformation, not the annihilation, of the present creation.'[2]

The main emphasis in verses 1–8, then, is on the continuity between the present universe which we know and the new universe which is going to be born at the second coming of Jesus Christ. Thus our Lord described the process as the 'regeneration, when the Son of Man sits on the throne of His glory' (Matthew 19:28). Likewise, Peter speaks of God sending Jesus, 'whom heaven must receive until the times of *restoration* of all things, which God has spoken by the mouth of all His holy prophets since the world began' (Acts 3:21, italics added). Again, it is a process of refining in which 'the elements will melt with fervent heat' (2 Peter 3:10,12). It is significant then that the Greek word translated 'new' four times in verses 1–8 is not the word for new in the sense of time, but of *quality*.[3]

As the vision unfolds, the first difference John saw between the old earth and the renewed earth was that 'there was no more sea' (v. 1). Its removal, of course, is not because of any evil in itself, because all material things are amoral. Rather, it is because its vast and dangerous expanses have always separated peoples from each other. Its absence, therefore, speaks of the removal of barriers and the uniting of all heaven's citizens.

> Then I, John, saw the holy city, New Jerusalem, coming down out of heaven from God, prepared as a bride adorned for her husband.   (v. 2)

The church is pictured as a 'city', and it is called 'holy' because its citizens are God's redeemed people, sinless and perfect. The church is also called 'New Jerusalem' in contradistinction to the old geographical Jerusalem in Palestine, which was God's dwelling place on earth under the law of Moses; but by Christ's work of redemption on the cross the Christian church has now become God's new and permanent temple

(1 Corinthians 3:16; 2 Corinthians 6:16; Ephesians 2:19–22; cf. Isaiah 62:3–5). Moreover, in a strange mixture of metaphors, the holy city is dressed as immaculately as a bride about to join her Groom, the Lamb, at the altar (19:7–9; Ephesians 5:23–32). It is also a picture of heaven being transferred to the new earth, and of Christ and His bride setting up home forever on the new earth. From this verse we learn that the glorified church after Christ's return is not going to spend eternity in a heaven far off in space, but on the new earth. This is made even clearer in verse 3:

> And I heard a loud voice from heaven saying, 'Behold, the tabernacle of God is with men, and He will dwell with them, and they shall be His people, and God Himself will be with them and be their God.'

This covenant promise of God to His believing people ('I will walk among you and be your God, and you shall be My people') is repeated with slight variations eighteen times from Exodus 6:7 to Revelation 21:3 where it is ultimately and permanently fulfilled (see also Leviticus 26:12; Jeremiah 7:23; 11:4; 24:7; 30:22; 31:1,33; 32:38; Ezekiel 11:20; 14:11; 36:28; 37:23,27; Zechariah 8:8; 13:9; and 2 Corinthians 6:16). God's presence will be experienced among His believing people in a way and to a degree they have never known before. It will be a relationship of perfect and joyful communion between the Creator and His glorified saints (or separated ones). Moreover, the unqualified presence of God with His people will guarantee absolute bliss:

> And God will wipe away every tear from their eyes; there shall be no more death, nor sorrow, nor crying. And there shall be no more pain, for the former things have passed away.   (v. 4)

Sin is the cause of every tear, because sin brings death, sorrow and pain to every soul it blights. But as a result of the redeeming work of God's incarnate Son on the cross, these former things 'shall not be remembered or come to mind' (Isaiah 65:17). And at last the twice-repeated promise shall be fulfilled: 'And the ransomed of the Lord shall return, and come to Zion with singing, with everlasting joy on their heads. They shall obtain joy and gladness, and sorrow and sighing shall flee away' (Isaiah 35:10; 51:11).

Then He who sat on the throne said, 'Behold, I make all things new'. (v. 5)

Here again, the continuity between the first creation and the new is emphasised. For God does not say: Behold, I make all *new* things; but 'I make all things new.' He is not promising to make something altogether new, but to make all the things He has already made, new; to renew or regenerate them. And the words that follow confirm this:

And He said to me, 'Write, for these words are true and faithful'.   (v. 5)

They are 'true' or reliable because God cannot lie (Numbers 23:19); and they are 'faithful' because in this preview of the new heaven and the new earth, and New Jerusalem coming down to the new earth, what God has promised 'is done!' There is nothing regarding the universe or His church that is now unfulfilled.

And He said to me, 'It is done! I am the Alpha and the Omega, the Beginning and the End'.   (v. 6)

Alpha is the first letter of the Greek alphabet and Omega the last, and so God is saying that what He starts He also finishes. The divine Beginning guarantees the divine End. Let sinners who are perishing from soul-thirst take heart. They can trust the promise of God:

I will give of the fountain of the water of life freely to him who thirsts.   (v. 6)

Although it is priceless, because it cannot be bought or earned, God offers it for free, because it was purchased for hell-deserving sinners at the enormous cost of Christ's suffering and death on the cross. To drink from this well of salvation is to drink from the inexhaustible outflow of God's infinite grace. God gives this invitation in the midst of this vision of the glory to come, because He does not want any reader to feel excluded. Indeed, He repeats His invitation in chapter 22:17. What a gracious God He is! His graciousness, however, is not to be taken for granted. Those who believe must not compromise with the world, but overcome it:

> He who overcomes shall inherit all things [all the marvellous blessings described in verses 2–4], and I will be his God and he shall be My son.   (v. 7)

The mark of God's covenant people is perseverance (Matthew 24:13; 2 Timothy 2:12; 4:10; Hebrews 10:38–39; 2 Peter 1:5–11; Revelation 2:7,11; 3:5,12,21). In the renewed creation, the Christian believer's sonship and heirship stems, not from himself, but from his union by faith with Christ, God's unique Son and heir (Romans 8:17; Galatians 2:20; 4:4–7). The unbeliever, however, will have no part or inheritance in the new heaven and the new earth.

> But the cowardly [who obey men rather than God], unbelieving [who refuse to trust in Jesus as their Saviour], abominable [who give themselves over to unnatural desires], murderers [who shed innocent blood], sexually immoral [who have sex outside marriage], sorcerers [who rely on astrology or evil powers instead of on God], idolaters [who worship things and not God] and all liars [who communicate falsehood in place of the truth] shall have their part in the lake which burns with fire and brimstone, which is the second death.   (v. 8)

Such persons exclude themselves from the new heaven and the new earth by excluding Jesus Christ from their lives. Verse 8 is not saying that there is no hope of salvation for anyone who has told lies or practised idolatry or even committed murder. Jesus said, 'I did not come to call the righteous, but sinners, to repentance'; and John tells us that 'the blood of Jesus Christ His Son cleanses us from all sin' (Mark 2:17; 1 John 1:7). So the forgiveness of sin and the gift of eternal life in the new heaven and the new earth are freely available to all sinners who have sincerely repented of their sin and believed in Christ.

Conversion, however, does not lessen in any way the need for every believer to pursue holiness (Hebrews 12:14). 'Heaven is gained through perseverance and not apart from it.'[4]

The security of holy Jerusalem, the Lamb's bride

Jerusalem, the capital city and centre of worship for the Old Testament church, is often spoken of as a place of safety and security: 'Those who trust in the LORD are like Mount Zion, which cannot be moved, but abides forever' (Psalm 125:1). In much the same way, the church, which is the Lamb's bride, is portrayed as absolutely secure.

> Then one of the seven angels who had the seven bowls filled with the seven last plagues came to me and talked with me, saying, 'Come, I will show you the bride, the Lamb's wife.' And he carried me away in the Spirit to a great and high mountain, and showed me the great city, the holy Jerusalem, descending out of heaven from God, having the glory of God.   (vv. 9–11)

The glory of the holy Jerusalem is the very glory of God radiating from the innumerable company of Christ's people who, by grace, have been perfectly transformed into His image and now constitute that city: 'Its radiance like a most rare jewel, like a jasper, clear as crystal' (v. 11, ESV). The picture is one of inexpressible beauty and splendour. Furthermore, the city John saw 'descending out of heaven from God' was not just magnificent, but *massive*:

> and showed me the great city, the holy Jerusalem … Also she had a great and high wall with twelve gates, and twelve angels at the gates, and names written on them, which are the names of the twelve tribes of the children of Israel: three gates on the east, three gates on the north, three gates on the south, and three gates on the west. Now the wall of the city had twelve foundations, and on them were the names of the twelve apostles of the Lamb.   (vv. 10,12–14)

It is similar to the vision of Jerusalem in Ezekiel 48:30–35, only

John's vision is fuller and richer. Both visions have their fulfilment, not in the millennium, but in the new heavens and a new earth. The names of the twelve tribes inscribed on the twelve gates represent the nucleus of the Old Testament church, and the names of the twelve apostles inscribed on the twelve foundations represent the nucleus of the New Testament church. Both make up the 'Lamb's wife … the holy Jerusalem.'

In John's vision 'the great and high wall' is meant to convey the *security* of the relationship of 'the holy Jerusalem' and her Bridegroom, the Lamb. The wall surrounding any city is specifically built to provide protection and security, but here the wall is not, in that literal sense, needed because all God's enemies have been destroyed. The wall is simply a symbol to remind believers that the church will be safe in the arms of Jesus for all eternity to come. The twelve angels who stand watch at the twelve gates signify the same thing. No one can enter the holy city who has not been redeemed by the blood of the Lamb. The church is complete and secure.

> And he who talked with me had a gold reed to measure the city, its gates, and its wall. The city is laid out as a square; its length is as great as its breadth. And he measured the city with the reed: twelve thousand furlongs [lit. stadia, about 1,380 miles in all, ESV mg]. Its length, breadth, and height are equal (vv. 15–16).

The scene continues to be highly symbolic. The 'gold reed' used for measuring the holy city signifies the divine accuracy of the measurements. God's 'gold standard' is being used, not the wooden or iron rod of a human surveyor. Its massive size is denoted by the figure 'twelve thousand stadia.' Being approximately 1,380 miles, that would be 'the distance between London and Athens, between New York and Houston, between Delhi and Rangoon, between Adelaide and Darwin. A city of this size is too large for the imagination to take in. John is certainly conveying the idea of splendour. And, more importantly, that of room for all.'[5]

Twelve is the number of the church, God's redeemed people: three (representing the Trinitarian God) times four (representing the four corners of the earth). Twelve times a thousand (representing a largeness or completeness predetermined by God) denotes the church which consists of 'a great multitude which no one could number of all nations, tribes, peoples and tongues … clothed with white robes' (7:9). So once again, in a different way, the security of the church is being pictured as a perfect cube 1,380 miles in length, height and width.

Of course, the Holy of Holies in the Tabernacle and the Temple was also a perfect cube, with each side just thirty feet long. It was the place where the shekinah glory of God's presence hovered over the Mercy Seat of the Ark of the Covenant. Only the high priest of Israel could enter the Holy of Holies, and then only once a year, on the Day of Atonement with the blood of a spotless and innocent animal to sprinkle on the Mercy Seat. So the imagery here is saying that Christ's bride, the church, 'the holy city, New Jerusalem', will itself be God's ultimate and final dwelling place for the rest of eternity. The presence of God will permeate its entire membership. He will be equally near to each and every member.

> Then he measured its wall: one hundred and forty-four cubits, according to the measure of a man, that is, of an angel (v. 17).

The symbolism here is rather harder to ascertain, for we were told in verse 12 that the holy city is surrounded by 'a great and high wall' to provide security and protection. But with a cubit measuring eighteen inches, the height of the wall at two hundred and sixteen feet would be completely out of proportion to the height of the city (1,380 miles). Seemingly, in this picture the wall of the city is not for defence, but for *demarcation*. The wall of one hundred and forty-four cubits marks the boundaries of the church of God.

So the security of the wall is not in its height or width, but in its function of eliminating any uncertainty as to who are within its ranks.

They are the elect; the ones God has chosen out of the world to give as an eternal possession to His only, beloved Son (Deuteronomy 7:6–8; John 15:16; 17:6,9,12; Ephesians 1:3–6; 1 Peter 1:1–2). The numbers twelve and one hundred and forty-four (twelve times twelve) denote God's gathering of believers from the four corners of the earth throughout the entire period of the Old and New Testament. All who have entered its gates from the north, south, east and west belong to Christ forever. As our Lord assured us: "All that the Father gives Me will come to Me and the one who comes to Me, I will by no means cast out' (John 6:37). The symbol applies not only now in this world, but in a far greater sense in the world to come. The added statement that the measurement of the wall is 'according to the measure of a man', even though carried out by an angel, tells us that it is just a human measurement incapable of calculating such a deep spiritual reality. Only 'the Lord knows those who are His', and therefore how many they actually are (2 Timothy 2:19).

> The construction of its wall was of jasper; and the city was pure gold, like clear glass. The foundations of the wall of the city were adorned with all kinds of precious stones: the first foundation was jasper, the second sapphire, the third chalcedony, the fourth emerald, the fifth sardonyx, the sixth sardius, the seventh chrysolite, the eighth beryl, the ninth topaz, the tenth chrysoprase, the eleventh jacinth and the twelfth amethyst.
>
> The twelve gates were twelve pearls: each individual gate was of one pearl. And the street of the city was pure gold, like transparent glass. (vv.18–21)

Having given us the measurements of the city and the wall surrounding it, the apostle John describes their beauty and costliness. The wall did not just contain jasper stones, but was built of jasper: the same material mentioned in chapter 4:3 when he says that the appearance of God was 'of jasper'. Similarly, he has described the city as 'having the glory of God' and 'her light was … like a jasper stone, clear as crystal' (v. 11). So the city and its wall is of jasper because the church is the creation of God and of His Christ and it shines with Their glory.

Indeed, John goes further and describes the glory of God radiating from the church in even more lavish terms: 'the city was pure gold, like clear glass', and so was its main street (vv. 18,21). That is impossible in this world where the laws of physics forbid a transparent metal! But in conveying the appearance of this city, this image is given. The twelve foundations supporting the wall, on which were written the names of the twelve apostles, 'were adorned with all kinds of precious stones' (vv. 19–20), not all of which are known to us. The gates of the city are also unbelievably magnificent, each one constructed out of 'one pearl'. The true splendour and indestructibility of the make-up of New Jerusalem exceeds the bounds that any of these poor earthly symbols can ever hope to convey, for the beauty of the Lamb's bride is the glory of God which is indescribable.

The intimacy between the Lamb and His bride

The only earthly symbol which can appropriately illustrate the intimate spiritual relationship between God and His people is the intimate union between a man and his wife. It is a symbol that has already been used in verses 2 and 9, but is now further developed in terms that will show how close and intimate the relationship between the Lamb and His bride will be in the new heaven and the new earth.

> But I saw no temple in it, for the Lord God Almighty and the Lamb are its temple. (v. 22)

There will be no need in the holy city to walk down the street of transparent gold to go to church and worship God, for being a perfect cube, the church is itself the Holy of Holies in which God's presence is equally and fully experienced by all. Wherever you are in that countless number of the redeemed, God and the Lamb will be as close to you as to anyone else, even the greatest of the saints. Indeed, the union of

God and His people will be so complete that it is not only they who are *His* dwelling place (1 Corinthians 3:16; Ephesians2:20–22; 1 Peter 2:5), but He will be *their* dwelling place or temple (v. 22; Psalm 90:1).

> The city had no need of the sun or of the moon to shine in it, for the glory of God illuminated it. The Lamb is its light.   (v. 23)

These words are not intended to give us astronomical details of the new heavens, but to magnify the uncreated light that radiates from the Person of God and is described as His glory. It is inseparable from Him, and therefore His immediate presence throughout the holy city removes any need of light from outside. It is another example of the intimacy of our relationship with God in the new creation. For in this dark world we do not walk in God's perfect light, and as a result our fellowship with Him and one another is often marred by sin and by ignorance (1 John 1:7–8). But in the perfect light of God's presence in the holy city there will be no more darkness or sin or ignorance. We shall see Him face to face and enjoy unclouded communion with God Almighty and the Lamb, and therefore with our fellow saints.

> And the nations of those who are saved shall walk in its light, and the kings of the earth bring their glory and honour into it … and they shall bring the glory and honour of the nations into it.   (vv. 24,26)

The use of the terms 'nations' and 'kings' is a further assertion of the holy city as a multinational, multiracial, multicultural community of redeemed people who will bring with them into the holy city this rich diversity, as predicted in Isaiah 60:3. The saved of each nation, race, class (even kings) and culture will each enrich the worship of God with their own contribution in the new heavens and the new earth. The intimacy between Christ and His wife will be open to the enrichment of these sanctified diverse cultural contributions to their marriage union. No contribution will excel any of the others. All will be equally perfect.

Verse 25, Its gates shall not be shut at all by day (there shall be no night there).

Again, the scene is one of intimacy; of unrestricted access between husband and wife. In this sin-cursed world a husband has to lock the doors of his house, especially at night, to protect his wife from harm. But in the new heavens and the new earth this will not be necessary; firstly, because it will have been purged forever from all evil that may have required the closing of the gates of the holy city. And secondly, 'There shall be no night there', since its light, as we have been told (v. 23), is the glory of the Lord God and the Lamb. It will be eternal day there, as foretold by the prophet Isaiah: 'Therefore your gates shall be open continually; they shall not be shut day or night … The sun shall no longer be your light by day, nor for brightness shall the moon give light to you; but the Lord will be to you an everlasting light, and your God your glory' (60:11,19).

> But there shall by no means enter it anything that defiles, or causes an abomination or a lie, but only those who are written in the Lamb's Book of Life. (v. 27)

Nothing spoils a marriage union like impurity and unfaithfulness, but nothing like that will mar the intimacy between Christ and His bride in the renewed universe. All evildoers will be confined to hell forever. Only those whose names are written in the Lamb's Book of Life will inhabit the holy city, for they are the ones that God has chosen, justified and glorified for this purpose. As predicted again by Isaiah, 'your people shall all be righteous' (60:21). It will be the ideal, unending honeymoon for the only perfect marriage ever.

The felicity of life in heaven on earth

Felicity is defined in the Oxford Dictionary as 'intense happiness', and in John's final scene of the new heaven being established on the new earth, we have a picture of Paradise regained: of the perfect happiness lost in Adam abundantly restored in Christ. So, we have the picture of the holy city, New Jerusalem, being a garden city. We are still dealing with earthly symbols that are very helpful, but at best can only faintly resemble the greater reality behind them. To be sure, when by grace we inherit the new heaven and the new earth, we shall exclaim with greater reason and more joyous surprise what the Queen of Sheba said to King Solomon: 'It was a true report which I heard in my own land … however I did not believe the words until I came and saw with my own eyes; and indeed the half was not told me' (1 Kings 10:6–7).

> And he [the angel] showed me a pure river of water of life, clear as crystal, proceeding from the throne of God and of the Lamb. In the middle of its street, and on either side of the river, was the tree of life, which bore twelve fruits, each tree yielding its fruit every month. The leaves of the tree were for the healing of the nations.   (22:1–2)

Water in the Bible is often used as a symbol of eternal life, and so in this scene we are being assured that the source of eternal life will be in plentiful and pristine supply in the new heaven and the new earth (Isaiah 12:3; 44:3; 55:1–2; John 4:10,13–14; Revelation 22:17). Moreover, this river flowing with life-giving water for the souls of humankind proceeds 'from the throne of God and the Lamb' who once again are seen as coequal. Its fountainhead is God the Creator who in the person of His incarnate Son became the 'Lamb that takes away the sin of the world', thus making the gift available, and the Holy Spirit Himself is the 'water of life'.

Our Lord Jesus Christ made this clear when He said, '"If anyone thirsts, let him come to Me and drink. He who believes in Me, as the Scripture has said, out of his heart will flow rivers of living water." But this He spoke concerning the Spirit, whom those believing in Him would receive; for the Holy Spirit was not yet given, because Jesus was not yet glorified' (John 7:37–39). This 'river of the water of life' was predicted by three of the Old Testament prophets. Joel said, 'A fountain shall flow from the house of the LORD' (3:18). Ezekiel also saw a vision of 'water flowing from under the threshold of the temple … along the bank of the river, on this side and that, will grow all kinds of trees … They will bear fruit every month, because their water flows from the sanctuary. Their fruit will be for food, and their leaves for medicine' (47:1,12). And Zechariah saw a day when 'living waters shall flow from Jerusalem' (14:8).

These prophecies are descriptive of the state of blessedness and happiness which will prevail not for a thousand years on this 'first earth', but universally and everlastingly in the new heaven and the new earth, after the destruction of Satan and all his followers. Both food and water are the staples of life, and so with the river from the throne of God and the Lamb flowing down the middle of the main street both the water of life and the tree of life are freely and readily available to all the redeemed. Little wonder that John says, 'They shall neither hunger anymore nor thirst anymore' (7:16). Moreover, with 'the leaves of the tree for the healing of the nations', no one will get sick or die anymore. The fruit of the tree of life is a symbol of life sustained and its leaves of health maintained.

> And there shall be no more curse, but the throne of God and of the Lamb shall be in it, and His servants shall serve Him. They shall see His face, and His name shall be on their foreheads. There shall be no night there: they need no lamp nor light of the sun, for the Lord gives them light. And they shall reign forever and ever. (vv. 3–5)

Paradise lost can only be restored when 'there shall be no more curse', for it was the curse that Adam's sin brought to the earth that turned its weal into woe (Genesis 3:17–19). This too was predicted by the prophets and will be realized in the final renewal of creation (Isaiah 11:6–9; 65:25; Zechariah 14:11). The Lamb of God made it certain when He offered Himself as 'the propitiation for our sins' (1 John 2:2), and 'redeemed us from the curse of the law, having become a curse for us' (Galatians 3:13). And, of course, with the removal of sin and its curse, 'the throne of God and of the Lamb' can now be transferred from 'the first heaven' to the 'new earth.'

How incredibly amazing! Who would ever have thought that the Triune God who is Spirit would ever leave His eternal spiritual dwelling place to make a new and permanent home on the new earth! But that will be yet a further manifestation of His marvellous grace and condescension to sinners who deserved only His wrath. And there before Him, we 'His servants shall serve Him.' The verb is in the future active tense meaning, 'His servants shall keep on serving Him' in the worship of praise and thanksgiving, and carrying out whatever plans He has for the new heavens and the new earth, which He has not yet made known. 'Heaven is not a place of indolent leisure, but a place where service is done, centring on God.'[6]

What is more, the blood-washed and blood-bought redeemed will 'see His face', which will surely be the climax of their happiness. This is what is called *the beatific vision*, and it will utterly satisfy the eager expectation of every believer (Psalm 17:15). This is confirmed by the statement, 'and His name shall be on their foreheads.' This is a symbol of belonging to God, and a pledge that none of those who comprise the Lamb's bride will be denied access to Him.

Indeed, the reason why the beatific vision will be so perfect, says John, is that 'There shall be no night there: they need no lamp nor light of the sun, for the Lord God gives them light.' This is not just a repetition of what has already been said in chapter 21:23 and 25. Rather, it is an explanation of why there will be no more theophanies or partial revelations of God from the 'lamp' of His word (Judges 13:16–22; Psalm 119:105). 'God is light', and in His immediate, eternal presence 'we shall see Him as He is' in His own uncreated, unsurpassed light, and (to quote Charles Wesley) 'be lost in wonder, love and praise!' (1 John 1:5; 3:2).

'And they shall reign forever and ever.' This is not a picture of the redeemed ruling over anyone, for all our Lord's enemies will already have been destroyed. It is another picture of their blissful and exalted final state. As the Lamb's wife, the saints are also 'joint heirs with Christ' (Romans 8:17). We share in His royalty. Our reigning is by virtue of our union with Jesus, who alone is 'King of kings and Lord of lords' (17:14; 19:16). We will not reign independently, but 'with Him', and it will be forever and ever because His kingdom will have no end (2 Timothy 2:12; Isaiah 9:7; Daniel 7:18,27; Luke 1:32–33; 22:28–30).

Such is the indescribable glory that awaits God's elect, the 'Lamb's wife', when they enter 'the holy city, New Jerusalem', in the 'new heavens and a new earth in which righteousness dwells' (21:2,9; 2 Peter 3:13). But these images convey only a shadow, a feint outline, of the reality that awaits us when our gracious God and Saviour, Jesus Christ, comes with power and great glory to make all things new. C.S. Lewis captures well something of what it will be like when the shadows give way to the substance. In the final paragraph of the last volume of his classic story, *The Chronicles of Narnia*, the three children and their parents have died in a railway accident and are in the real Narnia or heaven.

> The things that began to happen after that were so great and beautiful that I cannot write them. And for us this is the end of all the stories, and we can most truly say that they all lived happily ever after. But for them it was only the beginning of the real story. All their life in this world and all their adventures in Narnia had only been the cover and the title page: now at last they were beginning Chapter One of the Great Story which no one on earth has read: which goes on for ever: in which every chapter is better than the one before.[7]

24 The final curtain falls

²²:⁶Then he said to me, 'These words are faithful and true.' And the Lord God of the holy prophets sent His angel to show His servants the things which must shortly take place. ⁷'Behold, I am coming quickly! Blessed is he who keeps the words of the prophecy of this book.'

⁸Now I, John, saw and heard these things. And when I heard and saw, I fell down to worship before the feet of the angel who showed me these things. ⁹Then he said to me, 'See that you do not do that. For I am your fellow servant, and of your brethren the prophets, and of those who keep the words of this book. Worship God.' ¹⁰And he said to me, 'Do not seal the words of the prophecy of this book, for the time is at hand. ¹¹He who is unjust, let him be unjust still; he who is filthy, let him be filthy still; he who is righteous, let him be righteous still; he who is holy, let him be holy still.'

¹²'And behold, I am coming quickly, and My reward is with Me, to give to every one according to his work. ¹³I am the Alpha and the Omega, the Beginning and the End, the First and the Last.'

¹⁴Blessed are those who do His commandments, that they may have the right to the tree of life, and may enter through the gates into the city. ¹⁵But outside are dogs and sorcerers and sexually immoral and murderers and idolaters, and whoever loves and practices a lie. ¹⁶'I, Jesus, have sent

My angel to testify to you these things in the churches. I am the Root and the Offspring of David, the Bright and Morning Star.'

¹⁷And the Spirit and the bride say, 'Come!' And let him who hears say, 'Come!' And let him who thirsts come. Whoever desires, let him take the water of life freely.

¹⁸For I testify to everyone who hears the words of the prophecy of this book: If anyone adds to these things, God will add to him the plagues that are written in this book; ¹⁹and if anyone takes away from the words of the book of this prophecy, God shall take away his part from the Book of Life, from the holy city, and from the things which are written in this book. ²⁰He who testifies to these things says, 'Surely I am coming quickly.'

Amen. Even so, come, Lord Jesus!

²¹The grace of our Lord Jesus Christ be with you all. Amen.

(Revelation 22:6–21).

These final words of John are not just the end of the book of Revelation, but the end of the Bible itself. They are also very fitting words, as we shall see. God, through His servant John, has unveiled for us in scene after scene the chief forces behind the progress of history since the first coming of His Son to be the Saviour of the world; namely, the Lamb on the throne of God, the devil and his fellow-demons, the church of Jesus Christ, the harlot Babylon, Antichrist and the false prophet. With the second coming of Jesus Christ as 'King of kings and Lord of lords' in chapter 19 and the final judgment of the devil and all his wicked followers in chapter 20, the divine visions have reached a magnificent climax with the creation of 'new heavens and a new earth in which righteousness dwells' (2 Peter 3:13; Revelation 21:1).

Now, as we come to chapter 22:6–21, and the angel has finished unveiling the 'things which must shortly take place' (1:1; 22:6), he reminds John that the words he has heard are 'faithful and true' (v.

6; 21:5). What a welcome reassurance for us too! To quote Richard Brooks: 'We have read many strange things, many amazing things, many delightful things and many terrible things in this book. But one thing is sure: everything we have read is true—all the messages of salvation, all the warnings of judgment, all the statements about history! "Trustworthy and true" are two great words that characterize everything about God, and so everything about God's word.'[1]

The authority of Scripture

The angel continues, '"And the Lord, the God of the spirits of the prophets, has sent His angel to show His servants what must soon take place"' (v. 6b, ESV). God is the One who moves the spirits of the prophets to prophesy and gives men and women His word (2 Peter 1:21). Their spirits are so under the control of God that their words are His words. So, to take this last book of the Bible, the revelation which God gave to Christ, and which Christ gave to the angel, and which the angel gave to John, and which John has given to us, has not at any stage of its transmission lost any of its divine authority. What John has written in this prophecy is exactly what God said, no more and no less. A man and his word may be different, but God and His word are always the same. So the things which God 'sent His angel to show His servants … must shortly take place.' There will be no delay in beginning the train of events which will lead to the return of Christ, the final judgment and the new heaven and the new earth.

Christianity is a religion based on divine revelation. Nobody would know the truth about God and His purposes, had not God first acted to make Himself and His will known in the Bible. The term 'Bible' comes from the Greek word for 'book', but it is not a biblical word. The New Testament, referring to the Old Testament, speaks instead of 'Scripture', or 'the Scriptures', a Greek word which means 'writing'. Scripture is divine writing. Thus Paul can say in 2 Timothy 3:16, 'All Scripture [or 'every text of Scripture'] is inspired by God' (lit. 'breathed out from God', expired rather than inspired). This is what gives Scripture its authority over our lives. As J.I. Packer explains: 'What Scripture says, God says; for in a manner comparable only to the deeper mystery of the Incarnation, the Bible is both fully human and fully divine. So all its manifold contents—histories, prophecies, poems, songs, wisdom writings, sermons, statistics, letters, and whatever else—should be received as from God, and all that Bible writers teach should be revered as God's authoritative instruction. Christians should be grateful to God for the gift of the written Word, and conscientious in basing their faith and life entirely and exclusively upon it. Otherwise, we cannot ever honour or please Him as He calls us to do.'[2]

The finality and sufficiency of Scripture

The theme of the nature of Scripture is taken up again in verses 16, 18 and 19, so we will leave our explanation of the intervening verses to a suitable place below. Our Lord says to John, 'I, Jesus, have sent My angel to testify to you these things in the churches. I am the Root and the Offspring of David, the Bright and Morning Star' (v. 16). Jesus is repeating here what was said in the opening verse of this book; namely, that He has made known 'things which must shortly take place' by sending His angel to testify of them to John. He is speaking directly to John when He says 'to you', but 'to you' is plural, for the 'revelation of Jesus Christ' is not a private one. It is for Christians of every generation.

The angel has spoken on Christ's authority which is then spelt out for us. Jesus Christ is not only David's descendent or 'Offspring' ('a shoot from the stump of Jesse', Isaiah 11:1, ESV), He is also his ancestor or 'Root' (the cause of his existence, his Creator and God, Isaiah 11:10). Jesus also calls Himself 'the Bright and Morning Star'. The 'morning star' is the brightest star in the sky and it appears a few hours before dawn. Implicit in this self-description is the assurance that by His first coming (His incarnation, atoning death and resurrection) Jesus is the guarantee that the long night of sin will soon end, heralding the glory of eternal day (John 1:4–5,9,14; Revelation 21:23; 22:5).

Such supreme authority brooks no interference: 'For I testify to everyone who hears the words of the prophecy of this book: if anyone adds to these things, God will add to him the plagues that are written in this book; and if anyone takes away from the words of the book of this prophecy, God shall take away his part from the Book of Life, from the holy city, and from the things which are written in this book' (vv. 18–19). This solemn warning applies not merely to future scribes who will copy out the book of Revelation for future generations, but most particularly for 'everyone who hears the words of the prophecy of this book.' The book of Revelation is not the work of John's fertile imagination, but a 'prophecy' that comes from God. Every word in this book has been divinely revealed and is not to be tampered with by those who preach or teach it. The warning, coming as it does at the end of the prophecy, is the counterpart of the blessing pronounced at the beginning of the book on everyone who reads and hears and keeps what is written in it (1:3). And there is an appropriate balance in the punishment it prescribes. To the person who 'adds' to the words of this prophecy, 'God will add to him the plagues that are written in this book.' And from the person who 'takes away from the words of the book of this prophecy, God shall take away his part from the Book of Life.' Both punishments amount to the same thing: everlasting torment in hell.

If we think that the threat of plagues added and life taken away is too severe, Michael Wilcock has this explanation: 'If we believe that what God has said in His book is not sufficient for salvation, but that we need to make certain additions of our own if we are to be saved; or if we believe that some of the demands of God's book are superfluous, and we can get by without observing them; then we are not only saying

that we know better than Him—we are (which is much worse) acting
as if that were true. Rudeness He can forgive; but blind wilfulness is
the sin against the Holy Spirit. Of the curse that comes upon those
who alter the gospel to suit themselves, it will be said, with the most
terrible truth, that they have asked for it.'[3]

Something else, however, needs to be pointed out. This warning in
verses 18 and 19 may be seen as a claim that the book of Revelation
belongs to the canon of Holy Scripture, for there is a biblical precedent
to this warning. It has a history. Moses, the inspired writer of the first
five books of the Bible, issued similar warnings in connection with his
writings (Deuteronomy 4:1–4; 12:32); and not only with his writings,
but also in connection with those of the New Testament to come. In
Deuteronomy 18:18–19 God says to Moses, 'I will raise up for them
[the Israelites] a Prophet like you from among their brethren, and will
put My words in His mouth, and He shall speak to them all that I
command Him. And it shall be that whoever will not hear My words,
which He speaks in My name, *I will require it of him*' (italics added). It
is a reference to Jesus Christ's teaching ministry, now preserved for us
in the Gospels and perpetuated in the teaching of His apostles (John
4:25–26,29,39; 14:25–26; 16:12–15; Acts 3:22–23).

The same threat of divine judgment is thus applied to all who refuse
to comply strictly with any part of God's revelation in Scripture
(Deuteronomy 4:2–3; 18:19; Proverbs 30:5–6; Galatians 1:6–9). For
all the books of the Bible are equally inspired and not to be tampered
with. Nothing is to be *added*, for nothing is missing that should be
there; which negates the claims of books such as the *Apocrypha, the
Book of Mormon*, Mary Baker Eddy's *Science and Health*, and the
New World Translation of the Bible by Jehovah's Witnesses to be
on a par with the Bible. And nothing is to be *taken away*, for there
is nothing there that is incorrect or obsolete. The teaching of liberal
theologians and preachers who deny creationism, the virgin birth, the
penal substitutionary death of Christ, His bodily resurrection and

return, and the eternal punishment of the wicked in hell falls under this category and forfeits all hope of eternal life in the new heaven and the new earth. The sixty-six books of the Bible constitute the final and all-sufficient revelation of God which is 'able to make [us] wise for salvation through faith which is in Christ Jesus' (2 Timothy 3:15).

John again attempts to worship an angel

For thirty-three verses from chapter 21:1 the apostle John has been overwhelmed by the utterances of the angel who has been showing and explaining to him the glorious wonders of the New Jerusalem and the new earth. These amazing sights and sounds have been interrupted by majestic statements from the divine Christ (21:5–8; 22:7,12–13,16,20). The voice of the angel in verse 6 is immediately followed in verse 7 by the voice of the Son of God: 'Behold, I am coming quickly! Blessed is he who keeps the words of the prophecy of this book.' It must have been difficult for John to discern which of the dazzling personages was speaking at any one time. We can at least re-read the words to make sure who is speaking, but John did not have that opportunity. The sights and sounds followed in quick succession. Profoundly awed by our Lord's sudden and unexpected interjection in verse 7, the apostle inadvertently fell down before the dazzling personage (10:1) of the one he thought had made this glorious announcement. We are not told in verse 7 that another and different voice uttered the words, 'Behold, I am coming quickly.' In other words, 'though the angel and the Christ are distinct persons, yet their messages are indistinguishable.'[4] Unfortunately, he bowed down before the only person who was there—the angel. The announcement came from the throne of God where Christ is permanently seated.

John's action was well intentioned but misguided! And so for a second time (19:10) the apostle had to be rebuked for attempting to worship an angel. Angels are not only created beings, but fellow servants of God with the redeemed. 'Now I, John, saw and heard these things [21:1–22:6]. And when I heard and saw, I fell down to worship before the feet of the angel who showed me these things. Then he said to me, "See that you do not do that. For I am your fellow servant, and of your brethren the prophets, and of those who keep the words of this book. Worship God'" (vv. 8–9). It is a solemn warning that, given the sinful nature that remains with us until death, it is still possible to sin even in the holiest of exercises.

The imminence of Christ's return

It is a remarkable thing, to return to verse 7, that in this short passage at the end of the Bible our Lord warns us three times that He is 'coming quickly' (vv. 7,12,20). It is an echo of His teaching in His Olivet Discourse at the close of His earthly life: 'Watch, therefore, for you do not know what hour your Lord is coming … Therefore you also be ready, for the Son of Man is coming at an hour when you do not expect Him … Watch therefore, for you know neither the day nor the hour in which the Son of Man is coming' (Matthew 24:42,44; 25:13). Two thousand years have passed, but whatever scoffers may say, or however plausible the arguments of the critics who try to explain it away, our Lord's return will be *personal* and *imminent*. 'I' Myself, am coming, is the thrust of His word in verses 7,12 and 20. And I am coming 'quickly'. The Greek word means 'suddenly.' In chapter 16:15 Jesus says, 'Behold, I am coming as a thief. Blessed is he who watches.' It will not be a well-publicized or drawn out event. When Jesus Christ comes to raise the dead and judge the world, it will all take place 'in a moment, in the twinkling of an eye, at the last trumpet' (1 Corinthians 15:52). There will be no time for anyone to prepare themselves to meet God; no chance to repent or escape.

For those who are found watching and waiting for Christ's return there is a promised blessing: 'Blessed is he who keeps the words of the prophecy of this book' (v. 7b). The verb 'to keep' means to observe them with all one's heart. For those who not only read the book of

Revelation but obey its injunctions and heed its warnings there is a blessing, not just the blessing of a mind filled with knowledge of the future, but a life transformed with holy vigilance and expectancy (1:3; 2 Peter 3:11–12). This is the sixth of seven beatitudes that are scattered in this prophecy (1:3; 14:13; 16:15; 19:9; 20:6; 22:7).

Verse 10, 'And he said to me, "Do not seal the words of the prophecy of this book, for the time is at hand."' God, for His part, has nothing scheduled on His calendar but the return of Christ. This was not the case in Daniel's time when in chapter 8:26 God says to the prophet, 'the vision … which was told is true; therefore seal up the vision, for it refers to many days in the future' (see also Daniel 12:4). When Daniel wrote his prophecy God still had much to do in terms of the great saving events of the incarnation of His Son, His death and resurrection, His ascension and bestowal of the Holy Spirit. But now that these great acts of salvation have taken place, there is no other major event in the drama of redemption except Christ's return to judge the world.

So while Daniel was commanded to seal up the vision, now that the first coming of Christ has accomplished redemption and the Holy Spirit is applying it to the elect, John is told: 'Do not seal the words of the prophecy of this book, for the time is at hand.' According to the angel our Lord's return will be so swift that there will be no time for men and women to change their ways: 'He who is unjust, let him be unjust still; he who is filthy, let him be filthy still; he who is righteous, let him be righteous still; he who is holy, let him be holy still' (v. 11). What the wicked are at that terminal moment, so will the Lord find them. It is therefore imperative that while there is still time to repent, the words of this book remain open for all to read. Those who impenitently ignore its message can carry on in their unjust and filthy ways if that is what they are bent on doing, but they will not escape their just due from the returning Judge. Likewise, because Christ's return will be so sudden and unexpected, Christians must not 'be weary in well-doing' (Galatians 6:9; 2 Thessalonians 3:13). Let the righteous continue to do right and the holy remain holy, so that they may receive their promised reward.

The promise, therefore, of the imminent return of Christ made in verse 7 is now repeated with the added assurance that He who has been appointed to judge the world in righteousness on that day will have His reward with Him. Verse 12, 'And behold, I am coming quickly, and My reward is with me, to give to every one according to his work.' No one will be able to escape that judgment, not even the dead. 'Every one' is going to be rewarded or requited. The word translated 'reward' literally means 'wages or what is due.' And the word translated 'give' means 'to give back' or pay their wages. So the day of Christ's return will be a day of recompense in which Christ will bring with him rewards for the righteous and punishment for the law-breakers which they are to get back as their due, for He is a just God and Saviour. And it will be 'My reward', says Christ, because the words 'according to his work' really mean to give back what each person has done with Christ, whether he has received Christ as Saviour and Lord or rejected Him.

This is made clear in verses 14–15 if we may skip verse 13 for a moment. Christ's reward is a reward of grace to His followers, because it is what He has promised to all who put their trust in Him. The better Greek manuscripts read, 'Blessed are those who wash their robes, that they may have the right to the tree of life, and may enter by the gates into the city.' Throughout this book our acceptance with God is always ascribed to the Lamb who was slain and with His blood 'purchased men for God from every tribe and tongue and people and nation' (5:9; 7:14). The verb 'wash' is in the present tense and speaks of a continuous washing. The redeemed are comprised of those who keep on trusting in the cleansing power of Christ's blood derived from the complete satisfaction of the law's demands by His death on the cross of Calvary. Having reconciled them to God His Father by the shedding of His precious blood on their behalf, Jesus gives them the right to enjoy the tree of life from which all have previously been barred because of their sinfulness (Genesis 3:24).

They are now free at their Saviour's return to enter the gates of the holy city, New Jerusalem, which stand open to receive them. This will not be so for those who have rejected Christ's gracious offer. The angels at the gates will prevent all unbelievers from entering the holy city. They will remain 'outside' because by their refusal to commit themselves in faith to Christ they are 'filthy' in the sight of an all-holy God: 'But outside are dogs and sorcerers and sexually immoral and murderers and idolaters, and whoever loves and practises a lie' (v. 15). What does it mean to live and practise a lie? It means to believe the lie of our own righteousness before God. It means to carry on living as we are because we think we are quite good enough to pass muster with God. That is the lie that condemns all impenitent sinners to everlasting hell with the devil and his angels (1 John 1:5–9).

Who has the authority to make such serious judgments upon humankind? The answer in verse 13 is God in the person of His Son Jesus Christ: 'I am the Alpha and Omega, the Beginning and the End, the First and the Last.' In chapter 1:8 and again in chapter 21:6 it is God Almighty who claims these titles. But here in verse 13 the risen Christ is claiming them for Himself, for He is co-essential, co-equal and co-eternal with God the Father and the Holy Spirit in the blessed Trinity. And what our Lord Jesus Christ is saying here is that as the 'Alpha' (the first letter of the Greek alphabet) and the 'Omega' (the last letter), He is the One who created everything and will bring it to its predetermined end. He who had the 'first' word about the creation of those who have rejected Him, will also have the 'last' word about their destruction. The same applies to His relationship with the godly. What He has started in their conversion or regeneration, He will bring to fulfilment in their glorification in the new heaven and the new earth (Philippians 1:6; Jude 24).

All three titles set Jesus Christ apart from the entire created order. The culmination of history lies entirely in His hands, not ours. So for the third time our Lord assures us of His imminent return: 'He who testifies to these things says, "Surely I am coming quickly"' (v. 20a). And just as surely, His beloved bride and church fervently responds, 'Amen [Aramaic participle meaning "Let it be so"]. Even so, come Lord Jesus' (v. 22b). Christian hope and confidence does not rest in man's ability to create a new world order, but in the return of Jesus Christ who created all things in the beginning and will 'make all things new' at the end (John 1:3; Colossians 1:15–18; Revelation 21:5).

God's free offer of eternal satisfaction

Verse 17 is a good note on which to end our study of the book of Revelation: 'And the Spirit and the bride say, "Come!" And let him who hears say, "Come!" And let him who thirsts come. And whoever desires, let him take the water of life freely.' It consists of four invitations. The first two, some think, are addressed to Christ to return to the world, while the last two are addressed to the world to take of the water of life. It is more probable, however, that the first two invitations should be understood in the light of the last two as addressed to an unbelieving world.

The 'Spirit', of course, is a reference to God, the Holy Spirit, whose temple is Christ's church, the 'bride' (1 Corinthians 3:16; Ephesians 2:19–22; Revelation 21:2). By the Spirit's presence and power in the church, God issues the invitation through the bride's testimony to Jesus to come to Him who can give sinners the water of life (John 4:10; 6:35; Revelation 21:6; 22:1). Moreover, the duty of extending this gospel invitation to the world is not restricted solely to the church as a corporate body. It is also the duty of every single member of the church. Thus those who 'hear' and accept the invitation of the Spirit must repeat it to others. Then, just in case there may be some doubt, the gospel invitation is issued by John to all and sundry a further two times (v. 17bc). This is such an important and common biblical theme that it requires some further elucidation on our part (Isaiah 55:1; John 7:37–38; see also above).

Spiritual thirst is a universal phenomenon

Everybody wants a fully satisfying life, but can never attain it. Lasting satisfaction is an elusive goal for all humankind whatever our age. When we are children we cannot wait to become of age and do our own thing; but we soon find out that attaining majority is not all that it is cracked up to be. When we are at college we cannot wait to graduate and get a good job and all that goes with it; but even marriage, owning a home and having a family brings its stresses. So we plan and look forward to retirement; but going on leisure trips also loses its appeal after a while.

It is always at the next stage of life that we think satisfaction will be found. But like a mirage it always eludes us, and eventually the next thing is the grave. Paul Simon, the American folk song writer wrote these lines expressing the dissatisfaction people feel at the meaningless of life:

> On my wall my eyes can dimly see
> > The pattern of my life and the puzzle that is me.
> From the moment of my birth till the instant of my death,
> > There are patterns I must follow just as I must breathe each breath.
> Like a rat in a maze the path before me lies,
> > And the pattern never alters until the rat dies.[5]

What is the water of life Jesus offers?

The idea that earthly possessions, achievements or even relationships can satisfy our deepest desires and yearnings is a soul-destroying lie. The truth is that we were made in the image of God with a spiritual nature that can only find lasting peace and contentment in a right relationship with God, which by nature we do not want. We do not wish to be dependent on God, or to live in submission to Him. We want autonomy. We want to please ourselves, and thus our relationship with God is broken. We are at enmity with Him. Recognizing this problem sixteen hundred years ago, Augustine says to God on the opening page of his *Confessions*, 'You have made us for Yourself, and our hearts are restless until they find their rest in You.'

The fall of man has left him with what Blaise Pascal (1623–1662) describes as 'the mark and empty trace, which he in vain tries to fill from all his surroundings, seeking from things absent the help he does not obtain in things present. But these are all inadequate, because the infinite abyss can only be filled by an infinite and immutable object, that is to say, only by God Himself.'[6] Aldous Huxley called it a 'God-shaped blank' in every person. And it is this spiritual need that our Lord Jesus is referring to when He speaks of 'the water of life' (21:6). It is the life of God made real in the human soul by the Saviour's gift of the Holy Spirit at conversion (Acts 2:38–39).

The clearest statement of this truth is found in John 7:37–39 where Jesus says, '"If anyone thirsts, let him come to Me and drink. He who believes in Me, as the Scripture has said, out of his heart will flow rivers of living water." But this He spoke concerning the Spirit, whom those believing in Him would receive.' The Son of God offers Himself as the solution to the spiritual drought in every person's soul, for He is God manifested in the flesh (John 1:1,14; 1 Timothy 3:16). He does not offer us a new recipe, but a new relationship with Himself, God incarnate. Only He can make this offer to us, because only He is able to deal with the offence of our sin which has estranged us from God and separated us from Him (Isaiah 59:2; Romans 3:21–26).

God takes no pleasure in the suffering sin has brought to human beings (Ezekiel 33:11). He loves the world because He is a merciful and forgiving God, but He cannot let sin go unpunished (Exodus 34:6–7). To be a just God He must satisfy the just demand of His holy law: 'The wages of sin is death' (Romans 6:23), not just physical death, but eternal death for body and soul in hell (20:11–15). But to be just and forgiving at the same time, God became one of us in the person of His Son, Jesus. In Him God bore the full brunt of His righteous anger against our sin, so that 'He might be just and the justifier of the one who has faith in Jesus (Romans 3:26). Once forgiven through the Lord Jesus Christ, the living water of God's eternal life is available to us.

How are we to drink the water of life?

The answer is given three times in one word: 'come'. Come to whom? To the Lord Jesus Christ who has just claimed that He is the promised Messiah who came to give the water of life to perishing sinners: 'I, Jesus … am the Root and Offspring of David' (v. 16). He is the same Jesus Christ who revealed Himself as the Messiah to the Samaritan woman at Jacob's well, saying, '"Whoever drinks of this water [from Jacob's well] will thirst again, but whoever drinks of the water that I shall give him will never thirst. But the water that I shall give him will become in him a fountain of water springing up into everlasting life"' (John 4:13–14,25–26,42). To 'come' to Christ, of necessity, involves turning away from our old self-centred life of unrest and dissatisfaction (repentance), and turning to Christ for God's new life imparted by the Holy Spirit (faith). The promise made is: 'And whoever desires, let him take the water of life freely' (v. 17). It is not for sale. All the money in the world could not buy the forgiveness of our sins. It comes to us freely on the grounds of God's gracious, self-sacrificial offering of His Son on the cross as an atonement (a covering) for our sins. To come to Christ in faith is to come with empty, outstretched, cupped hands, trusting Him to give us His life-giving Spirit as He has promised. And He will! The Son has never turned any thirsting, trusting soul away empty-handed (John 6:36).

John's closing prayer for all God's people

'The grace of our Lord Jesus Christ be with you all. Amen' (v.21). Some manuscripts have 'with all the saints'. It is a fitting close not only for the book of Revelation, but also for the end of the Bible itself. John's prayerful and affectionate wish for all God's saints in every generation is the *benediction* of God's grace. From the beginning of our Christian life to the end, every believer is dependent on God's grace, by which John means God's mercy in showing favour and blessing to sinners who do not in the least deserve it. There can be no greater wish for other Christians than that the grace of God which chose them, saved them and is keeping them, should remain with them until their glorification in a new heaven and a new earth.

With that assurance we, like the original readers of *The Revelation of Jesus Christ*, may face the future with peace and contentment. Whatever troubles and hardships may lie ahead, the grace of the All-conquering Lamb of God will satisfy our every need. At the end of life's journey we too will be able to echo the words of Bunyan's Mr. Valiant-for-truth when his final summons came: '"I am going to my Father's; and though with great difficulty I am got hither, yet now I do not repent me of all the trouble I have been at to arrive where I am" ... When the day that he must go hence was come, many accompanied him to the river side, into which as he went he said, "Death, where is thy sting?" And as he went down deeper, he said, "Grave, where is thy victory?" So he passed over, and all the trumpets sounded for him on the other side.'[7]

We may even come to the point where like John Newton we are beginning to lose our faculties. The great preacher and hymn writer became very confused of mind near the end of his eighty-two years. At the final wedding service he conducted, he had to ask the congregation several times what he was supposed to do next in the order of the liturgy. A few days before he died, on December 21, 1807, he confided to one of his dearest friends: 'My memory is nearly gone; but I remember two things: that I am a great sinner, and that Christ is a great Saviour.'[8]

🍂 Notes

Introduction
1. Leon Morris, *Revelation* (Tyndale Press, 1969), p. 26.
2. William M. Ramsay, *The Letters to the Seven Churches of Asia* (Baker, 1963), p. 183.
3. Irenaeus, *Against Heresies*, v. 30. 3.
4. Eusebius, *Ecclesiastical History*, III, 18. 3 and III, xx.
5. William Barclay, *Revelation* (Saint Andrew Press, 1960), vol. 1, pp. 4–5.
6. Henry B. Swete, *The Apocalypse of Saint John* (Eerdmans, n.d.) p. cxl.
7. William Hendriksen, *More Than Conquerors* (Baker, 1956), pp. 13–14.
8. B. Sinclair Ferguson, *Daniel* (Word, 1988), p. 22.

Chapter 1. The opening curtain rises
1. William Shakespeare, *As You Like It*, Act II, Scene VII.
2. Michael Wilcock, *I Saw Heaven Opened* (Inter-Varsity Press, 1975) p. 34.
3. Philip Edgcumbe Hughes, *Revelation* (Inter-Varsity Press, 1990), p. 20.

Chapter 2. The all-majestic Judge overseeing His church
1. Leon Morris, *Revelation*, p. 52.
2. Robert H. Mounce, *Revelation* (Eerdmans, 1980), p. 75.
3. Thomas F. Torrance, *The Apocalypse Today* (James Clarke & Co., 1960), p. 12.
4. Hal Lindsey, *There's a New World Coming* (Coverdale House, 1974), p. 34.
5. John F. Walvoord, *Revelation* (Moody Press, 1966), p. 44.
6. Philip Edgcumbe Hughes, *Revelation*, p. 27.
7. Derek Thomas, *Revelation* (Banner of Truth, 2011), p. 15.
8. Richard Brooks, *The Lamb is all the Glory* (Evangelical Press, 1986), p. 24.

Chapter 3. Christ's letters to Ephesus and Smyrna
1. Robert H. Mounce, *Revelation*, p. 86.

2. John Stott, *What Christ Thinks of the Church* (Harold Shaw, 1990), p. 18.
3. Philip Edgcumbe Hughes, *Revelation*, p. 36.
4. Leon Morris, *Revelation*, p. 63.
5. Robert H. Mounce, ibid. p. 91.

Chapter 4. Christ's letters to Pergamum and Thyatira

1. Robert H. Mounce, *Revelation*, p. 95.
2. John Stott, *What Christ Thinks of the Church*, p. 46.
3. Philip Edgcumbe Hughes, *Revelation*, p. 47.
4. Leon Morris, *Revelation*, p. 71; and Richard Brooks, *The Lamb is all the Glory*, p. 39.

Chapter 5. Christ's letters to Sardis and Philadelphia

1. Leon Morris, *Revelation*, p. 75.
2. Philip Edgcumbe Hughes, *Revelation*, p. 57.
3. William M. Ramsay, *The Letters to the Seven Churches of Asia*, p. 392.
4. Robert H. Mounce, *Revelation*, pp. 114–115.
5. John Calvin, quoted in J. Blanchard, *Gathered Gold* (Evangelical Press, 1984), p. 85.
6. John F. Walvoord, *Revelation*, p. 87.
7. John Stott, *What Christ Thinks of the Church*, p. 107.

Chapter 6. Christ's letter to Laodicea

1. Philip Edgcumbe Hughes, *Revelation*, pp. 64–65.

Chapter 7. Is the church raptured before chapter 4?

1. Dispensational premillenialism holds to a two-stage return of Jesus Christ separated by seven years of tribulation for all except the raptured church, and followed by a literal fulfillment of the Old Testament prophecies to Israel of a future golden age on earth.
2. Hal Lindsey, *There's A New World Coming* , pp. 73,75.
3. John Walvoord, *Revelation*, p. 103.

Chapter 8. God enthroned supreme as Creator

1. Matthew Henry, quoted by Richard Brooks, *The Lamb is all the Glory*, p. 54.
2. Oxford Dictionary of Current English.
3. Thomas F. Torrance, *The Apocalypse Today*, pp. 36–37.
4. Robert H. Mounce, *Revelation*, p. 140.
5. Arthur W. Pink, *Gleanings in the Godhead* (Moody Press, 1975), p. 36.
6. Leon Morris, *Revelation*, p. 92.

Chapter 9. Christ enthroned supreme as Redeemer

1. Thomas F. Torrance, *The Apocalypse Today*, pp. 42–43.
2. Robert H. Mounce, *Revelation*, p. 144.
3. Leon Morris, *Revelation*, p. 98.

4.   Leon Morris, *The Cross in the New Testament* (Eerdmans, 1965), p. 358.

Chapter 10. The Lamb opens the seals

1.   Leon Morris, *Revelation*, p. 102.
2.   For further information see Brian A. Russell, *Christ's Return as King of Kings* (Grace Publications Trust, 2013), pp. 106–115.
3.   Thomas F. Torrance, *The Apocalypse Today*, pp. 58–59.
4.   Philip Edgcumbe Hughes, *Revelation*, p. 87.

Chapter 11. The sealing, security and bliss of believers

1.   John F. Walvoord, *Revelation*, p. 144.
2.   C.H. Spurgeon, *Treasury of David* (Zondervan, 1968), vol. 2b, p. 93.
3.   Philip Edgcumbe Hughes, *Revelation*, p. 96.
4.   Robert H. Mounce, *Revelation*, p. 172.
5.   Dietrich Bonhoeffer, *The Cost of Discipleship* (SCM, 1964), p. 79.

Chapter 12. God's trumpet blasts of warning

1.   Michael Wilcock, *I Saw Heaven Opened*, p. 88.
2.   Michael Wilcock, ibid. pp. 94–95.
3.   William Hendriksen, *More Than Conquerors*, p. 148.
4.   Philip Edgcumbe Hughes, *Revelation*, p. 110.
5.   C.S. Lewis, *The Problem of Pain* (Collins, 1966), pp. 81,83.

Chapter 13. The little book and the two witnesses

1.   Leon Morris, *Revelation*, p. 137.
2.   Leon Morris, ibid. p. 141.
3.   John MacArthur, *The MacArthur Study Bible* (Word, 1997), p. 2006.
4.   John MacArthur, ibid. p. 2006.
5.   Thomas F. Torrance, *The Apocalypse Today*, pp. 83,85,86.

Chapter 14. War in heaven and on earth

1.   Leon Morris, *Revelation*, p. 153.
2.   D.A. Carson, *These Last Days*, edited by Richard D. Phillips and Gabriel N.E. Fluhrer (P&R, 2011), pp. 19–20.
3.   C.S. Lewis, *The Screwtape Letters* (Collins, 1966), p. 9.
4.   A.T. Robertson, *Word Pictures of the New Testament*, (Broadman, 1933), vol. VI, p. 394.
5.   David Barrett and Tedd Johnson, *World Christian Trends* (William Carey Library Publishers, 2003).
6.   http://www.magichelix.com/core/human/fire/00.htm.

Chapter 15. Satan's agents in his war on the church

1.   G.R. Beasley-Murray, *Revelation* (Oliphants, 1974), p. 208.
2.   A.T. Robertson, *Word Pictures of the New Testament*, vol. VI, p. 397.

3.   Leon Morris, *Revelation*, p. 169.
4.   William Barclay, *Revelation* (Saint Andrew Press, 1960), vol. 2, pp. 126–127.
5.   John R.W. Stott, *The Gospel and the End of Time* (IVP, 1991), p. 172.
6.   Robert H. Mounce, *Revelation*, p. 261.

Chapter 16. The Lamb, the 144,000 and the harvest

1.   Thomas F. Torrance, *The Apocalypse Today*, p. 113.
2.   Quoted by C.H. Spurgeon, *Morning and Evening* (Nelson, 1994), January 17, morning.
3.   Leon Morris, *Revelation*, p. 186.
4.   Kenneth W. Osbeck, *101 Hymn Stories* (Kregel, 1982), p. 35.

Chapter 17. The seven bowls of God's wrath

1.   Philip Edgcumbe Hughes, *Revelation*, p. 169.
2.   J.I. Packer, *Knowing God* (Hodder and Stoughton, 1973), pp. 136–137.
3.   William Barclay, *Revelation*, vol. 2, pp. 157–158.
4.   Leon Morris, *Revelation*, pp. 193–194.
5.   Robert H. Mounce, *Revelation*, p. 304.

Chapter 18. The mystery of Babylon the great

1.   Leon Morris, *Revelation*, p. 209.
2.   Adrian Rogers, *Unveiling the End Times in our Time* (Broadman & Holman, 2004), pp. 195–196.
3.   Leon Morris, ibid. p. 212.
4.   Leon Morris, ibid. p. 213.
5.   Philip Edgcumbe Hughes, *Revelation*, p. 188.
6.   Michael Wilcock, *I Saw Heaven Opened*, p. 165.
7.   Robert H. Mounce, *Revelation*, pp. 319–320.
8.   Thomas Guthrie, quoted in J. Blanchard, *More Gathered Gold* (Evangelical Press, 1986), p. 19.

Chapter 19. The destruction of Babylon the great

1.   Andrew Murray, quoted in J. Blanchard, *More Gathered Gold*, p. 342.
2.   Billy Sunday, quoted in J. Blanchard, *Gathered Gold* (E.P., 1984), p. 338.
3.   Richard Brooks, *The Lamb is all the Glory*, p. 157.
4.   William Guanall, *More Gathered Gold*, p. 341.

Chapter 20. The church's Bridegroom and Victor Emmanuel

1.   Derek Thomas, *Revelation*, p. 152.
2.   C.H. Spurgeon, *My Sermon Notes* (Baker, d?), vol. 4, p. 397.
3.   Henry Martyn, quoted by John R.W. Stott, *Motives and Methods of Evangelism* (IVF, 1963), pp. 12–13.
4.   Philip Edgcumbe Hughes, *Revelation*, p. 204.

5.   Robert H. Mounce, *Revelation*, p. 347.

Chapter 21. Satan bound for a thousand years

1.   This chapter, with minor changes, has been taken with permission from my book, *Christ's Return as King of Kings* (Grace Publications, 2013), pp. 180–199.
2.   Papias extolled the fanciful notion that in the millennium each vine would have ten thousand branches, each branch ten thousand twigs, each twig ten thousand shoots, each shoot ten thousand clusters, each cluster ten thousand grapes, and that each grape would yield twenty measures of wine (see Irenaeus, *Against Heresies*, v. 33. 3)!
3.   *The New International Dictionary of the Christian Church*, Editor: J.D. Douglas (Paternoster, 1974), p. 674.
4.   Cornelis P. Venema, *The Promise of the Future* (Banner of Truth, 2009), p. 224.
5.   Quoted by Philip Edgcumbe Hughes, *Interpreting Prophecy* (Eerdmans, 1976), pp. 100–101.
6.   Anthony A. Hoekema, *The Bible and the Future* (Eerdmans, 1979), p. 226.
7.   Derek Thomas, *Revelation*, p. 161.

Chapter 22. Satan destroyed and the last judgment

1.   John Blanchard, *Whatever Happened to Hell?* (Crossway, 1995), p. 111.
2.   Anthony A. Hoekema, *The Bible and the Future*, p. 256.
3.   J.L. Dagg, *Manual of Theology and Church Order* (Gano Books n.d.), p. 356.
4.   Anthony A. Hoekema, ibid. p. 259.
5.   Henry Alford, *Apocalypse of John* in *The Greek Testament* (Moody, 1958), vol. IV, pp. 735–36.
6.   C.S. Lewis, *The Problem of Pain* (Collins, 1966), pp. 106–107.
7.   J.I. Packer, *Knowing God* (Hodder and Stoughton, 1973), p. 139.
8.   J.I. Packer, *Concise Theology* (Tyndale House, 1993), p. 260.

Chapter 23. A new heaven and a new earth

1.   This chapter, with minor changes, has been taken with permission from my book, *Christ's Return as King of Kings*, pp. 200–220.
2.   Cornelis P. Venema, *The Promise of the Future*, p. 461.
3.   Marvin R. Vincent, *Word Studies in the New Testament* (Eerdmans, 1989), Vol. 1, p. 139.
4.   Derek Thomas, *Revelation*, p. 175.
5.   Leon Morris, *Revelation*, pp. 250–51.
6.   Leon Morris, ibid. pp. 256–57.
7.   C.S. Lewis, *The Last Battle* (Lane, 1956), p. 165.

Chapter 24. The final curtain falls

1.   Richard Brooks, *The Lamb is all the Glory*, pp. 196–97.
2.   J.I. Packer, *Concise Theology*, p. 5.
3.   Michael Wilcock, *I Saw Heaven Opened*, p. 219.

4. Michael Wilcock, ibid. p. 215.
5. Paul Simon, *Patterns* (The Paul Simon Song Book, 1965).
6. Blaise Pascal, *Pensées* , trans. W.F. Trotter (University of Chicago Press, 1990) no. 425.
7. John Bunyan, *Pilgrim's Progress* (Lutterworth, 1944), p. 318.
8. Brian H. Edwards, *Through Many Dangers* (Evangelical Press, 1988), p. 191.